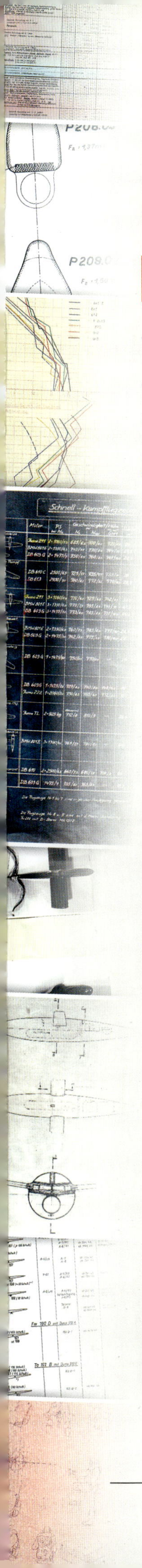

Preface

Britain became intimately familiar with the Luftwaffe's bomber fleet during the Second World War, particularly from September 1940 to May 1941 when it repeatedly attacked the nation's major ports and cities. Yet despite their evident need to drop the highest possible tonnage of bombs over Britain, it always struck me as curious that the Germans did not operate a heavy bomber of a sort equivalent to the British Avro Lancaster or Handley Page Halifax.

Instead, Germany fielded a range of smaller aircraft – the glass-nosed Heinkel 111, Dornier's slender Do 17 and the workmanlike Ju 88. They seemed to get the job done however, and having grown up with stories of the terrifying and deadly Blitz, it did not occur to me that the Germans might have been anything less than satisfied with their bomber fleet.

Years later, during the 1990s, I was amazed to discover the incredible variety of unusual 'secret project' aircraft apparently developed by German manufacturers during the war. There were rocket-powered interceptors aplenty, pulse-jet fighters, forward-swept wings, asymmetrical ground-attack aircraft, parasite fighters and more.

The purpose, context and even in some cases the true nature of many of these designs appeared to have become confused however, prompting me to write Luftwaffe: Secret Jets of the Third Reich in an attempt to provide some clarity.

While working on this project I naturally encountered many bomber designs, but lacking the space to do them justice, I set them aside. In truth, there were just as many puzzling aspects to German bomber development during the war as there were concerning jet fighters.

The more I read about these designs, the more conflicting claims, obfuscation, oddly recurring themes and outright misinformation I encountered. This publication is therefore an attempt, once again, to set the record straight using primary source material as far as possible.

There is one particular theme that seems to have cast a shadow over all studies of German wartime bomber development – what has come to be called the 'Amerika bomber'. Today, many German bomber projects are said to have been part of an 'Amerika bomber programme', this being a concerted effort throughout the war to build something capable of flying over to US, bombing it, and flying all the way back to a base in Europe.

However, among the records and archives I examined for this edition, there is seldom any mention of an attempt to build a bomber capable of reaching America. Reading the Germans' own technical reports, minutes of meetings, air ministry memos and dozens of other documents carefully preserved in British archives, one could be forgiven for thinking that the Germans never seriously considered flying a bomber all the way from Europe to attack the US.

Time and again, there are references to bombing Britain. There are laments that the Luftwaffe's existing types are not up to the job of doing just that, there is regret at the lack of a bomber that can fly high enough to avoid RAF interceptors, there is concern that the British are developing ever better navigation techniques for their own heavy bombers without fear of reprisal.

Similarly, there is constant debate and discussion about how best to find and sink the convoys plying the Atlantic with the supplies that are keeping Britain alive. The U-boats, it is said, urgently require help to do their job effectively – something that is better than the Focke-Wulf Fw 200, a repurposed airliner.

In fact, there was one attempt – during the early part of the war – to build a bomber capable of reaching America, but this hope seems to have faded very quickly and was never to be rekindled. All thoughts turned instead to Britain and how best to bomb it into submission.

With the 'Amerika bomber programme' myth removed from the equation, the story of heavy bomber development in Germany becomes a little more straightforward as I hope will be apparent.

As before, I found that the best place to begin my research was with a document called German Aircraft: New and Projected Types, which can be found in the National Archives at Kew in London. This factually accurate 'greatest hits' of German secret aircraft projects was compiled by British air intelligence in 1945 from captured documents and published in January 1946. Numbered among the 174 types and projects it covers are numerous bombers.

Dozens of other documentary sources were then added to establish a basic history of German bomber development. The focus has been mainly, though not exclusively, on large and long-range bombers and bomber projects, rather than ground-attack aircraft or smaller 'schnellbomber' types. This is primarily for reasons of space but also because those types tended to have more in common with fighters and therefore had a somewhat different development background.

It will also be noticed that this publication is somewhat lacking in tables of statistics and graphs. Contemporary documents are full of these occasionally useful graphics but there is rarely enough room for them in a publication that seeks to establish a cohesive historical narrative, rather than documenting every technical nuance and detail of aircraft that were never built.

Finally, no matter how interesting their features, no matter how innovative their design, it should not be forgotten that these projects were sponsored by the Nazi regime, and that their chief purpose was to bomb and destroy its opponents.

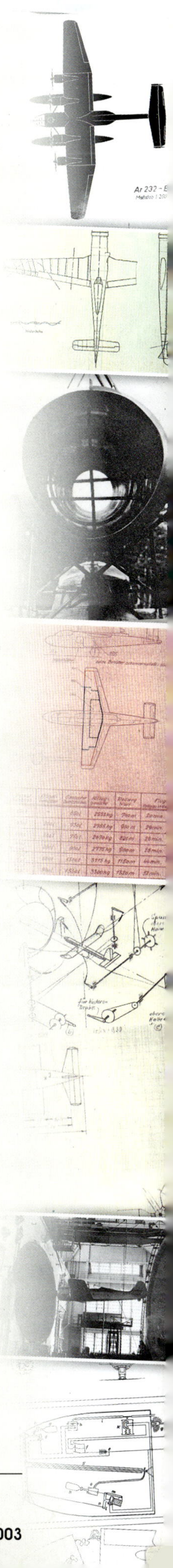

Contents

ABOVE: The distinctive form of a Junkers EF 130 in flight. In fact, numerous different configurations for the EF 130 were proposed, though none now survive save this one. Art by Ronnie Olsthoorn

FRONT COVER: A pre-production model Junkers Ju 287 A-0 prepares to bomb Allied advanced landing grounds in western Germany by Ronnie Olsthoorn. For more information about the Ju 287 see pages 78 and 106.

AUTHOR: Dan Sharp
DESIGN: atg-media.com
REPROGRAPHICS: Jonathan Schofield and Paul Fincham
PRODUCTION EDITOR: Jack Harrison
PUBLISHER: Steve O'Hara
ADVERTISING MANAGER: Sue Keily, skeily@mortons.co.uk
PUBLISHING DIRECTOR: Dan Savage
MARKETING MANAGER: Charlotte Park
COMMERCIAL DIRECTOR: Nigel Hole

PUBLISHED BY: Mortons Media Group Ltd, Media Centre, Morton Way, Horncastle, Lincolnshire LN9 6JR.
Tel: 01507 529529

THANKS TO: Simon Fowler, Chris Gall, Chris Gibson, Paul Malmassari, Paul Martell-Mead, Ronnie Olsthoorn, Alexander Power, Chris Sandham-Bailey, Daniel Uhr, Stephen Walton, Gary Webster and Tony Wilson

PRINTED BY: William Gibbons and Sons, Wolverhampton

ISBN: 978-1-911276-06-7

MORTONS MEDIA GROUP LTD

Arrested develop

Germany's Second World War bombers – an introduction

It was clear even before its formation in 1935 that the Luftwaffe was going to need a heavy bomber. After a couple of false starts, it seemed as though a world-beating design was firmly in the frame by the end of 1936...

ABOVE: Possibly the most important German aircraft of the Second World War – the Heinkel He 177. A great deal of time, effort and money was expended on it which might have been more profitably employed elsewhere. Worse still, for several years it seemed as though the He 177 might be just about ready to enter service even though it wasn't, fatally delaying the development of a more capable aircraft to replace it.

When Heinkel's P 1041 was declared the winner of the Fernbomber or 'long-range bomber' competition on October 16, 1936, the German military believed it to be the most advanced aircraft design of its type anywhere in the world.

It stood head and shoulders above the designs tendered for the first long-range bomber specification of two years earlier – the Junkers Ju 89 and Dornier Do 19. It was smaller, could fly higher and was dramatically faster, with a projected top speed of 366mph compared to 241mph and 196mph respectively.

This incredible advantage was secured through a series of innovative drag-reducing measures: the P 1041's Daimler-Benz DB 606 engines were linked in pairs, driving only two propellers; radiators to disperse their heat were replaced with a system of surface evaporation cooling; and the aircraft's defensive gun turrets were to be remote-controlled, allowing them to be smaller and lighter.

Taken together, these measures resulted in an extremely aerodynamically clean design. It was a revelation.

Equipped with the maximum bomb load that the other two could manage, 3500lb, it had a calculated range of 3600 miles compared to 1862 miles and 994 miles. There was every reason to believe, in 1936, that this remarkable aeroplane – soon to receive the official designation He 177 – would be able to carry out any strategic bombing mission deemed necessary.

But less than a year after work on the aircraft began, the German military came to understand that it might soon be required to fight a series of fast limited engagements against countries bordering or not too far from Germany. There would be no need for a long-range bomber, but it was thought that the He 177 might make a good anti-shipping bomber.

GERMAN BOMBER DEVELOPMENT TIME

• Early 1935	The RLM issues a specification for a Fernbomber or 'long-range bomber' to Junkers and Dornier.
• June 3, 1936	A meeting is held between representatives of the RLM, Junkers, Blohm & Voss, Messerschmitt, Henschel and Heinkel to discuss the Fernbomber specification. Following the meeting, a revised specification is issued by the RLM. Neither the Dornier Do 19 nor the Junkers Ju 89 as submitted to the earlier specification are able to meet it.
• August 1, 1936	Deadline for submission of preliminary designs by Junkers, Blohm & Voss, Messerschmitt, Henschel and Heinkel to meet the June 3 Fernbomber specification.
• Late summer 1936	Heinkel begins work on the He 119 as a technology demonstrator for its P 1041 Fernbomber design.
• October 16, 1936	The P 1041 is chosen as the successful design in the Fernbomber competition.
• October 28, 1936	First flight of the Dornier Do 19 V1 bomber prototype.
• January 1937	Henschel is given a contract to develop a high altitude test aircraft for the DVL. This becomes the P 30 and is later given the RLM designation Hs 128.
• April 11, 1937	First flight of the Junkers Ju 89 bomber prototype.
• April 29, 1937	Generalfeldmarschall Hermann Göring orders that the development of both the Junkers Ju 89 and Dornier Do 19 should cease.
• July 1937	First flight of the He 119 V1.
• August 6, 1937	Heinkel P 1041 mock-up inspected by the RLM.
• September 19, 1937	Hamburger Flugzeugbau receives a contract for three P 54 flying boat prototypes. This will become the Ha 222, later the BV 222.
• November 11, 1937	A revised mock-up of the P 1041, now designated the He 177, is approved.
• November 22, 1937	Adolf Hitler visits the Messerschmitt factory at Augsberg and is shown a mock-up of a very large four-engined bomber – presumably of the company's rejected submission for the Fernbomber competition.
• October 1938	An order is placed for six Heinkel He 177 prototypes. Henschel enters talks with the RLM to develop its Hs 128 for the military.
• Autumn 1938	The RLM decides that a larger flying boat transport than the BV 222 is needed and begins talks with Blohm & Voss about building what will become the BV 238.
• February 1939	Henschel receives an order for six prototypes of its militarised Hs 128 – the Hs 130.
• February 24, 1939	The order for Heinkel He 177 prototypes is doubled to 12.
• Mid-1939	Work commences on a version of the He 177 with four separate engines under the designation He 179.

ment

Attacking ships at sea required precision as well as the ability to avoid flak guns firing from the target. Therefore, it was decided that the He 177 should be fitted out for dive-bombing duties. However, the aircraft had not been designed with this in mind and Heinkel struggled to make the necessary changes. As the Second World War began, on September 1, 1939, the first He 177 prototype was being prepared for its maiden flight but the type was still a long way from being production-ready. And once flight-testing began, it emerged that the source of the aircraft's impressive specifications - the linked engines in their streamlined housings - was also going to be a source of serious and previously unforeseen problems.

With the He 177 mired in technical difficulties, the Luftwaffe had to rely entirely on its fleet of medium and dive-bombers - the Heinkel He 111, Dornier Do 17 and latterly Junkers' Ju 88 for the war's early engagements. The first two were already outdated and in need of replacement, while the Ju 88 required further development to make it suitable for service as an out-and-out bomber. A new specification had been issued in July 1939 for a 'Bomber B' to meet this need but the contest eventually ended in failure due to the non-availability of the necessary engines. The 1930s bombers just had to soldier on.

At the beginning of 1940, efforts were made to extend the range of both the He 177 and the Focke-Wulf Fw 200, an airliner refitted for maritime reconnaissance, so that the Luftwaffe could play a greater role in seeking out supply convoys travelling to and from British ports. Mid-air refuelling experiments were carried out and the design of each aircraft was examined in detail to establish whether additional fuel could be carried.

However, the experiments served only to highlight the technological challenges involved in mid-air refuelling and neither aircraft proved particularly well suited to further development. Tensions were now growing between Germany and America too, so a new long-range bomber requirement was issued during the summer, following the conquest of France.

This aircraft had to be capable, if needed, of taking off from Brest on the northwestern tip of what was now occupied France, delivering between three and five tonnes of bombs over American soil and returning safely. Such an attack would have paid dividends both in terms of propaganda and in forcing the Americans ▶

ABOVE: The Dornier Do 19 V1. Large and slow even by the standards of the time, on paper it was hopelessly outclassed by the brilliantly modern but highly complex Heinkel P 1041 – which would become the He 177.

ABOVE: While the nose of the Do 19 might look basic, it should be remembered that this was only the first prototype. Had it not been for the sparkling P 1041, the Dornier might have been developed further and formed the basis for a more advanced bomber later.

NE

• July 1939	The RLM issues a specification for a second generation medium bomber, 'Bomber B'. Preliminary designs are submitted by Arado, Dornier, Focke-Wulf, Heinkel and Junkers.
• July 6, 1939	Heinkel receives an order for 20 pre-production He 177s.
• August 1939	A total of 800 He 177s are ordered with a deadline for completion of April 1943.
• September 1939	Plans for the He 179 are dropped.
• September 1, 1939	The Second World War begins.
• November 20, 1939	He 177 V1 CB+RP makes its first test flight.
• February 1940	Dornier presents the Do 317 design to the RLM as its tender for Bomber B.
• February 13, 1940	Focke-Wulf presents its Baubeschreibung Nr. 225 Mittlerer Bomber – 2 x DB 603 project description to the RLM as its tender for Bomber B.
• Circa spring 1940	Heinkel drops out of the Bomber B competition.
• March 1, 1940	Focke-Wulf's Nr. 225 Bomber B aircraft receives the designation Fw 191.
• May 23, 1940	The Hs 130 V1 makes its flight debut.
• Mid-1940	The RLM issues a new specification for a Fernkampfflugzeug with a total maximum range of 15,000km. Focke-Wulf and Junkers are initially invited to tender, with Messerschmitt being brought on board shortly afterwards. Contracts are issued for two prototypes each of the Dornier, Focke-Wulf and Junkers designs to the Bomber B specification.
• November 29, 1940	The Junkers Ju 288 V1 makes its first flight, three and a half months ahead of rival Focke-Wulf's Fw 191 V1.
• January 22, 1941	The Luftwaffe General Staff call for comparative tests between the Fw 200, the He 177 and the Blohm & Voss BV 222 to assess their suitability to support the U-boat campaign against shipping in the Atlantic.
• March 5, 1941	Messerschmitt's P 1061 design is chosen as the successful design in the Fernkampfflugzeug competition. It is given the RLM designation Me 264 and a contract for six prototypes and 30 production examples is issued.
• March 18, 1941	The Focke-Wulf Fw 191 V1 makes its first flight.
• June 1941	Arado's E 340 design is knocked out of the Bomber B competition.
• July 14, 1941	Following the invasion of the Soviet Union, Hitler issues Führer Directive No. 32 (Supplement), restricting the allocation of non-war-essential military equipment development contracts.

ABOVE: Like the Dornier Do 19, the Junkers Ju 89 was made to appear slow and basic by the P 1041. Yet it was still faster and more capable than its immediate competitor and unlike Dornier and its Do 19, Junkers did not give up on the Ju 89. Instead, it was developed into the Ju 90.

ABOVE: The silhouette of the Ju 89 as seen from below is not entirely dissimilar to that of the Ju 90 it was later to become, which in turn became the Ju 290.

to invest valuable resources in setting up an extensive network of anti-aircraft defences. But its effect on Germany's immediate prospects would have been negligible.

Therefore, the desire to strike a blow against the continental USA quickly faded as the need to keep up attacks on Britain and to destroy its supply convoys grew ever more pressing. The Kriegsmarine's U-boats, successful as they were, simply could not find and sink ships fast enough to choke off Britain's lifeline.

Consequently, almost every large aircraft then in service or under development for the Luftwaffe was assessed for the anti-shipping role in early 1941, with particular consideration being given to whether in-development air-to-surface guided weapons such as the PC 1400X or Hs 293 could be carried. The requirement for an aircraft that could bomb America rapidly became a requirement for an aircraft to find and attack supply ships.

There was also a requirement for a bomber capable of flying over Britain at extremely high altitude, where it would be less vulnerable to interception. Suitable designs for each requirement were chosen, but with most factories in Germany already operating at maximum capacity on existing types, particularly as the invasion of the Soviet Union got under way, heavy bomber design and production was largely outsourced to subcontractors primarily in France but also in Italy, Holland and elsewhere.

Just as this programme was gearing up, on August 17, 1942, the first bombing raid to be carried out by American Boeing B-17s operating from British soil took place. The subcontractors' work progressed steadily but the liberation of France during the summer of 1944 automatically put an end to all hopes of building another large piston-engine aircraft for the Luftwaffe.

At the same time, aircraft production within Germany itself underwent a large-scale

GERMAN JET AIRCRAFT DEVELOPMENT TIMELINE

• **Summer 1941**	Inaccurate Messerschmitt figures result in a new Fernkampfflugzeug requirement being issued, with the necessary maximum range reduced to 12,000km. The order for 30 Me 264s is put on hold and the number of prototypes is reduced to five. Junkers' engine division announces that the Jumo 222 engine, upon which the Bomber B programme depends, is unlikely to reach full production. Focke-Wulf and Junkers' aircraft division are forced to consider radical alterations to their Fw 191 and Ju 288 designs in order to make them viable without the powerplant.
• **August 1941**	Plans are drawn up to equip the He 177 for mid-air refuelling to allow longer range operations. Messerschmitt is given leave to continue working on the Me 264.
• **December 1941**	The deadline for design submissions to the rerun of the Fernkampfflugzeug competition passes. The competitors are confirmed as a revised four-engined Me 264, a six-engined Focke-Wulf design, Junkers' Ju 390 and a revised version of the He 177. Entered but rejected are the BV 238, Ju 290 and a six-engined Me 264.
• **December 11, 1941**	Germany declares war on the United States.
• **Early 1942**	Production of the He 177 is scaled back until various problems with its design – particularly with its engines – can be overcome.
• **January 1942**	Blohm & Voss sets about outsourcing some of the BV 238 design work to French subcontractors and draws up preliminary plans for a land version, the BV 250.
• **Late January 1942**	Arado completes its E 470 project – an assessment of the possibilities for building long-range transports and bombers.
• **February 1, 1942**	An experimental squadron is formed to bring the He 177 into service with the Luftwaffe.
• **Februrary 15, 1942**	Generalfeldmarschall Erhardt Milch, the air inspector general in charge of aircraft production, asks the engineer responsible for aircraft development, Flugbaumeister Walter Friebel, whether any of the tendered Fernkampfflugzeug designs will have sufficient range for what is referred to as the 'Aufgabe Amerika' or 'America task'. He is told that they will not.
• **March 1942**	Five prototypes of the high-altitude Heinkel He 274 bomber are ordered, plus three prototypes of the Junkers Ju 390. Messerschmitt's success in the Fernkampfflugzeug competition is confirmed and work on the Me 264 bomber is expected to proceed to full production.
• **March 10, 1942**	The Junkers Ju 288 is officially declared the successful design in the Bomber B competition.
• **April 25, 1942**	Willy Messerchmitt proposes the Me 264 for a reconnaissance role – seeking out Allied convoys and dropping transmitter buoys to guide U-boats into the area.
• **July 13, 1942**	Part of the development of the He 274 is handed over to the SAUF (Société Anonyme des Usines Farman) company in Paris.
• **August 1942**	French firm SNCASO (Société Nationale des Constructions Aéronautiques du Sud-Ouest) is subcontracted by Focke-Wulf to carry

programme of reorganisation. Twenty aircraft types were cancelled, including the He 177, and efforts were concentrated on building as many fighters as possible to combat the waves of American and British bombers now pounding Germany on an almost daily (and nightly) basis. Development work focused on interceptors that could waylay the bombers as they arrived and shoot down as many of them as possible.

This was not the end of German ambitions to build an effective bomber however. During the autumn of 1943, a competition had been held to produce a jet bomber capable of outpacing enemy fighters. The liberation of France in 1944 brought work on the winning design, the Ju 287, to a halt, but a few months later – in November 1944 – a design submission by Messerschmitt brought about a new competition. It was proposed that a fast four-engined jet bomber, built quickly, might succeed in flying over to Britain and destroying the British and American bomber fleets on the ground. It would be so fast that no British or American fighter would be able to stop it. And if enough damage could be done to the Allies' bombers and their bases, they might be forced to pause or even halt their bombing campaign – providing Germany with much needed respite.

Unfortunately, developing Messerschmitt's design, the P 1107, would take months or even years so the almost fully developed Ju 287 was resurrected to compete against it, resulting in the third of the last three German aircraft design competitions of the war – the other two being for a single-jet day fighter and a twin-jet all-weather night fighter.

Much to the chagrin of Messerschmitt and Junkers, a third design was added to the contest at the last minute – the Horten XVIII flying wing. An intensive four-day conference towards the end of February 1945 concluded that there was much to recommend the Horten design, while Messerschmitt's calculations relating to the P 1107 failed to add up. The Ju 287 had few demonstrable advantages over the others but was chosen to enter production in any case, simply because it required the shortest development time.

By now, however, it was far too late for any new aircraft to enter production, the war in Europe ending only two-and-a-half months later.

Germany never managed to build a dedicated strategic bomber, despite vast expenditure on numerous projects and the construction or partial construction of several prototypes. This ▶

RLM BOMBER REQUIREMENTS WITH COMPETING DESIGNS

FERNBOMBER (LONG-RANGE BOMBER)
Date: 1936
Competitors: Heinkel P 1041 (He 177)
Messerschmitt design
Henschel P 26
Junkers design
Blohm & Voss design

BOMBER B
Date: July 1939
Competitors:
Arado E 340
Dornier Do 317
Focke-Wulf Fw 191
Junkers Ju 288

FERNKAMPFFLUGZEUG (LONG-RANGE COMBAT AIRCRAFT) FIRST TRY
Date: Late summer 1940 to March 1941
Competitors:
Focke-Wulf Fernkampfflugzeug
Junkers design (possibly EF 100 or derivative)
Messerschmitt P 1061 (Me 264)

FERNKAMPFFLUGZEUG SECOND TRY
Date: Mid-1941 to March 1942
Competitors:
Focke-Wulf Fernkampfflugzeug (revised)
Heinkel six-engined design
Junkers Ju 390
Messerschmitt Me 264
Blohm & Voss BV 238/250

FERNERKUNDER (LONG-RANGE RECONNAISSANCE AIRCRAFT)
Date: March 1941 to March 1942
Competitors:
Junkers Ju 290
Focke-Wulf Fw 300

HIGH-ALTITUDE BOMBER
Date: 1941 to March 1942
Heinkel He 274

FERNKAMPFFLUGZEUG FINAL PHASE
Date: Winter 1942 to May 1943
Competitors:
Focke-Wulf Fernkampfflugzeug (becomes Ta 400)
Messerschmitt Me 264
Heinkel He 277

STRAHLBOMBER (JET BOMBER)
Dates: Autumn 1943 to September 1944
Competitors:
Blohm & Voss P 188
Arado E 395
Junkers EF 122 (Ju 287)

LANGSTRECKENBOMBER (LONG-DISTANCE BOMBER)
Dates: November 1944 to March 1945
Horten XVIII
Junkers Ju 287
Messerschmitt P 1107

	out design work on the Fw 300. At around the same time, Blohm & Voss contracts Breguet to build two prototypes of its BV 144 civil transport.
• **September 15, 1942**	SAUF in France is ordered to construct a mock-up of the He 274.
• **October 1942**	Willy Messerschmitt continues to promote the six-engined version of the Me 264. Milch doubts the company's performance estimates, stating: "This Me 264 merely offers propaganda value."
• **November 1942**	Focke-Wulf compels a group of French designers from SNCASO to work at a company facility in Lage, Germany, on its Fw 300 design. Arado begins to assess swept wing forms under the project designation E 560.
• **December 23, 1942**	The Me 264 V1 RE+EN makes its first test flight.
• **February 1943**	Focke-Wulf compels a further group of SNCASO designers to join the Fw 300 team at Lage – bringing the total number of French designers working there to 150.
• **February 20, 1943**	Heinkel completes the transfer of the entire He 274 project to SAUF.
• **March 1943**	Heinkel proposes a new version of the He 177 with four separate BMW 801 engines and enlarged wings. All work on the Fw 191 is brought to an end.
• **March 5, 1943**	Focke-Wulf presents the RLM with a new bomber description – Baubeschreibung Nr. 262 Fernkampfflugzeug mit 6 x BMW 801E-Motoren.
• **March 18, 1943**	Hermann Göring tells senior figures in Germany's aircraft manufacturing and technology industry that they are failing and calls for a bomber that can function as well as the RAF's best bombers.
• **March 19, 1943**	Junkers begins an extensive wind tunnel test programme to assess swept wing shapes.
• **March 23, 1943**	Me 264 V1 suffers a collapsed undercarriage leg on landing and is too damaged for flight trials to continues.
• **May 1943**	Series production of the Me 264 is cancelled. Focke-Wulf is finally awarded a development contract for its Fernkampfflugzeug. The Baubeschreibung Nr. 262 aircraft is designated the Ta 400, although subcontractors are told that it is to be called the Fw 300A.
• **May 23, 1943**	Adolf Hitler calls together Ernst Heinkel, Claude Dornier, Willy Messerschmitt, Kurt Tank of Focke-Wulf, Walter Blume of Arado, Heinrich Hertel of Junkers and Richard Vogt of Blohm & Voss to ask them personally about the technical situation regarding the development of new aircraft for the Luftwaffe.
• **June 1943**	The Bomber B programme is cancelled.

ABOVE: When the He 177 was chosen to be Germany's strategic bomber, the type of war it was expected to fight was land-based. Britain's declaration of war on Germany came as an unwelcome surprise and left the RLM and the Luftwaffe scrambling to come up with an aircraft that could help U-boats track down and destroy convoys ferrying supplies across the Atlantic – such as the one pictured here.

ABOVE:The Fw 200 had been designed to a Deutsche Lufthansa specification and made its first flight shortly after Heinkel's P 1041 had been chosen as the winner of the Fernbomber competition. During the early stages of the war, the militarised Fw 200C version enjoyed unexpected levels of success in attacking Allied shipping but it struggled with the manoeuvres it was required to perform and several were destroyed as a result of structural failure.

ABOVE: The Focke-Wulf Fw 200 Condor was a civilian airliner pressed into service as a long-range reconnaissance and maritime patrol aircraft – primarily due to the lack of any other type capable of doing the job.

ABOVE: As the war progressed, it was hoped that a long-range patrol aircraft armed with newly developed guided anti-shipping missiles such as the unpowered PC 1400 X or 'Fritz X' could help turn the tide in the Battle of the Atlantic. But building a suitable and satisfactory launch aircraft proved almost impossible.

failure can be attributed in part to the ambitious design of the He 177 and the amendments subsequently made to it. Under other circumstances, development of the type might have been halted despite the large sums already spent on it, but the need to bring it into service was so pressing that the Germans persevered.

GERMAN JET AIRCRAFT DEVELOPMENT TIMELINE

• **June 7, 1943**	Junkers begins wind tunnel testing its swept wing EF 116 design against that of the Ar 234.
• **July 1943**	Series production of the Me 264 is reinstated by direct order of Adolf Hitler. Arado begins to assess flying wing aircraft forms under the project designation E 555. Junkers proposes a stopgap long-range bomber design – the Ju 488. Work on the latter is subcontracted to French firms.
• **July 21, 1943**	SAUF in Paris is told to build two prototype and four pre-production He 274s – rather than the five prototypes originally ordered from Heinkel more than a year ago.
• **August 11, 1943**	Arado produces a report outlining the possibilities for building a two-seat jet bomber.
• **Autumn 1943**	The RLM issues a requirement for a long distance jet bomber to attack England and invites tenders from Junkers, Arado and Blohm & Voss. Ernst Heinkel sets to work on the He 277 bomber with four separately mounted engines. Arado begins to consider ways in which its Ar 234 jet reconnaissance design can be scaled up under the project designation E 395.
• **September 8, 1943**	First flight of the Dornier Do 317 V1 – long after Dornier has lost the Bomber B competition and three months after the whole competition has been scrapped.
• **September 30, 1943**	Wind tunnel testing of the EF 122 swept wing bomber design begins at Junkers.
• **October 1, 1943**	Focke-Wulf draws up plans to send another 60 French designers to work at its Lage facility on the Ta 400.
• **December 22, 1943**	Focke-Wulf chief executive Kurt Tank and production manager Willi Kaether meet Conrad Haberstolz, the German armaments ministry's representative in Italy and a former Focke-Wulf executive, to discuss building parts of the Ta 400 in Italy.
• **January 1944**	Junkers is awarded a contract to build at least one prototype of its EF 122 fast bomber design under the designation Ju 287. Heinkel is ordered to develop its P 1068 jet bomber design as a matter of the utmost urgency so that it can be rushed into production, combining it with the work already carried out by Arado on its E 395 to ultimately create the He 343.
• **January 11, 1944**	Heinkel proposes combining Me 264 wings with the He 277's fuselage to create a new long-range bomber but this idea is dropped before the end of the month.
• **February 1944**	Tank travels to Como to discuss the outsourcing of Ta 400 production to Italian firms.
• **April 1944**	Focke-Wulf signs a deal with Italian firms Fiat, Breda and Piaggio to build sections of the Ta 400.
• **April 8, 1944**	The Hs 130 programme is finally abandoned.
• **April 14, 1944**	The repaired Me 264 V1, now fitted with BMW 801 MG/2TC-1 engines is rolled out, ready for flight testing to recommence.
• **April 15, 1944**	Messerschmitt draws up fresh plans to use the Me 264 as a long-range reconnaissance aircraft.
• **May 1944**	The Junkers Ju 290B and Ju 390A-1 are cancelled.
• **Spring to early summer 1944**	The BV 238 V1 flying boat begins flight testing.
• **June 10, 1944**	Representatives of Focke-Wulf meet representatives of SNCASO in Paris to discuss progress on designing the Ta 400's fuel tanks.

Thereafter, Germany's ever-changing wartime circumstances only served to exacerbate the problem. By the time consideration was given to a replacement or successor it was already too late. It must be remembered that designing a successful bomber was much more difficult than designing a successful fighter – which in itself was no easy feat.

Bombers typically required four engines working in unison and all the systems associated with them; they needed large fuel tanks positioned correctly to prevent unwanted changes in the aircraft's centre of gravity and handling as they drained; they required defensive turrets, either manned or controlled through an electrical or hydraulic system; their undercarriage and structure had to be strong enough to cope with massive loads and with the strain of violent manoeuvring during combat and they had to carry systems to allow for the accurate delivery of their load when they reached their target.

Putting all of this together took time. And tailoring it to a particular mission specification took even longer. At the beginning, Germany needed a high performance strategic bomber. Then it needed an extremely long-range bomber for hitting fixed targets on the American east coast. Then it needed a long-range bomber and reconnaissance aircraft capable of finding and attacking mobile targets in the Atlantic. Then a jet bomber that could hit fixed targets either in England or on the Continent.

The companies attempting to meet these challenging requirements were all simultaneously being stretched to the limit by the rigours of fighter development and mass-production. It is little wonder that work on heavy bomber projects was outsourced to foreign subcontractors. Yet even if the work had been handed to the French firms at the very moment that the government of France agreed an armistice with the Germans, there would have scarcely been enough time to design, prototype, thoroughly test and manufacture the complex aircraft they were contracted to produce before they were liberated in August 1944.

It has been argued that the German designers continued to work on bomber projects right up to the end of the war because they hoped to avoid being press-ganged into joining the army, or that they were deluded, or that they hoped to curry favour with the Allies when the inevitable collapse came. But no one in Germany was preparing for absolute defeat at the beginning of 1945. The Allies had yet to penetrate the borders of Germany itself. Although they were acutely aware of losing their French 'allies' and the constant air-raids, the aircraft manufacturers cannot have known how swiftly their nation's remaining ground defences would be swept aside.

They were corporate bodies, embedded in a network of supply chains and part of a vast industrial complex, attempting to fulfil their contractual obligations and build the aircraft that their country's aviators so desperately needed. In so doing, they created the designs featured in this publication. ●

ABOVE: A test launch of a Hs 293 guided anti-shipping missile from a Heinkel He 111. The aircraft could only carry one and its range was limited. An aircraft with greater endurance that could be equipped with multiple missiles might have been able to wreck havoc across the Atlantic.

ABOVE: The 'prototype' of the Junkers Ju 287 was little more than a flying testbed made from the fuselage of a He 177, the tail of a Ju 188, and wheels from crashed B-24 Liberators, with new wings added. Nevertheless, it represented the most viable option for a new Luftwaffe bomber towards the end of the war.

• **June 1944**	The first 20 pre-production Arado Ar 234B-0 aircraft are delivered.
• **July 3, 1944**	The He 277 is now cancelled, although Ernst Heinkel receives no notification that this is the case.
• **July 18, 1944**	The Me 264 V1 is destroyed in a bombing raid.
• **August 1944**	Eugen Sänger proposes a sub-orbital rocket bomber in his Über einen Raketenantrieb für Fernbomber report.
• **August 8, 1944**	The Ju 287 V1 is flown for the first time.
• **August 18, 1944**	Work on the Ju 488 ends when French contractor Breguet's facility near Toulouse is liberated.
• **August 25, 1944**	Development of the He 274 and construction of the two prototypes comes to an end at SAUF as Paris is liberated by the Allies.
• **September 6, 1944**	The Ta 400 is cancelled.
• **September 23, 1944**	Hitler orders Messerschmitt to cease all work on the Me 264.
• **September 28, 1944**	Final flight test of the Ju 287 V1.
• **November 1944**	Willy Messerschmitt proposes a four-turbojet bomber design, sparking a new long distance bomber competition.
• **November 21-22, 1944**	A meeting of the Entwicklungshauptkommission discusses the Ju 287 and at the end of talks its development "hangs in the balance".
• **Winter 1944**	Work on Arado's E 555 and E 560 programmes has come to an end.
• **January 26, 1945**	Messerschmitt issues a brochure for the P 1107 jet bomber. The specification contained within is then assessed using data gathered from the Ju 287 test programme. A date is set for a full comparison between the two types – February 20-23 – and in the meantime the Horten XVIII is added to the comparison.
• **February 10, 1945**	Focke-Wulf publishes Kurzbeschreibung Nr. 28, featuring details of fast bomber, bomber carrier and self-sacrifice aircraft devised by executives at Daimler-Benz.
• **February 20-23, 1945**	A conference is held at Dessau to compare the detailed features of the Messerschmitt P 1107, the Ju 287 and the Horten XVIII. There is no clear 'winner'.
• **March 31, 1945**	Heinkel's technical design department is evacuated from Vienna, ending work on all projects.
• **April 8, 1945**	British forces overrun Focke-Wulf's Bad Eilsen design facilities, ending work on all projects.
• **April 21, 1945**	American forces overrun Junkers' headquarters at Dessau, ending work on all projects.
• **April 29, 1945**	American forces overrun Messerschmitt's Oberammergau design facilities, ending work on all projects.
• **Early May 1945**	Arado's Brandenburg facility is overrun by Soviet troops, ending work on all projects.
• **May 3, 1945**	British forces overrun Blohm & Voss's headquarters in Hamburg. It is likely that work on all projects ended some time in mid-April.

Birth of the 'Flam

Fernbomber – Heinkel He 177

When Heinkel's He 177 was first unveiled as the P 1041 it was a technological dream come true. But the dream became a nightmare when its advanced design proved to be a little too far beyond the state-of-the-art.

Throughout the 1930s and even into the 1940s, Ernst Heinkel Flugzeugwerke prided itself on building fast aircraft. It began with the He 70 mail plane. This relatively small transport first flew in December 1932 and was all about speed.

Every aspect of its design was tailored to this purpose: flush rivets were used to give it a smooth skin, it had a retractable undercarriage - unusual at the time - its pilot and radio operator sat one behind the other to allow a narrow fuselage and its engine used ethylene glycol rather than water so it could have a smaller radiator.

The result of all this careful aerodynamic design and technical innovation was a world beater. Its top speed never came close to challenging the highly specialised racing aircraft of the day - the world air speed record in December 1932 was 407.5mph - but it could manage a consistent 222mph over 1000km carrying a 1000kg payload, which was a world record in itself.

During 1934, the He 70 design formed the basis for the larger He 111 bomber, which incorporated many of its aerodynamic features such as its elliptical inverted gullwing and small rounded control surfaces. Initially shown to the world as an airliner, the He 111 was billed as the 'fastest passenger plane in the world'. Heinkel was getting a reputation for building large aircraft capable of a remarkable turn of speed.

In 1935 the RLM issued a specification for a Langstrecken-Grossbomber or 'long-range heavy bomber'. Only two firms were invited to tender designs - Dornier and Junkers. Each was famous for producing large heavy aircraft, Dornier with its Do X and Junkers with the G.38, both of which first flew in 1929.

The companies' Langstrecken-Grossbomber proposals, the Do 19 and Ju 89, were duly submitted and deemed promising enough to warrant the commissioning of prototypes. However, despite being modern enough designs they were unimaginative, the former being intended as a stablemate for the speedy new Do 17 medium bomber and the latter a progression from the Ju 86 bomber about to enter service.

Neither was particularly fast and each had at least one particularly unappealing design flaw. The Do 19 was intended to have heavy two-man gun turrets, the weight of which hampered its already weak performance, and the Ju 89 suffered from longitudinal instability.

By 1936 it was evident that other companies felt far better performance could be achieved and on June 3 that year a second heavy bomber specification was issued with stringent requirements, particularly with regard to speed, that superseded those of the Langstrecken-Grossbomber.

The new Fernbomber or 'long-range bomber' would have to be able to carry 500kg of bombs 5000km with a top speed of 500kph at an altitude of 5500m. Neither Langstrecken-Grossbomber design came close on range or speed, although each could carry a heavier bomb load.

Dornier was not invited to tender, its design having been the worst of the two Langstrecken-Grossbombers, but Junkers was to be given a second chance since its Ju 89 was shaping up to be a promising basis for a new transport aircraft. The other firms included in the competition, eager to try their hand at designing a strategic bomber, were Dornier's rival in the seaplane business Blohm & Voss, the up-and-coming Messerschmitt, Henschel - an industrial giant with aviation ambitions - and Heinkel.

It's certain that all five firms put forward designs but today little is known about four of them. Junkers most likely fielded another

ABOVE: The Heinkel He 177 was designed for speed. Instead of two propellers on each wing, it had only one – driven by two linked engines. Its fuselage was streamlined and even its unusual undercarriage, where each pair of main wheels retracted in opposite directions, was designed to allow the use of thinner wings. Compared to its opponents in 1936, the design was light years ahead.

ABOVE: As a company, Heinkel set out to associate itself with fast aircraft during the early 1930s. The He 70 mail carrier was one of the firm's earliest attempts to create an aerodynamically clean design that could achieve impressive speeds with the relatively underpowered engines then available.

ABOVE: Designed and worked on at around the same time as the P 1041/He 177, the He 116 long-range mail carrier was another example of Heinkel's aerodynamic design philosophy.

ng Coffin'

ABOVE: Although it was ostensibly designed as an unarmed fast reconnaissance aircraft, the He 119 served as a hastily conceived and constructed technology demonstrator for the He 177's proposed power plant – the Daimler-Benz DB 606 – and its evaporative cooling system. The V1 pictured here is fitted with a conventional radiator under its nose because the evaporative system was not yet ready.

ABOVE: It is uncertain how many He 119s were built but the figure is likely to be three or four, with at least one of them being sold to Japan. The one depicted here is believed to be the He 119 V3 before it was converted to operate as a seaplane. Testing of the He 119 revealed early problems with both the DB 606 engine and the cooling system intended for the He 177.

version of its Ju 89, now in the process of becoming the Ju 90; Messerschmitt probably offered an early incarnation of its P 1061; Blohm & Voss may well have offered a design related to its four-engined BV 142, itself based on the four-engined Ha 139 floatplane, and Henschel served up its P 26, which eventually provided the basis for what became the Hs 130.

What is certain, however, is that Heinkel's P 1041 beat every other competitor hands down. Where the He 70 had combined a number of innovative but relatively uncomplicated features to produce an impressive top speed, the P 1041 managed not only a hugely impressive top speed but also immense range and loading capacity. And it did this by combining a number of cutting edge technologies which in 1936 only existed on paper.

In order to allow for thin wings and to prevent drag-inducing nacelles, the four necessarily large main undercarriage wheels were each mounted on separate legs - one retracting towards the fuselage and one towards the outer wing when the undercarriage was raised after take-off.

The engines proposed for the P 1041 represented the aircraft's biggest technological leap forward however. Heinkel had been working with Daimler-Benz on the new DB 606 - which was composed of two 1100hp DB 601s sitting side-by-side, connected via a single gearing system to a single propeller shaft. It was expected to produce more than 2000hp at take-off, so with two of them the P 1041 would be propelled by 4400hp of power.

Two engines running together in such a confined space generated a lot of heat, but rather than fit drag-inducing radiators, Heinkel's designers proposed an evaporative cooling system. The water/antifreeze coolant was pressurised so that it could remain liquid above its usual boiling point. Fully heated, it was then ducted away and depressurised, becoming steam. This was condensed by running it through pipes in the wing where it was exposed to the cold air outside the aircraft. Liquid again, it was fed right back into the engine to repeat the process.

The aircraft would be so fast that defensive armament could be light - just one manned MG 131 machine gun in each of the nose, tail, upper and lower fuselage positions.

The RLM adjudicators gambled on Heinkel's proven track record of turning out high-speed aircraft boasting cutting-edge features and aerodynamics that were the envy of the world. In fact, the mid to late 1930s were a golden age for the firm - at the same time that the P 1041 was being considered, the company was simultaneously working on the new He 115 floatplane and the He 116 extreme long-range mail plane, as well as upgrades to existing designs such as the He 111. It seemed perfectly reasonable to expect great things.

Nevertheless, the P 1041's engines were a risk. When it became clear in late summer 1936 that the RLM was particularly keen on its Fernbomber submission, Heinkel set about designing and building what amounted to a technology demonstrator - the He 119. Ostensibly a reconnaissance aircraft, this incorporated both the engine intended for the P 1041 and the cooling system that was meant to go along with it.

The design was rushed into production, paid for out of Heinkel's own funds, and the V1 prototype first flew in July 1937. The He 119 was a highly unusual design that looked as though it was built purely for speed. A monoplane with a single propeller at its nose, it lacked any sort of cockpit 'bulge'. Instead, the area of fuselage immediately aft of the propeller was extensively glazed. The DB 606 was positioned in the centre of the aircraft, over the wings, and connected to the propeller by a very long drive shaft that ran right through the centre of the crew compartment.

By now, another Heinkel design was being worked on which was also to use the evaporative cooling system, the He 100 fighter - a specially modified version of which eventually succeeded in breaking the absolute world air speed record on March 30, 1939, at 463.919mph. ▶

ABOVE: A close-up view of the He 119's extraordinary cockpit – where the drive shaft for the propeller passed between the crewmen. This is thought to be another view of the V1 with modified radiator.

ABOVE: Ernst Udet, in charge of the RLM's development section, was a close personal friend of Ernst Heinkel. He found himself in an awkward position when the chief of the Luftwaffe's General Staff, Hans Jeschonnek, decided that the He 177 which Udet had approved ought to be redesigned as a dive-bomber.

ABOVE: The Luftwaffe's rising star Hans Jeschonnek. Although he lacked the influence to simply order that the He 177 be made capable of dive-bombing, as the chief of the Luftwaffe's General Staff, he successfully persuaded the RLM – against the better judgement of its technical specialists – that this needed to happen.

The first P 1041 mock-up was inspected by RLM representatives at Heinkel's Rostock-Marienehe headquarters on August 6, 1937. Changes were requested - better visibility for the crew, better positioning of the gun turrets and a clearer layout of cockpit instrumentation - but these issues were quickly resolved and the revised mock-up was approved for production on November 11, 1937. The design received the official designation He 177.

Then company owner and founder Ernst Heinkel had a discussion with Ernst Udet, his close personal friend and head of the RLM's aircraft development section, about the new

ABOVE: A Heinkel He 177 in flight. Efforts to give the aircraft an effective dive-bombing capability resulted in long delays, but the type's unreliable engines were an even bigger cause for concern.

aircraft. Heinkel recalled in his autobiography, Stürmisches Leben or 'Stormy Life': "In the corner of my conservatory, he said to me: 'In future there won't be any more multi-engined bombers unless they can attack as dive-bombers. The He 111 is the last horizontal bomber. By its accuracy, a medium-sized twin-engined machine which, in a dive, can hit the target with its bomb load of 2000lb, has the same effect as a four-engined giant which carried 6000-8000lb of bombs in horizontal flight and can only drop them inaccurately.

"'We do not want these expensive, heavy machines which eat up more in material than a medium, twin-engined dive-bomber costs. Junkers has completed his first twin-engined Stuka, the Ju 88. We can build two or three with the same amount of material that a four-engined machine needs and achieve the same bombing effect. Jeschonnek is absolutely delighted. Furthermore, with the cheap super-Stukas, we can build up the numbers the Führer wants'."

Based on these revelations about preferring accurate two-engined 'super-Stukas' over inaccurate, heavy and

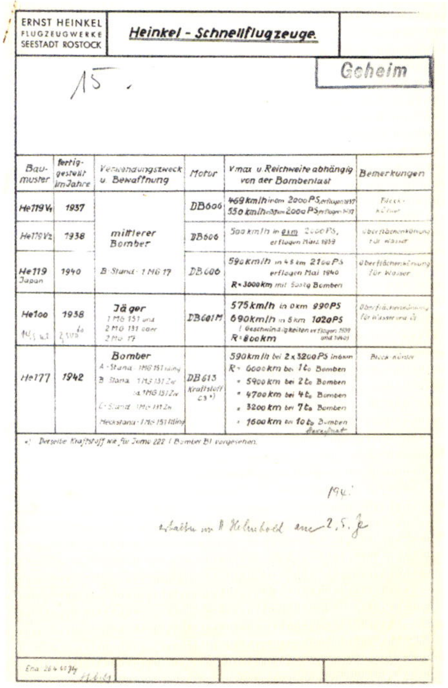

ERNST HEINKEL FLUGZEUGWERKE SEESTADT ROSTOCK

Heinkel - Schnellflugzeuge.

Geheim

15

Baumuster	fertiggestellt im Jahre	Verwendungszweck u. Bewaffnung	Motor	Vmax u. Reichweite abhängig von der Bombenlast	Bemerkungen
He 119 V1	1937	mittlerer Bomber	DB 606	469 km/h in 0 km 2000 PS, erflogen 1937 550 km/h in 4.5 km 2000 PS erflogen 1937	[illegible]
He 119 V2	1938		DB 606	500 km/h in 0 km 2000 PS, erflogen März 1939	Oberflächenkühlung für Wasser
He 119 Japan	1940	B-Stand: 1 MG 17	DB 606	590 km/h in 4.5 km 2100 PS erflogen Mai 1940 R = 3000 km mit 500 kg Bomben	Oberflächenkühlung für Wasser
He 100	1938	Jäger 1 MG 151 und 2 MG 131 oder 2 MG 17	DB 601 M	575 km/h in 0 km 990 PS 690 km/h in 5 km 1020 PS (Geschwindigkeiten erflogen 1939 und 1940) R = 800 km	Oberflächenkühlung für Wasser und Öl
He 177	1942	Bomber A-Stand: 1 MG 151 [illegible] B-Stand: 1 MG 131 Zw. u. 1 MG 151 Zw. C-Stand: 1 MG 131 Zw. Heckstand: 1 MG 151 [illegible]	DB 613 Kraftstoff C3 *)	590 km/h bei 2 x 3200 PS in 6 km R = 6000 km bei 1 t Bomben " 5900 km bei 2 t Bomben " 4700 km bei 4 t Bomben " 3200 km bei 7 t Bomben " 1600 km bei 10 t Bomben	[illegible]

*) Derselbe Kraftstoff wie für Jumo 222 (Bomber B) vorgesehen.

1941

ABOVE: This Heinkel document, dated April 26, 1941, shows the company's 'fast aircraft'. The list shows only three He 119s, with the He 119 V2 and He 119 Japan both listed as floatplanes. Next on the list is the He 100 fighter, followed by the He 177 – due to enter service in 1942.

expensive machines, Heinkel became concerned about the future of the He 177.

He wrote: "When Udet told me that the four-engined bomber was dead, I could not help thinking of the He 177. 'What about our 177?' I asked. 'If the four-engined bomber is no longer of any interest, there's no use our continuing to develop it'. He hesitated for a moment. 'Jeschonnek and the General Staff,' he said, 'unfortunately cannot see any way in which we can use it. Nobody is thinking of a war against England. The 'iron man' (as he called Göring) had full discussions with the Führer before taking the decision to concentrate all our means on the twin-engined Stuka. A war with England is absolutely out of the question. If anything happens, it will be a scrap with Poland or Czechoslovakia. The Führer will never let it come to a war which spreads outside the European continent.

"'For the only conflicts we are likely to be involved in, therefore, we only need a medium bomber with a small range and small bomb-load, but with the increased dive-bombing accuracy that we've now got with the new Ju 88. We can build as many as the Führer wants, in order to impress England and France, so they will leave us, whatever happens, in peace. We'll go on developing the He 177 for research purposes. Perhaps later we can use it as a long-distance machine for the navy, but it must be able to dive, or else it won't stand a chance'."

Heinkel was rather nonplussed by this: "'A giant plane like that,' I objected, 'can't be a dive-bomber.' 'But in practice the machine is twin-engined,' said Udet, 'and if the twin-engined Ju 88 can be a dive-bomber, why can't the He 177?' 'Because it's nearly twice as heavy'."

Heinkel went on to add: "This conversation with Udet was, in view of later events, probably the most serious I ever had with him. If what he said was true, the Luftwaffe was trying to meet Hitler's requirements in the confidence of there being no war with England or, at worst, a local war in the east, by building only medium dive-bombers. As their range could never be more than 300-odd miles, they would be inadequate in any war fought over the British Isles or at sea.

"Dropping the heavy bomber was a gamble based on England staying out of the war. It would be a catastrophe if we found ourselves fighting England without them."

Having said all that, Heinkel added: "The new line which Udet now announced to me was not followed consistently in the ministry's actions. The Technical Department continued to experiment with

ABOVE: Low to the ground and seemingly very narrow and compact, the He 177 was actually fractionally longer and wider in span than the Avro Lancaster.

four-engined long-distance bombers, such as were being developed by me in the He 177."

Eleven days after the He 177 design was approved for production, on November 22, 1937, the He 119 V1 set a new world record by carrying 500kg and 1000kg payloads 1000 miles at an average speed of 313.538mph. Unladen but with a conventional radiator in place of its unfinished cooling system, the same aircraft had already achieved a top speed of 351mph – the top speed of the first production Supermarine Spitfires, introduced the following year, was 362mph.

Making another record attempt on December 16, the V1 suffered engine failure and was destroyed in the resulting crash. It is believed that a total of four He 119s were built, but while they succeeded in making the case for the DB 606 engine through their incredible turn of speed, they also demonstrated its unreliability and showed how difficult it was to maintain.

An order for six He 177 prototypes was placed with Heinkel in October 1938.

Heinkel himself later wrote: "I proposed to the RLM on November 19, 1938, that they should not base everything on the success or failure of the rapidly tested double engine in the He 119, but should also authorise a second and third prototype of the He 177 as a normal four-engined aircraft, with four single Jumo 211s.

"This proposal was turned down flat by the General Staff, which gave the following reasons: 'The efficiency of the He 177 in dive-bombing depends upon the use of only two power units. The normal four-engined plane cannot be used as a dive-bomber. A development in that direction is consequently ruled out'."

In spite of this, Heinkel pressed ahead with a four-separate-engines version of the 177 during 1939 under the RLM designation He 179. On February 24, 1939, the number of He 177 prototypes on order was increased to 12 and on July 6 a further order for 20 pre-production aircraft was placed. In August, Heinkel received a full production order for 800 aircraft, to be fulfilled by April 1943. Work on building the He 177 prototypes was now well under way.

The following month, on September 4, the bomber's design underwent another major revision. It was decided that instead of heavy manned turrets – which might also pose problems during a dive-bombing attack – the He 177's defences would be changed to consist mostly of remote-controlled guns. Without the need to provide space for the gunner, turrets could be small and flat to reduce drag, particularly in the ventral and dorsal positions.

In addition, they could all be controlled from the armoured cockpit using a sophisticated system of hydraulics. Only the gun in the nose was to be operated by a crewman. All this necessitated a significant redesign of the cockpit, however.

Still, with the He 177's development rapidly gathering pace, the He 179 project was cancelled on September 12, 1939, less than a fortnight after the outbreak of the Second World War. By now, the He 119 programme was winding down and it was all too apparent to the company that fitting a pair of DB 606s to the He 177 was going to cause serious problems.

During the first flight of the He 177 V1 prototype, at the Rechlin Test Centre on November 20, 1939, the oil temperature of its DB 606s soared well above the recommended maximum limit – to 1200°C. This problem persisted as tests continued into 1940, with the second prototype first taking to the air on April 21, 1940.

Other problem areas included instability, vibrations, undercarriage weakness and poor brakes. Diving trials commenced with the V3 on April 24, 1940, but due to its tail being inadequately balanced the rear control surfaces developed severe flutter and the aircraft crashed, killing the pilot and two crew.

On April 26, the V1 had to make a crash landing after one of its engines failed. The V2 was destroyed when it crashed into the Baltic near Rostock, this time killing four men including the pilot.

No further testing could take place between until September 4, around four months later, when He 177 V4 flew for the first time. The V5 flew on September 30, 1940, and the V1 was reportedly repaired and ready to fly again in late December. The V6 joined them on December 18.

By February 1941, there were seven airworthy prototypes with five more close to full readiness. But on June 8, 1941, V4 suffered an engine fire which resulted in the destruction of the aircraft, though the pilot survived. As the programme of tests continued, this problem became increasingly serious.

At the Luftwaffe's Rechlin test facility, it was determined that since the engines were so tightly packed into a confined space, and so close to the leading edge of the wing, there was insufficient room for all the necessary fuel lines and oil pipes. Bent and stressed, these pipes tended to leak at their connection points, which meant the nacelle was usually awash with flammable liquids.

In addition, when the aircraft was flown at high altitude, oil in the engine tended to foam up. This reduced its lubricating properties and caused the engine con rod bearings to disintegrate. When the rod eventually tore through the engine case, oil flooded out onto the hot exhaust – starting the fire.

Despite these unresolved problems, deliveries of production model He 177A-1 aircraft commenced in December 1941. And this was only the beginning of the aircraft's troubled service history, its horrifying tendency to burst into flames earning it the nickname 'Flaming Coffin'. ●

ABOVE: How the He 177 was envisioned operating. The aircraft shown here, coded TM+1F, is test-launching a Blohm & Voss L10 torpedo. As an anti-shipping weapon, the He 177 was not a success. In the event of an engine fire, its crew would have had little chance of escape out over the open ocean.

Medium bomber mess

Bomber B – Arado E 340, Dornier Do 317, Focke-Wulf Fw 191 and Junkers Ju 288

The anticipated performance of the large He 177 put the Luftwaffe's existing medium bombers – the He 111, Do 17 and even the Ju 88 – to shame. It was clear that a modern replacement for these types would be needed but who would build it?

The new medium bomber specification issued in July 1939 called for a twin-engined design capable of carrying a 2000kg bomb load 3600km with a top speed of 600kph - fewer bombs, shorter distance but faster even than the He 177. It also had to be capable of dive-bombing and was expected to be powered by either Daimler-Benz DB 604 or Jumo 222 engines. A crew of three in a pressure cabin was also stipulated.

The former powerplant, with its cylinders arranged into a unique 'X' shape, had an anticipated power output of 2500hp, while the latter had six inline banks of four cylinders and an output of 2465hp. It was the astonishing potential of these engines that made the whole Bomber B programme worthwhile, certainly in comparison to the Junkers Ju 88, powered by two Jumo 211s at 1400hp each, and Dornier Do 217 with its BMW 801s producing 1540hp each.

When it is mentioned in 1939 documents, the new specification is referred to as 'Kampfflugzeug B', but by 1941 it had become Bomber B. Five companies were initially approached to tender designs for it: Arado, Dorner, Focke-Wulf, Junkers and Heinkel. However, it has been suggested that the specification was actually written around an existing Junkers proposal, since a mock-up for the firm's entry, the Ju 288, had already been built and inspected by the end of July 1939. The other companies had barely put pen to paper on their designs by this point - though Dornier had also been given a head start.

HEINKEL DESIGN

There was concern from the outset that Heinkel already had more work than it could cope with in developing the He 177 but nevertheless the company managed to produce a brochure on its Bomber B entry by November 16, 1939. Like many other Heinkel projects, nothing of this appears to have survived beyond scattered references in correspondence and elsewhere, so precisely what it looked like is unknown.

Even its designation is questionable. One Heinkel letter, written by company designer Robert Lusser, refers to it as the P 1035, but that number appears in other surviving Heinkel documents as referring to the He 100. Since the He 100 first flew in January 1938 and its designation could easily have preceded the He 177 (P 1041) and been P 1035, the Heinkel Bomber B may actually have been P 1045.

In any case, Lusser seems to have felt that Heinkel's design was never taken seriously, and that the RLM had only asked it to submit a design in order to generate additional ideas for the two predetermined front runners - Dornier and Junkers. Heinkel withdrew entirely in around April 1940.

ARADO E 340

Just as Heinkel was dropping out Arado presented its Bomber B entry, designated E 340, to the RLM on April 5, 1940. The brochure showed an unusual twin-boom tail design with a wingspan of 23m and 18.65m in length. It had no fewer than five weapons positions - all of them controlled remotely from the three-man pressurised crew compartment by a single gunner using periscopes to direct his fire.

Twin-MG 81 turrets were positioned just aft of the cabin, one on top of the fuselage and the other underneath, each of the tail booms had an MG 81 mounted in a rotating dome on its tip and the rear fuselage was fitted with a single MG 131.

Fuel was carried in six tanks - two in the central fuselage, one in each wing section between the central fuselage and the booms and another in each wing outboard of the booms. The forward fuselage tank could carry 750 litres, the rearward fuselage tank 2000 litres. The inner wing tanks carried 1385 litres each and the outer wing tanks 725 litres each.

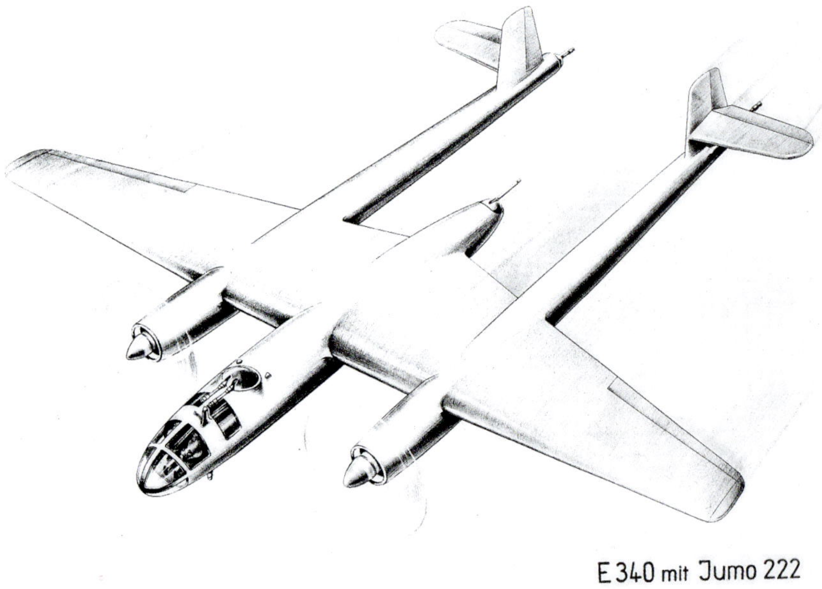

LEFT: Contemporary artwork depicting Arado's Bomber B – the E 340. Its unusual configuration does not appear to have been counted against it, but it was still the first design to be knocked out of contention.

LEFT: Junkers Ju 288 V9 pictured during a test flight in June 1942.

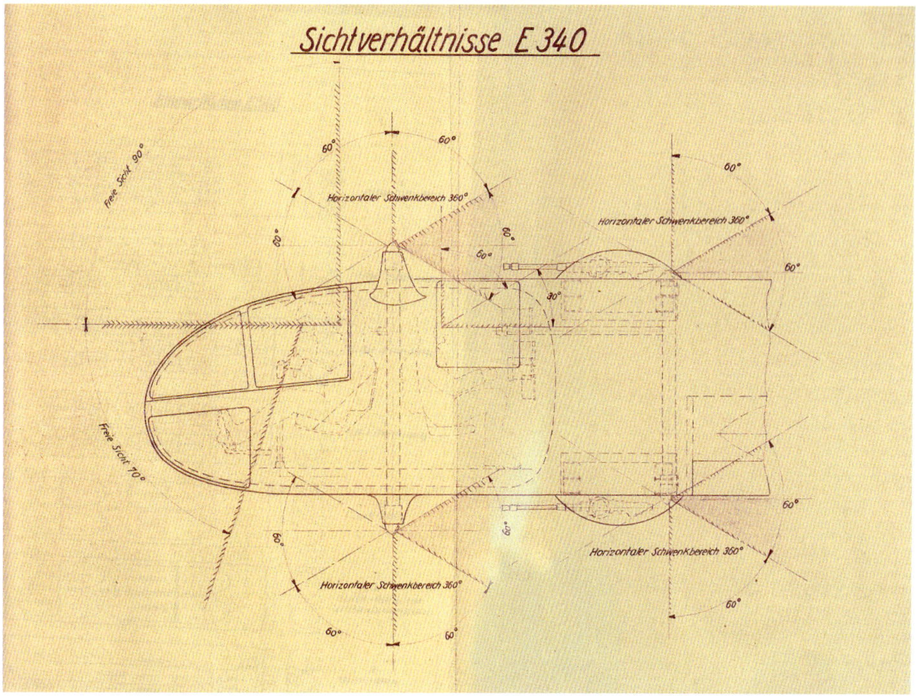

LEFT: Fields of vision for the E 340's gunner via a pair of periscopes are shown in this brochure drawing.

Bomb load options were 28 x SC 50 bombs for a total load of 1400kg, six SC 250s totalling 1500kg, six SD 500s for 3000kg, four SD 1000s at 4000kg, four LMA III mines at 2800kg, two LMB III mines at 1800kg, two LMA IIIs and two LMB IIIs at 3200kg or a single 1000kg torpedo.

Drawings showed how the E 340 could be powered by either two Jumo 222 or two DB 604 engines on the forward ends of the booms, and the undercarriage mainwheels retracted in just behind them. Although the design was unusual and relied on a hi-tech hydraulic system to operate its defensive weapons, the E 340 was designated the Ar 340 some time prior to December 1940.

At this point a mock-up of the Ar 340 was inspected by eight RLM men and a representative of weapons manufacturer Rheinmetall-Borsig. It generally met with their approval, although it was suggested that the bomb bay should be slightly enlarged to accommodate an optional load of eight SC 250s rather than just six. By this point Arado had upgraded the Ar 340's weaponry – two MG 131 each in the main fuselage upper and lower turrets and an MG 151 in the central rear position.

A total of 10 prototypes had been ordered from Arado and there were discussions with the Rheinmetall-Borsig representative about which hydraulic system would be best installed in the Ar 340 V3.

The precise date of the Ar 340's cancellation is unknown but there is no further mention of it as an ongoing project beyond June 1941.

DORNER DO 317

Alongside Junkers, Dornier was invited to participate in the Bomber B programme before the official offer to tender was presented, due to the success of its Do 217 medium bomber – which was superior even to the new Ju 88 when it first flew in 1938.

Perhaps because of this new bomber, Dornier seems to have had little interest in pressing ahead with its entry for Bomber B, the Do 317, with any great haste.

Despite being involved from an early stage, its first draft for the Do 317 was not presented to the RLM until February 1940. Nevertheless, the RLM quickly ordered six prototypes.

Another possible reason for Dornier's tardiness may have been some awareness of the slow progress being made on the Jumo 222 and DB 604. If neither engine was going to be available, and there were no performance gains to be made over the Do 217, there was little point in building a replacement for it.

Reluctantly therefore, Dornier pressed on and drew up plans to fit the Do 317 with DB 606 engines – the same as those proposed ▶

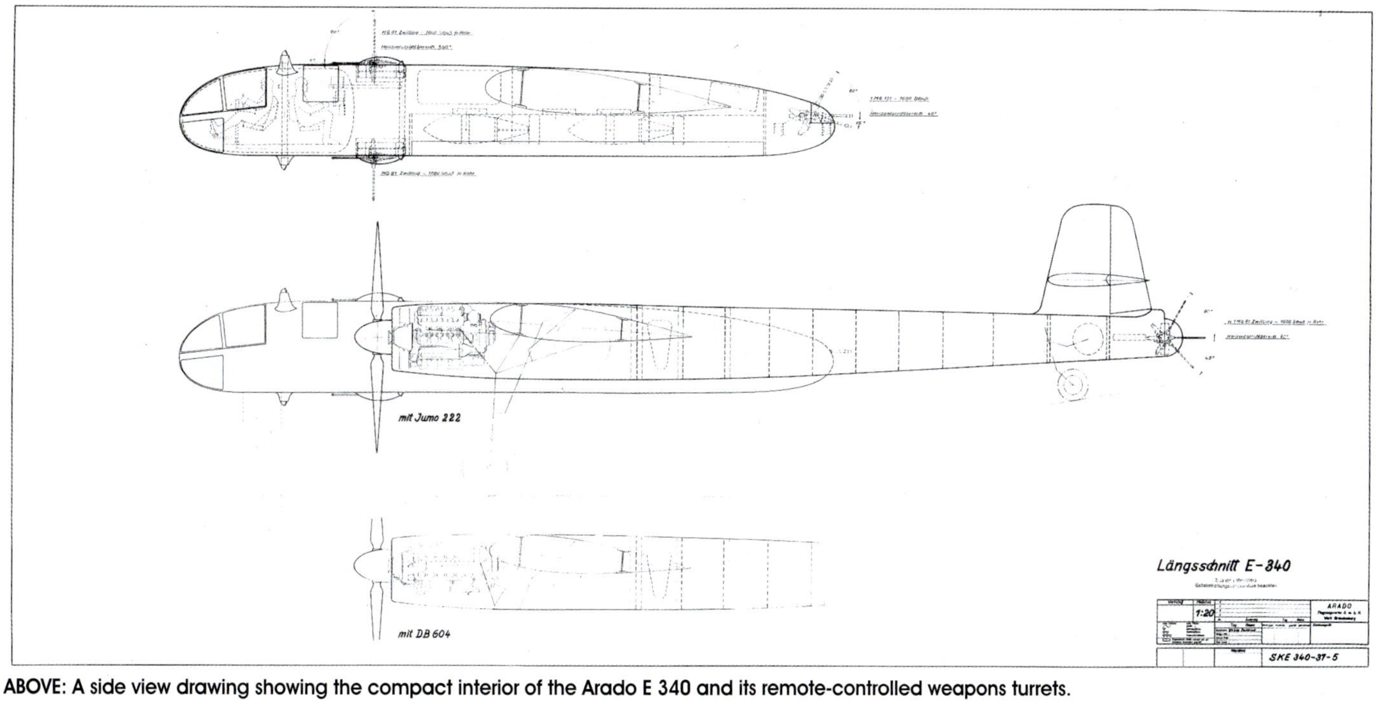

ABOVE: A side view drawing showing the compact interior of the Arado E 340 and its remote-controlled weapons turrets.

BELOW: The E 340 is typically depicted in period drawings with its turrets pointing forwards, but they were capable of rotating through 360°. Art by Daniel Uhr

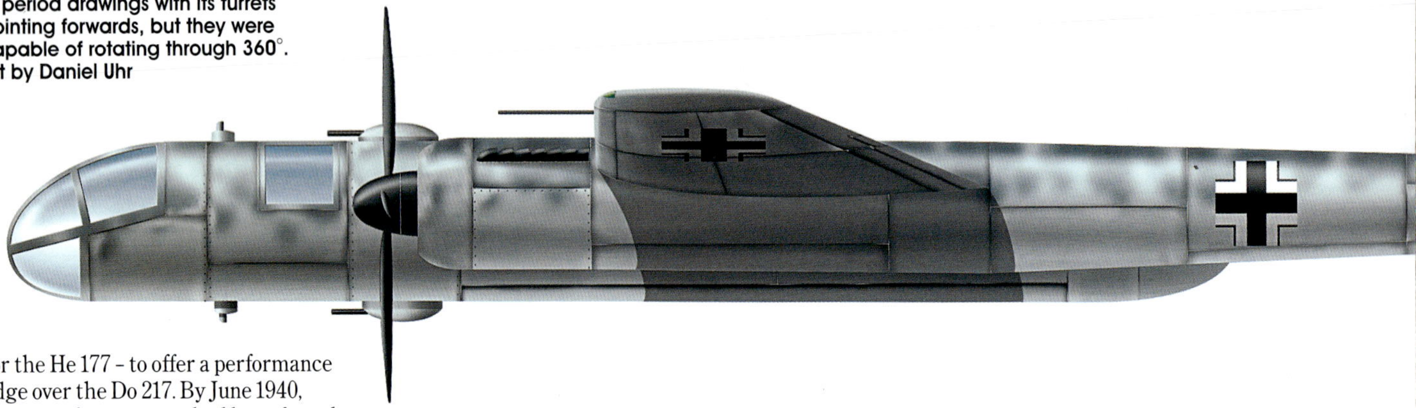

for the He 177 - to offer a performance edge over the Do 217. By June 1940, however, the company had been forced to specify BMW 801s for the Do 317 prototypes.

Mock-ups were inspected by the RLM, personnel from the Rechlin test centre and a group of sub-contractors on Thursday, October 17, and Friday, October 18, 1940. The result was a requirement to improve the type's turret armament and an order to speed up work on the aircraft's sighting devices and forward armament positioning. The mock-up seems to have been in a poor state of readiness for the visit, since the bomb bay was incomplete and armour positioning had not been indicated.

Complaints about this seem to have stung Dornier into action and a second inspection was scheduled for the following Tuesday and Wednesday - presumably giving the works team three days to make the mock-up ready. Three days later, an even larger group of 29 inspectors turned up to look it over.

It was remarked that the Do 317 mock-ups bore a distinct similarity to the Do 217 E-2 - which was being worked on in parallel.

The RLM noted in January 1941 that the Do 317 did not meet the basic requirement for landing speed. Dornier pointed out that the problem had already been faced during development of the Do 217 and solved using double-slot flaps.

On March 15, 1941, a first flight date of January 1942 was proposed for the Do 317 V1, with V2 following in February, V3 in March, V4 in May, V5 in July and V6 in August. Series production of the Do 317A was planned to begin at the end of 1942 with one example to be built in October, three in November and another six in December.

ABOVE: Dornier's unloved Do 317 V1 pictured on September 8, 1943, the day of its first flight – long after the design had been defeated in the Bomber B competition.

But by the end of 1941, it was evident that neither the Jumo 222 nor the DB 604 was going to be ready any time soon. The DB 606 had suffered crippling development problems and fitting the BMW 801 was deemed pointless. Therefore, plans were submitted to the RLM on January 1, 1942, for a Do 317 powered by DB 610s - a pair of linked DB 605s rather than DB 603s.

The new version of the aircraft was also to have a pressure cabin and remote controlled turrets. The nose weapon, an MG 81 Z, was also present and correct. Wingspan was enlarged and the type could carry a greater payload too.

By June 1943, the Do 317 V1 was almost ready but had not yet flown - some four years after the Bomber B programme began. It still had not flown by August, whereupon the RLM ordered that all parts for the yet-to-be-assembled Do 317 V2 should be scrapped and the type cancelled in its entirety.

The V1 finally flew, fitted with DB 603 engines, on September 8, 1943, at Friedrichshafen. The flight lasted 32 minutes with a second taking place on September 13 and a third on September 17. Shortly thereafter it was unceremoniously scrapped and its engines donated to one of 200 incomplete Do 217Ms that sat around the Dornier works awaiting engine deliveries.

The design of the Do 317 evolved through numerous different design variations, with the shape of its wings,

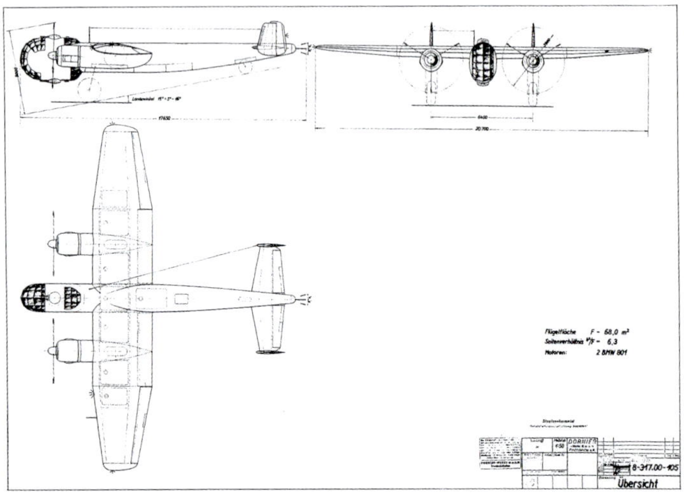

ABOVE: The Dornier Do 317 as it appeared in January 20, 1940, based heavily on the Do 217. It is shown here with a pair of BMW 801 engines.

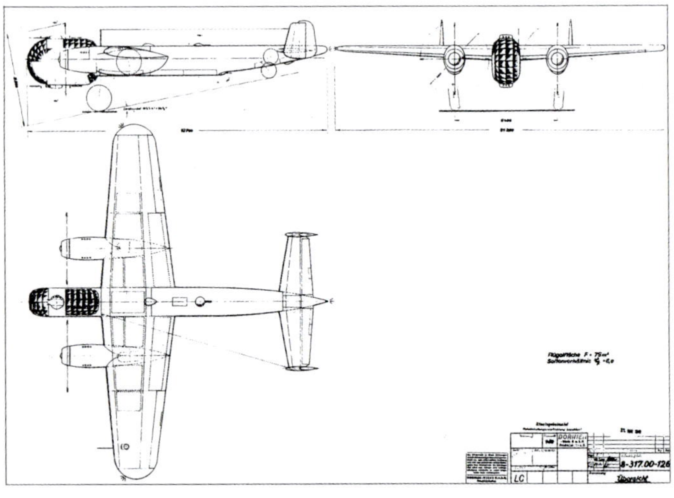

ABOVE: By May 21, 1940, the Do 317 design had changed significantly – its crew cabin, fuselage and wings were all different. Here it is powered by a pair of Jumo 222 engines.

fuselage and crew cabin being dramatically altered as time wore on. It is therefore difficult to present a firm set of dimensions for the type. In 1942, however, it had a fuselage length of 18.8m and a wingspan of 26m.

FOCKE-WULF FW 191

While it had not been one of the companies invited to tender for the Fernbomber requirement in 1936, Focke-Wulf had, nonetheless, been aware of the competition and had gone so far as to design its own Fernbomber.

There was little realistic prospect of the Focke-Wulf Fernbomber entering production but the company used the opportunity to experiment with pressure cabin arrangements and assess the possibilities for a bomber type aircraft.

In October 1939, somewhat later than the other contenders, the firm joined the Bomber B competition and began to work on its proposed design.

This was first described in Baubeschreibung Nr. 225 Mittlerer Bomber - 2 x DB 603 of February 13, 1940. Four crewmen would sit in a pressure cabin in the nose, having climbed up a ladder through the bomb bay to get in.

If they needed to leave in a hurry, they could open the rear door to the pressure cabin, open the bomb bay doors, and jump. The pilot and radio operator got seat cushion parachutes, while the others received back parachutes.

Below and to the front of the crew in their positions would be an MG 81 Z 7.92mm machine gun. Above them would be a Plexiglas dome for sighting the rearward-facing mid-upper and mid-lower electrically actuated remote-controlled turrets. The former had an MG 81 Z or MG 151 and the latter a pair of MG 131s.

The Nr. 225 aircraft was 18.45m long with a wingspan of 25m and an all-up weight of 18.4 tonnes, including two tonnes of bombs. A top speed of 605kph (376mph) was achieved at an altitude of 6km or 19,700ft.

All this was met with the RLM's approval and Focke-Wulf was given a development contract for two prototypes plus eight pre-production machines, with the aircraft receiving the official designation Fw 191 on March 1.

A fresh project description - Baubeschreibung Nr. 230 2 mot. Kampfflugzeug Fw 191 - was published on May 16, 1940. The design outlined here was very similar to that of the Nr. 225 but with a pair of Jumo 222s as an option if they were preferable to the DB 603s. It was offered as 'option A': a bomber or dive-bomber, or 'option B' as a reconnaissance platform with either Rb 50/30 and Rb 20/30 or Rb 75/30 or Rb 20/30 cameras.

Despite the engine options being outlined in the report, Focke-Wulf itself was already lining up a pair of BMW 801Cs for use in the Fw 191 V1, later amended to BMW 801 M-1As.

The bomb bay was 5645mm long and 1158mm wide and the internal mountings allowed a range of different bombs to be loaded.

Representatives of the RLM inspected a mock-up of the Fw 191's crew compartment on August 13, 1940, and suggested only minor amendments.

On November 22, 1940, Focke-Wulf decided to reduce the number of electromechanical actuators on board the Fw 191 and replace them with more reliable hydraulic systems. This left 26 out of 44 systems electrically controlled.

The total order for Fw 191s had risen, by December 30, 1940, to 10 prototypes, 20 pre-production machines and 80 A-1 full production examples. Work on the V1 was reported to be 80% complete at Focke-Wulf's Wenzendorf facility on January 31, 1941, with the V2 at 50%. Work on building the V3 commenced on February 6. A little more than a month later, on March 11-12, the prototypes were fitted with dummy Jumo 222s and inspected by Focke-Wulf and Junkers staff to ensure that the design of the aircraft would marry up with the design of the engine when it was eventually delivered.

The V1, which lacked a full pressure cabin, first flew on March 18, 1941, at 3.34pm for 16 minutes. Further flights took place between April 5 and 19.

A delegation from Japan were Focke-Wulf's guests on May 14, 1941, and they were allowed to see the Fw 189, Fw 187 and Fw 200 - but not the Fw 190 or Fw 191.

Tests on the first Fw 191 pressure cabin, fitted to the V2 prototype, began on May 23 and continued for a week. Air leaks were found everywhere. It was decided, after various failed attempts to fix these, that the V2 should be rushed through to flight testing without a full pressure cabin. A static airframe would be used for further pressure cabin tests instead.

By May 30, 1941, Focke-Wulf was struggling to get more Fw 191s built. The company told the RLM that it would have to strip resources away from series production of the urgently needed Fw 189 reconnaissance aircraft to get the work done, and the RLM decided that the Fw 189 had priority.

Focke-Wulf was forced to make major changes to its design and testing programme in August 1941 ▶

ABOVE: The Focke-Wulf Fw 191 V2 with its BMW 801 engines being run up during January 1942. The type's unusual observation blister, fitted above its pressure cabin, is visible.

ABOVE: The Do 317 in profile. The engines shown are those that were fitted to the V1 – DB 603s. The distinctive triangular tailfin was a feature of the final form but the crew cabin, fuselage and wings had changed again by 1943. Art by Daniel Uhr

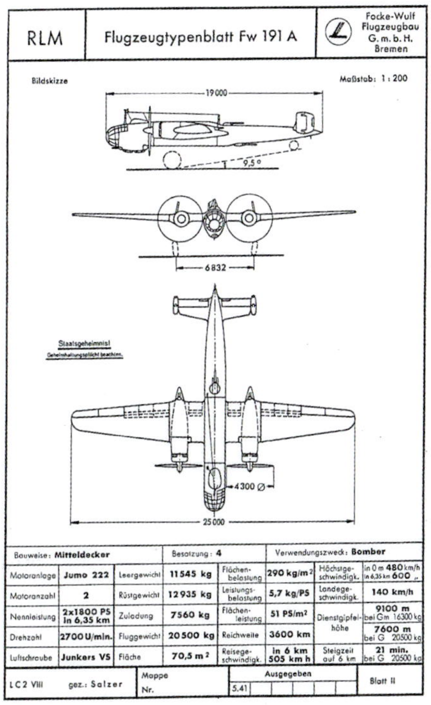
RLM | Flugzeugtypenblatt Fw 191 A | Focke-Wulf Flugzeugbau G.m.b.H. Bremen

Bildskizze

Maßstab: 1 : 200

19 000

9,5°

6832

Staatsgeheimnis!

4300 Ø

25 000

Bauweise: Mitteldecker			Besatzung: 4			Verwendungszweck: Bomber	
Motoranlage	Jumo 222	Leergewicht	11545 kg	Flächenbelastung	290 kg/m²	Höchstgeschwindigk.	in 0 m 480 km/h in 6,35 km 600 „
Motoranzahl	2	Rüstgewicht	12935 kg	Leistungsbelastung	5,7 kg/PS	Landegeschwindigk.	140 km/h
Nennleistung	2x1800 PS in 6,35 km	Zuladung	7560 kg	Flächenleistung	51 PS/m²	Dienstgipfelhöhe	9100 m bei Gm 16300 kg
Drehzahl	2700 U/min.	Fluggewicht	20500 kg	Reichweite	3600 km		7600 m bei G 20500 kg
Luftschraube	Junkers VS	Fläche	70,5 m²	Reisegeschwindigk.	in 6 km 505 km h	Steigzeit auf 6 km	21 min. bei G 20500 kg

LC 2 VIII gez.: Salzer	Mappe Nr.	Ausgegeben 5.41	Blatt II

RIGHT: An RLM type sheet for the Fw 191 as it was expected to appear fitted with its intended Jumo 222 powerplants. The fuselage length is given as 19m – a figure which was to change numerous times while the type was in development.

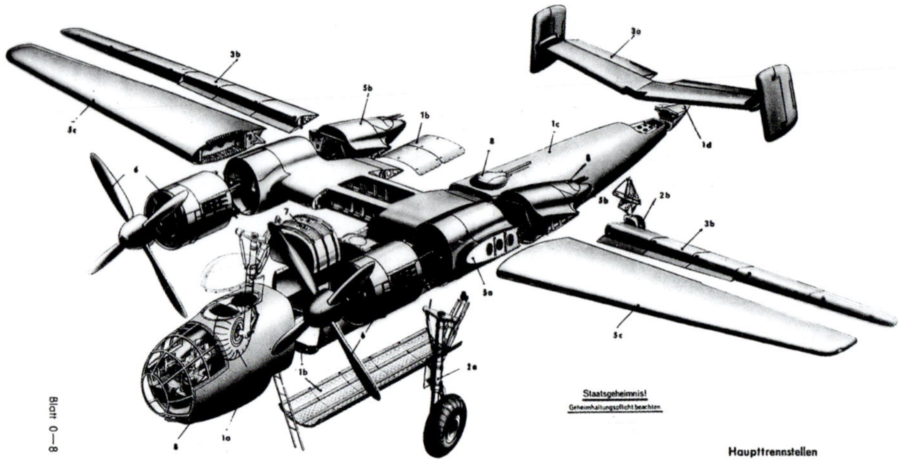

ABOVE: Brochure drawing, from Baubeschreibung Nr. 230, showing how the Fw 191's component parts were designed to fit together.

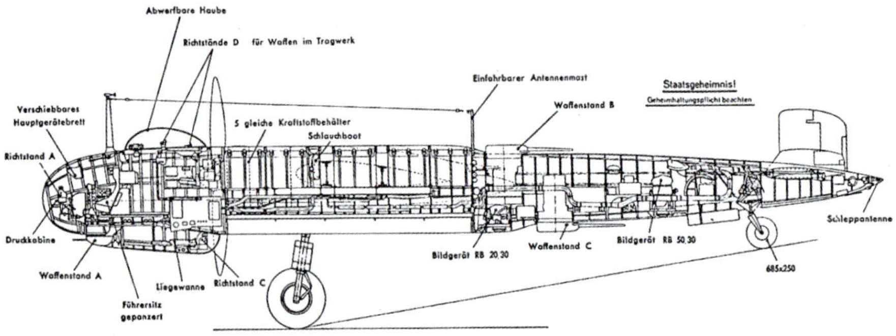

ABOVE: A side view of the Fw 191 showing the position of its fuel tanks in the centre fuselage, its electrically actuated rear turrets, its pressure cabin and its tail-mounted Rb 50/30 camera.

when Junkers announced that the Jumo 222 was no longer expected to enter full production. Fitting a different engine would require changes to the engine nacelles, the landing gear and the wings themselves.

Focke-Wulf also began to consider whether a four-engine design would now be necessary using either the DB 606 or 610 doubled engines, or single engines such as the DB 601 or 605.

Flight testing with BMW 801s up to this point had revealed that the Fw 191 suffered from flutter around its flaps and each successive attempt to cure it had failed. In November, it was decided that Fw 191 V13 would test a pair of DB 606 linked engines as a prototype for the Fw 191B-0 production aircraft, which was to be powered by two DB 610s. A mock-up of the V13 was examined by representatives of both the RLM and the Luftwaffe's Rechlin test centre on December 16, 1941, and a wide range of alterations were ordered. Further inspections took place on December 18 and then January 6 and February 23, 1942. At this point a set of detail revisions to the seating arrangements was ordered, along with more armour and measures to improve visibility.

By this point both Dornier and Arado were effectively out of contention and it was a straight contest between Junkers and Focke-Wulf. On February 27, 1942, it was proposed that the Ju 288, being more than a year ahead of the Fw 191 in development terms, should be selected as the Luftwaffe's Bomber B. Reichsmarschall Hermann Göring approved this decision on March 6, 1942.

Four days later, Focke-Wulf was told the bad news: the Ju 288 would go forward into full production while the Fw 191 would only be built as a series of 18 prototypes – V1 to V18.

The Fw 191 V3 had finally been completed by now and was being used for engine tests with prototype Jumo 222s. It was cleared for flight testing on April 20, 1942, but it remained on static engine-testing duties, then vibration test duties.

Despite the Bomber B decision going against the Fw 191, Focke-Wulf produced Baubeschreibung Nr. 248 Fw 491 on July 6, 1942, which proposed that the Fw 191 be fitted with a quartet of Jumo 211Js to create the Fw 491. This would make the aircraft two tonnes heavier overall, resulting in a corresponding loss of performance – but it would mean that all the development effort put into the Fw 191 would not be wasted. This came to nothing.

Only four Fw 191s were completed: V1, V2, V3 and V6. The V7 was in final assembly when the programme was cancelled and never reached 100% complete. The V4, V5, V8, V9, V10, V11 and V12 were all a varying stages of completion before being stripped and scrapped. All work on the Fw 191 was stopped in March 1943 and the last surviving prototype, the V6, was scrapped some time before April 24, 1944.

JUNKERS JU 288

From the outset, Junkers had a significant advantage in the Bomber B competition. It had begun work on its EF 72 project in 1937 as a projected replacement for the Ju 88 – which had made its first flight on December 21, 1936.

As the Bomber B specification was being issued to the other firms, Junkers was already preparing the necessary drawings to move from the mock-up stage to construction of the first prototype of what had been designated the Ju 288. It was anticipated that the V1 would make its first flight in October 1940 with full production commencing at the start of 1942.

In its initial Ju 288A form, the Junkers aircraft was the smallest Bomber B design with a wingspan of 22m and a length of 16.6m – compared to 26m and 18.8m for the Do 317, 25m and 18.45m for the Fw 191 (later 26m and 19.63m), and 23m and 18.65m for the Ar 340.

Its pressure cabin was narrow, with the gunner positioned some distance back from the pilot, the bombardier seated on the bottom of the fuselage between them. Initial armament was comparatively light – a pair of forward-facing MG 81s beneath the pilot's feet and two remote controlled turrets. The first was just in front of the rearward facing gunner on the upper fuselage and the second was on the underside of the rear fuselage, not far from the tailwheel.

The Ju 288 was always intended to fly with a pair of Junkers' own Jumo 222 engines, rather than the competing Daimler-Benz design, but it was apparent by mid-1940 that the 222 programme was encountering significant difficulties. As a result, the Ju 288 V1 first flew a month behind schedule on November 29, 1940, powered by a pair of BMW 801Gs.

It was followed by the V2 on March 1, 1941, the V3 on April 18, 1941, and the V4 on May 17, 1941 – all of them powered by BMW 801G engines. The V5, fitted with Jumo 222A/Bs, first flew on October 8, 1941, and was also fitted with mock-up defensive gun positions.

Throughout 1941 and 1942 an increasing number of Ju 288 prototypes took to the

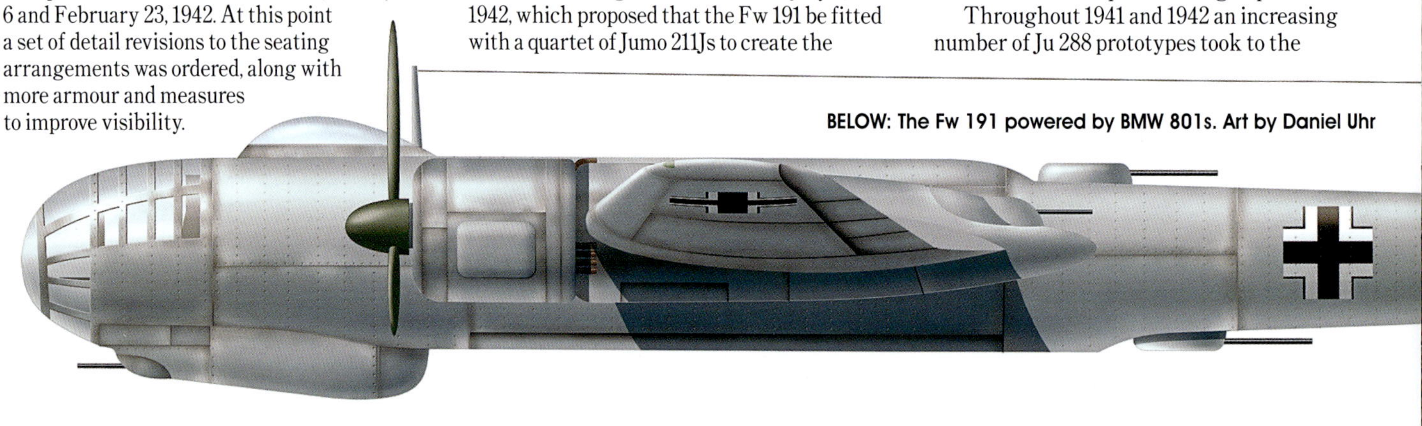

BELOW: The Fw 191 powered by BMW 801s. Art by Daniel Uhr

ABOVE: The Junkers Ju 288 V2, powered by BMW 801s, pictured in July 1941 beside the Ju 88 V16 prototype.

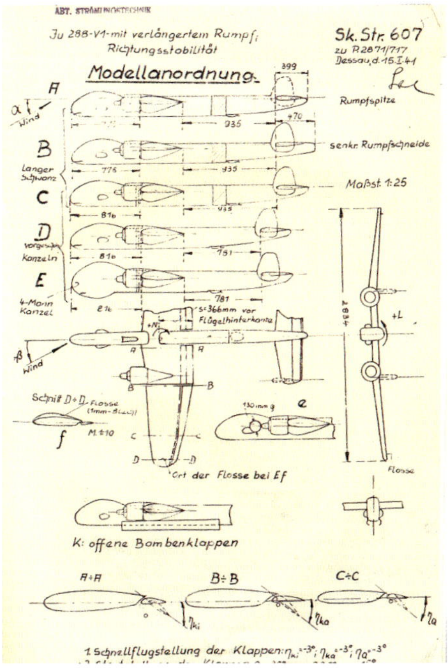

ABOVE: Junkers had the opportunity to thoroughly test its aerodynamic designs at its in-house wind tunnel facilities. These company drawings from January 15, 1941, show the range of different forms being assessed for the Ju 288.

air, with the V14 being the last to receive Jumo 222s. V11 and V13 were fitted with DB 606 linked engines – with the unsurprising result that the V13 suffered engine problems on May 13, 1943, and crash-landed. In all, 22 were built and flown up to October 9, 1943.

Junkers, being so far ahead of its competitors, won the Bomber B competition and the result was officially announced on March 10, 1942. The full extent of the Ju 288 programme falls beyond the scope of this publication, with so many examples being built and tested.

A wide range of production variants were planned too, including the Jumo 222A/B-powered 288A, the Jumo 222C/D-powered 288B, the DB 610-powered 288C, a version fitted with a huge 355mm Gerät 104 'Münchhausen' cannon for sinking Allied supply ships, a high-altitude version, a version fitted with a 280mm Düka 280 cannon, again for destroying ships, and a heavily armed bomber version powered by DB 610C/D engines.

Large scale plans were drawn up to create components supply chains involving 32 manufacturing groups and it was proposed that from June 1943 to December 1945 80 aircraft a month would roll out of Junkers' factories ready for testing followed by front line service. Five subcontractors - Arado, Dornier, Heinkel, Henschel and Siebel - were also to have begun production of the Ju 288 to varying degrees, resulting in a planned total of 8640 examples being built by the end of 1945.

Ultimately, however, the Ju 288 suffered the same fate as its rivals when it was cancelled towards the end of 1943. The engines that would have made its existence worthwhile, the Jumo 222 and the DB 610 failed to reach full reliable production status and without them it lacked any advantage over types powered by BMW 801s or DB 603s.

Huge efforts had been made and huge sums of money had been spent with little to show for any of it. But there remained other bomber developments in progress... ●

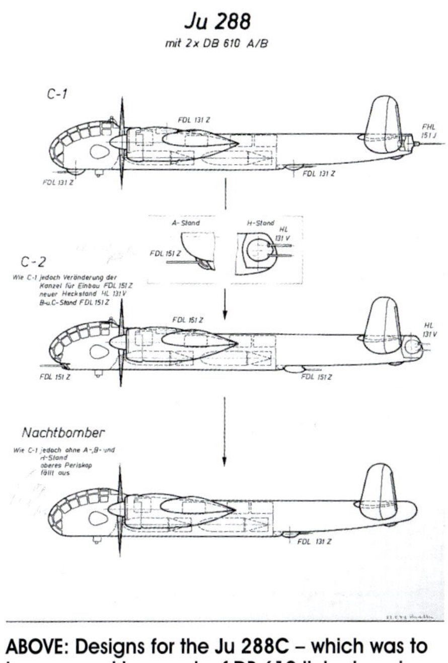

ABOVE: Designs for the Ju 288C – which was to be powered by a pair of DB 610 linked engines. The C-1 and C-2 had different tail turret arrangements, while the night bomber version was far less well armed, with only a lower fuselage FDL 131 Z turret to ward off enemy night fighters.

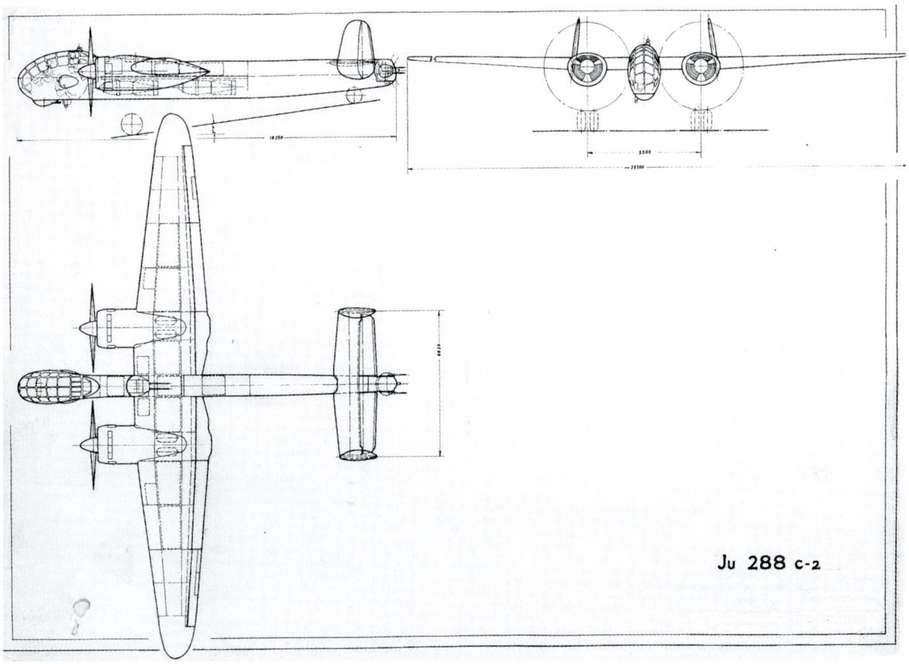

ABOVE: This three-view drawing of the Ju 288C-2 shows the manned tail turret, the positions of the three crewmen inside the pressure cabin and, in the forward and top-down views, shows the very broad nacelles necessary for the DB 610s – the engine consisting of a pair of DB 605s positioned side-by-side.

High-flying birds

Höhenfernaufklärer – Henschel Hs 130

Henschel's P 26 design failed to win the Fernbomber competition but went on to provide the basis for a series of pressure cabin-equipped research aircraft. These were to produce invaluable data for the construction of high-altitude bombers.

ABOVE: Where it all began. After Henschel's bid for the Fernbomber competition was defeated by Heinkel, the firm's bomber design was used as a vehicle for this DVL-designed pressure cabin.

During the late 1920s, Germany became interested in ways of safely increasing the altitude at which aircraft could fly.

To this end, the Deutsche Versuchsanstalt für Luftfahrt (DVL) or 'German Research Institute for Aviation' commissioned the building of the country's first high-altitude test aircraft with a pressurised crew compartment, the Junkers Ju 49, which first flew in 1931.

The compartment worked but made the aircraft heavy with extremely poor visibility. Despite being able to reach a maximum altitude of 41,000ft, the aircraft had a top speed of only 136mph and a fixed undercarriage which further hampered its performance. No records were set and it was clear to the RLM that more research was needed.

When it became evident that Henschel's P 26 four-engined bomber design was not going to succeed against Heinkel's P 1041 in the Fernbomber competition, in January 1937, the RLM handed the company a development contract to create a testbed for high-altitude engines instead.

A new project number, P 30, was used and this received the RLM designation Hs 128 - which had originally been intended for the P 26. In line with the thinking that resulted in the He 177, Henschel worked hard to keep the Hs 128's design as streamlined and aerodynamically clean as possible by careful positioning of the engines and their accessories.

Only Henschel's third twin-engined design after the Hs 124 heavy fighter/fighter-bomber and Hs 127 bomber, the all-metal Hs 128's tail unit was conventional and its wings had a slight dihedral. The fixed landing gear was given spats to minimise drag and the fuselage had a circular cross section. Power was supplied by two Daimler-Benz DB 601s developing 950hp each, linked to a TK.9 turbocharger, and driving four-bladed propellers. The key feature of the Hs 128, however, was its pressure cabin. This was designed by the DVL to significantly improve upon that of the Ju 49, with a target altitude of 55,000ft.

The design seemed so promising that in October 1938 the RLM began discussions with Henschel about developing it into a three-man high-altitude military aircraft capable of sustained flights at 49,000ft - well above the ceiling of potential enemy interceptors. A contract for six prototypes was placed with Henschel in February 1939. Two versions were envisioned - the Hs 130A reconnaissance aircraft and the Hs 130B bomber. Similar in appearance to the Hs 128, the Hs 130 was an all-metal monocoque with a circular cross section. Rather than having a pressure cabin installed in its nose, the entire nose of the aircraft was the pressure cabin, bolted onto the rest of the aircraft. Fuel tanks and an equipment or bomb bay were fitted into the fuselage behind it. A retractable undercarriage was added, with the main legs withdrawing into the engine nacelles. Wingspan was 95.2ft.

The first Hs 128 V1 took its maiden flight on April 11, 1939. It was then transferred to the Rechlin test centre in June and presented to Adolf Hitler and an audience of military

BELOW: The Henschel Hs 128 experimental high-altitude aircraft. Designed to pick up where the Junkers Ju 49 had left off, the Hs 128 proved to be less successful than expected.

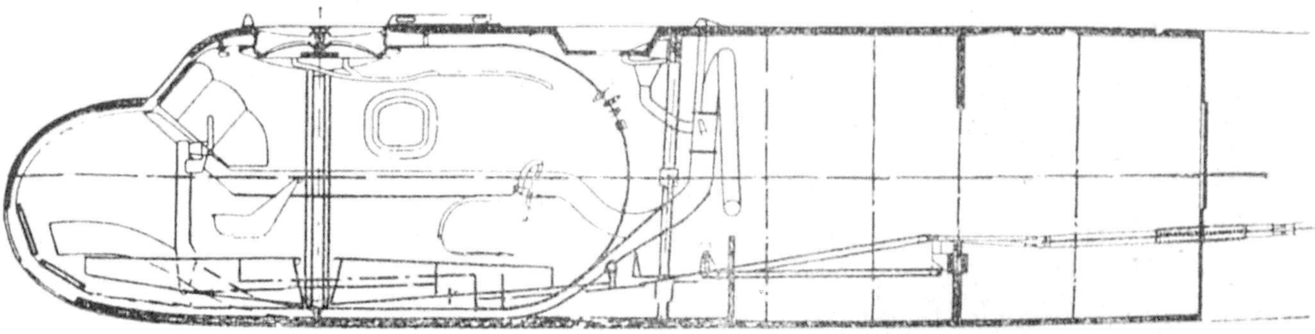

ABOVE: Henschel drawing showing how the Hs 130A's controls could be operated from within the nose-mounted pressure cabin. Also visible are the cabin's roof hatch and parts of its heating system – essential for high-altitude flight.

and industry representatives on July 3. During August, it was flown to an altitude of 31,000ft. Work on the second Hs 128 prototype was delayed as the company was required to prioritise its P 40 ground-attack aircraft design, designated the Hs 129. The Hs 128 V2 was largely finished by August 1939 but final completion was delayed by a problem with its engines. The intention was to fit it with a pair of Jumo 210Gs linked to a TK.16 turbocharger, but since the latter had been cancelled it was fitted with DB 601s instead.

The V1 was handed over to the DVL on March 8, 1940, and the V2, having first flown on March 20, followed it on May 7. On May 23, the Hs 130 V1 was flown for the first time and in June the proposed Hs 130B bomber version was discontinued. The V1 was flown by Oberstleutnant Theodor Rowehl, commanding officer of the Versuchsstelle für Höhenflug (VfH), on July 29 to assess its suitability for high-altitude reconnaissance. Work progressed rapidly, and by October 1940 the V1 had been joined by the V2. The V6 was delivered in mid-December. In each case, however, the type's DB 601 engines proved inadequate and proposals were drawn up to try the Jumo 208, DB 605 and DB 603. Most were retrofitted with the DB 605.

The prototypes flew without armament but provision was made for the fitment of two 900 litre external fuel tanks, or alternatively the carriage of two 500kg bombs.

With the demise of the Hs 130B, two more versions were proposed – the Hs 130C bomber and another reconnaissance version, the Hs 130D, which was to be powered by diesel-fuelled Jumo 208s. Contracts were issued for the development of both. The first of four pre-production Hs 130A-0s, serial number 3007, equipped with DB 605 engines was ready by December 20 and three more, numbers 3008-3010, were finished by April 1941. All of these aircraft, plus the six prototypes, serials 3001-3006, were then sent to various test and training facilities.

The Hs 130C went into production in 1941 and 10 out of a planned total of 30 were eventually built. The type was substantially the same as the Hs 130A but differed in having a much more heavily glazed pressure cabin with gun turrets capable of rotating 360° both above and below it. Another remote-controlled gun was to be fitted in the tail. It was powered by a pair of BMW 801Js and could carry 2000kg of bombs in a large fuselage compartment in line with its wings. Top speed was 320mph at 40,000ft and maximum range was 3100 miles.

In August 1941, development of the Hs 130D was halted and eight part-finished airframes put ▶

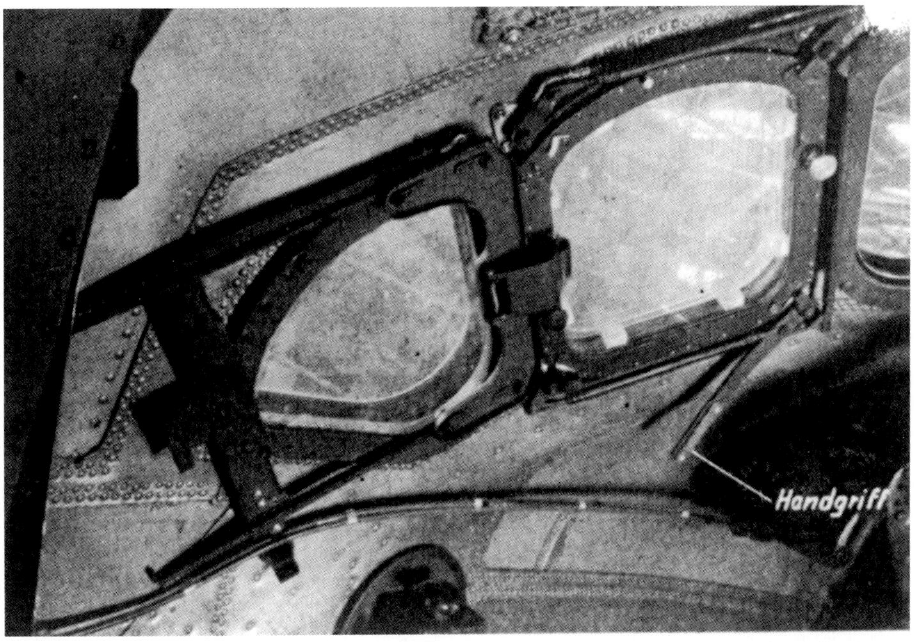

ABOVE: Great care was taken in constructing the Hs 130's pressure cabin. This view shows the heavy support structures in place behind the thick cockpit windows – and the lever that could be used to open one of them.

ABOVE: One of the less appealing features of the Hs 130A was the roof-mounted crew access hatch. In the event of an emergency, as at least two crews found to their cost, it was very difficult to use.

ABOVE: One of the Hs 130A-0 aircraft. It is similar in general appearance to the Hs 128 but features a retractable undercarriage and revised pressure cabin.

ABOVE: With the Hs 130B bomber version cancelled before it was built, attention switched to the Hs 130C – a high-altitude bomber capable of carrying a 2000kg payload. A wind tunnel model shows the large upper gun turret 'bulge' on its pressure cabin.

into storage. Work on yet another, significantly revised, variant - the Hs 130E - commenced on September 1. This was a larger aircraft thanks to a lengthened fuselage and longer wings, up to a span of 108.2ft, and it was fitted with a pair of liquid-cooled V12 DB 603C engines. A third engine, a DB 605T, was fitted inside the fuselage to drive a two-stage supercharger providing compressed air for the others. The bomb bay was smaller than that of the Hs 130C thanks to the presence of the DB 605T.

The Hs 130E mock-up was inspected and approved just eight days later on September 9. The Hs 130D airframes were scrapped on January 22, 1942, and the first Hs 130E-0, serial number 13 0051, began initial test flights in August.

During a flight up to 41,000ft on December 17, 1942, the aircraft's port engine began to shudder and smoke. The fire could not be extinguished and quickly spread to the wing. The crew attempted to escape - the pilot managing to crawl out of the awkward hatch in the cabin ceiling - but the other two crewmen were killed.

Following the accident, the RLM called for the pressure cabin to be redesigned with an escape hatch on its underside and for the Hs 130E to have defensive armament fitted since Germany was now regularly being overflown by enemy aircraft at high altitude.

Meanwhile, Hs 130A-0 serial 3009, built with DB 605C engines, was converted to DB 601Rs in 1943 before being transferred to Peenemunde and used for tests involving the Hs 293 glide bomb. The 10 completed Hs 130C airframes were scrapped.

There was a second fatal accident on September 24, 1943, when the third Hs 130E-0, serial number 13 0053, suffered an engine fire at low altitude and crashed at Diepensee in Brandenburg with no survivors. Eventually, the fifth Hs 130E managed an altitude of 47,500ft but on April 8, 1944, the Hs 130 programme was finally abandoned and all surviving examples were scrapped.

Henschel's design offices were based at Schönefeld airfield in Berlin and much of the company's paperwork was destroyed or captured by the Soviets at the end of the war. One of the company's engineers, Otto Oeckl, was interrogated by the British after the war

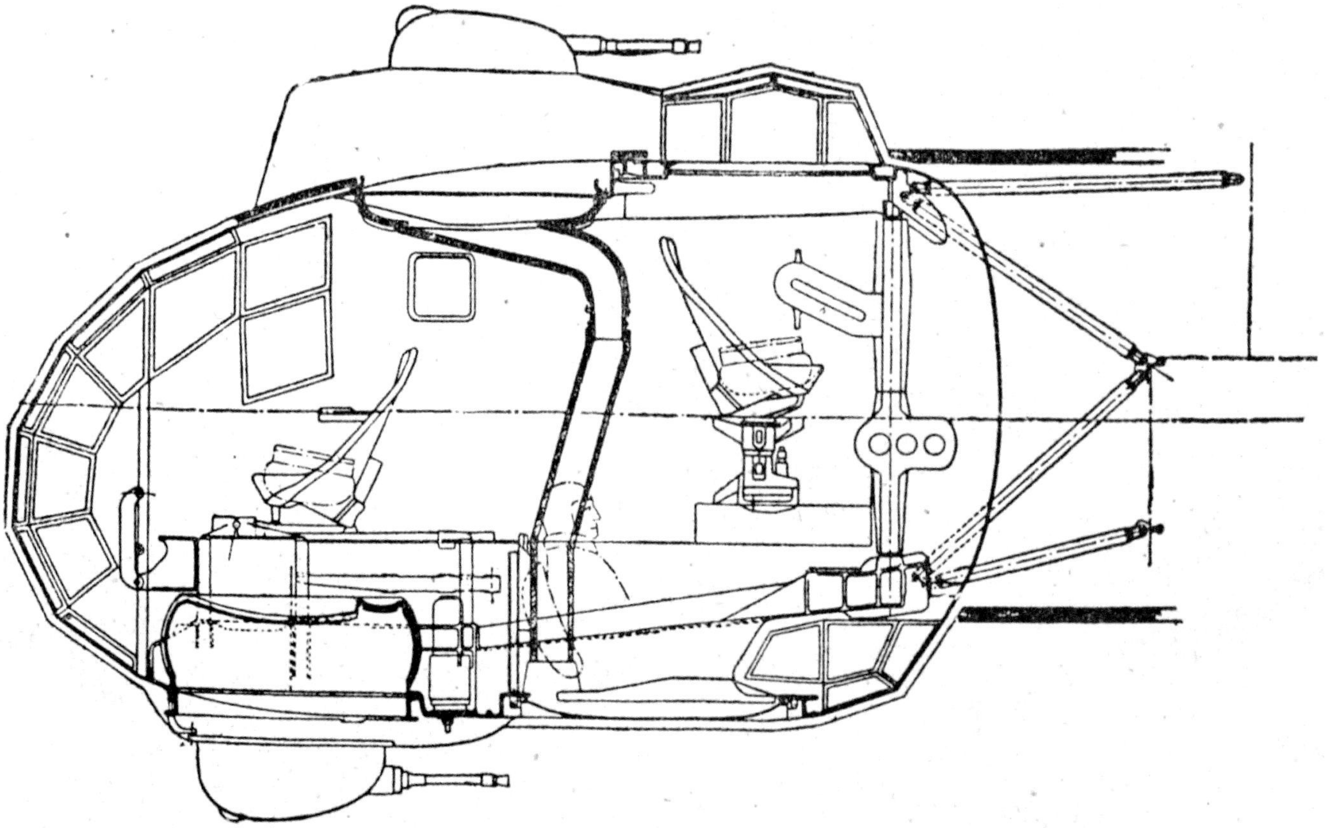

ABOVE: Like the Hs 130A, the Hs 130C bomber was designed to have a pressure cabin that could easily be bolted on to its airframe or removed and swapped for another one if necessary. This Henschel drawing shows its internal layout – note the bombardier's well-cushioned position on the base of the cabin.

ABOVE: The only known photograph purporting to show a forward view of an Hs 130C. If it is real, it has been heavily retouched. Other photographic evidence suggests that this might, in fact, be a detailed Henschel factory scale model.

and was asked directly about the Hs 130.

Regarding the Hs 130A, the summary of his response states: "Only 16 of these aircraft were built, but they were not a success. Of all metal construction they were powered by two DB 605 standard engines with four-bladed propellers. Built to study the problems of high-altitude flying. The aircraft were definitely underpowered for their purpose, as they were intended to reach an altitude of 13,500m. Nothing like this altitude was ever reached, but exact altitude on test was not known by source.

"Hs 130C. Same as Hs 130A but with plexi-glass nose and BMW 801K engines. Twelve built but again failure."

The British summary report on German projects, German Aircraft: New and Projected Types, includes all three 'built' versions of the Hs 130.

It states: "Although none of the projected sub-types of the Hs 130 ever became operational, this high-altitude aircraft aroused considerable interest when it was

ABOVE: The lengthened Hs 130E as viewed from the side. Like all the other members of the Hs 130 family, it failed to live up to expectations.

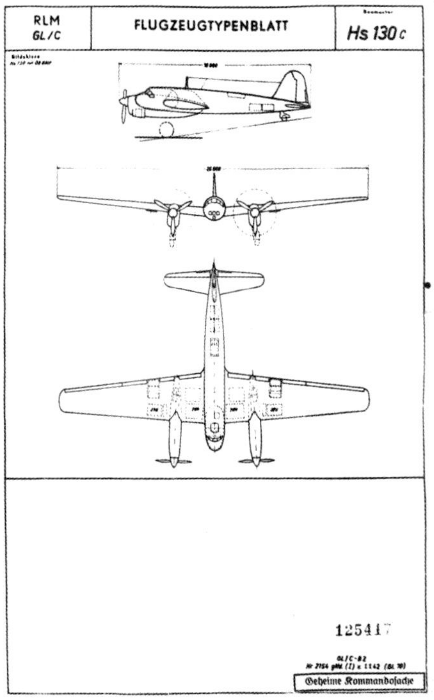

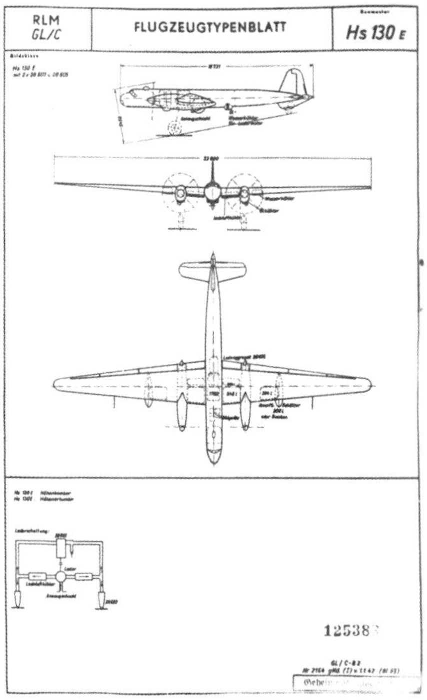

first identified. Performance figures from official German sources are now available. The sub-type A-0 has a pressure cabin for a crew of two and is powered by two DB 605B engines with GM 1 power-boosting installation.

"Hs 130C high-altitude bomber. Although placed by the Germans in this category the Hs 130C hardly qualifies for inclusion among high-altitude bombers when judged by present-day standards.

"Henschel Hs 130E high-altitude bomber. The bomber version of the Hs 130E is generally similar to the reconnaissance aircraft but the normal flying weight has been increased to 39,600lb. The maximum range with 1000kg bomb load is 1400 miles at 47,500ft." ●

FAR LEFT: Labelled 'Hs 130C' this type sheet appears instead to depict the Hs 130A.

LEFT: The Hs 130E took the basic structure of the Hs 130A and stretched it. The fuselage had additional sections added and the wings were also lengthened by 13ft in total.

The USA bombers

Fernkampfflugzeug

When Britain declared war on Germany in September 1939, two thorny problems had to be addressed: how to sever the island nation's supply lines and how to strike back at the USA if it intervened. Nothing in the Luftwaffe's existing stable was up to either task, so a new requirement was issued...

After a stunning round of victories that saw all resistance on the European continent subdued, Germany faced the question of what to do about Britain – a last pocket of defiance shielded by the strong tides and unpredictable storms of the English Channel.

With an ever growing fleet of medium bombers available and the He 177 waiting in the wings, the Luftwaffe was not unduly concerned about the prospect of bombing Britain itself. But when it came to finding and destroying the supply ships that regularly brought it the means to carry on the fight, there were few aircraft with anything like the necessary range and endurance.

There was also a secondary problem which was, if anything, more worrisome: America. On November 4, 1939, President Franklin D Roosevelt had successfully managed to get the Neutrality Act of 1939 passed which weakened the traditional American position of isolationism and allowed US-made arms to be traded with Britain and France. Then on June 3, 1940, as France was teetering on the brink of collapse under the German onslaught, the US government approved the sale of surplus small arms ammunition and 'obsolete' American weapons to Britain.

To the Germans, it began to seem as though America might well enter the fray on the side of the Allies. If that happened, there was no realistic plan in place for aerial bombardment of the American mainland and certainly no aircraft capable of carrying it out.

The best evidence for what happened next comes from a summary written on May 12, 1942, by Generalleutnant Eccard, Freiherr von Gablenz. He was actually writing about a requirement for a long-range aircraft issued in mid- to late 1941, but in doing so he recalled a competition launched by Ernst Udet shortly after fall of France in 1940.

He wrote: "At the outset it is necessary to describe briefly the considerations and proposals which brought about the present projects. In 1940, as a result of the situation in the Atlantic and the increasing tensions with the United States, work began to increase the range of the He 177 and Fw 200.

"The proposal came from Generalluftzeugmeister Udet, since at the time the General Staff did not require aircraft of that type. The minimum range required, in the case of America, was 12,000km (the distance from Brest to New York and return), which would also be sufficient for Atlantic operations and other trans-oceanic missions. To this minimum range was added 1500km as a technical reserve, providing a total range of 15,000km. A three- to five-ton bomb load plus normal armament and armour were also required.

"Focke-Wulf and Junkers carried out in-depth analyses of these requirements and came up with aircraft having an all-up weight of between 100 and 140 tons. They proposed large, but as yet unavailable, engines and a development period of at least three or four years.

"Focke-Wulf was also asked to provide an additional design for a trans-oceanic fast aircraft. The suggestion was for a machine of wooden construction equipped with four BMW 801 engines and a light armament. The project was worked through to completion and met the specifications. No order was placed because Focke-Wulf had no capacity for development and the use of wood seemed too risky.

"At the same time, because of current development on the Me 261, Messerschmitt had received a similar invitation to tender, and the Me 264 variant was offered to the RLM in mid-1941. The design was so much better than its competitors as regards weight and performance that it was subjected to a lengthy evaluation before final acceptance."

Besides the Me 261 and 264, it is difficult to determine precisely which designs von Gablenz is referring to. It is certain that Focke-Wulf and Junkers came up with the first designs to meet the requirement however, and that the Messerschmitt Me 264 joined them later, in mid-1941, whereupon it was evaluated and chosen as the successful design.

FOCKE-WULF FERNKAMPFFLUGZEUG

It seems likely that Focke-Wulf's entry for this competition was a design that the company referred to as the Fernkampfflugzeug or 'long-range combat aircraft'. It was common for Focke-Wulf to give its projects names which

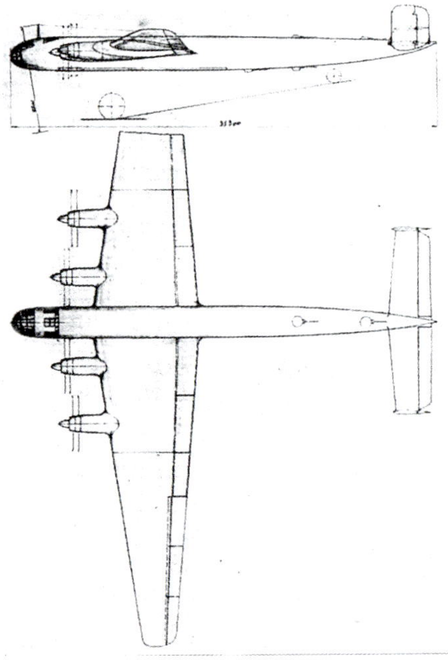

Above: The earliest known iteration of the Focke-Wulf Kampfflugzeug. The company would work on a type with that name almost continuously until the autumn of 1944 when its final dramatically different form, the Ta 400, was cancelled.

BELOW: Asked to design an aircraft capable of flying from occupied France to America and back, Focke-Wulf came up with this design. It was heavy and powered by four huge BMW 803 engines, each driving four-bladed contra-rotating propellers. Art by Chris Sandham-Bailey

ABOVE: The mighty BMW 803 engine was composed of two 801 engines mounted back-to-back. These contemporary BMW images show the 3800hp engine being tested. The monstrous gearbox is visible just behind the rearmost propeller. Focke-Wulf designed a number of aircraft around this powerplant but in the end it failed to live up to expectations and its development was halted.

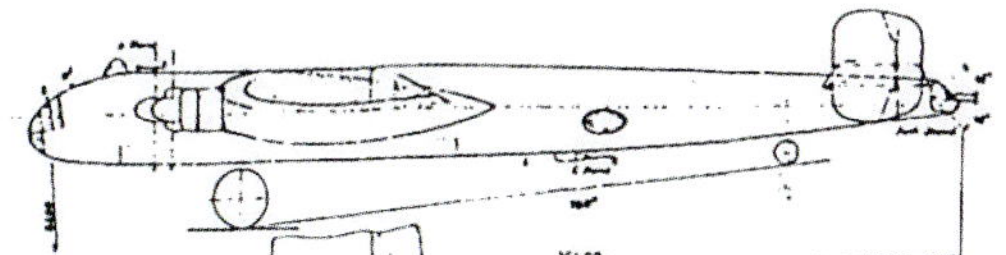

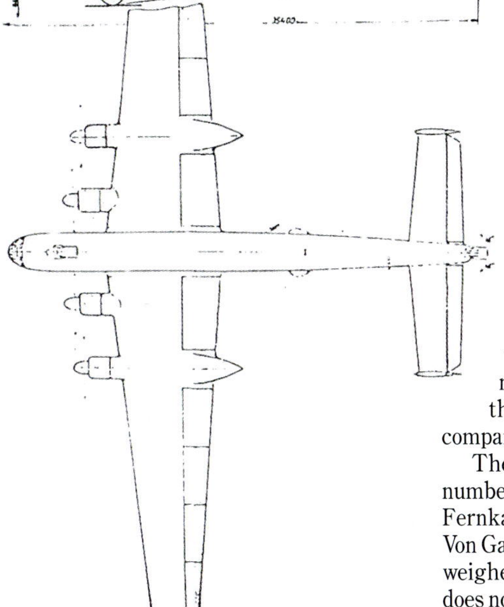

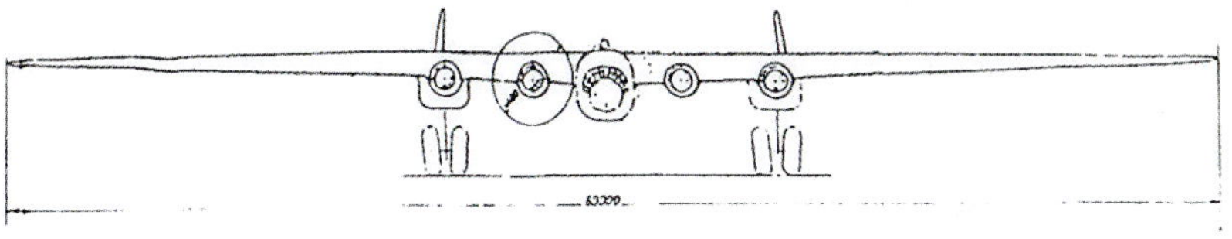

Above: At the same time that it was asked to produce a heavy Atlantic-crossing bomber, Focke-Wulf was also tasked with designing a fast trans-oceanic aircraft made of wood and powered by four BMW 801s. The project was completed but the design was deemed too risky to build.

directly referenced the requirement for which they had been submitted, rather than giving them a 'P' or 'Projekt' number like Heinkel or Messerschmitt.

In general Focke-Wulf gave its projects absolutely literal names, rather than project numbers, such as 'Zwei mot kampfflugzeug' when referring to the two-engined bomber that was the Fw 191. This was then linked to a Baubeschreibung number. The Baubeschreibung or specification document outlined the project in sufficient detail to give a good understanding of its essential points. If no RLM designation had been given to the design, it was referred to within the company by its Baubescheibung number.

The Baubeschreibung and drawing numbers of Focke-Wulf's earliest Fernkampfflugzeug are unknown however. Von Gablenz states that the submitted designs weighed in the order of 100 to 140 tons but does not give dimensions or engine types. The Focke-Wulf Fernkampfflugzeug has been described as weighing 81 tons, but it is evident that it may well have weighed much more than that – particularly given its four enormous BMW 803 engines, each of which weighed three tons in its own right.

The BMW 803 was effectively a pair of BMW 801 engines mounted back-to-back driving contra-rotating propellers with the aid of a monstrous gearbox positioned between the engines and the props. It boasted 28 cylinders and was liquid-cooled.

All-up weight estimates for the Focke-Wulf Fernkampfflugzeug have ranged from 118.5 to 126 tons.

The aircraft was certainly a giant, measuring 35.3m from end to end. It had a long-legged undercarriage and was defended by two pairs of turrets – one pair on the upper fuselage and the other underneath it.

It would be tempting to suggest that the wooden trans-oceanic fast aircraft mentioned by von Gablenz as having been designed by Focke-Wulf is in fact the Fw 300, but this design is mentioned separately later on in the document and no known version of the Fw 300 was ever intended to have BMW 801 engines. However, Focke-Wulf did produce another long-range design of similar dimensions to the Fernkampfflugzeug that was to be fitted with a quartet of BMW 801s. This is more likely to be the aircraft von Gablenz makes reference to and many of its features reappear in later drawings.

JUNKERS' DESIGN

If the Focke-Wulf entry for the Fernkampfflugzeug competition is obscure, then the Junkers design is doubly so. Described by von Gablenz as sharing similar characteristics ▶

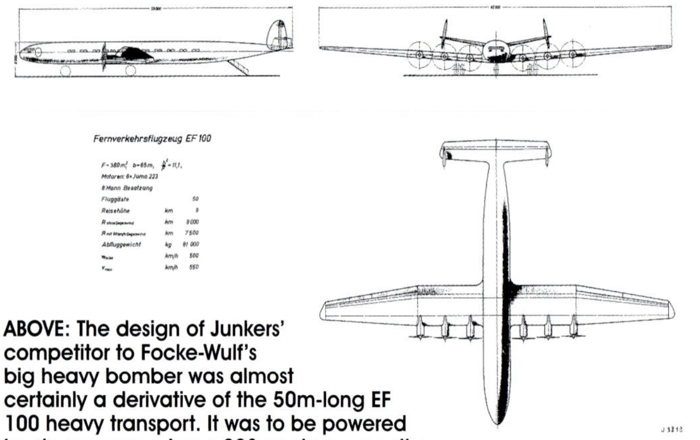

ABOVE: The design of Junkers' competitor to Focke-Wulf's big heavy bomber was almost certainly a derivative of the 50m-long EF 100 heavy transport. It was to be powered by six enormous Jumo 223 engines – another powerplant that was unavailable in 1940 and expected to take years of further development before it could be brought to full production.

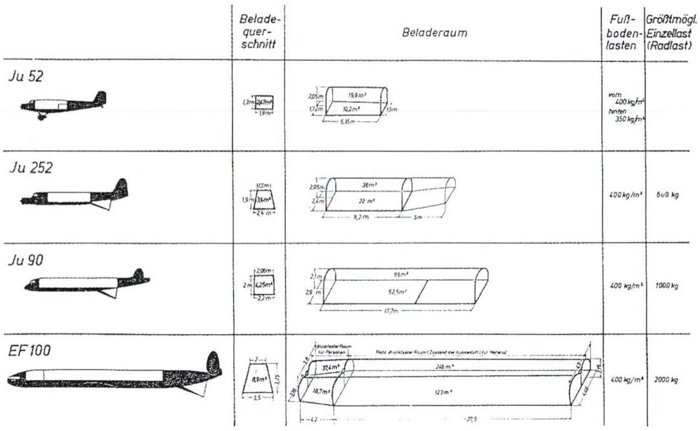

ABOVE: A Junkers drawing showing the sheer scale of the EF 100 when compared to some of the company's existing transport aircraft.

ABOVE: The huge Jumo 223 engine undergoing tests at Dessau. It was a 24-cylinder design with four banks of six cylinders arranged in a rhomboid pattern. Power output was expected to be 2500hp.

to those of the Focke-Wulf design, the Junkers aircraft would have been very large and very heavy. Perhaps the only known design that might have come close to an all-up weight of between 100 and 140 tons is the EF 100.

This goliath would have been nearly 50m long with a wingspan of 65m and, remarkably, an all-up weight of only 81 tons. Although most of what is known about it relates to a transport version, it appears that a military version was also contemplated. Like the 35.3m Focke-Wulf Fernkampfflugzeug, this would have been fitted with both upper and lower turrets. Development of the EF 100 is said to have ended in 1941, which would fit with von Gablenz' account.

MESSERSCHMITT ME 264

Although not one of the companies initially chosen to work on designs for a Fernkampfflugzeug, Messerschmitt seems to have been given an opportunity to revive the P 1061 four-engine design previously rejected during the Fernbomber competition in favour of the He 177. By all accounts, Willy Messerschmitt himself was determined to expand his company's interests from designing small nimble fighters into contesting the potentially more lucrative field of transport and bomber production.

The invitation to tender alongside Focke-Wulf and Junkers, months after they had begun their in-depth studies came as a result of Messerschmitt's work on the Me 261 long-range aircraft. This had started out as P 1062 and had been worked on in parallel with the P 1061. But where the latter had been rejected, P 1062 had succeeded in attracting a contract for three prototypes.

Like the He 177, the Me 261 was to be powered by a pair of DB 606 engines. Unlike the He 177 it was designed for operations where pure long-range ability was the essential attribute rather than payload-lifting. As a consequence, while its projected range was 20,000km or 12,000 miles, the carrying capacity of its narrow fuselage was minimal. This limited its potential uses to reconnaissance, passenger transport - up to eight people - or light bombing duties.

By now the Me 261 V1 had made its first flight, on December 20, 1940, and the results were so promising that Messerschmitt felt confident of delivering on its promised performance. This was enough to buy entry into the Fernkampfflugzeug competition.

The P 1061 was revised and brought back to the table. As with the Me 261, an expected range of 20,000km was given - 5000km more than the requirement called for - but this time using new Daimler-Benz DB 603 engines. There would be room for a two- to five-ton payload and defensive armament too.

The P 1061 was substantially smaller than the Focke-Wulf Fernkampfflugzeug and most likely smaller than the Junkers design too, with a length of just 21.3m. It appeared to offer a

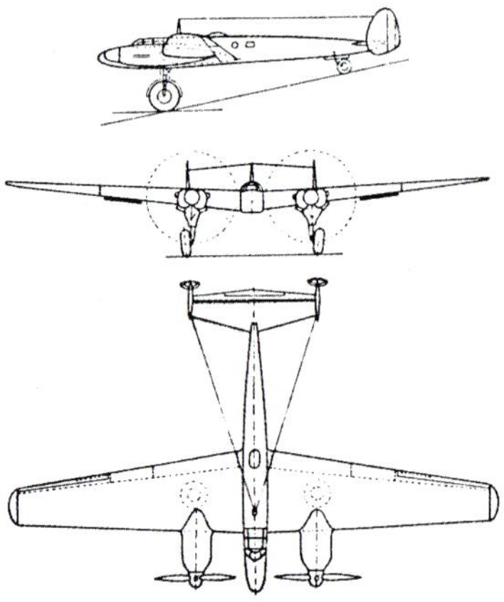

ABOVE: Messerschmitt's Me 261 design. This was promising enough to convince the RLM that Messerschmitt could be trusted to produce a complex bomber design. It later transpired that this trust was misplaced.

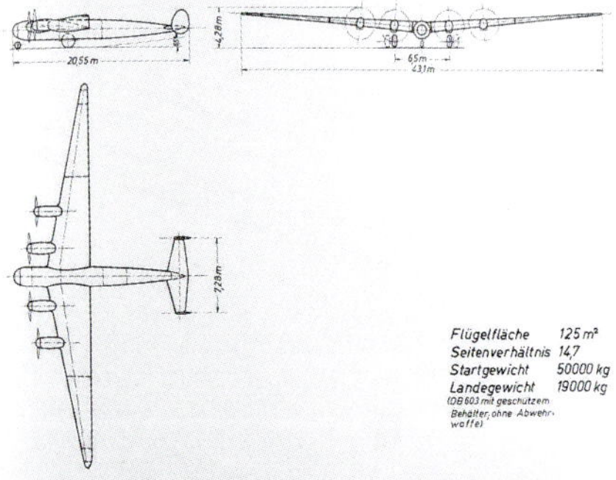

ABOVE: A very basic outline of the Me 264 from the company's December 1941 brochure – produced after the design had already been approved for prototype production, and then found to be substantially less capable than originally stated by its designers.

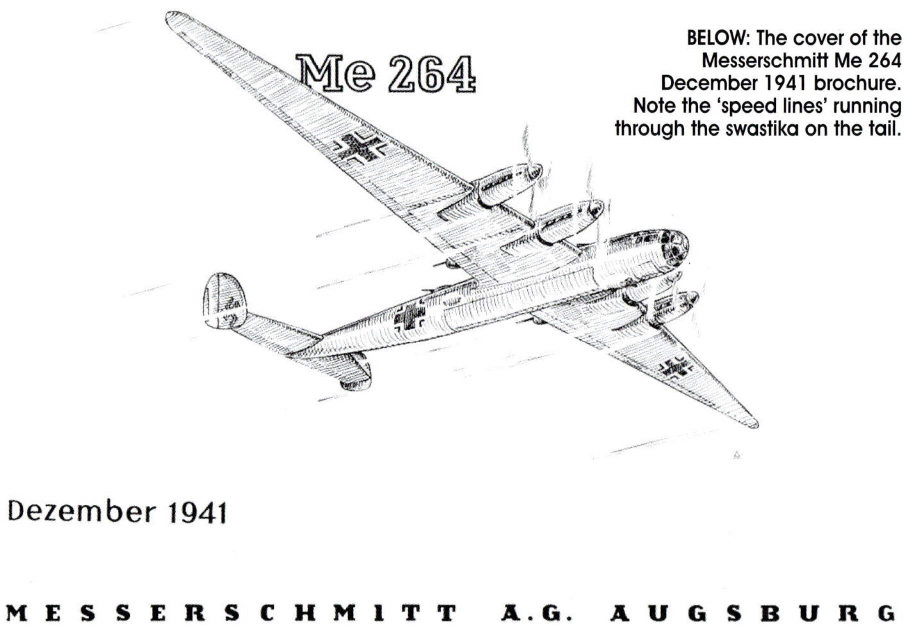

BELOW: The cover of the Messerschmitt Me 264 December 1941 brochure. Note the 'speed lines' running through the swastika on the tail.

ABOVE: Art from the Me 264 brochure. The aircraft in this form required an enormous undercarriage. Later on, versions of the Me 264 were intended to use some form of take-off trolley instead of their own undercarriage. By the time the aircraft came in to land it would be much lighter – having used most of its fuel and dropped its bombs – allowing the undercarriage to be smaller.

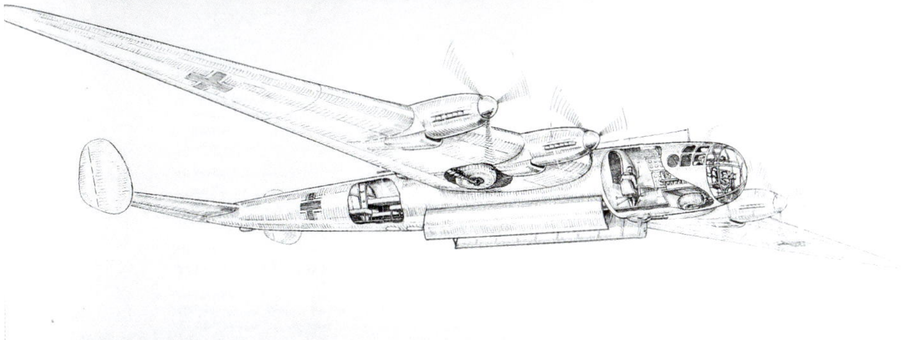

ABOVE: Another piece of concept artwork from the Me 264 brochure. Spread over a 'fold-out' section, this drawing shows bunk beds in the rear fuselage – essential for keeping the crew fresh during those long transatlantic flights. Or nearly transatlantic.

huge leap forward in performance compared to its competitors in the same way that the He 177 had five years earlier. It won the competition and prototypes were ordered. The type was designated Me 264 and Messerschmitt wasted absolutely no time in making preparations to build the first prototype.

But then the RLM, carrying out due diligence checks on the Me 264, discovered that Messerschmitt's numbers did not add up. It was apparent that the aircraft would never be able to fly nonstop from Brest to New York with any substantial payload and return. It would be unable to fly 15,000km, let alone the stated 20,000km.

This came as a tremendous blow to Messerschmitt, particularly to the personal reputation of Willy Messerschmitt himself. At this time, mid-1941, he was under increasing pressure as the Me 210 heavy fighter test programme suffered one embarrassing setback after the next.

However, in spite of everything, without Willy Messerschmitt there would have been no Me 109 and many still had faith in his genius. Von Gablenz therefore wrote: "Because Messerschmitt lacks experience in building heavy aircraft, and also because, in the opinion of the RLM technical specialist, the Me 264 plan-form was too narrow, the design could not be adopted as the standard long-range bomber for the Luftwaffe and other firms had to be invited to tender."

With work on the first Me 264 prototype already under way, the whole competition was going to have to be run again. ●

THE 'AMERIKA BOMBER' MYTH

For years there has been much debate about the 'Amerika Bomber'. Today frequent reference is made to an 'Amerika Bomber' programme and numerous German bomber projects are regularly associated with it. But there is no contemporary evidence for a programme using that term.

However, there are several references in contemporary British intelligence reports indicating that the Me 264 had indeed been given a nickname by German personnel. Was this the 'Amerika Bomber'?

A.I.2.(G) Report No. 2208 of December 26, 1943, states: "The information which has been received concerning the Me 264 is of a rather spectacular nature. It was originally believed that this was to be a twin-engined aircraft but more recent reports describe it as a four-engined long-range recce-bomber. Particular emphasis is laid upon range, which has been variously indicated as 9300 miles; 6200 miles (with four-ton load); and 'sufficient to attack the USA'. There has also been a reference to sleeping accommodation for four out of a total crew of nine."

A later account, A.D.I.(K) Report No. 169/44 of April 18, 1944, says: "Two P/W [prisoners of war] who were at Lechfeld during the summer of 1943 had seen an aircraft which they referred to as a Me 264 at that airfield. It appears that one aircraft of this type was standing in the open at Lechfeld airfield for several months up to August 1943 when it suddenly disappeared.

"It aroused P/W's interest owing to its reputed prodigious range; it was usually referred to as the 'USA Bomber', as it was supposed to be capable of attacking the United States, and one P/W asserts that it has been flown to Tokyo and back."

A.D.I.(K) 1346 dated October 18, 1944, refers to the "Me 264 'York Bomber'" presumably meaning 'New York Bomber'.

The most oft-stated reference for the Me 264 as being the 'Amerika Bomber' comes from a speech given by Hermann Göring at his Carinhall retreat on March 18, 1943. He is quoted as saying: "I well remember that at Augsburg – it was exactly a year ago – I was shown an 'Amerika Bomber' that really called for nothing more than to be put into mass production." In fact, word for word, the original transcript actually says: "I remember – it is years ago now – when I was in Augsburg, I was shown an 'America' aircraft which had only to be put into large-scale production."

This interesting speech is reproduced in its entirety elsewhere in this publication. So there appears to be no contemporary source that puts 'Amerika' and 'Bomber' together. Where, then, does this common 'secret projects' term come from?

The earliest verified reference appears on p15 in the November 1952 issue of American magazine *Flying* and is used in reference to a postwar Soviet-supervised Junkers design, the EF 132. It states: "More German scientists and equipment arrived and more German aircraft and engine plants took roots in Russian soil. Professor Doctor Schiebe, Freundel, Wocke, Hartmann and hundreds of others went to work on different projects, such as the most secret Luftwaffe plan of transatlantic bombing with the JuEF 132 – The 'Amerika Bomber'."

There is scant evidence from the 1960s but writing in his highly influential 1970 work The Warplanes of the Third Reich, William Green stated that the Me 264 was 'dubbed unofficially the Amerika-Bomber'. Green was writing at a time when most if not all documents and reports relating to German projects were still classified and unavailable. He therefore did what he could with what he had.

No doubt as a consequence of this description, Herbert Molloy Mason stated in his 1973 book, The Rise of the Luftwaffe, that the Me 264 was known as the Amerika-Bomber, and in his 1978 Illustrated Encyclopedia of 20th Century Weapons and Warfare, Bernard Fitzsimons said the Me 264 was 'popularly called' the Amerika-Bomber. In the 1987 Smithsonian Book of Flight, Walter J Boyne also uses 'Amerika Bomber' to refer to the Me 264.

Nathan C Goldman, writing in 1992, used the term to refer to Eugen Sänger's suborbital bomber, as did NASA writer A M Springer in 2003. In 1999, Isolde Baur called the Me 264 an 'Amerika-Bomber' in her biography of her husband, Messerschmitt test pilot Karl Baur.

Perhaps most influentially in recent times, David Myhra referred to the Horten XVIII as an Amerika Bomber in his 1998 book Secret Aircraft Designs of the Third Reich. This followed his interview with Reimar Horten in 1980, where Horten stated: "The Ho 18 was to have been a very long-range all-wing bomber which Walter and I were ordered to design and build for Hermann Göring in April 1945. The project already had a nickname – it was being called the 'Amerika-Bomber'."

This evidence is discussed in more detail elsewhere in this volume, but suffice to say that only Göring and perhaps Horten himself ever used the 'nickname' since the XVIII was entered for a competition that was meant to result in a bomber capable of attacking England and, to a limited degree, supply vessels in the Atlantic.

Following Myhra's lead, Walter J Boyne also refers to the Horten XVIII as the 'Amerika-Bomber' in his 2002 Air Warfare encyclopaedia, as does Jean-Denis G G Lepage in his 2009 Aircraft of the Luftwaffe, and Lance Cole in his 2015 Secret Wings of World War II.

The preliminary bomber

Arado E 470

With the Fernkampfflugzeug competition in the process of being rerun, Arado was asked to provide an independent assessment of just how feasible it was to build an extremely large aircraft for transatlantic operations. The result was project E 470...

Arado was a little different from the other German aircraft manufacturers. Where the likes of Heinkel, Messerschmitt and Focke-Wulf remained private concerns even during wartime, Arado had been a wholly owned tool of the Nazi state since 1936.

The previous owner, Heinrich Lübbe, had been forced to hand over his firm after refusing to join the Nazi party. Thereafter the state poured huge sums into Arado, transforming it into a pliable and ego-less 'in house' manufacturer for the government. In practice, this meant that Arado spent much of its time and effort building the designs of other companies.

It also meant that whenever the private companies failed or the government felt that they could not be trusted, Arado was there to act as a fallback. Junkers was also a government brand but where Arado had been pumped up from relatively humble beginnings, Junkers had been a vast concern beforehand and managed to retain some of its original character.

Following the embarrassing failure of the original 1940-41 long-range bomber competition, the RLM realised that its own experts knew too little about what was possible and what problems might arise in the design and construction of extremely large aircraft.

Therefore, Arado was tasked with carrying out some research on the subject ahead of the contractors' due date for their revised long-range aircraft proposals in the spring of 1942. It was particularly asked to look at whether large transport aircraft might reasonably be converted for use as bombers.

The resulting report, Analysis of the Design of a Large Transport Aircraft, Project E 470, was broken down into three areas - an analysis of structures and weights, an examination of range and endurance potential, and some suggestions for 'preliminary projects'.

The analysis of structures and weights tried to work out how values such as area loading, power loading and stress classification changed when you took a 16-ton aircraft design and then scaled it up to 120 tons. Different component 'weight groups', such as engines, undercarriage and structural strengthening were examined at different points along the overall weight curve to see

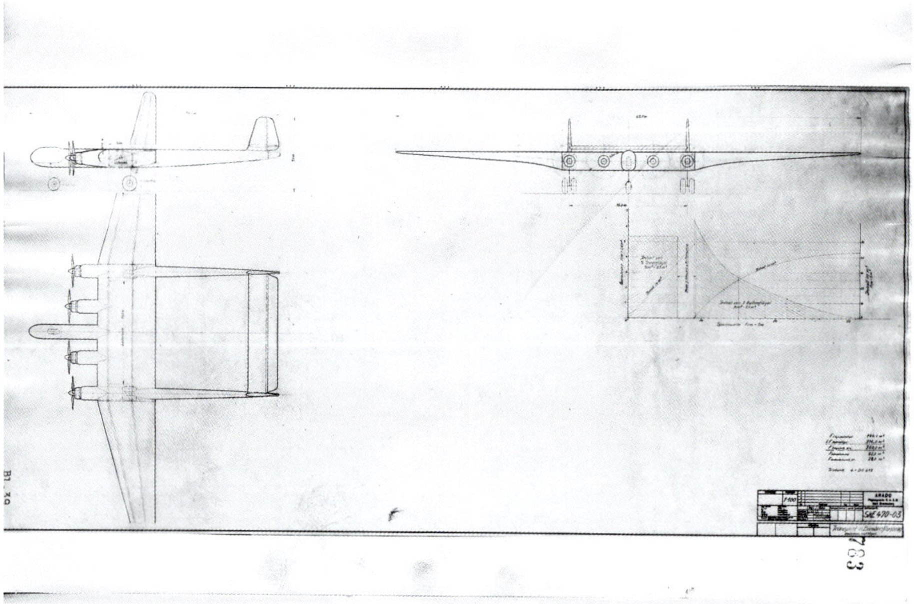

ABOVE: What the accompanying report refers to as the Arado E 470 'Variant E', is described as a 'transport and bomber aircraft – load space in wing' in the drawing's own information panel. Since it was intended primarily to illustrate a concept, rather than as a buildable project, the design is lacking in detail.

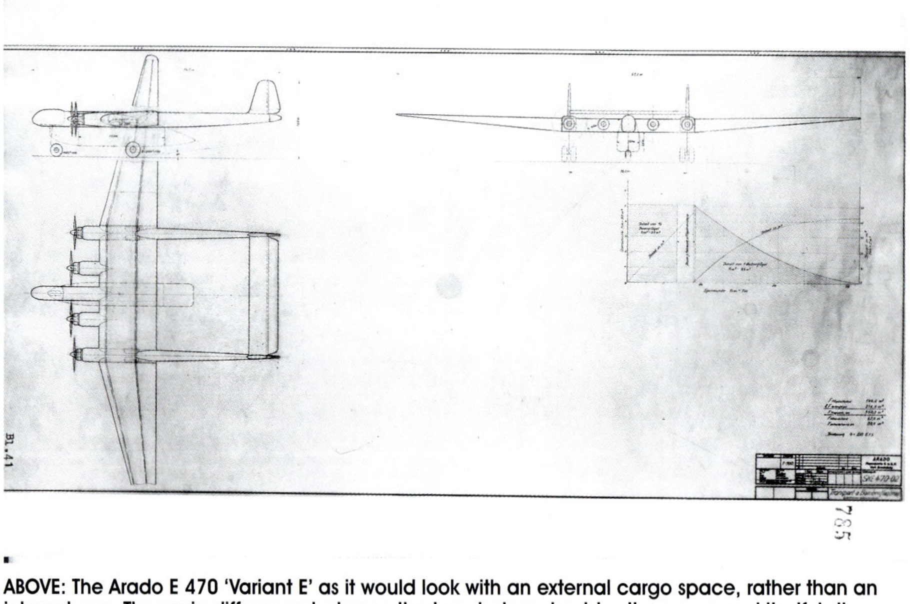

ABOVE: The Arado E 470 'Variant E' as it would look with an external cargo space, rather than an internal one. The main difference between the two designs, besides the cargo pod itself, is the undercarriage – this version of the aircraft layout requiring an additional metre of height.

BELOW: The Arado E 470 'Variant E' imagined as a real aircraft, with a very thick fuel-bearing wing. Art by Daniel Uhr

how they needed to change, e.g. more engines or larger undercarriage, and what proportion of the total weight they then represented.

During the course of this work, it became increasingly apparent that the key to carrying large loads over long distances was to put as much of the aircraft's fuel as possible into its wings, leaving the fuselage free for cargo. A bomber such as the He 177 had small wing tanks with the bulk of its fuel carried in the fuselage.

Under a heading of 'Increase in payload for equal structural weight, by load distribution over the span', the report states: "The considerations applied hitherto, to the effect of increasing aircraft dimensions on structural weight and attainable payload, were valid for centrally-applied loads.

"If it becomes possible to distribute the payload more suitably, e.g. by distributing the fuel weight over the span, the payload can be considerably increased by only a slight increase in the structural weights.

"A simple mathematical calculation shows that the design of a dual-purpose aircraft is possible, if the payload consisting principally of fuel, is distributed over the wingspan, the tanks being taken into use successively from inboard outwards."

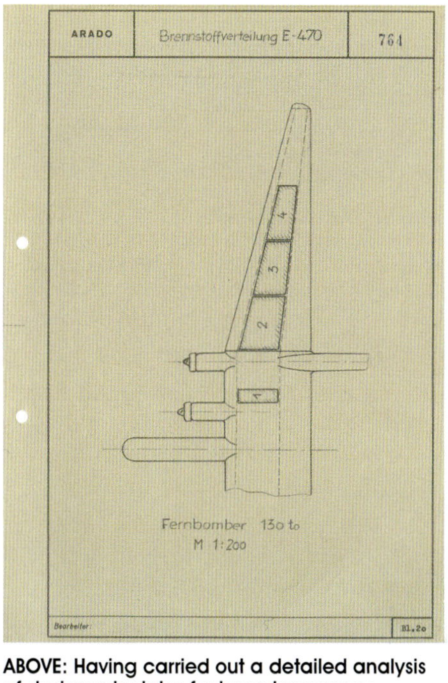

ABOVE: Having carried out a detailed analysis of design principles for large long-range aircraft, Arado believed it was critical that as much fuel as possible should be stored in the wings. This would leave the fuselage and central portion of the aircraft free for bombs or cargo.

With a central space left free for cargo, the report noted: "It may be said, that no unfavourable effect on the performance will result from adaptation of a transport aircraft for long-range bombing, owing to the consequent weight increment".

Combining this idea with the work carried out on scaling and weights, the Arado engineers put forward four sets of stats, each one representing a different theoretical aircraft. None of these were actually drawn and nor were they meant to be - they were simply numbers to be played around with to see how altering one variable affected the others.

Variants A and B each had a wing aspect ratio of 7.5, meaning they had relatively short, broad wings, while Variants C and D had an aspect ratio of 12, meaning they had longer, narrower wings.

All four were assessed on the basis that they used DB 613-type engines. Of the two short-wing examples, Variant A had four engines while B had six. Of the long-wing variants, C had four engines and D had six.

Having two basic wing types and two basic engine configurations generated four different sets of stats. For example, the four-engine short-wing variant was the lightest, while the six-engine long-wing type was the heaviest.

The four were then assessed based on them having to carry a 44,100lb payload, 'centrally applied' over a distance of 2200 miles. In this instance, the short-wing six-engine variant needed to carry the most fuel but could also carry the largest amount of cargo. The long-wing four-engine type needed the least fuel but correspondingly carried the smallest cargo.

Next, the variants were assessed with an 11,000lb cargo, centrally applied, carried a distance of 9300 miles. In this scenario, the short-wing six-engine variant would have a whopping all-up weight of 172 tons.

At the bottom of the chart, the report notes: "These figures show that the long-range alternative requires an aspect ratio of at least 12, under the given conditions, the required engine power after take-off being 11,200hp.

Under a heading of 'Analysis of an aircraft with thickened mid-wing cargo space (Variant E)', the report then states: "After these preliminary investigations, a design for a transport aircraft was developed. Since the dimensions of the required wing unit were quite considerable, it was suggested to develop the cargo space as a portion of the thickened mid-wing section.

"The design development led to selection of the following data: four DB 613 engines, wingspan 63m, aspect ratio 11 and equipped weight 55,000kg."

Two different loadouts were then looked at - one with 37,500lb of fuel and 44,100lb of cargo for a range of 2100 miles at 248-275mph, and one with 152,100lb of fuel and 11,000lb of cargo for a range of 9400 miles at 172-249mph. A further note then states: "With jet thrust boosters built in the wings, partially lowered during combat, an increase in speed is possible."

Speed with four unspecified Junkers-type jet engines operating at '100% performance' is given as 340mph. Six of these increased it to 359mph. Fitting four Daimler-Benz type jet engines to assist would give a speed of 356mph, or 383mph with six.

Under the heading 'Analysis of an aircraft design with supplementary cargo space', the report says: "Appendix 4 illustrates an alternative design with supplementary cargo space. As already mentioned, this design is less favourable than Variant E in the transport aircraft version. The layout of the cargo space, however, is probably simpler.

"As a long-range bomber without cargo space, it is aerodynamically somewhat cleaner than Variant E. A just appreciation of the pros and cons of the two arrangements is, however, only possible by a detailed analysis, which was outside the scope of the present work.

"To conclude, it may be said that the combination of a transport aircraft for large, centrally-carried loads over distances of average length, with a long-range bomber layout, is quite practicable."

In essence, Arado designed the E 470 not as a viable proposition to compete against other firms' projects and be approved or denied by the RLM, but rather as a means of helping readers more easily grasp the results of calculations and conclusions on the design of large long-range aircraft.

The twin-boom layout shown in the two drawings attached to the report was simply the easiest way of accommodating a 'thickened mid-wing cargo space'.

The report itself is undated, but one of the drawings included is dated November 1941, while two of the graphs each bear the same illegible signature and the dates January 15, 1942, and January 18, 1942. Quite what influence the Arado report and the aircraft layouts it suggested had on the outcome of the long-range aircraft design competition of mid-1942 will never be known. ●

The Atlantik

Fernkampfflugzeug second try

With the first design of the Me 264 found to be less capable than its manufacturer had claimed, it was decided that the competition to find an extremely long-range bomber for the Luftwaffe would have to be run again.

ABOVE: The only Messerschmitt Me 264 prototype to fly – coded RE+EN. A contract was placed for prototypes after the Me 264 design won the Fernkampfflugzeug competition in 1941, only for the company to be humiliated when the RLM demonstrated that its calculations on range were inaccurate. The competition was run again, and the Me 264 won again, but although the V1 was eventually completed the V2 was destroyed in a bombing attack before it could fly and the V3 was never finished.

Messerschmitt had failed to produce a bomber capable of flying to America and back but there was some sympathy for the company's efforts. It was felt that attacking America was less important than having an aircraft that could fly across the Atlantic looking for and sinking British supply vessels.

As a result, the original requirement for a range of 15,000km was relaxed somewhat and the original three companies plus Heinkel were invited to submit tenders in mid-1941 for the revised specification.

In his report of May 12, 1942, Generalleutnant Eccard, Freiherr von Gablenz, wrote: "In order that this new round of designs could be realised within reasonable time limits, the range requirement was reduced to between 11,000km and 12,000km with a total payload of five tonnes for bombs, armament and protection, and the specification stipulated six DB 603 engines working singly and not paired up, availability for these being promised within one or two years.

"The aircraft was not to be over-large; what was not wanted was too much of a jump as regards weight, dimensions and characteristics etc. and for the aircraft to be the successor to the He 177 within a reasonable period.

"A range of 11,000-12,000km provides enormous possibilities for the Battle of the Atlantic; in the event of operations against America it is planned to increase the range by refuelling in the air. A second aircraft of similar or the same type would fly out with the first and refuel it to the maximum take-off weight at about the 3000km mark, providing the necessary radius of action to the target and return. Preparations are in hand to work out a satisfactory refuelling procedure and a method of effecting the mid-air rendezvous."

Given that the technology required for effective in-flight refuelling had not yet been developed, as von Gablenz would have been well aware, it is evident that attacking America was not the central focus of this new long-range aircraft. It could, however, join the Battle of the Atlantic as soon as it was available.

Von Gablenz went on: "These new guidelines laid down in mid-1941 led to the present projects by Focke-Wulf, Heinkel and Junkers as follows. Heinkel: 90 tonnes all-up weight, 260 square

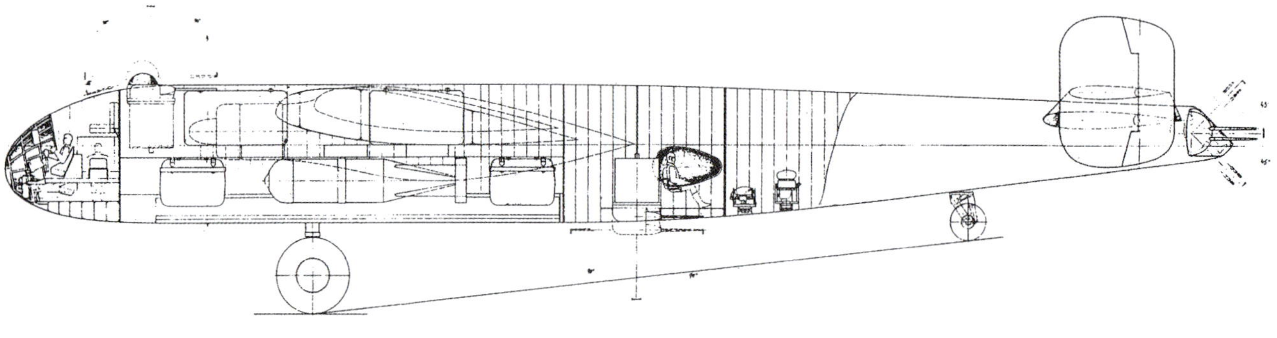

ABOVE: A side view of the Focke-Wulf Baubeschreibung Nr. 242 long-range bomber showing interior detail.

Bomber

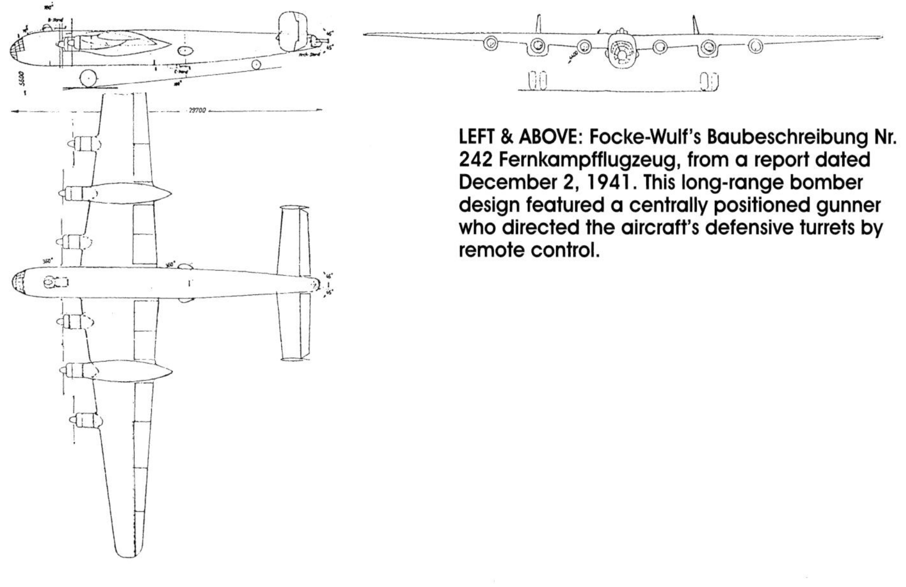

LEFT & ABOVE: Focke-Wulf's Baubeschreibung Nr. 242 Fernkampfflugzeug, from a report dated December 2, 1941. This long-range bomber design featured a centrally positioned gunner who directed the aircraft's defensive turrets by remote control.

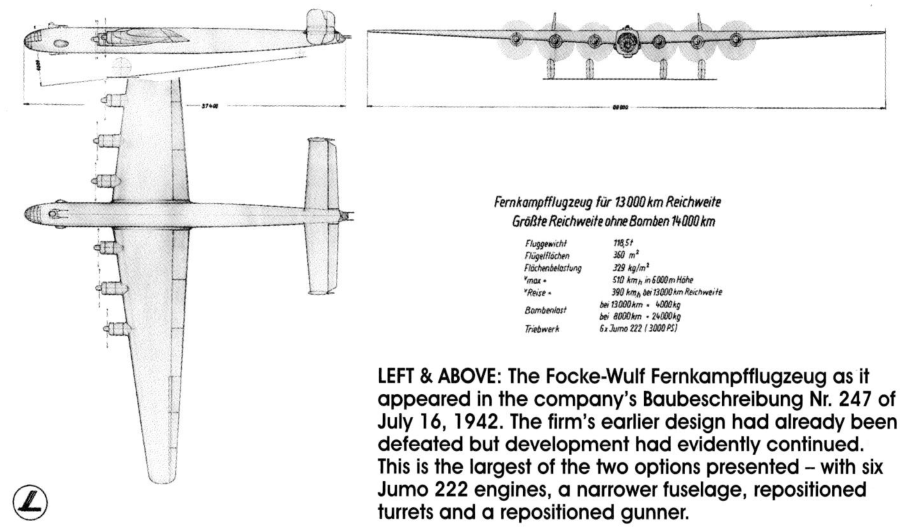

LEFT & ABOVE: The Focke-Wulf Fernkampfflugzeug as it appeared in the company's Baubeschreibung Nr. 247 of July 16, 1942. The firm's earlier design had already been defeated but development had evidently continued. This is the largest of the two options presented – with six Jumo 222 engines, a narrower fuselage, repositioned turrets and a repositioned gunner.

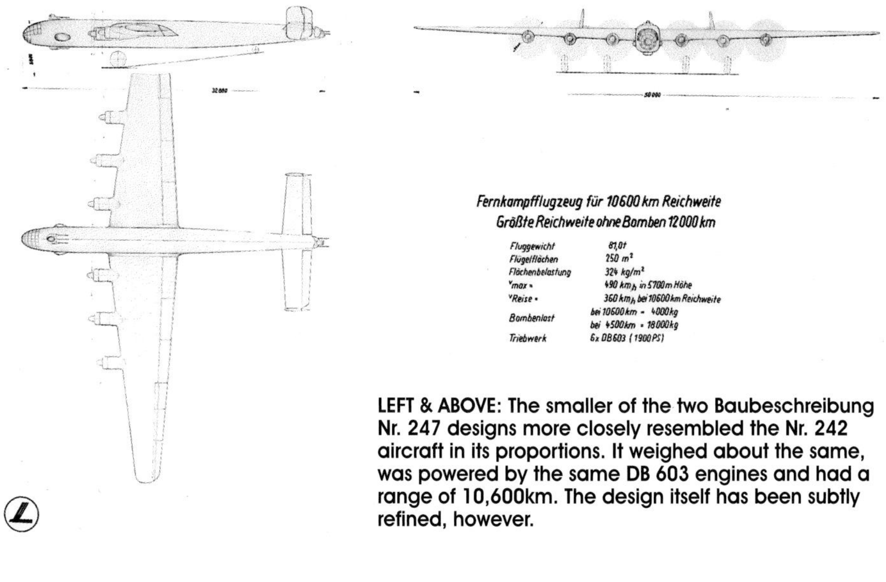

LEFT & ABOVE: The smaller of the two Baubeschreibung Nr. 247 designs more closely resembled the Nr. 242 aircraft in its proportions. It weighed about the same, was powered by the same DB 603 engines and had a range of 10,600km. The design itself has been subtly refined, however.

metres wing surface, 11,000km range, five tonnes payload, 4.3 tonnes armament and armour.

"Focke-Wulf: 80 tonnes all-up weight, 250 square metres wing surface, six DB 603 engines, range 10,000km, payload five tonnes, 3.8 tonnes armament and armour. The prototypes for these two proposals would not be available before mid-1944, thus operational readiness will lie some time before 1945.

"Junkers: This is an aircraft designated Ju 390, designed for rapid development and created by lengthening the wings and fuselage of the Ju 290. All-up weight 74 tonnes, six Jumo 213 or BMW 801 engines, range 10,000km, payload five tonnes, 4.3 tonnes armament and armour.

"The Junkers' proposal has the advantage that it would be ready before all the others and it can be used as a transport with a 25-tonne payload. A Ju 390 prototype could be ready by the end of 1942. The first true prototype could be available by the end of 1943, so that testing and operational readiness would occur in 1944."

Focke-Wulf's 80 tonne design was a revised Fernkampfflugzeug and was detailed in the company's Baubeschreibung Nr. 242 of December 2, 1941. It had, as the specification required, six DB 603 engines, plus three remote-controlled turrets – one just aft of the cockpit on the upper surface, one in the tail, and a third in the centre of the aircraft's underside. Seated just in front of the latter was a lone gunner who was provided with a large observation blister on either side. This would enable him to direct the fire of the aircraft's guns onto their targets.

On March 21, 1942, Focke-Wulf issued a full proposal for this design in readiness for a final decision from the RLM on the outcome of the competition.

The nature of the Heinkel design remains a mystery. There are no known drawings of a Heinkel bomber with six engines but the company is known to have come up with at least one such design. A list of project numbers and one-line descriptions compiled for the Americans shortly after the war states that P 1064 was a long-range bomber powered by six piston engines. The high project number – Heinkel's project numbering system was chronological in that the most recent project had the highest number – suggests that P 1064 was probably much later than 1941-42 and may have been related to the He 277.

That means nothing is known about the 1941 six-engined Heinkel bomber design. A little more is known, however, about the third competitor: the Ju 390.

This was a six-engined development of the Ju 290 which, when von Gablenz was writing, had yet to make its first flight. Or rather, it had yet to make its first flight as the Ju 290 V1, since the Ju 290 was itself a modified Ju 90 – a development of the Ju 89 which had already undergone years of work and extensive testing. There is no doubt that of these three designs, the Ju 390 was the safe option.

Yet there were two further contenders. Von Gablenz wrote: "To these details of the six-engined projects we must compare the now confirmed Me 264 data and the possibilities of the BV 238.

"Me 264 first variant: All-up weight 50 tonnes, four DB 603 engines, range 13,000km, payload three tonnes, two tonnes armament and armour. ▶

Heinkel-Projekte

P	He	Verwendungszweck	Triebw.	P	He	Verwendungszweck	Triebw.
1054		takt. Transporter	2 x Otto	1075		Fernaufklarer (Do335Z)	4 x Otto
1062		Jager	1 x Otto	1076		Jager	1 x Otto
1063		Schnellbomber (1 Mann)	2 x TL	1077	Julia	Jager	1 x RGer
1064		Fernbomber	6 x Otto	1078		Jager	1 x TL
1065		Arbeitsflugzeug (3 Mann)	2 x Otto	1079		Nachtjager	2 x TL
1066		Arbeitsflugzeug (2 Mann)	2 x Otto	1080		Lorin - Jager	Lorin
1067		Schnellstbomber	2 x Otto				
1068	343	Bomber	4 x TL				
1069		Jager	1 x TL				
1070		Bomber(Nurflugel)	2 bezw. 4 x TL				
1071		Jager(unsym.)	2 x Otto				
1072		Fernbomber	4 x Otto				
1073	162	Jager	1 x TL				
1074		Jager (1u. 2 mot. Druckschr.)	2 x Otto				

ABOVE: A list of Heinkel late war projects compiled for the Americans in 1945 after the firm's designers were taken into custody. No drawing of a Heinkel bomber with six 'Otto' or piston engines appears to have survived but the company certainly produced at least one – the P 1064. The Germans referred to piston engines as 'Otto' engines after German internal combustion engine pioneer Nikolaus Otto.

up the idea of trans-oceanic operations."

Again it is apparent that despite Messerschmitt's earlier failure to provide accurate performance figures, von Gablenz still preferred the Me 264 with its "now confirmed" data. GLZM is an abbreviation for Generalluftzeugmeister, the air inspector general in charge of aircraft production, Erhard Milch.

The fifth possibility was the Blohm & Voss BV 238 flying boat, which was at this stage still nearly two years away from its first flight.

A brief mention is then made of the Focke-Wulf Fw 300 and Junkers Ju 290, which will be examined in a different chapter, before von Gablenz turns his attention back to the Me 264 and more problematic matters regarding these enormous aircraft.

"On the outbreak of war with the United States, the idea of operating against America directly without refuelling was naturally pursued as it had been previously. The first theoretical solution was proposed by Messerschmitt in the autumn of 1941 with the following design: Me 264 six-engined variant: All-up weight 70-80 tonnes, six DB 603 engines, range 15,000km, payload five tonnes, approximately four tonnes armament and armour.

"The solution was theoretical because of the firm's under-capacity. Mention must be made of the special characteristics associated with these trans-oceanic aircraft and their performance. They require long runways (on average a 2km run before take-off). On grounds of weight only about two-thirds of the fuel tanks can be protected.

"The aircraft are fitted with landing gear: a jettisonable undercarriage is provided for

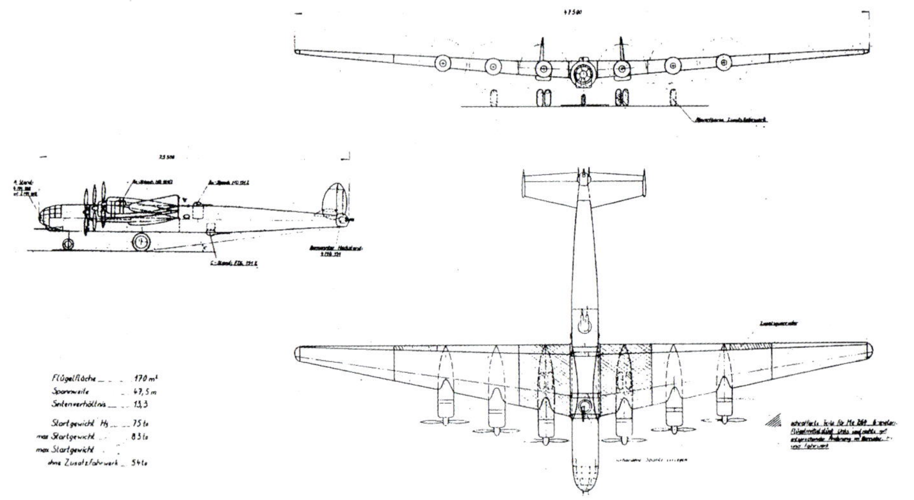

ABOVE: Messerschmitt drawing showing the Me 264 with six engines. The company would continue to revise the design of its failed bomber until the autumn of 1944 in the hope of securing a firm production contract and the allocation of a suitable subcontractor to build it.

"Me 264 second variant: All-up weight 47 tonnes, four BMW 801 engines, range 12,000km, payload two tonnes bombs as reconnaissance aircraft, three tonnes armament and armour possible.

"Me 264 third variant: All-up weight 43 tonnes, four Jumo 211 engines, range 11,500km, no bombs, 1.4 tonnes armament and armour.

"Investigation has shown that contrary to the assertion made by the firm, the America return flight direct is probably not possible with so little reserve. However, compared with the other proposals, the lesser all-up weights and materials requirement, plus four engines as against five or six, the design is so much better that in the opinion of the GLZM this is the aircraft to order and accordingly attempts will be made to resolve the difficulties of under-capacity at Messerschmitt.

"If it is possible to resume the interrupted course of development work on the Me 264, then we can have the prototypes this year, get the programme of flight testing over with during 1943, and have the machines operational in 1944. The simplifications to the design suggested by the RLM technical centre (normal unpressurised cockpit, proven engines, no bomb-aimer's position) were made so that development could be continued despite the under-capacity at Messerschmitt (which would otherwise involve very long delays in production or cancellation of the contract) and to get the aircraft into the air.

"Furthermore, on account of the increasing delay in trials and introduction of the DB 603 engines, it is not expected that the engines will be ready for the 30-hour endurance run in 1943/44.

"Even the Me 264 will need mid-air refuelling on the America route but this is possible with the alternative engines. Especial value is placed on this assurance as, according to the GLZM-Staff at a meeting with the Chief of General Staff, it was assumed by the GLZM that fitting alternative engine types and simplification of the Me 264 would mean giving

BELOW: The six-engined Me 264 design was rejected as offering little improvement over its four-engined counterpart. Art by Daniel Uhr

ABOVE: The Me 264 V1 prototype was obsolete before it was even finished. Development work continued however, and some argued that it ought to have been rushed into production, but this was not to be.

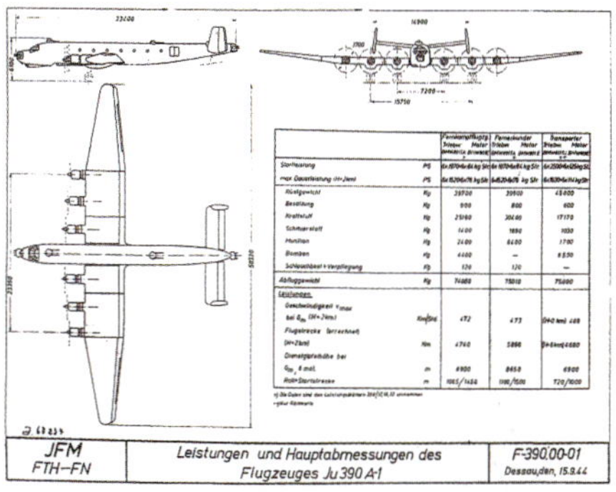

ABOVE: Junkers drawing from September 15, 1944, showing proposed versions of the Ju 390 – long-range bomber, long-range reconnaissance and transporter. The basic design had changed little since it was first proposed in 1942.

take-off. Tactically, problems of stability and lack of manoeuvrability rule out dive-bombing. For nuisance raids against American land targets, night bombing will be in the horizontal attitude. In operations over the sea, the size of the aircraft is particularly disadvantageous.

"Normal aerial torpedoes are envisaged but remote-controlled missiles would be best. Planning and development work is in hand to launch small parasite aircraft from these very large aircraft to carry out attacks. Test aircraft of this type are under construction and the basic trials regarding mounting them on the mother aircraft have been partly completed and should be finished during the course of the year.

"The parasite aircraft will be very small (6sq m as against 14sq m of the Bf 109) jet-propelled single-seaters designed for flights lasting from 30 minutes to an hour. They should be especially suitable for direct attacks on shipping using one or two bombs of 1000kg aggregate weight. Experiments to solve the problem of how the mother aircraft can recover the parasite are also in hand.

"Besides bombing, the parasite aircraft can be used to defend against enemy fighters. A Ju 390 for example can carry two parasite aircraft. The aircraft can be rearmed with bombs aboard the mother aircraft."

The immense take-off distances required, the lack of fuel tank protection, the jettisonable undercarriage and the lack of manoeuvrability meant that none of these aircraft was a particularly appealing prospect. It is possible that this was the impression von Gablenz was attempting to give to this report's intended recipient – and his brief discussion of parasite aircraft only serves to enhance the idea that expending a huge amount of time and money designing an aircraft capable of extremely long range operations was a mistake.

He finishes his report by recounting what had "been approved": "To summarise therefore, in accordance with the suggestions of the GLZM in the area of trans-oceanic aircraft, the following have been approved:

1) The four-engined Me 264 will be proceeded with as the quickest possible solution for operations against the United States.

2) The necessary mid-air refuelling procedure will probably be worked out during 1942.

3) For distances up to about 10,000km, the Ju 390 is best (heavier loads, better armament, parasite aircraft).

4) Investigations with the object of achieving a return flight to and from America without refuelling (six-engined Me 264) will be stepped up.

5) Use of the Ju 290 for distances up to 8000km will be investigated with a view to using the aircraft to refuel the four-engined Me 264."

So Focke-Wulf and Heinkel were to be ruled out and the Me 264, in some form, was regarded as the best option if operations against the US were deemed necessary. But for the all-important Battle of the Atlantic, to help cut off Britain's supplies, the Ju 390 was best – even if the 'parasite aircraft' were unlikely ever to reach operational readiness. And the Ju 290 was to take part in air-to-air refuelling 'investigations'.

With the Ju 290 already close to airworthiness, Junkers was told to proceed with a development programme for the Ju 390. Messerschmitt's contract to build prototypes of the Me 264 remained in place along with the provisional commitment to build 30 aircraft.

Despite being defeated in the revised long-range bomber competition, Focke-Wulf was evidently not disheartened and continued to work on its Fernkampfflugzeug. Another project report, Baubeschreibung Nr. 247 of July 16, 1942, shows a second revision of the Baubeschreibung Nr. 242 aircraft. This time the large nacelles that had been fitted to the Nr. 242 aircraft's mid-wing engines were deleted and the gunner's observation blisters were moved to the front of the aircraft – presumably so that he could sit with the rest of the crew rather than being isolated mid-fuselage. In addition, the mid-lower turret was moved to sit directly beneath the front-upper turret. This would make it easier to link them together and to direct their fire via the remote control system.

Two different versions of the Nr. 247 bomber appear in the same report – one that was powered by six DB 603s, weighed 81 tonnes and measured 32.88m from end to end, with a range of 13,000km carrying bombs, and another weighing 118.5 tonnes and measuring 37.4m long, powered by six Jumo 222s. This was capable of 10,600km carrying bombs. Wingspan was 50m for the former and 60m for the latter.

While Focke-Wulf seems to have foreseen a future in designing enormous long-range bombers, Heinkel did not: it appears thereafter to have concentrated its efforts mostly on four-engined designs. But what of the BV 238 and its wheeled counterpart, the BV 250?

From boat to bomber

Blohm & Voss BV 238 and BV 250

One of the largest German bombers proposed during the war started out as a flying boat military transport. The BV 238 and its 'land' version, the BV 250, were regularly offered by Blohm & Voss to meet large long-range aircraft requirements…

ABOVE: Cover of the BV 238 brochure from June 1943. This details not only the unarmed BV 238A but also the heavily-armed Seefernaufklärer version.

The aircraft division of Hamburg-based ship-builder Blohm & Voss, established as Hamburger Flugzeugbau in 1933, had already made a name for itself in the field of flying boat design by the time of the Fernkampfflugzeug competition.

Early on, the firm had gained valuable experience in building large aircraft out of aluminium by winning a contract to make Junkers Ju 52 fuselages under licence.

In his autobiography Weltumspannende Memoiren eines Flugzeugkonstrukteurs or 'Globe-spanning memoirs of an aeronautical engineer', Blohm & Voss chief designer Richard Vogt recalled how, in 1933, "all prominent heads of the German aircraft factories were summoned by the RLM so that it could obtain information about their production facilities.

"It was a pleasant surprise as the first person in the elevator to meet Dr Dornier. He knew of my new job as chief engineer of the Hamburger Flugzeugbau. What he did not know, yet could foresee, was the fact that we would soon be the two competitors in the design and construction of large seaplanes.

"The meeting at the RLM was only interesting to me because of the opportunity to meet all of my future competitors. I had nothing to do with the technical aspects of the meeting. The Government showed us its programme to build a large number of three-engined Junkers Ju 52s, which should serve as a transporter as well as a bomber.

"Blohm & Voss was given a big piece of the hull construction. The experience of this production allowed us to obtain the necessary knowledge for the construction

ABOVE: The only Blohm & Voss BV 238 to be completed, the V1, seen at anchor during its initial test programme in 1944.

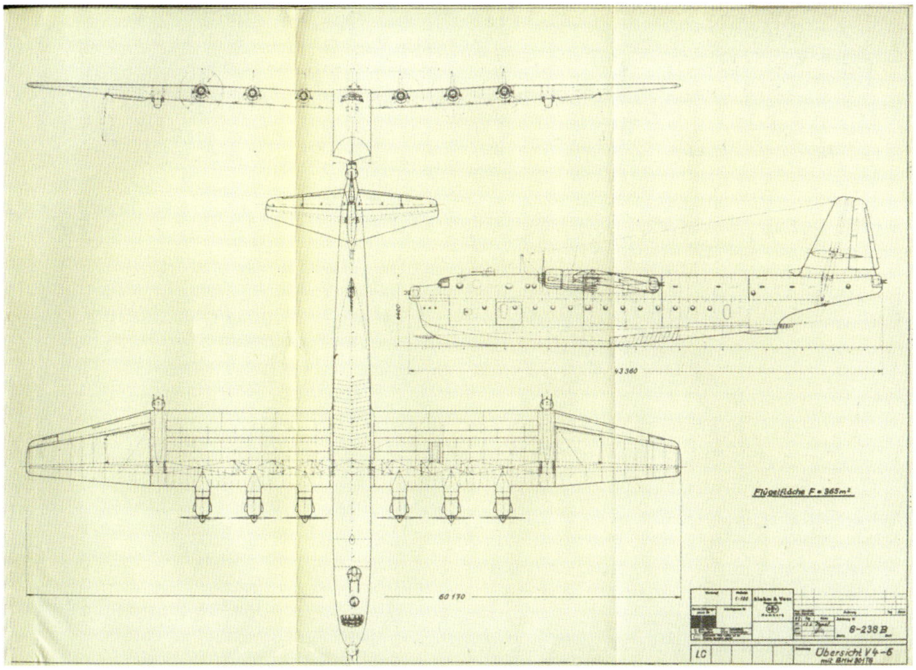

ABOVE: Featuring six gun turrets, the BV 238 B was intended for long-range reconnaissance missions in support of the German U-boat fleet – seeking out Allied supply vessels. The turrets were not the only difference from the BV 238 V1; the 'B' version was to be powered by six BMW 801TGs engines, rather than Daimler-Benz DB 603s.

ABOVE: Art from the frontispiece to the BV 250 brochure, dated March 1942. The BV 250, initially known as the 'BV 238-Land', was offered for four different potential roles – transport, bomber, long-range bomber and long-range reconnaissance.

of aircraft parts made of aluminium."

When Lufthansa invited tenders for a flying boat to operate three new transatlantic routes in late 1936, Hamburger Flugzeugbau submitted a design alongside efforts from Dr Claude Dornier's company, a long-established and world renowned builder of flying boats, and Heinkel. The first Hamburger Flugzeugbau offer was the P 45 – a large six-engined aircraft with a retractable wheeled undercarriage which could be launched from a body of water using a 'take-off boat' which it left behind on the water once it had lifted off.

Dornier offered the Do 20, based on the antiquated Do X design of 1929, while Heinkel put forward the smaller, lighter, four-engined He 120. Lufthansa was not convinced by any of these, so Vogt and his engineers revised their proposal and submitted the P 54 instead. This was a much more conventional six-engined flying boat.

Lufthansa awarded a contract for three prototype P 54s to Hamburger Flugzeugbau on September 19, 1937. Development of the type for production, with the RLM designation Ha 222, began in early 1938. It was to have a relatively narrow 36.5m long fuselage, straight 46m span wings constructed using a tubular spar containing six fuel tanks, six 1200hp Bramo 323-R Fafnir radial engines, and retractable stabiliser floats on at the ends of its wings.

Less than a year later, the RLM decided that a large military transport flying boat was needed – larger even than the Ha 222, now known as the BV 222 after the company's name was changed to Blohm & Voss Flugzeugbau.

Company designer and flying boat project leader Hans H Amtmann, wrote in his

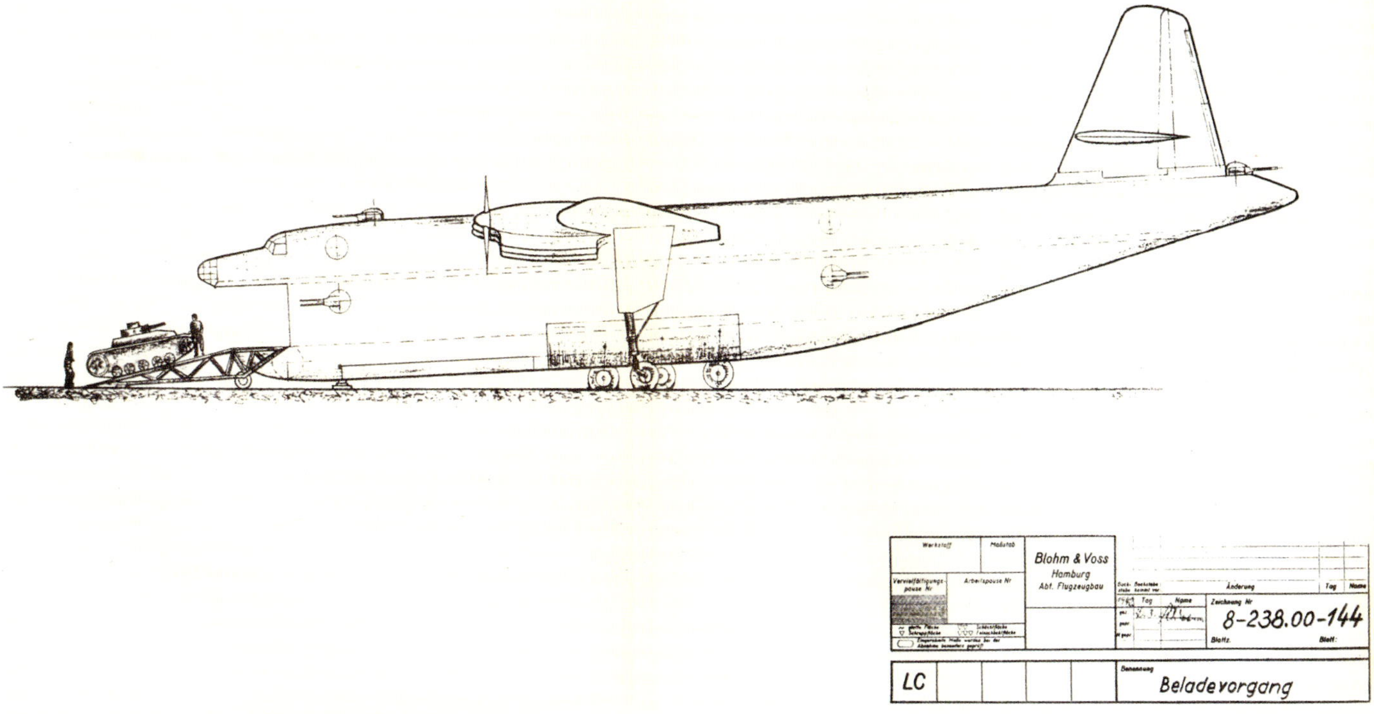

ABOVE: The BV 250 as a transport. This drawing illustrates the design's innovative front-loading doors. With the nosewheel retracted, the aircraft could 'kneel' forwards onto a jack so that vehicles could drive up a ramp into the cargo hold.

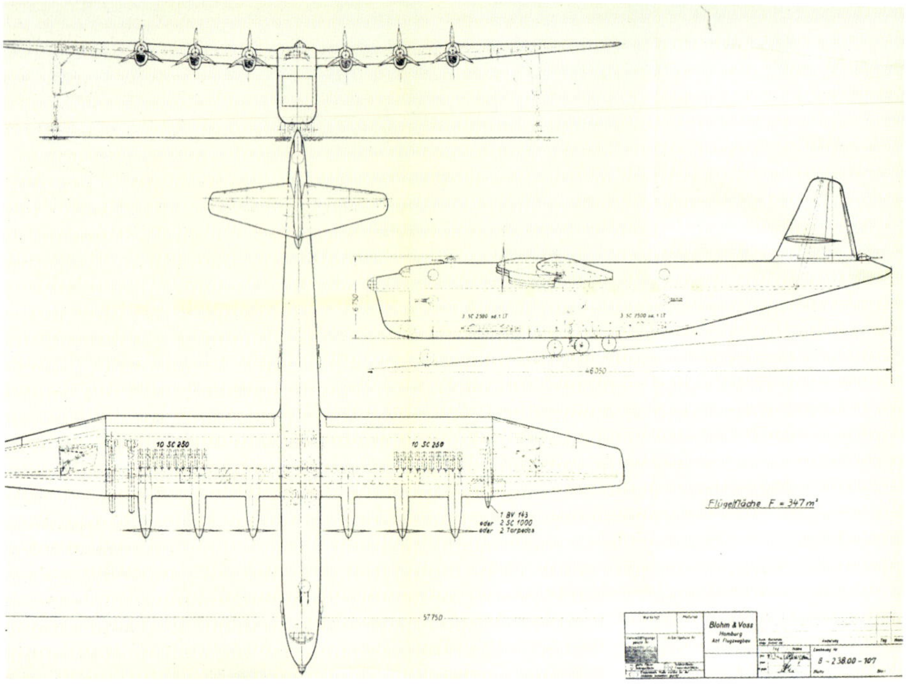

ABOVE: Fitted out as a bomber, the BV 250 could accommodate huge loads both under its wings and in bomb bays both fore and aft the central undercarriage in its fuselage.

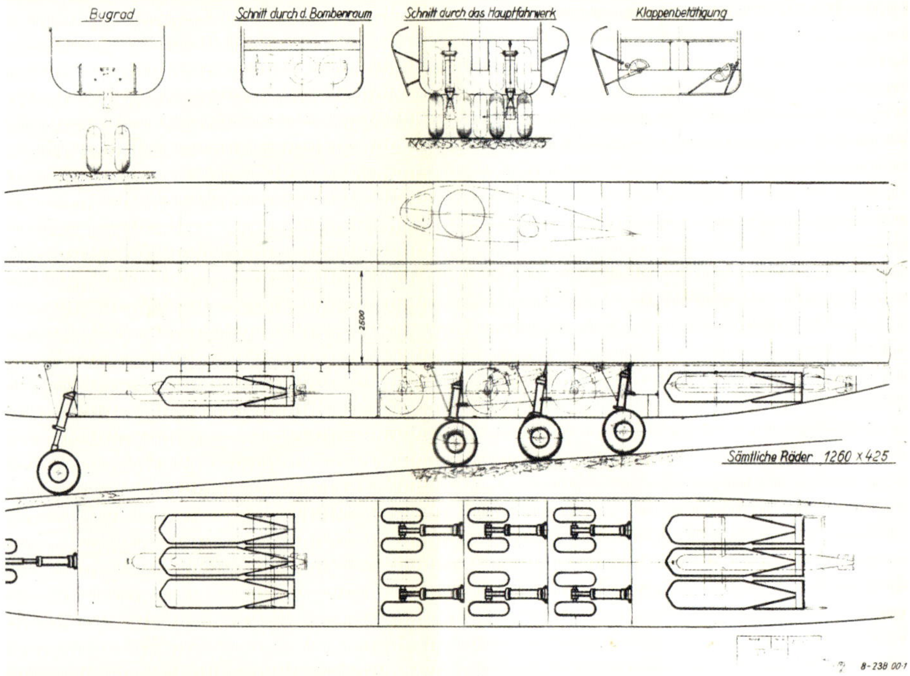

ABOVE: Blohm & Voss drawing showing the positioning of the BV 250's undercarriage in relation to its two internal bomb bays.

autobiography, The Vanishing Paperclips: "The RLM issued a request for a large flying boat. In spite of the fact that Erhard Milch, the powerful secretary to the Air Minister Göring, wanted this flying boat developed and built by the Dornier company, the technical staff of the Air Ministry selected our design and the contract went to our company.

"The preliminary design of this boat developed into the largest flying boat at that time, the 100 tons BV 238. This boat was actually a blown up BV 222 but designed from the beginning as a military transport."

Vogt apparently derived some satisfaction from defeating Dornier again and the company was awarded a contract in early 1942 to design and build six prototypes. Structurally, the BV 238 was largely a scaled-up BV 222 – with a fuselage measuring 43.35m long, about 120% of the original, and a wingspan of 60.17m, up to 130%. It was to be powered by six DB 603s and would require a crew of 10.

Between January and March 1942, Blohm & Voss arranged for some of the BV 238 design work to be carried out by a French subcontractor, arranged for some students to build a manned flyable 1:4 scale model of the BV 238 and set out designs for a 'land' version which had an ordinary undercarriage in place of a boat hull and floats.

The latter was outlined in a brochure dated March 1942, apparently a revised version of one previously produced some time during the preceding two months. In the foreword, it states: "In January this year we made the RLM aware of the possibility of building a land aircraft for maritime patrol and the large flying boat BV 238 simultaneously."

Benefits of doing this included additional construction and development expenses of only around 10-15%, use of common materials and parts including wings, engines, tail, controls, equipment and weapons, no need for extra testing and "immediate solution to the urgency palpable shortly after the testing of the flying boat". Presumably the latter meant that, built as a land aircraft, once it was on the ground there would be no need to secure it against the wind and waves.

The brochure further noted: "After first announcing the project to the person in charge of the RLM, we have revised it again. Compared to the first proposal, the chassis has a more conventional nosewheel and also we were able to enlarge the clear cargo space without additional resistance to 2.5m by using different wheel dimensions."

The cover of the brochure has the words 'BV 238-Land Grossraumtransporter Bomber-Fernbomber Fernaufklärer' on it but with a single black line through '238-Land' and the number '250' added above.

The BV 250 detailed inside was indeed offered in four different configurations – large transporter, bomber, long-range bomber and long-range reconnaissance. Ranges were, respectively, 1242 miles carrying 10 tonnes of fuel and 42.4 tonnes of cargo, 4100-5400 miles with 31.7 tonnes of fuel and 20 tonnes of cargo, 6200-8070 miles with 47.1 tonnes of fuel and four tonnes of cargo and 6830-8700 miles with 50.9 tonnes of fuel and no cargo.

Under its wings alone, the bomber version would be able to carry either twenty 250kg bombs, four 2000kg bombs, four 1000kg mines, four 1100kg torpedoes, two BV 143 rocket-assisted glide bombs, two Hs 293 radio-controlled bombs or two Hs 294 radio-controlled bombs.

In its fuselage it would be able to carry a further six 2000kg bombs, six 1000kg mines or six 1200kg torpedoes.

The load for the long-range bomber is simply described as "four tonnes of bombs".

As with the BV 238, the six engines would be DB 603s but unlike the BV 238 the undercarriage would consist of six sets of two mainwheels directly under the central fuselage, plus a double nosewheel and a single wheel on the end of a very long leg at the end of each wing.

For defence there were six gun turrets – a HD 151 Z on the upper part of the fuselage towards the front, an unspecified turret on either side even closer to the front, another HD 151 Z on the tail and another pair of unspecified turrets on either side towards the rear.

The precise reaction to this alternative take on the BV 238 is unclear but around two months later on May 12, 1942, Generalleutnant Eccard, Freiherr von Gablenz brought up the BV 238 in his report ahead of a decision on the second round of the Fernkampfflugzeug competition.

After discussing large bomber designs from Focke-Wulf, Heinkel, Junkers and Messerschmitt he turned his attention to Blohm & Voss's large flying boat.

Presumably referring to both land and sea versions, he wrote: "BV 238: All-up weight 100 tonnes, 350 square metres wing surface, range 10,000km, payload five tonnes bombs, 5.3 tonnes armament and armour. As regards the BV 238, these values correspond closely

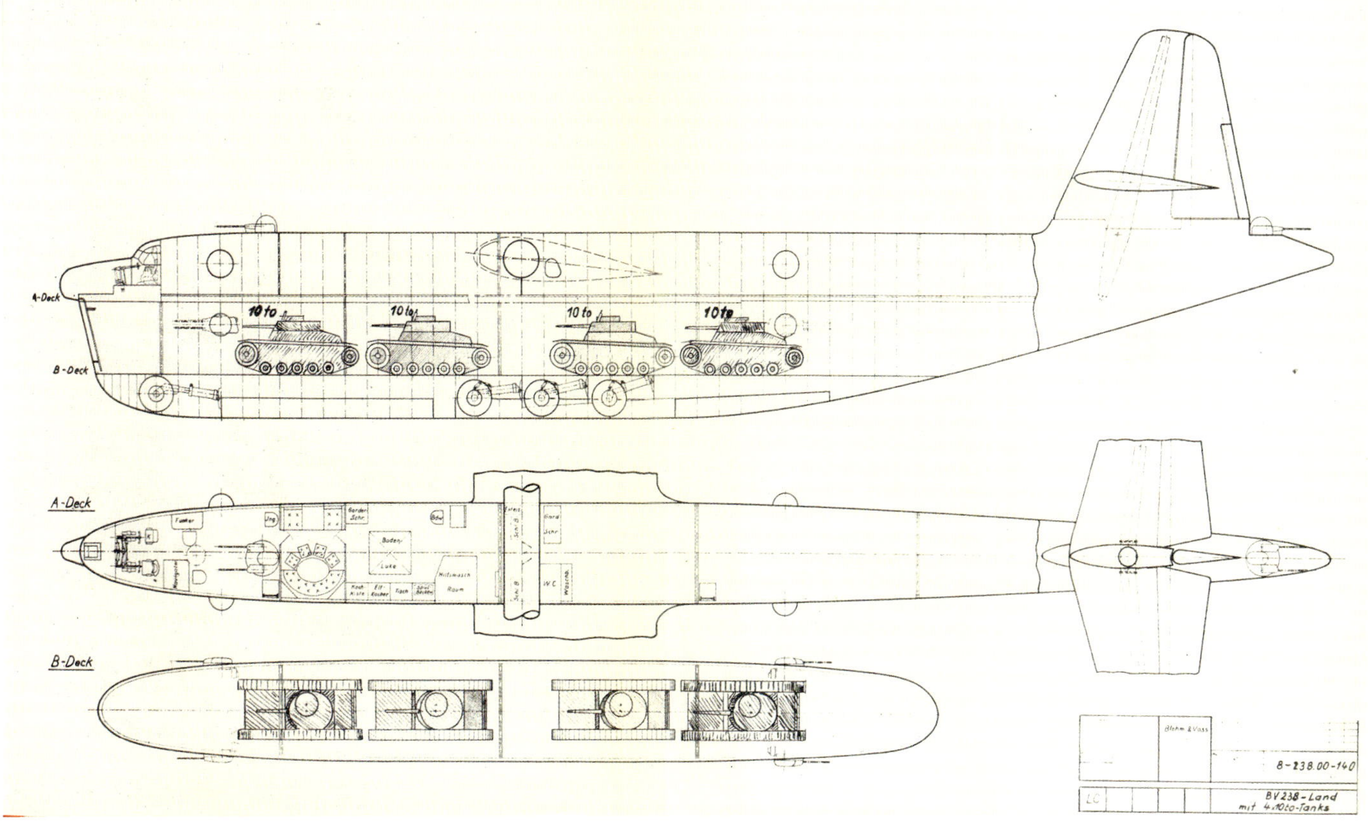

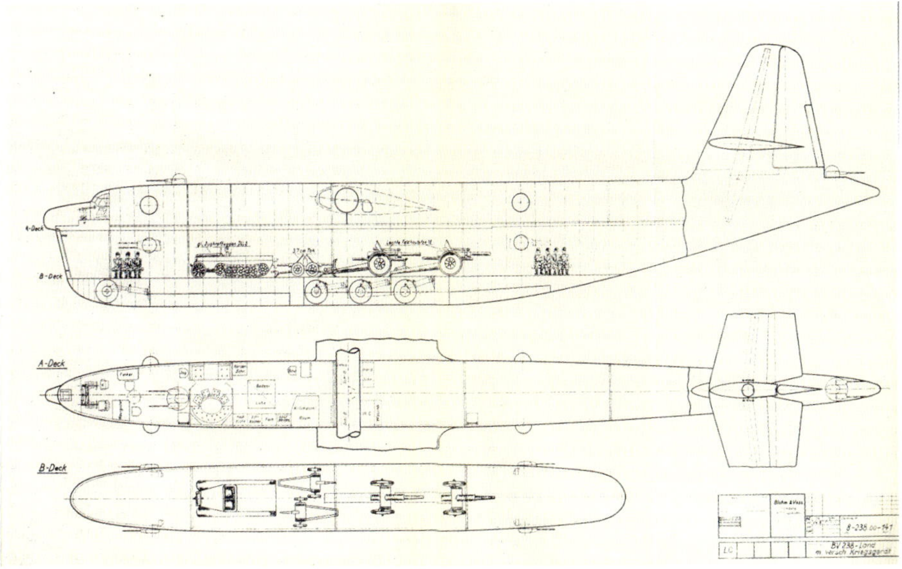

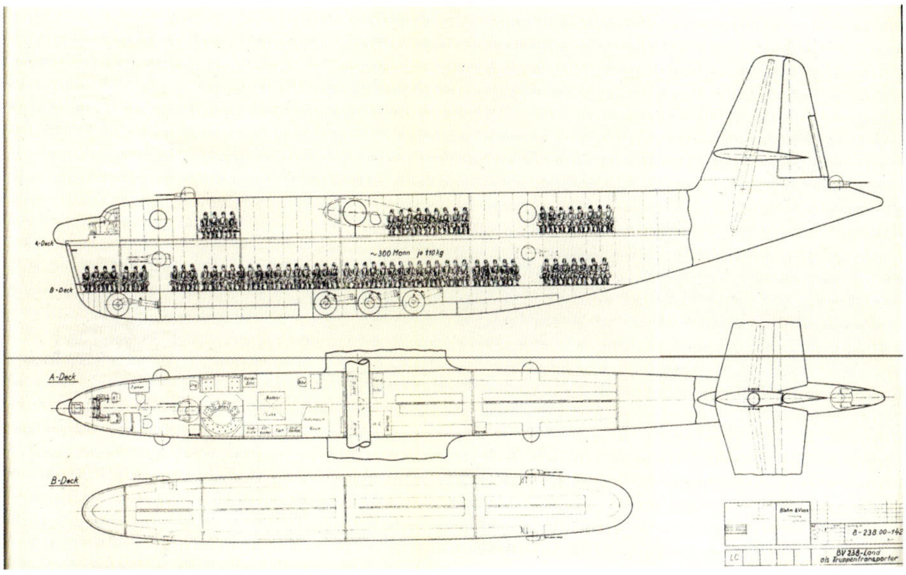

ABOVE & LEFT: As a transport, the BV 250 was flexible enough to accommodate loads ranging from four 10-tonne tanks to 300 fully-equipped soldiers.

to the specification and no great advantage is offered by this design against the others.

"Although the aircraft can be used for long distances over land as well as the sea, the GLZM suggests using the aircraft mainly in the transport role, since he understands that long-range flights over land will be better served by smaller and lighter wheeled aircraft designs and that aircraft the size of the BV 238 should then only be built if it is essential for transporting heavy loads."

The 'GLZM', Generalluftzeugmeister Erhard Milch, had seemingly never wanted the BV 238 built in the first place, so it is not surprising that he had no desire to see it progress to front line service. Nevertheless, development of the aircraft continued, though only in its seaplane form.

The manned flyable 1:4 scale model was successfully built by students at the Flugtechnische Fertigungsgemeinschaft Prag – though it took until early 1944 to complete. The model, known as FGP-227, initially had a fixed wheeled undercarriage. Damaged in a loading accident, it finally made its first flight that September at Travemünde on the coast to the north-east of Hamburg. It had a fixed undercarriage and was powered by six 400cc ILO two-stroke engines, each producing 22hp at 3000rpm. It had a wingspan of 15.25m and its fuselage was 12m long.

As the students were beginning work on the model, French designers working for the Société nationale des constructions aéronautiques du sud-ouest or SNCASO at Chatillon-sous-Bagneux in Paris commenced work on designing the BV 238's tail unit, outer wing floats, jigs and tools. ▶

According to CIOS report No. XVII-1, German Activities in the French Aircraft Industry, between March 1942 and September 1942, the Chatillon drawing office spent a total of 110,000 hours on the tail and floats with 100% of the work completed. The firm's stress office spent 24,000 hours on the same components, starting at the same time but finishing four months later - in January 1943. Preparing the drawings for the jigs and tools took 30,350 hours but the actual manufacturing of them was done in Germany.

According to British intelligence report ADI(K)/606 of November 4, 1944, construction of the first BV 238 did not take place at Blohm & Voss's own Finkenwerder facility at Hamburg either. It states: "BV 238 6-engined flying boat. One completed by end of May 1943, dismantled and sent to Finkenwerder, where it was reassembled."

BIOS final report No 254, entitled simply 'German Aircraft Industry' points out that "a Blohm & Voss 238 boat was also being built at Bremen by a subcontractor named Weser Flugzeugbau. This factory is in the American

ABOVE: Taxiing across a lake, the BV 238 V1 performs for the camera during its trials. Note the angular camouflage pattern painted onto its gigantic hull.

ABOVE: Two different views of the three DB 603 engines mounted on the BV 238 V1's starboard wing with inspection hatches open.

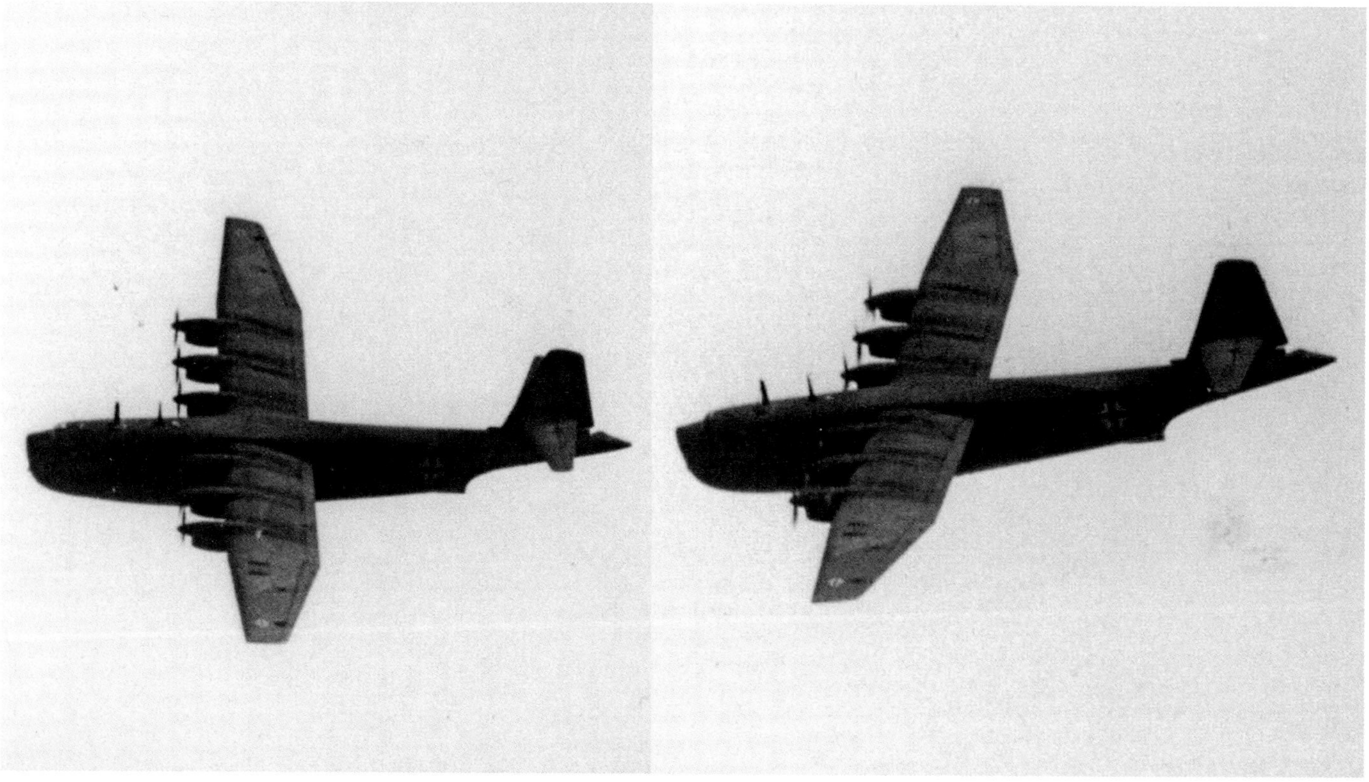

ABOVE: The BV 238 V1 in flight. The type apparently handled well for such a large aircraft.

zone. The detail parts such as frames, rib pressings, etc. for this sub-contractor were supplied from the Steinwarder works".

It seems, therefore, that two sets of tools and jigs for the BV 238 were constructed, the first set going to Bremen where Weserflug built the BV 238 V1. This was then taken apart and sent to Blohm & Voss at Finkenwerder, where it was reassembled.

In the meantime, a new brochure for the type was issued by the company in June 1943. It was entitled BV 238 Seefernaufklärer Bomber und Grossraumtransporter and set out details of the BV 238A – encompassing only the first three unarmed examples – and the BV 238B, effectively the V4, V5 and V6 which were all to be Seefernaufklärers or 'long-range maritime reconnaissance aircraft' with full turret defences fitted. These were to include a nose-mounted HL 131 V, an upper forward fuselage-mounted HD 151 Z, an HL 131 V on the rear of each wing, an HL 131 V in the tail and an SL 131 on either side – all hydraulically operated.

A note in the brochure says that "for use as a transporter and bomber there will be a change in the armament and equipment. Details have not yet been determined".

The BV 238 V1's reassembly date is unknown, as is the precise date of its first flight, although this is generally thought to have taken place some time between March 1, 1944, and mid-June 1944. After a series of apparently successful tests, the BV 238 programme was halted in August 1944 – perhaps as a result of the liberation of Paris – and the sole BV 238 was flown to a lake and hidden.

Amtmann wrote: "Two of these boats were built, one was flight tested and at the end of the war it was hidden, camouflaged in a side arm of a big lake, the Schaalsee, near the town of Lübeck." Here it was apparently discovered by Allied fighters four days before the end of the war and sunk.

A representative of British aircraft manufacturer Short Bros, chief production engineer W Swallow, interviewed Blohm & Voss head of production Otto Gaats in some detail about the BV 238 in September 1945 at the B&V headquarters at Finkenwerder.

He wrote: "It would appear that this man, who was in charge of all aircraft production for Blohm & Voss, had not been interviewed by anyone previously.

"He stated that the construction of the 90 ton type 238 boat was basically the same as the 40 ton type 222 boat. Thirteen of the type 222 boats, which was designed well before 1939, had been built."

He then states that "one type 238 had been flying for two months when it was sunk by Allied fighters four days before the end of the war". This is presumably a misunderstanding, since it is certain that the BV 238 V1 was flying by the middle of 1944. Gaats perhaps meant that the aircraft had only flown for two months before being mothballed and then eventually sunk. This would place the date of the first flight as late as June 1944.

Swallow went on: "The second 238 was being assembled at Finkenwerder, the hull is about 60% complete and the main planes barely started. The third 238 is about 80% complete at Bremen.

"Brief production facts regarding the 222 boat are as follows: production time for the hull bare in the gantry was reduced to six weeks, working day and night. Production man hours for aircraft bare (i.e. without equipment and motors) averaged 350,000 after initial boats. Regarding the type 238, Gaats stated that the total time to build the first boat in the shops, working day and night, was 14 months.

"I did not find out how much time had been spent on design, but due to the similarity of the 238 to the previous type 222, it must have been a fairly straightforward design job.

"The whole of the jigs and tools for the 238 boat had been completed and these took 600,000 man hours to make. I touched upon the prevention of corrosion in flying boats from a production point of view and Gaats said that no precautions other than painting were taken, despite the fact that Blohm & Voss were not allowed to use alclad sheet.

"He mentioned that they had extensive corrosion troubles until they had a special paint made for them. They applied two coats of this paint and he spoke very highly of it. In connection with this and the extent to which one can rely on the chief designer Vogt, I mentioned corrosion to the latter and he said they just used the paint specified by the Air Ministry and did not mention this paint which Gaats said had been specially developed for Blohm & Voss.

"At the end of the short interview with Gaats I asked him what had been his biggest production handicap during the war and he replied very expressively 'paperwork'."

Alclad is a type of corrosion-resistant aluminium sheet. Regarding the BV 238's construction, Swallow wrote: "The interior of the hull is free from bulkheads which must considerably help in laying out alternative seating combinations when used as a passenger machine. The floor sheeting on the lower desk is riveted and access for inspecting the bilges is through man-holes in the floors. This must be cheaper than the detachable floors used by us.

"A large portion of the boat skinning is of relatively thick gauge which gives good riveting conditions. It would appear that the main stressed structure of the hull is formed by the bottom, two flat sides and the upper deck because the structure above the upper deck is of a relatively light design."

Swallow also made a note, wandering through the Blohm & Voss facility of "small scale models of current types". He said: "A number of models were seen in one of the offices. Most striking of these was a model of a civil version of the BV 238 on which large panels were cut out and replaced with Perspex to show the interior fittings and decorations." ●

BELOW: A rear view of the BV 238 V1 at its moorings.

Son of Condor vs the Mighty Dessauer

Fernerkunder

Development of the Junkers Ju 89 continued despite its cancellation as a bomber and it became the Ju 90 transport. At the same time, Focke-Wulf drew up plans to replace its Fw 200 with something larger and more capable – the Fw 300 transport. Both firms hoped for military interest in their designs. The battle lines were drawn…

Design proposals for the Luftwaffe's first strategic bomber were requested in early 1934 and within a few months both Junkers and Dornier had been awarded contracts to build prototypes based on their proposals.

The first two Junkers Ju 89s were intended as bombers from the very beginning but in November 1935 the RLM noted that the V3 was to be a civilian transport version for Lufthansa. The following year, both the Ju 89 and Dornier Do 19 bombers were cancelled as the new Fernbomber specification called for a far more advanced design - resulting in the He 177.

Nevertheless, the Ju 89 V1 was first flown on April 11, 1937, the V2 on August 12 and the V3 on August 28. In the meantime, the Ju 89 V3 had received its own distinct type number - becoming the Ju 90 V1. This was essentially the wings, engines, tail and undercarriage of the Ju 89 attached to a much more spacious new fuselage.

Given a factory nickname of 'Der Grosse Dessauer', since it was enormous and had been built at Junkers' Dessau factory, the Ju 90 V1 began a programme of 100 hours' testing conducted jointly by the manufacturer and the Lufthansa airline. The V2, nicknamed 'Preussen' or 'Prussian' and fitted with air-cooled BMW 132 engines in place of the V1's Ju 89-derived DB 600s, first flew on December 2, 1937.

Part of the V1's testing regimen involved devices being fitted to the aircraft which artificially produced vibrations to simulate the effects of flutter.

During one such test on February 7, 1938, the vibration device failed and could not be switched off. The result was the loss of the aircraft and the death of flight test engineer Alfred Hahnemann, whose parachute failed to open in time.

The V2 began its 100 hours on May 26, 1938, and completed them without undue difficulty. There then followed an endurance test to demonstrate the aircraft's potential to the world's press. It was to fly in stages from Dessau to South America but during a stage in Africa on November 26, 1938, it suffered a technical malfunction and crashed with six further deaths.

In all, eight Ju 90 prototypes were built, followed by 10 series production aircraft - three of which were themselves later used as test airframes.

Towards the end of 1939, the RLM issued a specification for a new military transport. Junkers regarded the Ju 90 as an ideal platform for this and therefore offered up a suitably modified design. Not to be outdone, Focke-Wulf presented a proposed upgrade of its own Fw 200 airliner to serve as the Ju 90's main competitor - the Fw 300. It was Junkers, however, that won the development contract.

As a result, it militarised the Ju 90 V6 and V7, which were next on the production line, by giving them redesigned wings and BMW 801 engines. Another key feature was

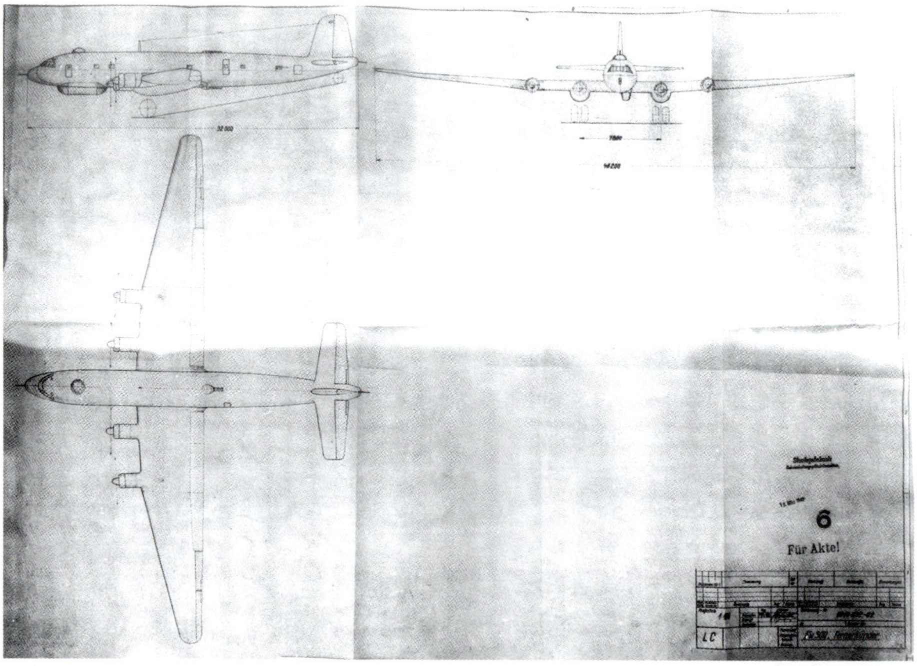

ABOVE: Focke-Wulf's heavily-armed Fw 300 Fernerkunder or 'long-range explorer' reconnaissance design. The drawing, number 1016 032-02, is dated March 19, 1942.

ABOVE: The first Junkers Ju 90, Der Grosse Dessauer, had originally been the Ju 89 V3. With a new fuselage, it retained the aborted bomber's wings, tail and undercarriage. In this way, the Ju 89 lived on.

ABOVE: While the Ju 90 entered limited production as an airliner, some of its prototypes were used to develop features for a military version. The Ju 90 V8, D-AQJA, DJ-YE, was used to test weapons positions – specifically an upper turret, underslung gondola and tail position.

LEFT: The Ju 290 V1 had originally been Ju 90 V11 before receiving different wings, fuselage modifications and tail alterations to become the first of a new breed.

a rear loading ramp which could be opened wide enough for vehicles such as half-tracks or staff cars to be driven on board. Work was also carried out on the provision of turrets which could carry defensive armament.

During late 1941, the RLM issued another specification, this time for a Fernerkunder or 'long-range explorer' - a reconnaissance aircraft with the endurance to seek out Allied convoys crossing the Atlantic and replace the Luftwaffe's stopgap fleet of Fw 200Cs.

Once again, Focke-Wulf offered a modified version of the Fw 300 and Junkers drew up plans for a more substantial adaptation of the Ju 90 for military purposes. Since Focke-Wulf already had the number 190 for its Fw 190 fighter, the upgraded Ju 90 received the designation '290'. In his report of May 12, 1942, Generalleutnant Eccard, Freiherr von Gablenz, wrote: "Ju 290: All-up weight 50 tonnes, range 8750km, payload five tonnes. Modifying the transport version is not a major job according to the files.

"A more thorough evaluation of the possibility of this aircraft becoming a long-range bomber is being undertaken since the data look very favourable."

He also wrote: "It remains to add that Focke-Wulf is working on a four DB 603-engined long-range bomber designated Fw 300 which is to have a range of 7500km with capacity for five tonnes of bombs and only 2.5 tonnes given to armament and armour.

"The model was originally designed for civilian service but was not ordered since it offered no significant advantage over the Ju 290."

Once again, Junkers had been successful. It seems that the Fw 300 was destined to always be runner-up to the descendants of the Ju 89. By the summer of 1942, Junkers was already making preparations for series production of the Ju 290.

The Ju 290 V1 first flew on July 16, 1942. It had started out as the Ju 90 V11 prototype for the Ju 90A-1 transport but later underwent extensive modification at Dessau - being fitted with the new wings and four BMW 801 engines already trialled on the Ju 90 V7, in place of the Ju 90's BMW 132s. Its fuselage was also fitted with rectangular windows, rather than round ones and its vertical tail surfaces were changed to incorporate a new squared-off shape.

The V3 made its first flight on October 16, followed by the V2 on December 7. A further four prototypes followed, up to V7, while series production of the Ju 290A-1 had already commenced. From the end of 1942 to June 1944 production continued but only in tiny numbers.

The full history of the Ju 290 falls beyond the scope of this publication but it is worth considering the very limited success of the type's various versions.

The A-1 was an unarmed transport with perhaps five examples built; the A-2 was a transport/reconnaissance type with relatively light defensive armament, three built; the A-3 was a pure reconnaissance aircraft, five built; the A-4 was another reconnaissance version, five built; the A-5 was a reconnaissance/bomber type with the ability to carry guided weapons externally, such as the Hs 293, and 11 were built. The A-6 was another transport version but no examples were made; the A-7 was another reconnaissance/bomber with the ability to mount up to three guided weapons externally, 13 made, and the A-8 was a heavily armed reconnaissance bomber but none were made. It is believed that three A-9s were also made, bringing the overall production total to around 50 examples.

FOCKE-WULF FW 300

Even before the Fw 200's campaign against British and Allied shipping began in mid-1940, Focke-Wulf had been working on its proposed replacement. The Fw 300 had originally been drawn up as another airliner at the behest of Deutsche Luft Hansa in 1940.

Its design was outlined in Focke-Wulf Baubeschreibung Nr. 236 of October 11, 1940, by which point it had already been given the RLM designation Fw 300, suggesting that it had first been proposed much earlier. Certainly, by February 1941, the company was already working on design drawings for the Fw 300 V1 prototype. One drawing dated February 21, 1941, shows the aircraft as being 31.13m long with a wingspan of 46.2m.

Plans to bring the Fw 300 into either civil service or military service as the Luftwaffe's new transport foundered however, thanks in part to the Ju 290, and the V1 was never built. When it became clear that the Fw 200 could operate successfully as a military type though, it naturally followed that the Fw 300 ought to have the same potential.

Therefore Focke-Wulf resurrected the type as a proposed long-range military reconnaissance aircraft for the RLM's Fernerkunder requirement. The firm issued a report on December 9, 1941, entitled 'ViermotorigerFernerkunder Fw 300 für Einsatz Über See' or Four-engined long-range explorer Fw 300 for use over the ocean.

This offered a short description of the Fw 300 as a fernerkunder powered by four DB 603 engines and measuring 32.2m long with a wingspan of 46.2m. It was to have an all-up weight of 104,500lb and a range of 5000 miles. Maximum flight duration would be 22 hours at an average speed of 224mph and an altitude of 20,000ft.

The crew of five or six men would be housed in a pressure cabin, operating a formidable ▶

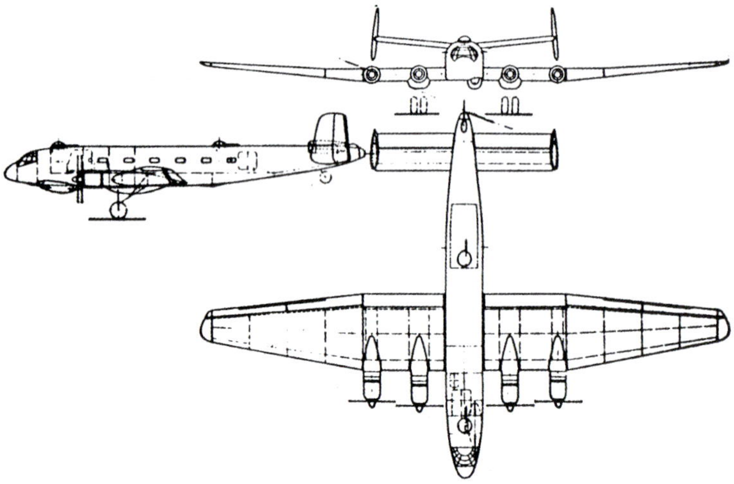

ABOVE: A drawing copied from an original German document by British intelligence in 1945 to appear in the German Aircraft: New and Projected Types report of January 1946. It is labelled 'Ju 290A' but appears more specifically to depict a Ju 290A-5.

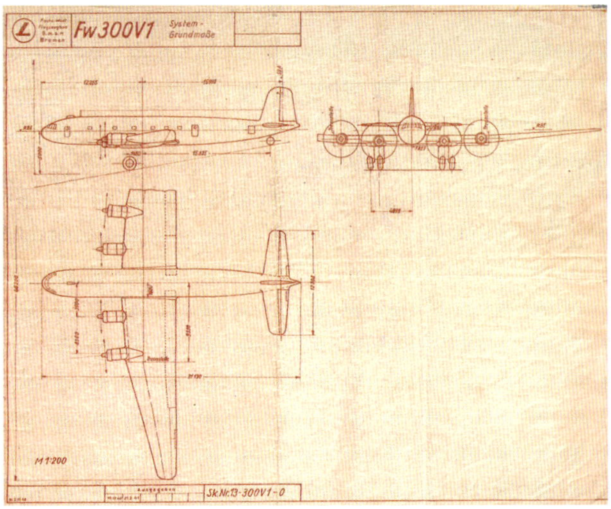

ABOVE: The earliest known drawing of the Fw 300, this design for the V1 prototype dated February 21, 1941, appears to show an unusual undercarriage arrangement – four mainwheels on four separate legs.

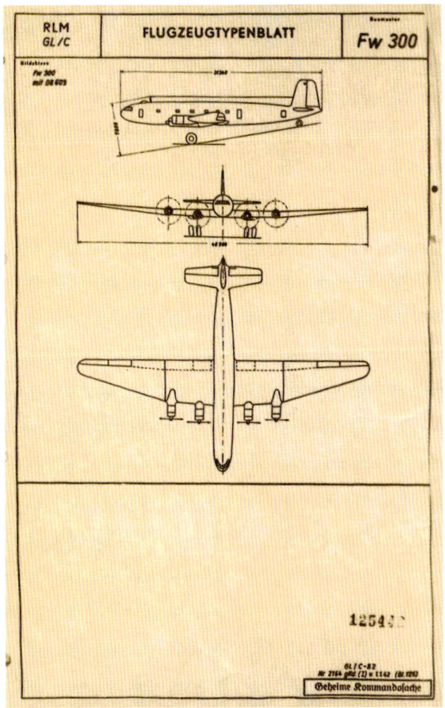

ABOVE: The RLM type sheet for the Fw 300 features the same unusual undercarriage arrangement as the V1 drawing but also a slightly broader wingspan at 46.3m compared to 46.2m for the V1. The fuselage is also slightly longer at 31.34m, compared to the V1's 31.13m. For scale, the Ju 290A-5 measured only 28.64m from end to end, with a wingspan of 42m.

arsenal of defensive weaponry. This consisted of a single 20mm MG 151 in the nose, two MG 151s in the mid-upper turret, another two in the mid-lower turret, another single MG 151 in a tail turret and two MG 131s in side mountings. All six positions would be controlled remotely from the crew cabin.

At the back of the same report is a page on the 'Mittleres Langstrecken-Verkehrsflugzeug Fw 300' or medium to long-range airliner Fw 300. Four different engine options were presented for this - four DB 603s, Jumo 213s, Jumo 222s or BMW 802s. The crew of five would again be provided with a pressure cabin and maximum carrying capacity was 40 men.

Three months later, on March 18, 1942, Focke-Wulf issued another report, this time entitled 'Fernkampfflugzeug Fw 300 mit 4 x Jumo 222 CD', which offered the Fw 300 as a bomber capable of carrying up to six SC 2500 bombs. Maximum range with this huge load was just 2850km however. With one SC 2500 it would be able to manage 7500km. An alternative payload was suggested too - up to five Henschel Hs 294 guided anti-shipping missiles. This variant apparently failed to find favour, however, and on April 8, 1942, Focke-Wulf issued yet another report: 'Fw 300 - Langstreckeneinsatz mit DB 603C' or Fw 300 - Long-distance operations with DB 603C.

This stated: "For military special operations of the aircraft Fw 300 with engines DB 603C loading of the aircraft is proposed as 54,000kg take-off weight. With this take-off weight the rate of climb to around 1000m is 1.75m/sec. The required take-off roll distance with no wind and 2000PS off power on each engine is 1140m.

"The safe load factor is 2.6 when the load is made so that when departing about 12,000kg of fuel is stored within the structure. An additional 12,000kg in the form of weapons, ammunition, supplies, container system other cargo can be loaded into the fuselage.

"If a secure load factor of 2.0 is considered adequate, the total load in the fuselage can be increased to about 19,000kg at the expense of loads in the structure.

"The chassis is designed for a landing weight of 42,000kg at a stop speed of 4.5m/sec. Another overload of the aircraft to about 60,000kg seems possible. In this case, rate of climb to 1000m is 1.0m/sec. The take-off roll increases to about 1500m. The safe load factor is about 2.0. The greatest possible range would be about 14,000km."

A range of 14,000km or 8700 miles would have made the Fw 300 an attractive proposition if pure range had been the most important quality.

Behind the scenes, as with the BV 238, a significant part of the design work on the Fw 300 was actually carried out by French designers working for the Société nationale des constructions aéronautiques du sud-ouest or SNCASO at Chatillon-sous-Bagneux in Paris. According to the German Activities in the French Aircraft Industry report: "The Germans showed great interest

ABOVE: The most famous Ju 290 of them all was this A-4 model, WNr. 290110165, PI+PS. Captured by the Americans, it is seen here in France having been painted with USAAF markings ahead of its journey across the Atlantic to the United States. It would later be daubed with the slogan 'Alles Kaputt'.

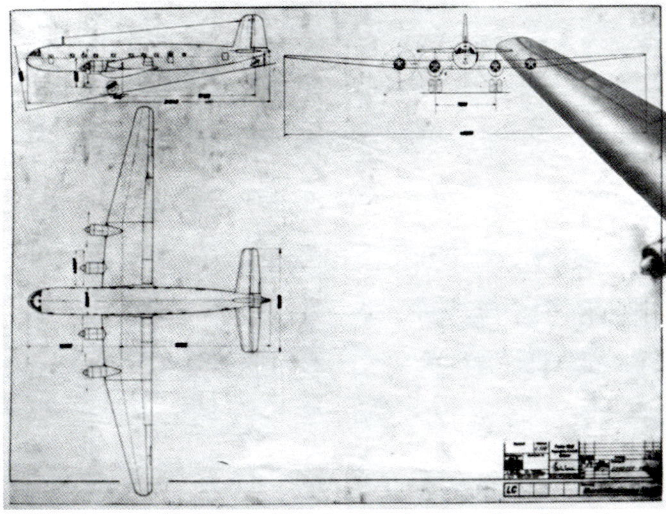

ABOVE: This early 1942 Focke-Wulf drawing shows another different version of the Fw 300's cabin windscreen, now with three small portholes set above it. A more conventional two-leg main undercarriage arrangement is also now depicted.

ABOVE: Focke-Wulf concept art from its April 1942 report on the Fw 300. The version shown features the three small portholes in the pressure cabin's roof.

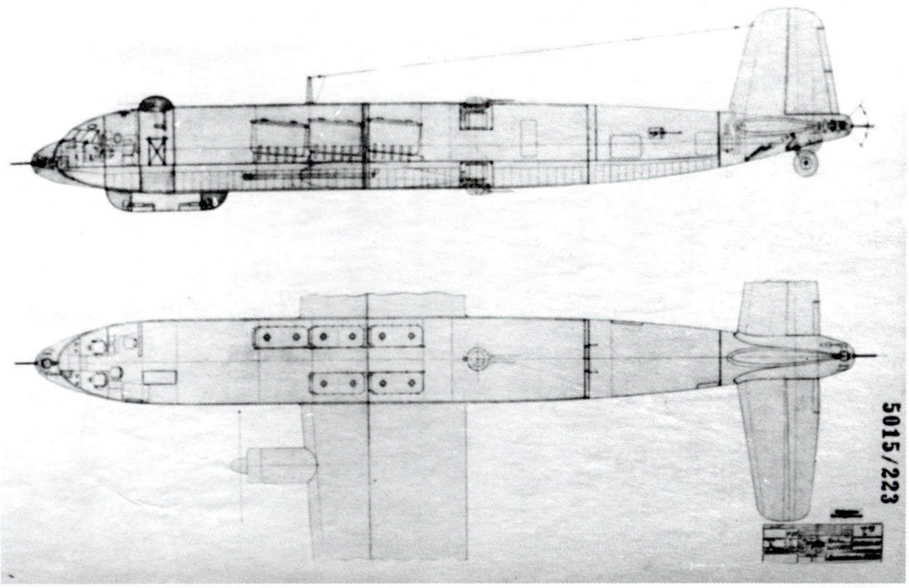

RIGHT: The internal layout of the proposed Focke-Wulf Fw 300 Fernerkunder version. The various weapons positions can be seen clearly, as can the five large fuel tanks positioned within the fuselage.

in the firm's design office and in January 1941, this was expanded and became known as the Groupe Technique de Chatillon. Instruction for the expansion came direct from the RLM and Focke-Wulf, and all work done was under German control.

"By August 1941 the group had increased to a total of about 300 personnel, and it was then composed of the following three sections: a drawing office, which was by far the largest of the three, and numbered about 240, a stress office, and a jig and tool design office. The group was particularly concerned with three main classes of aircraft, each corresponding to a particular phase of the war.

"During phase one, which lasted from the formation of the group until the summer of 1942, they were employed by Focke-Wulf on design studies of commercial aircraft, in particular the Fw 206 and the Fw 300. When the Russians entered the war the programme altered completely and the group was then put on modifications to existing military types.

"Moreover, during this phase, the group was no longer under the sole control of Focke-Wulf, but worked in addition for Junkers and Blohm & Voss. The types concerned were the Fw 189, Fw 190, Ju 138, BV 238, Ju 290. Finally, in 1943, this phase came to an end and from mid-summer until the time of liberation, the group was engaged on the design of new military types, especially the Fw 300A."

According to an appended chart, the SNCASO/Groupe Technique de Chatillon drawing office spent a total of 160,000 hours working on the Fw 300, starting in 1941 and finishing in September 1942, with the detail design of the aircraft 70% complete. The stress office spent 58,000 hours working on it, starting in February 1941 and finishing in July 1942, and assessing the wings, part of the fuselage, the tail unit and the undercarriage. And finally, the jig and tool section spent 17,900 hours on the Fw 300, completing just 10% of the necessary work.

Beyond September 1942, the Fw 300 seems to have been finally abandoned. ●

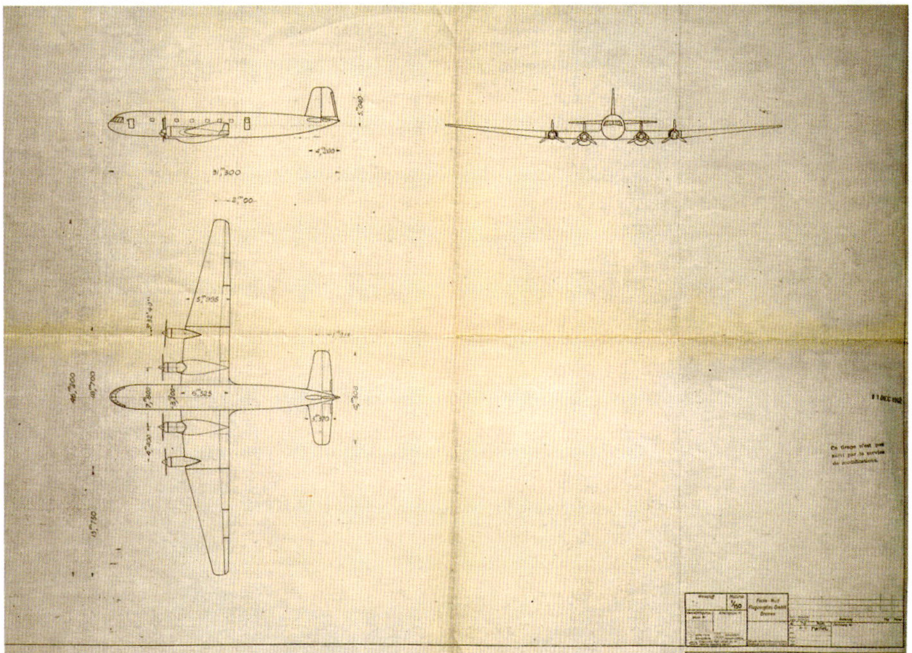

ABOVE: Drawing of the Fw 300 originating from French designer 'Mollet' at SNCASO in Paris, dated November 11, 1941. The dimensions are very nearly the same as those of the V1 from earlier in the year but this time the wraparound windscreen is wider and deeper, stretching closer to the crew access door. Larger fillets have also been added to the rear of each wing where it joins the fuselage.

Le avion stratosph

Heinkel He 274

With Henschel struggling to make its Hs 130 aircraft work during the late summer of 1941, proven bomber-builder Heinkel was contracted to construct an aircraft capable not only of flying high enough to avoid defending fighters but also of carrying a significant bomb load. Already at maximum capacity however, Heinkel needed a little help from some 'friends'.

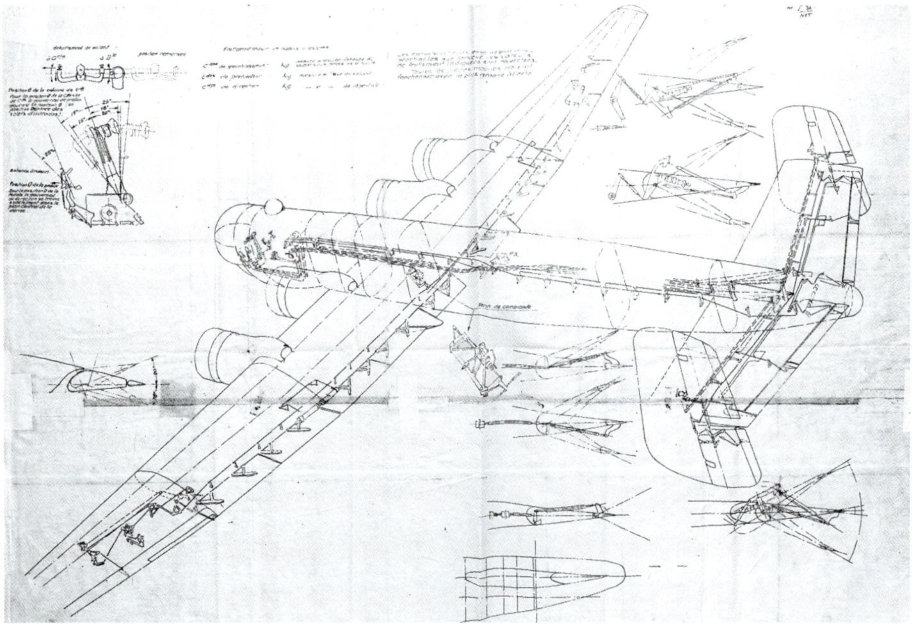

ABOVE: An enormous Farman factory drawing of the He 274 showing the mechanical operation of its control surfaces.

When the Germans occupied France in 1940, they suddenly found themselves in control of a second modern aviation industry - one that had previously been run in parallel to their own. During the months that followed, they took stock of the facilities and capabilities that the French possessed and resolved to make full use of them.

As the Luftwaffe fought the British and readied itself for the attack on Russia in early 1941, factories across Germany worked flat out to build up and replenish stocks of existing fighter and bomber designs, with the manufacturers' engineers and designers struggling to keep pace with the demand for ever more modern aircraft.

Extra manpower was needed in all areas and the French and their facilities were available. Therefore, the large German manufacturers sent government-sanctioned delegations to meet with their French counterparts. Several teams of designers were ordered to pack up their belongings and move to Germany while others were set tasks within their own company premises.

Among those French firms was Avions Farman, a company founded by brothers Henri and Maurice Farman in 1908. The French aviation industry was nationalised in 1936 and Henri retired a year later but Maurice, now in his 60s, remained in charge of what had been the Farman works in Suresnes, Paris. His son Marcel became the company's chief engineer. By 1941, the Farmans were back in charge of their own company under the name Société Anonyme des Usines Farman (SAUF).

That autumn, the Farman works was allocated to Heinkel to help with the design and manufacture of a heavily modified new version of the He 177 - which would be given the RLM designation He 274 in December 1941.

In his autobiography, Ernst Heinkel wrote of his first meeting with Marcel Farman, who represented his aging father and his company: "Only one other four-engine variant of the He 177 was developed by us, in the occupied Farman works in Paris.

"It was a high-altitude bomber, the He 274, intended to fly between 40,000 and 50,000ft.

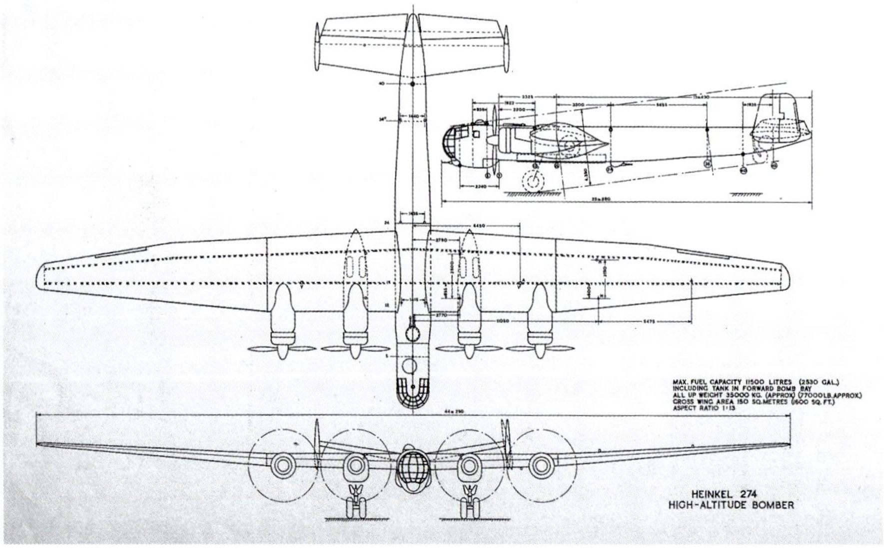

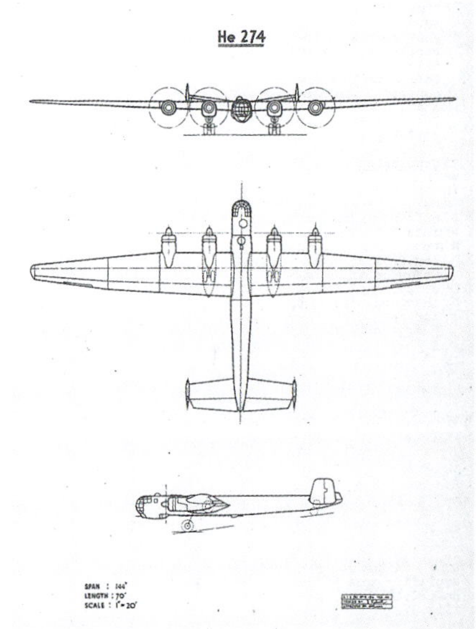

ABOVE: Copies of original French and German drawings of the He 274 produced by British intelligence.

erique

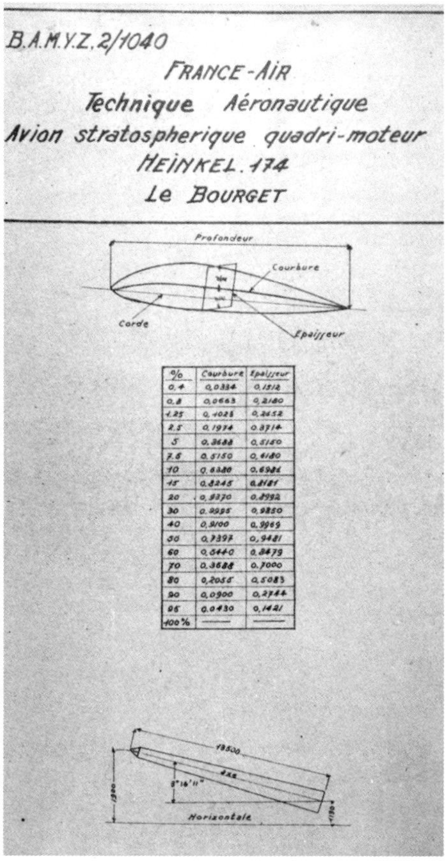

ABOVE: French note on the He 274, or 'He 174' as given here.

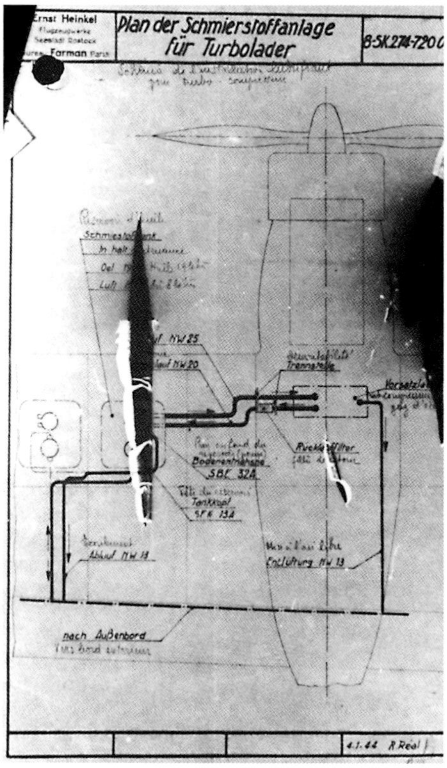

ABOVE: Heinkel drawing 8-SK.274-72008 showing part of the He 274's oil system – with annotations in French and 'Farman Paris' printed in the top left, below 'Ernst Heinkel'.

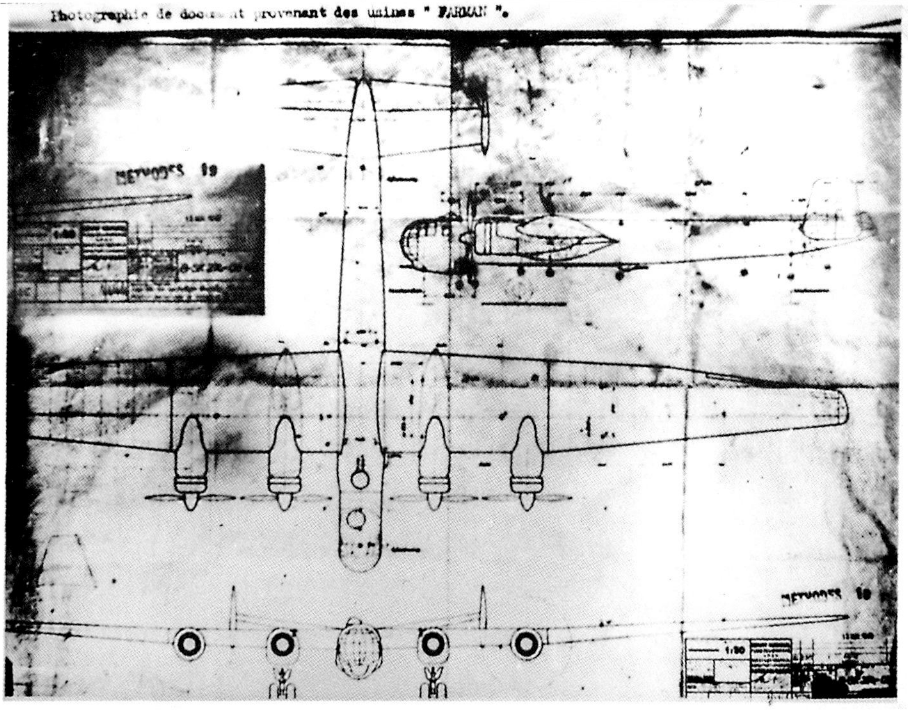

ABOVE: A photograph of a French-annotated Heinkel drawing showing the He 274's general layout.

After an uphill struggle, it was completed only after the end of the war in the West, and underwent its test flights with the new French Air Force in 1945. For Farman, this task had served only one purpose – to employ as many of his men as possible and to prevent them being sent to work outside France.

"When young Farman paid me a visit to discuss this machine in 1941, he remarked that I treated him as a real partner and not as a national of a conquered land. He said this while we were in my factory club room and repeated it over coffee in my own garden, where we chatted quite freely and honestly. 'Would you,' he asked later, 'as a German in my situation, have behaved differently?' I could only reply 'No.' I do not know whether he was ever thanked for what he did in this way."

The He 274 had started out as the He 177H – a version of the He 177A-4 – but it quickly became clear that the original wing design suffered from flexing problems and did not lend itself easily to extension. Entirely new wings were therefore proposed and the RLM approved. Further modifications included four separate DB 603A engines and the double set of tail fins and rudders that this configuration required. A pressure cabin was essential.

All of the initial design work on the He 274 was completed in Germany from December 1941 to July 1942, when the whole project was handed over to Farman for further development.

Allied Intelligence note A.I. 61220 of December 1943, from an unnamed source inside the Farman factory, reported: "Prototype Heinkel H.08-274. This is a heavy bomber with a crew of four. The prototype is at the moment under construction at the Farman factory at Suresnes. Two fuselages have been constructed side-by-side. One will serve for static tests, very shortly. The other, for actual flying, is now receiving its fittings to be despatched in about two months' time, to Rostock, where the engines and armament will be fitted and the flying trials commenced.

"In the construction of the centre section, two petrol tanks form an integral part of the assembly. The tightness of the riveting is ensured by a cotton fabric covered with a pasty film, of which a sample and the method of use will shortly be disclosed to us. The tail units, complete and finished, were sent to Rostock a month ago. The undercarriage is retractable. The Germans are distrustful about disclosing the armament. The information we have been able to receive, shows the existence of two turrets, a cannon support and a bomb-rack. Other data will be given later, if possible. The actual drawings of the aircraft will be disclosed in a few days' time."

In April 1944, the French resistance managed to pass another note to Allied intelligence from the Farman source. Filed by the British as A.I. No 82082, it was dated March 26, 1944, and read: "Information on stratospheric aircraft Farman He 274 being built in the Farman factory at Suresnes. This aircraft will have a weight of 77,500lb and a loading of 11lb per hp. It will be fitted with two superchargers, one of which is a new turbo-blower sent specially from Germany and having a special interest.

"The service ceiling of this aircraft would be 39,400ft and its speed fully loaded would be 342mph. At this moment, essential parts are missing, for example, for installation of cockpit, for the oleo-pneumatic system, for the locking of the undercarriage and for air-cooling of parts of the turbo-blower. These parts were to have arrived two months ago, but have not yet been received. They cannot be made in France and are to be brought by transport aircraft from Vienna (Austria) where they are made.

"The transport of these parts should take place during the first fortnight of May. When these parts are available, two months will be necessary for definite assembly. The engine cowlings are still in the manufacturing stage; only the primary parts have been finished."

The next paragraph appears to be a comment from the resistance themselves: "This aircraft, which from first impressions appears to be difficult to manoeuvre, seems to be interesting to follow because flying at a speed of 342mph at 39,400ft appears to be of some ▶

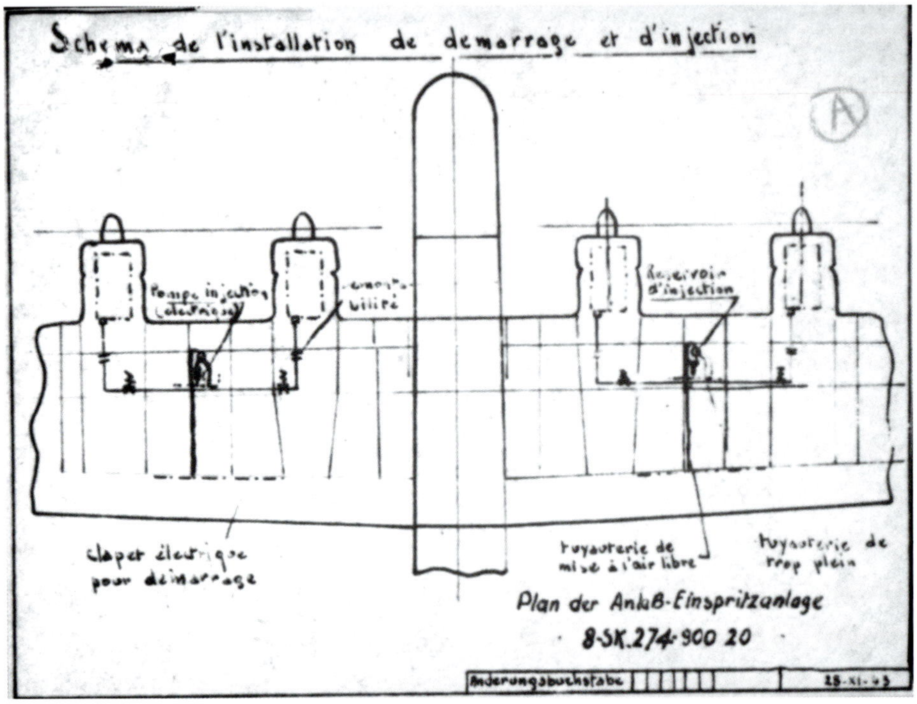

ABOVE: Another example of German-French cooperation – the French designer has used a German title for what is evidently a Farman drawing, despite its Heinkel-derived drawing number.

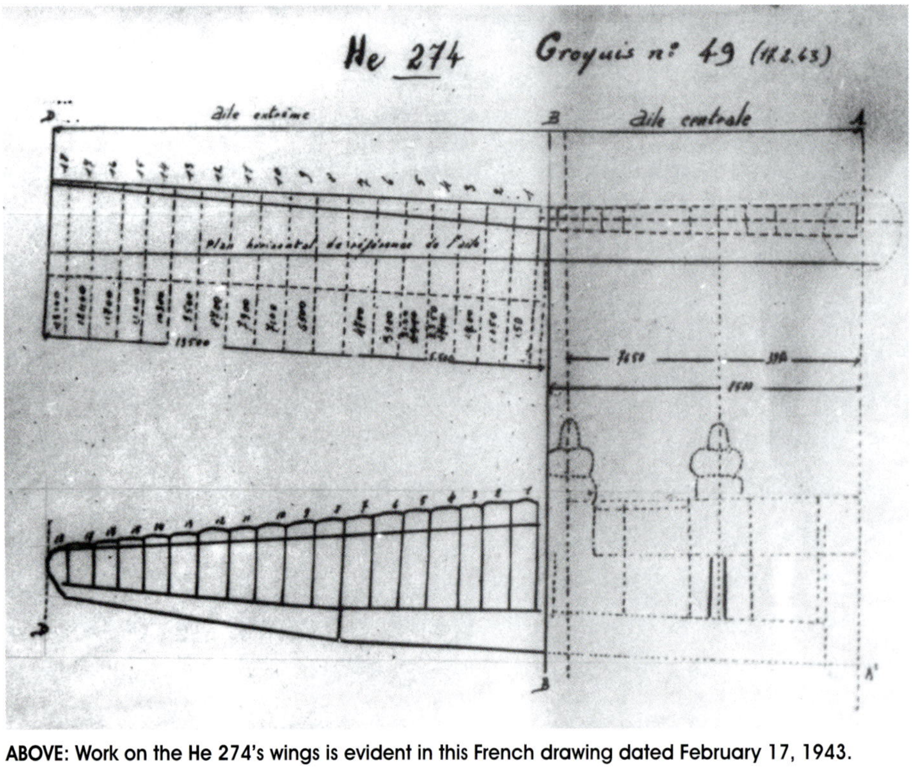

ABOVE: Work on the He 274's wings is evident in this French drawing dated February 17, 1943.

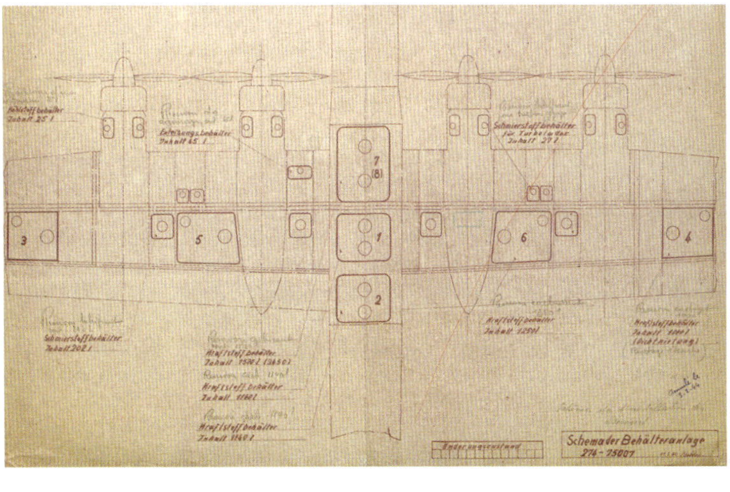

LEFT: An original Heinkel drawing of the He 274 dated May 21, 1942, but with French annotations.

danger. Attached are two plans of the factory with indications of the situation of the aircraft, the path of patrols, control box, telephone, archives containing plans [underlined], locality of German and French guards, etc."

On August 29, 1944, four days after Paris was liberated, Allied investigators visited the Farman factory and reported back on what they found: "The factory is a fairly small one employing about 1500 workers. It has facilities for working sheet metal but none for casting or extensive machinery. For the last three years all the work done had been on prototypes for the He 274, the first of which had been nearly completed. There were also finished and unfinished airframe parts for five other prototypes, as well as the nose section of an He 277, which was left uncompleted.

"The Germans had begun to install the engines in the first prototype when they had to leave and on August 18, 1944, they demolished the three engines already fitted as well as all the others which were ready for fitting into the second prototype except for one which was left in its case. The explosions damaged the airframe of the first prototype slightly as well as bringing down much of the glass and tiles of the factory roof.

"A complete set of jigs for the manufacture of the airframe parts was left undamaged in the factory. These were of Heinkel design but built in Paris and consisted chiefly of large diameter steel tubing welded together. All parts such as engines, instruments, castings, undercarriages, armament and radio were imported from Germany.

"A fairly complete set of detailed construction and assembly drawings had been hidden in the works when the Germans destroyed most of the other documents and these are available there if required. A set of general arrangement and assembly drawings was obtained from the Bureau des Etudes in Paris where other Farman personnel had been engaged. These are being taken to UK by Major Logan USAAF together with this report.

"It appeared that most of the drawing work had been done in Paris under the supervision of a German staff. Such modifications as were necessary were sent to Germany for approval. Wind tunnel tests on scale models were also carried out there and the results incorporated in the prototypes. As a result of such tests the tailplane dihedral had been increased to the present rather large amount and while on the first prototype the fins were set at right angles to each half of the tailplane, on the second they were to be vertical. The fuselage was also lengthened 2m after some experiment.

"The Farman staff stated that no other prototypes of the He 274 were known to exist and that if successful a limited series of 20-40 was to have been built. They had very little exact knowledge of the aircraft characteristics or performance as the Germans only told them as little as possible about it."

What the French did know was that the pressure cabin fitted to the He 274 was intended for a crew of four and that its defensive armament consisted of three remotely controlled turrets.

According to the report, "the pressure cabin which is built into the aircraft structure and is not a readily detachable unit has double walls with glass wool lagging in between them, and double 'plexiglass' windows. The

ABOVE: The completed He 274 is readied for a fight under new ownership after the war's end.

ABOVE: Boasting an impressive wingspan, four engine layout, pressure cabin, conventional landing gear and a 370mph top speed, the He 274 represents, perhaps, what the He 177 might have been. It is flown here by the French.

ABOVE: Up close with the impressive He 274 on a French airfield. The poor visibility offered by the pressure cabin's thick-rimmed double-glazed windows is readily apparent.

pilot and co-pilot/navigator sit side by side well up in the nose. The flight engineer sits behind the first pilot and the radio operator sits behind the second pilot under the sighting cupola which is slightly offset to starboard.

"Air for the cabin is supplied by two Roots type compressors, one on each inner engine, and a branch pipe takes air to the space between the double windows."

There were 8mm thick plates welded to the pilot's seat, protecting his back, head and shoulders, plus a 4mm plate under the seat itself. A dinghy recess was lined with 5mm armour at the back, sides and bottom.

According to USAAF report No. A-133 of November 6, 1944: "We were told that considerable trouble had been met with the pressure cabin, the first version leaking badly, particularly at rivet holes. The second version, as now fitted, was better, but the leaks had not been fully cured."

The four engines were DB 603A-2s, although it had been intended to fit DB 603Gs. These had two-stage superchargers – the first stage being turbo driven and the second gear-driven. There were seven fuel tanks, four in the wings and three in the fuselage. The British report stated that each of the two main undercarriage legs consisted "of a massive welded Y-shaped member carrying one wheel with 1220 x 445 tyre on either side of it on a levered suspension system. The undercarriage retracts rearwards and is completely enclosed in the inner nacelles when up. A retractable tail wheel, tyre size 780 x 290 is used".

The turrets were electrically operated. The dorsal and ventral ones each had a pair of MG 131s in it, while the chin turret had only a single MG 131. The dorsal turret was sighted from a rotating cupola in the top of the pressure cabin, slightly offset from centre, while the ventral turret was "controlled by the flight engineer lying on the floor and sighting through the lower rear windows". The chin turret was controlled by the pilot or co-pilot.

Another British report, Foreign Aircraft Bulletin No. 24, said: "The main entry and exit is through a single hatch about 2ft 6in diameter in the floor just behind the nose, with an internal toggle-operated release mechanism. It is possible that an emergency exit could be made through two small windows above and in front of the pilots' seats.

"Vision. The windows and nose are of double plexiglass panels, hot air being blown through the intervening space to prevent frosting. Visibility is poor since the panels are separated by metal frames about 2 in wide. A large dome is fitted in the top of the cabin behind the pilot's seat. This also is of two layers of plexiglass, but frosting is prevented by a porous plug, packed with a dessicating chemical, inserted in the inner layer. The dome can be rotated and has a flat bullet-proof glass insert."

This same report gave the type's range as 2200 to 2500 miles, its ceiling as 36,000ft and maximum speed at that altitude as 370mph. A full bomb load was 8800lb.

When the war was over, the French found new undamaged engines for the He 274 V1 and completed it. The aircraft was then re-designated the AAS 01A and used for high-altitude research, starting in early 1946.

The V2 was also completed and first flew in December 1947. Both aircraft were scrapped in 1953. ●

The steel bomber

Blohm & Voss P 163

When it became evident that Germany was running short of 'strategic materials' from which to build its aircraft, including light metals such as aluminium, Blohm & Voss came up with an unusual bomber design that made extensive use of steel…

From the late 1930s and into the 1940s, Blohm & Voss had experimented with asymmetrical designs - particularly the BV 141, which had competed unsuccessfully against the Arado Ar 198 and Focke-Wulf Fw 189 for a reconnaissance aircraft contract.

The competition had ended in 1940 with the Fw 189 being declared the winner, but Blohm & Voss did not give up on the BV 141 and saw it was a template for future designs. Blohm & Voss Flugzeugbau, a subsidiary of the Hamburg shipbuilder, had a reputation for offering up highly original concepts and ideas by this time under the leadership of chief designer Richard Vogt.

Vogt seems to have encouraged his team to come up with solutions to aeronautical problems that defied convention and rather than only offering these when asked to tender for a contract, B&V wrote them up and submitted them unsolicited to the RLM for consideration.

One such idea was the P 163. Evidently, B&V had spotted an opportunity in Germany's shortage of the materials most commonly used to build aircraft at that time, particularly aluminium. What if a bomber could be made

Arbeitsflugzeug
BV-P 163

Bomber, Erkunder, Abwurfslastenträger

B&V

LEFT: An artist's impression of the P 163 in flight adorns the title page of the Blohm & Voss project brochure. The central fuselage contains the aircraft's engine, fuel and payload, while the pilot is seated in the port gondola and the defensive gunners are housing in the compartment on the opposite wingtip.

ABOVE: Blohm & Voss designed and built the asymmetrical BV 141 during the late 1930s as a reconnaissance type. One example would later serve as a test vehicle for the P 163 project.

largely from steel without suffering any significant performance penalty compared to more conventional types?

The P 163 brochure begins: "The rearrangement of using steel instead of light metal becomes the focus of attention of our war-restricted aircraft production. But it is no secret that the achievements of today's aircraft are due to light metals to a significant extent. The move away from them and the use of steel is therefore not possible without substantial material and construction research and will also still be feasible only in a limited percentage of the components without degrading performance.

"One can but approach the problem from a completely different angle and search for types, or rather configurations, which offer such an advantage that you can afford to use the heavy building material without making sacrifices. Certainly one would - assuming such an overall concept - achieve significant savings if light-metal could be used later on. But that does not seem the most essential aspect of the urgent change to another material at the moment.

"For the purposes of these considerations, here a design is proposed in which bombers

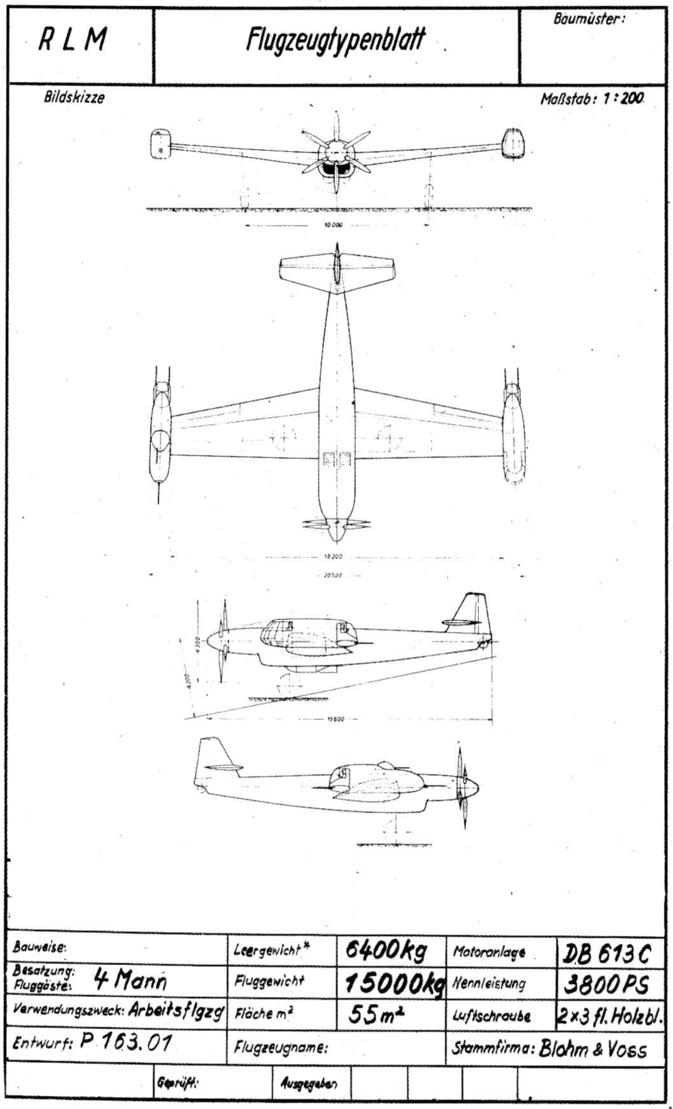

ABOVE: This 'RLM' type sheet is actually a page from the project brochure and shows the P 163 fitted with a Daimler-Benz DB 613C engine – a pair of DB 603s working side-by-side and driving contra-rotating props.

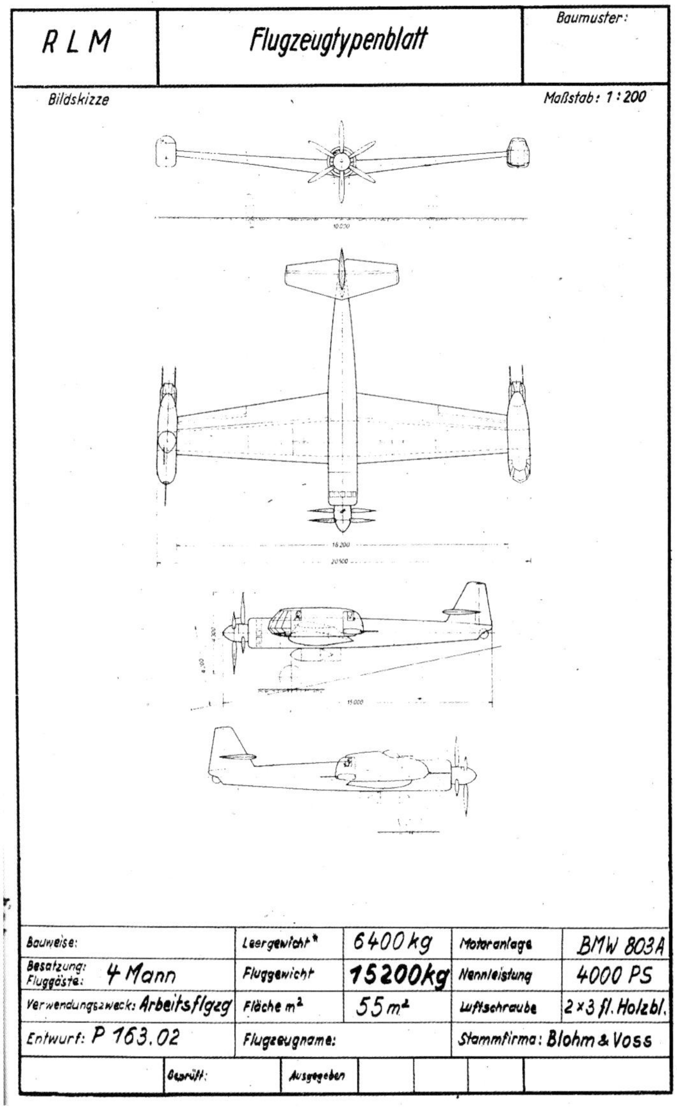

ABOVE: The P 163.02 was essentially the same as the P 163.01 but was powered instead by the mighty BMW 803A. Presumably unbeknownst to B&V, at around this time BMW was giving serious consideration to abandoning the engine's development all together.

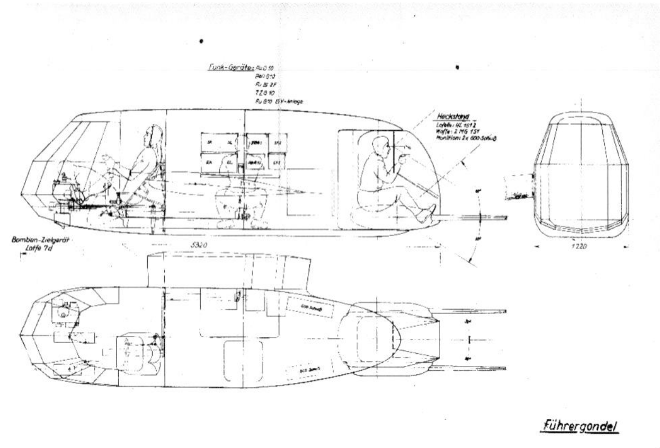

ABOVE: A side view of the pilot's cabin. Behind him, facing sideways, is the navigator/bomb aimer and to the rear is a defensive turret which, again, would be operated by the second crewman.

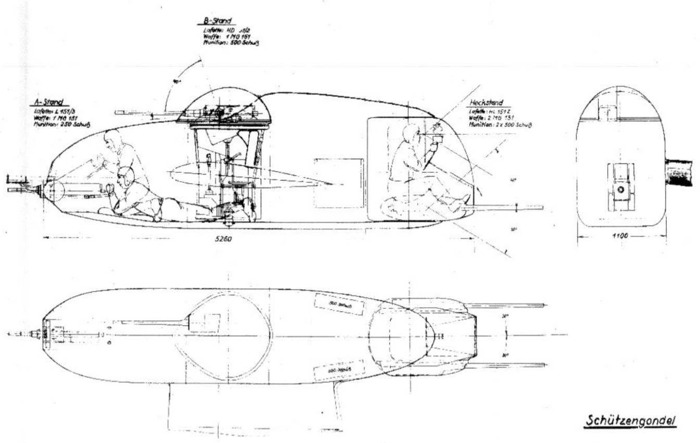

ABOVE: The P 163's defensive gondola, housing three weapons positions – a rear turret, upper turret and forward weapons mounting. Two crewmen would have manned these between them.

can immediately be constructed largely from steel without additional research and without excessive sacrifices of power. The later results of successes in the area of steel development, or a later return to lightweight alloys will bring the bomber a superior weight advantage."

It was here that the brochure's anonymous author had to ask the reader to bear with him as he got on to the subject of Blohm & Voss's unorthodox proposed solution to the problem.

"Such a lofty goal cannot of course be achieved through small modifications in the design that can bring only small improvements in the load of the main structural members. You have to have the courage to make a substantial change in layout," he wrote.

"Essentially, the weight of the airframe is now determined by the wing and the wing area in relation to the fuselage section. For the wing on a conventional aircraft it is essential that loads are concentrated in the wing centre section, for example between the fuselage and engine nacelles, and that therefore the wide-span wing's task it is to carry these loads to a large extent on the free overhangs. Technically speaking, this means a strong increase of the bending moments to the centre and the other result is a steep increase of the wing weight.

"This load distribution you can radically change if you put a due share of the total load to the outside of the wing tip. That is what we have achieved here, with the pilot and defensive weapons placed in separate battle gondolas at the wingtips. The two crew gondolas, each with about a ton of weight, reduce the bending moment at the wing root by about 44%."

The report's author suggested that both the wing spars and planking could be made from steel.

"Of course, taking such steps results in a number of consequences but fortunately in this particular case the effect of these is beneficial on the whole. The biggest benefit is to defence. From the battle gondolas at the wingtips the field of fire is excellent.

"Weapons positioned here on suitable mountings can protect the upper and lower rear attack sector. A turret can protect both the upper hemisphere and the forward area. Just as impressive as the gunners' view is the view from the pilot's cockpit and for the bombardier. Also aerodynamically the new design is not unfavourable. The position of the gondolas at the wingtips reduces the vortices on the outer part of the wing and has a positive effect on lift.

"A conventional bomber has three defensive positions, and the most poorly defended areas are the forward fuselage and the two engine nacelles. We have a double motor in a short very well-shaped hull and two less well-shaped battle gondolas. The small advantage or disadvantage of one or another solution will depend in these circumstances only on the importance you attach to a good or better defensive armament."

Two different engines were proposed for the P 163. The P 163.01 had a single DB 613C – a pair of coupled DB 603s – while the P 163.02 had a BMW 803A. Each engine drove a pair of contra-rotating propellers. The proposed layout for the aircraft had another significant advantage which the mechanics tasked with working on the He 177's engines would have readily appreciated: easy access.

In addition, the two gondolas could easily be reconfigured or even removed and replaced without any need to tamper with the central fuselage structure, which without having to house crew now had a handy space available for carrying additional fuel. The report notes: "It is a happy peculiarity of the new bomber that further alternations can be made to the battle gondolas without opening the entire fuselage – the work can be carried out very easily.

"Since we could place the crew in the battle gondolas, this obviously left room in the central fuselage for a large steel-protected fuel capacity. This gives the advantage of bare steel usage and the double use of the building material gives a corresponding saving in structural weight and production time.

"Almost more important is the operational simplification – reinforcing cutouts, overlays, covers, services and circuits will be replaced by at least half a dozen rubber tanks. In addition, these central fuselage tanks will still be protected by the power plant in front of them. We have taken full advantage of this and housed the bullet-sensitive water cooler in an extremely convenient location.

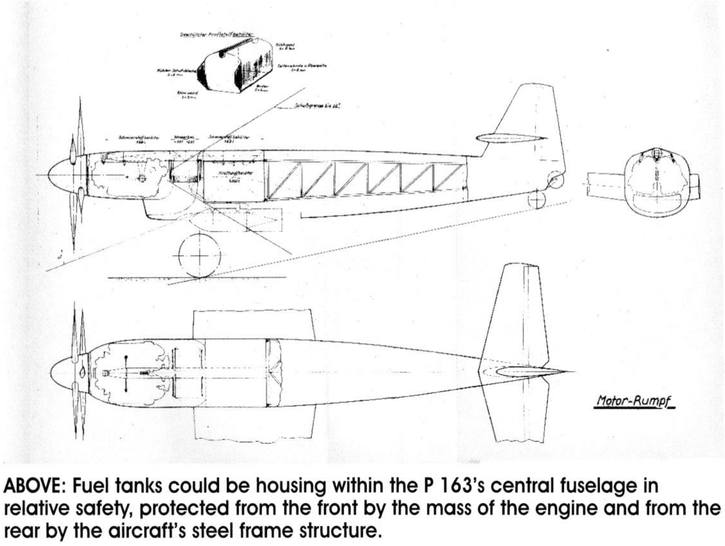

ABOVE: Fuel tanks could be housing within the P 163's central fuselage in relative safety, protected from the front by the mass of the engine and from the rear by the aircraft's steel frame structure.

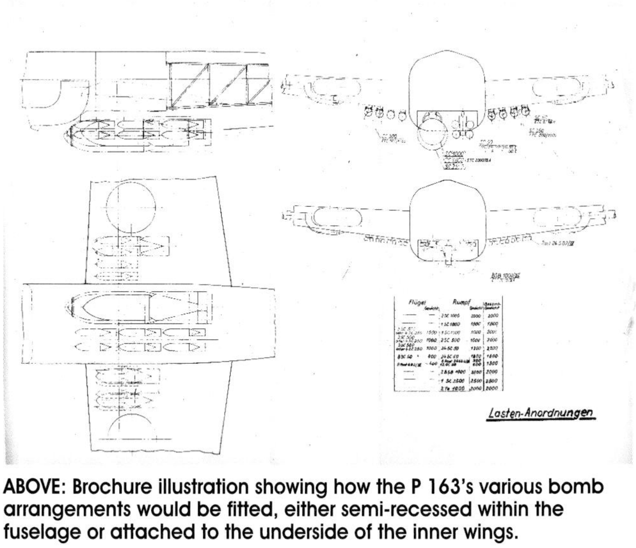

ABOVE: Brochure illustration showing how the P 163's various bomb arrangements would be fitted, either semi-recessed within the fuselage or attached to the underside of the inner wings.

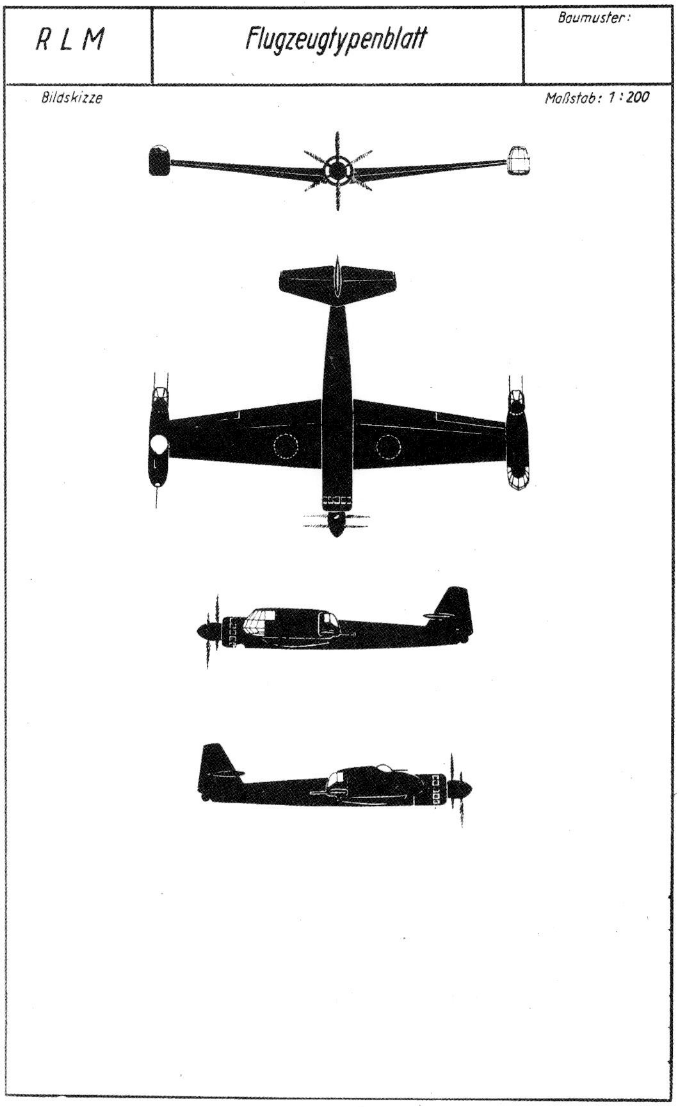

ABOVE: A silhouette type sheet featuring the P 163.

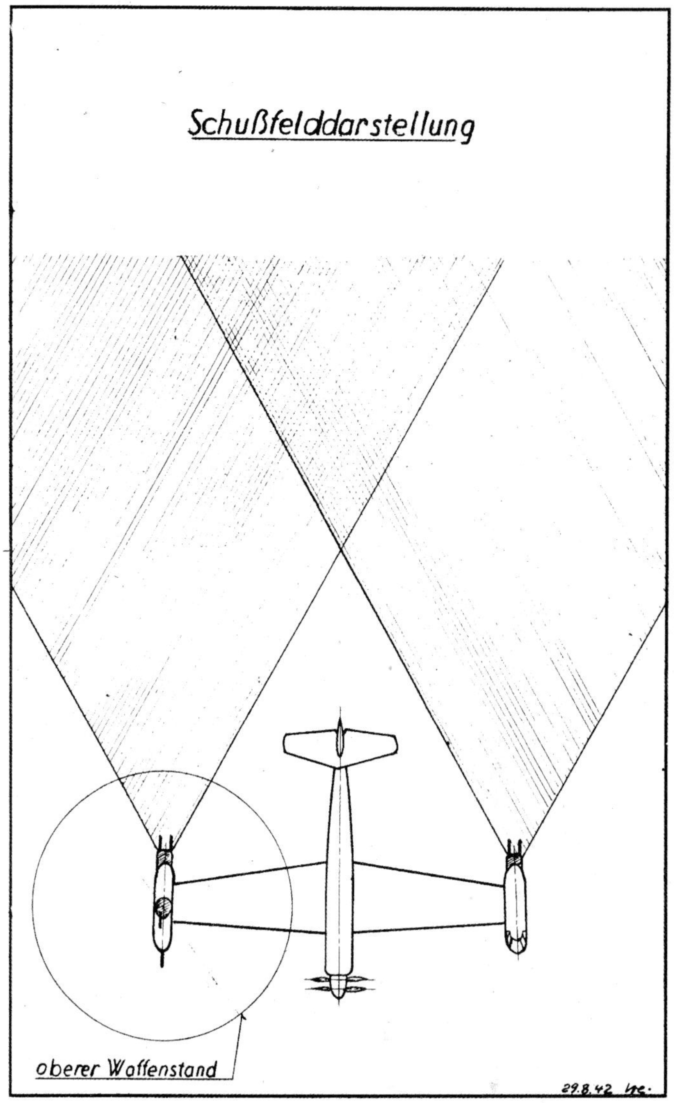

ABOVE: One of the chief advantages claimed for the P 163, besides its economical steel structure, was the fields of fire offered by its twin rear gun turrets. The upper gun turret offered a 360° field of vision.

"The adjoining tank-carrying fuselage end will be constructed as tubular steel truss with a fabric covering. Thus, the overall plan is also advantageous from the viewpoint of constructional separation in easy to assemble groups of components that allow for mass production in a unique way.

"All these substantial benefits are available assuming that airmen can agree to the aeronautical handling of such an unusual machine. You must keep an open mind if you are to free yourself from conventional habits. We have already proven that this is possible in a preliminary test on a BV 141, which we have provided with a wingtip gondola, from which we have controlled the aircraft."

No photographs survive of a BV 141 modified in the manner stated but in a 1998 interview Blohm & Voss designer Hans Amtmann said that conceiving such a radical test aircraft was not an unusual occurrence: "This was not an exception, as every idea had to be drawn up and discussed. Those discussions required tremendous concentration and knowledge in almost every field, which made them very interesting.

"An unusual arrangement of the pilot's and gunner's compartments was suggested for a proposed bomber design, the P 163 project. This had nacelles at each wingtip, giving the pilot the best possible view and the gunners the best field of fire. A wingtip pilot's nacelle was tried on a BV 141 with excellent results."

The BV 141 apparently had a second crew compartment fitted, rather than having the existing one moved along down the wing. This additional cabin lacked flight controls and was purely used to acclimatise pilots to the experience of being in such an unusual position.

The P 163 brochure sheds further light on Blohm & Voss's activities when it stresses that "the performance graphs have been set out on the basis of the published RLM guidelines about uniform project documentation. We had to dispense with the proposed presentation due to insufficient information provided by the manufacturers regarding fuel consumption".

This suggests that B&V had previously put forward proposals that did not conform to the RLM's guidelines and perhaps did not include all the information that the RLM wanted.

The result, however, is a very comprehensive brochure issued towards the end of August 1942. Drawings within it are dated August 7 and August 18. Information included on the DB 613 was taken from a Daimler-Benz document dated May 11, 1942.

The P 163 was to carry a load of 2000-2500kg with a range of 2000km at maximum engine power. Top speed at an altitude of 20,000ft was 300mph. Nine different bomb load possibilities were offered, ranging from a single SC2500 under the fuselage to 24 SC50s under the fuselage plus another eight under the wings.

Defensive armament was to include a rear-facing manned HL 151Z turret on the pilot's gondola mounting a pair of MG 151s with 500 rounds each, another one with the same weapons on the defensive gondola, plus a remote-controlled HD 151/2 turret on the top of the defensive gondola with 500 shots and an L 151/3 weapons mount at the front of the defensive gondola with a single MG 151 and 250 rounds.

Quite what B&V hoped to gain by putting forward the P 163 bomber design is uncertain. The RLM seldom responded positively to suggestions that came 'out of the blue'. But this seems to have done nothing to deter Vogt and his team, who continued to submit ideas for unusual aircraft arrangements right up until the very end of the war – though by that point the firm was often in the running for potentially lucrative development contracts such as that of the Strahlbomber, which had perhaps been the goal all along. ●

Absolute bitterness

Reichsmarschall Hermann Göring, March 18, 1943

ABOVE: Reichsmarschall Hermann Göring.

With much of the Luftwaffe engaged in fighting on the Eastern Front, the organisation's leader Reichsmarschall Hermann Göring took the opportunity to speak to the heads of Germany's most important technological development companies about the progress made so far in updating the nation's warplanes. The audience for what Erhard Milch would later describe in his diary as a "major onslaught" included Milch himself, Ernst Heinkel, Willy Messerschmitt, Claude Dornier, Heinrich Hertel of Junkers, Siemens director Friedrich Lüschen, Fritz Nallinger of engine maker Daimler-Benz, General of Luftwaffe communications Wolfgang Martini, chairman of the special commission on radar Dr Karl Rottgardt, national director of radar research Johannes Plendl, radar and night fighter commander Josef Kammhuber and newly promoted Colonel in the Luftwaffe General Staff Dietrich Peltz.

This is a direct transcript of the opening address Göring gave to the conference at his country retreat, Carinhall near Berlin...

Gentlemen, I have called you together again today to speak about the entire situation on the technical side of the Luftwaffe and to inform you of my views on this subject and, most important, those of the Führer as well. It would have been very agreeable if I could have commenced my remarks today by acknowledging and thanking you for your efforts.

However, I find myself unable to do this if I am to continue speaking frankly - quite the reverse. I can only express to you my absolute bitterness about the complete failure which has resulted in practically all fields of aeronautical engineering - bitterness too that I have been deceived in the past to an extent such as I had experienced only in variety shows at the hands of magicians and illusionists - such has been the hocus-pocus which everybody has used to take me in.

Whenever future problems were under discussion everyone already had the most fantastic things ready and it was then only a matter of production before they could be brought into service. Some things which were reported to me as being absolutely ready even before the war are still not available.

We lag so far behind enemy industry, or rather the technology of many fields of industry, particularly radar, that it is absolutely childish to attempt to draw a comparison. I am not forgetting that there had been a marked improvement. In no way do I fail to appreciate that we went into action with aircraft which in their time were something and were superior to enemy types.

I by no means fail to recognise that even today the Me 109 is still an aircraft of very high performance. However, it has now reached the peak of its performance; no further improvement is possible: the aircraft cannot take a more powerful engine, whereas the British began to improve the Spitfire series very early with the result that this aircraft is now absolutely and unquestionably superior to the Me 109.

I in no way fail to appreciate that the He 111 was a good aircraft in the first year of the war, but today it can be used only as a transport in Russia. I particularly emphasise that the Ju 87 was a fantastic gamble, with the result that today this aircraft can come into its own only in the East, while it has absolutely no chance against the enemy in the West and cannot be used against him in any way unless it is escorted by so many fighters that there is no longer any justification for the operation.

Even the Ju 88 is an aircraft which was thoroughly up to standard in the first years of the war and which today can only just be used at night for operations against Britain on rare occasions when conditions are especially favourable. I am not dealing with the Eastern theatre at all and now refer only to the West when I mention the enemy. However, all these were aircraft which were available at the beginning of the war, since when I might well say that I have witnessed one reverse after the other - crises of almost catastrophic proportions.

Shortly after war broke out it became evident that the [Messerschmitt] 110 was no longer equal to the demands made upon it. I was then told of the [Messerschmitt] 210 miracle aircraft which was to supersede every other type. I was promised this aircraft years ago. As a result of the confidence placed in it, development of other aircraft was stopped, which later proved to be an awful blunder. This aircraft was probably one of the greatest disappointments we have ever had, for as a result of the hopes based on it measures were taken which in their total effect set us back to a colossal extent.

I remember – it is years ago now – when I was in Augsburg, I was shown an 'America' aircraft which had only to be put into large-scale production. It was alleged that the aircraft would fly from here to the east coast of America and back and from Azores to the west coast of America and back etc. etc. and would also carry a large load of bombs. They told me that in all seriousness. At that time I was still trusting enough to at least go half-way towards believing that something of this kind was possible. Today I know that it is, of course, impossible.

I was promised a heavy bomber, the He 177, which should have been with the squadrons a year ago. Following a series of calamities I was told that if there was no need for this aircraft to dive it would be the best kite in the world and could be issued to squadrons instantly. I at once said that there was no need for it to dive, as there was no intention of it being used in this way.

However, every time we attempted operations with this type there were only catastrophic losses which were not brought about by the enemy. More than a year has passed now and even if the contraption is produced in a reasonably serviceable version in a year's time it will probably be obsolescent anyway. There is otherwise absolutely no immediate prospect of this situation being eased or the state of inferiority in which we now find ourselves being alleviated to any extent.

These are the aircraft. I do not wish to speak about all the other future projects. They may be all very fine, but I have been given time limits which cannot be questioned at the moment and will take an awfully long time to put into effect. Perhaps the [Messerschmitt] 410 will bring some relief. However, you cannot blame me if I am very sceptical about this too and prefer to wait for results.

Furthermore, it has not been possible to design our fighters in such a way that they can also be used at night. Although some of the aircraft may have good points, they are nevertheless very difficult to service and require airfields of a very high standard – otherwise they are always bursting tyres etc. – which is of course a further extremely serious impediment where operations are concerned.

Fun has been made of the enemy's backwardness and his slow four-engined crates etc. Gentlemen, I would be extremely happy if you could reproduce one of these crates in the immediate future. I would then have at least one aircraft with which something could be achieved. You know for a fact that in addition to night attacks the enemy does not hesitate for an instant to carry out daylight operations with these four-engined crates, which have excellent armament and terrific stability, and in spite of our so-called ultra-modern fighters he gets through everywhere.

It seems monstrous when I recall that the British – although they were not blessed with aluminium, but on the other hand were not so short of it as us – built a wooden aircraft at the right moment, which, moreover, is almost incredibly superior and unrivalled in speed. Today these aircraft stooge back and forth over Germany, sometimes on reconnaissance, but at others not hesitating to carry out very heavy attacks without incurring the slightest loss.

Here I am then, empty-handed, as far as aircraft are concerned. I do not know if anything can be done about this in the immediate future. Worst of all is the dead loss of the 177, as this means that essential reconnaissance for U-boat activity cannot be carried out and operations against enemy shipping with special-purpose bombs etc. will not be possible either. It is not only that the appearance of this aircraft is a year behind schedule, but that there is moreover no likelihood of its becoming operational for the present, and that an aircraft which has been in development for years should now suddenly present difficulties such as cannot be explained. I find this incomprehensible too.

However, the situation as regards engines appears to be even worse if anything. Once again there has been one promise after another, but comparatively few have been kept. To take just one example – by the time the [BMW] 801 had been developed after extensive operational experience to the point at which it was comparatively serviceable and would outlast several operations without needing to be changed, the enemy had already gone far ahead in terms of horsepower. Thus, just when the engine was at last beginning to become fit for operational employment it had once again already been long outclassed.

When I turn to water-cooled engines I find that here too the promised line of development has not been followed. I can see nothing exceptional in achieving an increase in horsepower by coupling together two engines and passing this off as a new engine – quite apart from the fact that I can do nothing with this crazy contraption as its suspended cylinders and unfortunate exhaust system make its employment against the enemy impossible.

A series of fires has already caused loss of life. But apart from this again, this nailing together of two engines has produced further immense difficulties. They dare to give me an engine which cannot be serviced at all operational stations and which at the slightest trouble must have its entire power unit dismantled before the engine can even be reached. The demands I made years ago for 2000, 3000 and even 4000 horsepower have not been met in the slightest degree. All that is still in the distant future.

I do not wish to imply that the fault lies with industry alone. I am aware – and I regret having to confess this – that in past years my own department has been very much at fault and that the field marshal [Milch] and his new colleagues have only just succeeded in restoring order. I initiated a court martial investigation just to obtain a general survey of the situation. This survey showed me not only how great was the ministry's inefficiency, but also gave me some idea of the extent of industry's inefficiency. It is as if the brains of our designers had suddenly dried up and they were no longer capable of producing anything else, or as if they took such a childish delight in the aircraft which they had produced that they did not consider it at all necessary to give their minds to new designs. I could read page after page of this court martial investigation to illustrate to you the really incredible dilatoriness in this field.

In addition, there has been a complete lack of farsightedness on the part of those controlling industry. There are always disputes in factories between the works manager and the owner and his designers. These designers are always being changed etc. etc. Nobody has given a thought to the broad, general policy and I really must declare that things have gone by far the best at factories where the state, that is ourselves, is the owner.

I am always being told a great deal about contractors; energy and private initiative etc. I can only assure you, gentlemen, that I have not noticed much of this, at least not on your part. As I said before, factories under our control, i.e. state-owned, have not worked in a bureaucratic manner; on the contrary, the best work has been done in these factories. If all goes well and you, gentlemen, produce your ancient types and achieve a certain increase in output, then this will be gratifying and I will commend it, but in the final analysis it is really nothing to shout about. These are types which were more or less obsolete at the outbreak of war. However, this is not a particularly outstanding effort.

There have of course been difficulties and you too, gentlemen, have frequently been afflicted by such difficulties. However, I too have spent some time carefully thinking over these difficulties and at no time have they assumed such proportions as to provide the slightest justification for allowing such an absolute standstill to occur in the development of airframes and engines. Moreover, I would have expected that in view of the much-vaunted initiative of private contractors, far more extensive preparations for retooling at the right moment would have been made than has been the case. Once again, this has been carried out most intensively and efficiently in the state-owned factories.

As regards armament we have managed passably well. However, in this case too it is absolutely essential that more powerful aircraft armament be produced as quickly as possible. Once again the designers should have come to this conclusion on their own initiative when they knew that the enemy was turning out increasingly powerful and heavily armoured aircraft.

I once again emphasise: let nobody come and tell me that the aerodynamic performance of our aircraft is far superior to that of the enemy's four-engined aircraft. All that is of no interest to me; I am interested only in practical results. I would exchange all of your brilliant designs for even a handful of these "old crates", as I have said before. With these I would at least be able to carry out operations which unfortunately are not possible with your aircraft.

However, the radar situation is by far the worst. It is really desperate. It must of course be plainly admitted that the British and Americans are leaps and bounds ahead of us in this field. I have always taken this into account as a matter of course and it has always been evident; however, frankly speaking, I did not believe that they were so far ahead of us. I had hoped that although we were lagging, we would at least manage to keep the gap from widening. I recall just one example – and it is probably the most absurd one to come my way since I have ▶

been in charge of the Luftwaffe. Just less than a year before the war they dared to demonstrate something to the Führer and myself and state that it was a recognition device and was to be installed immediately in all aircraft.

When German aircraft were approaching, our flak etc. would be able to identify them as such with the aid of this device. I asked if this device would be put into service quickly and was told that it would be fitted in all aircraft immediately. Now, four years later, we still have no aircraft equipped with a recognition device. The enemy has been using this device since the beginning of the war, but we have not. If our people have still not had any ideas I regret that I am not able to help them. You cannot get blood out of a stone. However, instead of being so arrogant, they should at least have set their hand to copying what the enemy had. At least I would then have a device by now, albeit of the most primitive type conceivable.

It is a disgrace that we should still be without a recognition device for our aircraft in the fourth year of the war. This is the greatest scandal that has ever occurred in the aeronautical field. They are always bungling about with things, but can never agree upon a definite line of development, while even I, as the person responsible for the Luftwaffe, can see when this device could be produced in its crudest form. I am always being told about miraculous things, but on the basis of experience I can only say in all honesty that whenever I attend any demonstration or projects are put to me it always turns my stomach – I can assure you that – for I know that it is all only wishful thinking and God knows when it will be produced, and even if it reaches this stage it will certainly already be long obsolete.

In my opinion there is really nothing more simple than a recognition device such as this. But we cannot manage it, we just cannot damn well manage it. At all events we are not getting it into the aircraft. You can go and embalm your recognition device, for if I do not get it in my aircraft I will have nothing to do with it. The enemy navigates with deadly accuracy and far and deep into our land. He drops bombs from above the clouds, in the clouds and below the clouds. He is always producing new radar devices.

His aircraft fly in close formation at night and he holds his squadrons together. If I ask then if it may be assumed that the British have the device I am told: Yes, that may be assumed. We have also found a device, but have not yet perfected it. I have long been aware that the British have all these devices. What installations we do have can be jammed by the enemy every five minutes. Night fighter technique is still the same as a year ago and has not been developed in the slightest degree; on the contrary, successes are diminishing. We have not got the right aircraft for the job.

This also applies in other respects. Always promises! If somebody comes to me and says we have here the Giant Würzburg and the Seeburg radar plotting table and are now building the Gigant and the Mammut and what have you – well, I have not yet seen these new things and would rather not believe in them until I do see them. At all events I have only one thing to say now: enemy aircraft fly about over Germany as they please and only a fraction of them are located, even where there are radar installations. Something or other goes wrong with these installations every five minutes.

I can only take the final product and determine what is fact. I observe that the enemy can fly around on a clear day such as this without even being seen or located. They also come over in the dirtiest weather and approach the target out of the clouds, fighters and all. However, not even our reconnaissance aircraft can get through any more as they are picked up by the enemy from the moment they take off from the French bases. This is really ideal organisation, but of course it is possible only because they have the equipment over there.

Now I have been informed quite coolly that it is feared that the enemy has another new device with the aid of which he can carry out precision bombing through cloud as he can tell immediately if he is over buildings of any appreciable size. He will soon be able to tell whether it is a tank factory or an aircraft plant down below. They accept all this as resignedly as the will of God and when I get excited they say that we have too few workers! Gentlemen, we do not have too few workers, but too few brains to invent the devices which are required.

It is an absolute certainty that there will be a gradual increase in output. We have made every effort possible in this sphere. We have constantly fed more workers into the industry. However, the production targets demanded of the radar equipment industry are so idiotic that they can hardly be discussed. I can of course discuss only such figures as lie within the bounds of possibility and not of such proportions that whole divisions would have to be disbanded merely to supply the radar equipment industry with workers. The radar equipment industry will have to go over quickly to modern methods of production. I have often seen the sets. They do not appear to be so imposing; they are just wires, more wires and a bit of something else – the whole thing is really remarkably primitive.

I do not wish to speak about the Eastern theatre of operations as we are on absolutely equal terms there and are superior in some respects. Instead, we must deal with the enemy in the west and in this respect I simply have the following observations to make: today the enemy flies over the Reich at will to whatever depth he pleases and with an enormously heavy bomb load, whereas the range of our aircraft decreases with every year of the war.

In 1940 my aircraft could fly on average at least as far as Glasgow, but this is no longer possible today. Ranges are becoming shorter and shorter instead of longer. I remember when the plans for the Ju 88 were submitted they drew me the most wonderful pictures showing how this machine would fly back and forth west of Ireland to attack enemy shipping. However, the aircraft has not once reached Ireland to this day. You must understand my unbounded anger. What was delivered is absolute rubbish.

Ranges are becoming shorter and bomb-loads smaller. The most trifling things and the slightest modifications cause difficulties and delay the time taken to deliver aircraft, which is almost incredibly long. Moreover, aircraft are delivered in a half-finished condition and have to be completed when they reach the squadrons. Some new modification is necessary every five minutes because fresh defects are always appearing. That really is a fine kettle of fish for you!

Our past achievements have certainly not been inconsiderable. However, at that time my outlook was different. Gentlemen, I must tell you quite frankly that it is as if an absolute stagnation had set in since the aircraft which we had at the beginning of the war were developed. Nobody has had any really new ideas. I will certainly concede that the Fw 190 could perhaps be considered as a very effective fighter-bomber. However, in this case too the side-tanks have recently been replaced by peculiar things which have reduced the speed of the aircraft to such an extent that the whole advantage has been lost.

The enemy has copied many things from us and then made a monkey of us. He first adopted the German ideas which came his way and then developed them extensively. You remember, gentlemen, that I spoke of the high-altitude bomber and the high-speed bomber even before the war. At that time I offered tax-free million mark awards to designers and others who could produce something serviceable. Throughout the war I have constantly reminded them that high-altitude and high-speed bombers are two types which would give us a certain advantage again.

For a high-altitude bomber I had to use the Ju 86, one of the oldest crates which were generally available for a few weeks to fill the gap. It carried a 50kg bomb at certain altitudes. In the case of the high-speed bomber our people made it very easy on themselves; a bomb was slung under the fastest fighter and the high-speed bomber was ready. Now a fighter is not a bomber, but this did not bother them in the slightest. Only in this way could my repeated demands be fulfilled.

With very few exceptions the projects which are in development are still things of the future and cannot be produced until the end of 1944, 1945 or 1946. Gentlemen, these are things which were being discussed even before the outbreak of war. I therefore conclude that in all these years you have not made any progress in this sphere either. In the field of jet propulsion too, everything was available before the war. At the time when I asked how soon the finished product would be ready I was told in 18 months to two years. Now, on receiving really positive information, I understand that it will be ready in two years. That's what it looks like.

I now have to produce the means whereby at least some kind of counterstroke may be delivered in view of the constantly increasing number of British bombers. Do not deceive yourselves, gentlemen; the British will carry out attacks with an ever-increasing number of these slow four-engined 'crates' or whatever else I have heard them called, which some of you hold in such contempt. He will deal with each and every city. It makes no difference at all to him; he can navigate to Munich or Berlin with the same precision and he can reach Warsaw and Vienna. Nothing bothers him; he can manage it without difficulty.

The night fighters are successful on some occasions and unsuccessful on others. The flak can only play a defensive role or have a deterrent effect. The endurance of the enemy aircraft is colossal. The equipment with which they have to navigate to hit the target even in bad weather is ideal, while our instruments are always going wrong so that the night fighters are always coming to grief and cannot do much about it. This, of course, is a severe strain on the entire war situation.

I have therefore decided to concentrate operations against Great Britain and to intensify them to the maximum degree, especially as the initiative in this matter has been taken by the Fuhrer himself. If I am, unfortunately, still obliged to leave the overwhelming majority of Luftwaffe formations in the East and South, the balance must be restored to a certain extent by other means: imaginative alternation of method of attack, the utmost exploitation of opportunities etc. I have therefore taken personal control of this matter and have selected a very young officer [Peltz] who in my opinion possesses all the qualities required to undertake this gigantic task.

Moreover, I have offered this officer the fullest co-operation and support in technical matters in so far as the present increased consideration for front-line requirements will allow. Our standards of submarine warfare have reached their present advanced stage because in spite of all the restrictions imposed by the departments of the Ordnance Branch of the War Ministry, the Admiralty and industry, operational experience has had a directly fruitful effect and has produced the weapon required.

This must also apply in the operations against Britain; the man himself must make demands as to how he requires his aircraft and what further development is necessary. All these demands made in the case of operations against Britain can also be applied in operations against Russia.

Unfortunately, there is one thing which I cannot change - the singular lack of progress in development. I have already told the Führer that I am no designer or technician and therefore unfortunately cannot produce aircraft or develop engines and equipment myself. I can therefore only make the proposals which are necessary to at least create the basis for a further limited advance in development.

Thus, as the situation stands, I must rely on the people who are here for this purpose and who have undertaken this task. However, I must once again express my extreme bitterness that so little has been achieved all along the line in this field. I do not know whether this speed will result in you gentlemen being shaken out of your lethargy to some extent so that something may at last be produced. Personally, I have no very great hopes of this as the lack of achievement has lasted too long and has become too ingrained.

I do not know why you should get a great many ideas now after producing nothing for years on end. One thing is sure - and you cannot dispute it - and that is the absolute superiority in the technical development of airframes, engines and instruments, particularly radar instruments, on the part of the British and Americans. This is the only irrefutable fact and all the rest was no more than a lot of tripe which you were always drumming into my ears. I was always being told that this was being improved and the other was being produced.

Now I know what has been produced. It is, of course, not only a matter of devising something new and better, but also of creating the basic conditions so that it may then be produced with the necessary dispatch and in the required quantity. At this point I should like to state most emphatically that I am rather more at ease since this matter was taken over by Field Marshal Milch with his outstanding powers of organisation. An enormous number of points have been clarified. Everything has begun to take on a definite shape again. I have dismissed the people who have been in control until now.

Thus, I hope that there will now be an improvement. However, the field marshal is also not a designer and has just as little inclination to be one as I have. He can only fulfil his enormous task, that is to maintain the aircraft industry on a reasonably well-balanced basis, if support is really forthcoming from all sides. I have never hesitated and have always been prepared to give real achievement its reward and I will continue to do so in the future. On the other hand, however, if all else fails I will not shrink from making any changes in personnel which I or the field marshal consider necessary. I will do this whether or not it is in accordance with regulations.

I am not going to be held up by minor details in this matter; you can rest assured of that. I cannot act otherwise. I would like to have said a great many fine things to you, but I have done that long enough. It would now be nothing more than falsity. The facts are as I have described them. I have considered and am still considering in all seriousness whether we could achieve our purpose most quickly merely by blindly copying the best British four-engined bomber.

Admittedly the thing is slow, but it is also extremely stable and can carry a colossal bomb load. At the same time it has an incredible range. I cannot do much with what you are giving me at present. Even if the 177 is produced what am I to do with it? It can hardly get its nose past the hangar doors and cannot even reach Glasgow. The same applies to the [Ju] 188. Even the fighters can reach London and I do not need your bombers for that. It is enough to drive one to despair! Year after year has gone by and you have plodded away at the same old things.

First an engine is drilled out a bit more, but this against results in other disadvantages. Then the wing-tips are snipped off or something else is done. But a new aircraft which can really do the job does not materialise. Tell me the name of such an aircraft, I ask you! Perhaps we have one unbeknownst to me. I know of no such aircraft or engine. I know only one thing: we have the 801 which, although it has not yet reached the peak of reliability, is nevertheless a really well-tried engine. Its performance is just short of 1800 horsepower. Even the [DB] 605's performance is not a great deal better than this. Although I now have an engine, it cannot be fitted in the 109 as the airframe is not strong enough.

This is how the situation stands. I deliberately put it to you in such clear and blunt terms. You can form your own impressions. The most absurd example is that of the recognition device, which is a problem that practically any amateur handyman would certainly have solved long ago. However, gentlemen, you always want to do things on an exceptionally grandiose scale. I would be content if the device were made with more modest materials and to a more simple design, for I would at least get it eventually. None of you gentlemen can contest what was said to me before the war.

I can still name the place where the device was demonstrated to us. In any case the net result is that we have no aircraft fitted with a recognition device. Whenever aircraft approach we do not know whether they are ours or the enemy's. The enemy is never in doubt, and you will not dispute that either. All of his aircraft are equipped with a recognition device. Whenever I enquire I am always told that we have the recognition device. However, I am not interested in where it is but only in whether it is in my aircraft. But it is not in any of the aircraft, or is that not so general? ●

'I HAVE CONSIDERED... BLINDLY COPYING THE BEST BRITISH FOUR-ENGINED BOMBER'

While Göring's speech pulls no punches in highlighting the failures of the German aviation industry across the board, it is included here because of what it says about bombers. Indeed, the relative performance of German and British bombers appears to be at the root of his dissatisfaction.

Early on, he mentions the 'America' aircraft at Augsburg – a reference to the Messerschmitt Me 264 – and bitterly laments its inability to achieve the ranges promised. This, however, is his only mention of such an aircraft and he speaks of it as being "years ago".

He brings up the Heinkel He 177 more frequently, calling it a "dead loss" and describing the missions it was most urgently needed to perform: reconnaissance to help U-boats locate Allied supply convoys and operations against Allied shipping using "special-purpose bombs" – in other words guided anti-shipping weapons such as the Henschel Hs 293 and Ruhrstahl PC1400 X aka Fritz X.

Set against these failures, he holds up Britain's four-engined bombers as examples of how a bomber should be built and the qualities it ought to have. These include "excellent armament and terrific stability", "a colossal bomb load" and "incredible range". The virtues of Britain's four-engined bombers are brought up four times, with Göring even expressing a desire to simply copy the best British design in order to quickly provide Germany with an effective bomber.

Furthermore, it is evident that even by March 1943, Britain was still seen as Germany's most dangerous enemy, rather than America. Beyond a brief mention as a failure of the recent past, there is no further discussion of attacking America. All efforts, Göring's audience are told, are to be focused on attacking Britain.

Aircraft are to be designed with fighting the British in mind – anything that works against the British will undoubtedly work against the Soviets too. The "very young officer" appointed to review the situation in the west was Peltz, who seems to have struggled to get to grips with his brief.

Development

Fernkampfflugzeug final phase

With several heavy bomber designs in limbo and in the wake of Reichsmarshall Herman Göring's bitter tirade concerning the state of bomber development in Germany, a final round of decision-making on these piston-engined giants-in-waiting was begun during the spring of 1943.

Heinkel had largely given up on designing a successor to its disastrous He 177 by early 1943. Messerschmitt had continued to develop the flawed Me 264 but had yet to successfully complete a fully functional prototype and Focke-Wulf continued working on its Fernkampfflugzeug despite the abject failure of its earlier incarnations.

Junkers was slowly building Ju 290s but its attention and its priorities had shifted elsewhere, particularly with the success of the jet engines developed by its Jumo division.

Yet there was still a strong desire within the German high command - coming in no small part directly from Adolf Hitler himself - to build a heavy bomber capable of taking the fight to Britain and the British. Göring had made it plain during his bullish Carinhall address that he wanted a bomber and soon.

It just so happened that Focke-Wulf, having refined its Fernkampfflugzeug, was perfectly placed to take advantage of this. Even before a reassessment of the competing designs took place from March to June - it was not a new competition as such - Focke-Wulf had already prepared two parallel projects - described in Baubeschreibung Nr. 261 and Nr. 262, dated March 5, 1943.

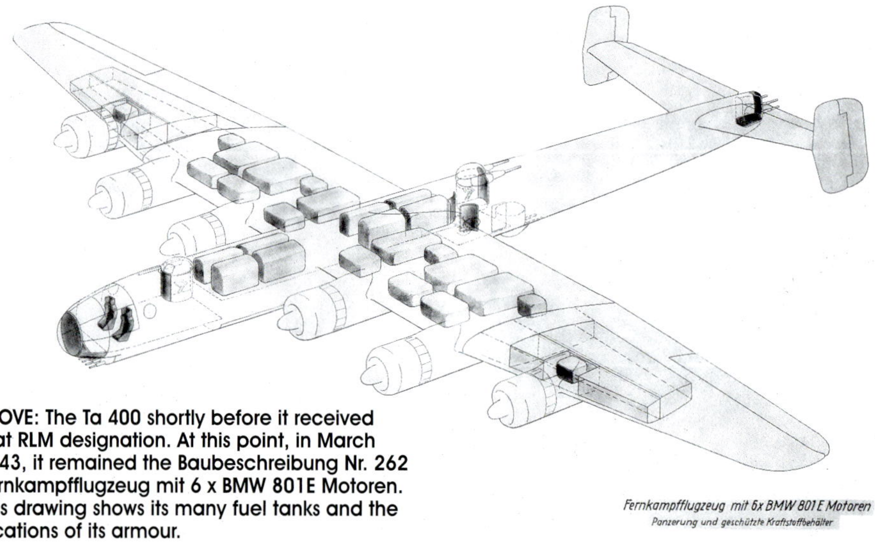

ABOVE: The Ta 400 shortly before it received that RLM designation. At this point, in March 1943, it remained the Baubeschreibung Nr. 262 Fernkampfflugzeug mit 6 x BMW 801E Motoren. This drawing shows its many fuel tanks and the locations of its armour.

ABOVE: The official Focke-Wulf Ta 400 logo, from the cover of a company folder.

FOCKE-WULF TA 400

The Baubeschreibung Nr. 261 Fernkampfflugzeug mit 4 x BMW 801E-Motoren design was a long-range reconnaissance and bomber aircraft which was, unsurprisingly given its typically matter-of-fact Focke-Wulf name, to be powered by four BMW 801Es. It featured a central fuselage with room for 10 tonnes of bombs, that ended just aft of the wings, and tail surfaces mounted on twin booms which extended far out to the rear.

Defensive armament was very heavy, with four MK 108 30mm cannon divided between two independently rotating chin turrets, a manned tail turret - on the stump end of the fuselage - with four MG 131s, and both upper and lower fuselage turrets too.

In contrast to this unusual arrangement, the Baubeschreibung Nr. 262 Fernkampfflugzeug mit 6 x BMW 801E-Motoren aircraft took a more traditional form. Its wing shape was almost the same as that of the Nr. 261 design but extended to accommodate its six engines.

With a single long fuselage, the Nr. 262 aircraft's defences were even more impressive. It mounted the same chin turrets and tail turret as the Nr. 261 but had two upper fuselage power-operated turrets. The one nearest the front was an HD 151/2 type mounting a single MG 151 20mm cannon, while the one towards the rear was an HD 151 Z with a pair of MG 151s fitted.

Beneath the fuselage and slightly further back than the latter turret was an FDL 151 Z, also fitted with a pair of MG 151s. These two rearward turrets were both to be controlled remotely by a gunner seated just ahead of them within the fuselage. Where previous Fernkampfflugzeug designs had seen the fuselage gunner provided with a pair of very large Perspex observation blisters, this time the blisters, though still present, were much smaller.

Like the Nr. 261 design, maximum bomb load was to be 10 tonnes but a brief note also stated that further droppable loads could be carried beneath the aircraft's wings - a reference to the Henschel Hs 293 and Hs 294 guided anti-shipping missiles shown in two of the drawings accompanying the report.

The introduction to Baubeschreibung Nr. 262 shows how Focke-Wulf intended to pitch the design: "The tasks of naval warfare today require an aircraft that can be used to support the submarine fleet. The ways hell

in which it can support the submarines are: 1) In providing reconnaissance over large areas of the Atlantic. 2) In defence against enemy aircraft that would seek to disrupt the operations of our submarines.

"Furthermore, the required aircraft should be equipped with droppable weapons on its own, to be able to carry out effective attacks on enemy shipping targets over a range of about 9000km. This task resulted in the present design of an aircraft which is designed to be suitable for use as scout, destroyer and bomber.

"The aircraft is designed as a cantilever monoplane with six air-cooled double radial BMW 801E engines. It has a retractable landing gear, which consists of a nose wheel and four single chassis which are arranged under the inner engine nacelles. The rudder is a double tail."

It was to have a wingspan of 42m, the fuselage was 28.2m long and the aircraft stood 6m tall at rest with its undercarriage extended.

At the end of May 1943, Focke-Wulf presented its Baubeschreibung Nr. 262 aircraft, chosen in favour of the Nr. 261 alternative, and this time was awarded a development contract - but as usual there was no full production order. And there was another problem: with its factories at maximum capacity churning out Fw 190s and its designers already fully engaged on a host of fighter-related projects such as the Ta 154, how would Focke-Wulf get one or more Baubeschreibung Nr. 262 prototypes designed, let alone built?

In this respect, the company believed it had an ace up its sleeve - the French designers at SNCASO in Paris who were part of the Groupe Technique de Chatillon (GTC). As previously related, this 300-strong team had been largely under Focke-Wulf's exclusive control from January 1941 to the summer of 1942 and had worked extensively on the Fw 300.

Following the cessation of work on the Fw 300 and into early 1943, Focke-Wulf had been forced to share the GTC with Blohm & Voss and Junkers, but with confirmation that the Baubeschreibung Nr. 262 would go forward under the new RLM designation Ta 400, in honour of charismatic managing director and chief designer Kurt Tank, Focke-Wulf was able to wrest back full control and set them to work on what they were told was called the Fw 300A.

This rather unsubtle piece of misinformation seems to have successfully confused Allied intelligence, who believed for a while that the Ta 400 was some sort of advanced Fw 300 development - rather than an entirely different design.

The GTC drawing office spent an incredible 300,000 hours working on the wings, tail and undercarriage of the 'Fw 300A' - almost double the amount of time spent on the Fw 300, starting

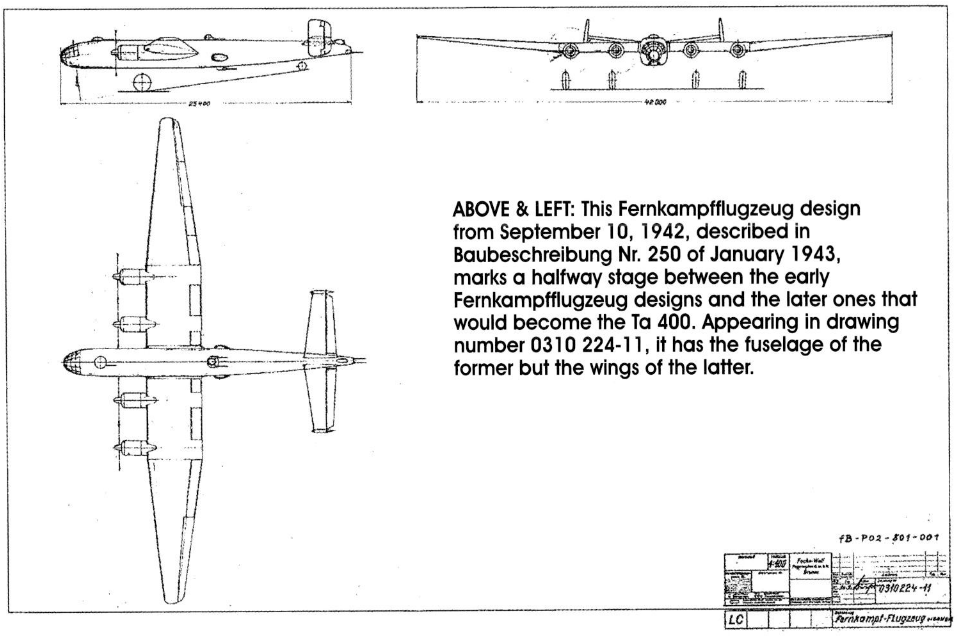

ABOVE & LEFT: This Fernkampfflugzeug design from September 10, 1942, described in Baubeschreibung Nr. 250 of January 1943, marks a halfway stage between the early Fernkampfflugzeug designs and the later ones that would become the Ta 400. Appearing in drawing number 0310 224-11, it has the fuselage of the former but the wings of the latter.

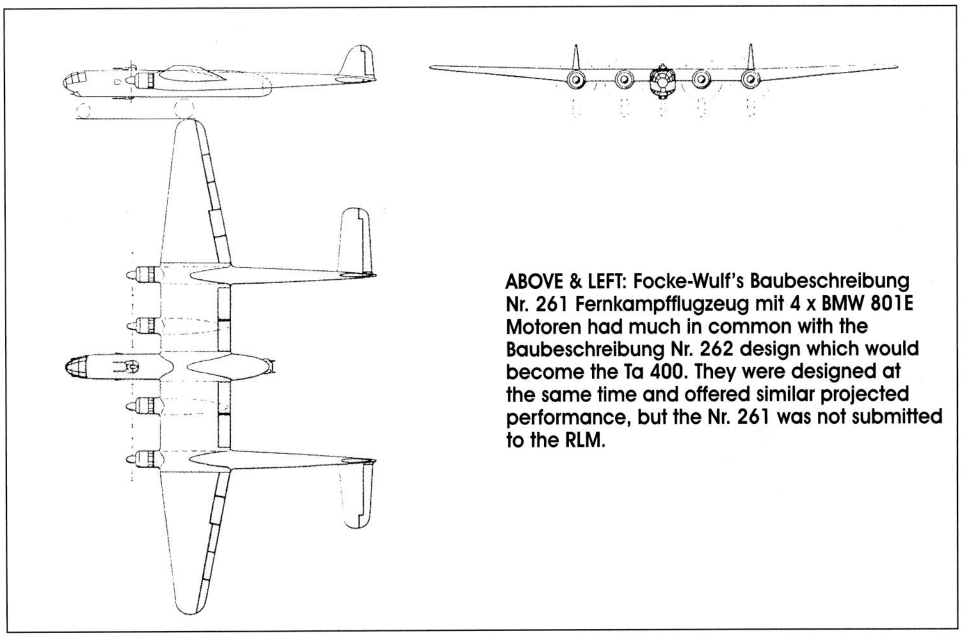

ABOVE & LEFT: Focke-Wulf's Baubeschreibung Nr. 261 Fernkampfflugzeug mit 4 x BMW 801E Motoren had much in common with the Baubeschreibung Nr. 262 design which would become the Ta 400. They were designed at the same time and offered similar projected performance, but the Nr. 261 was not submitted to the RLM.

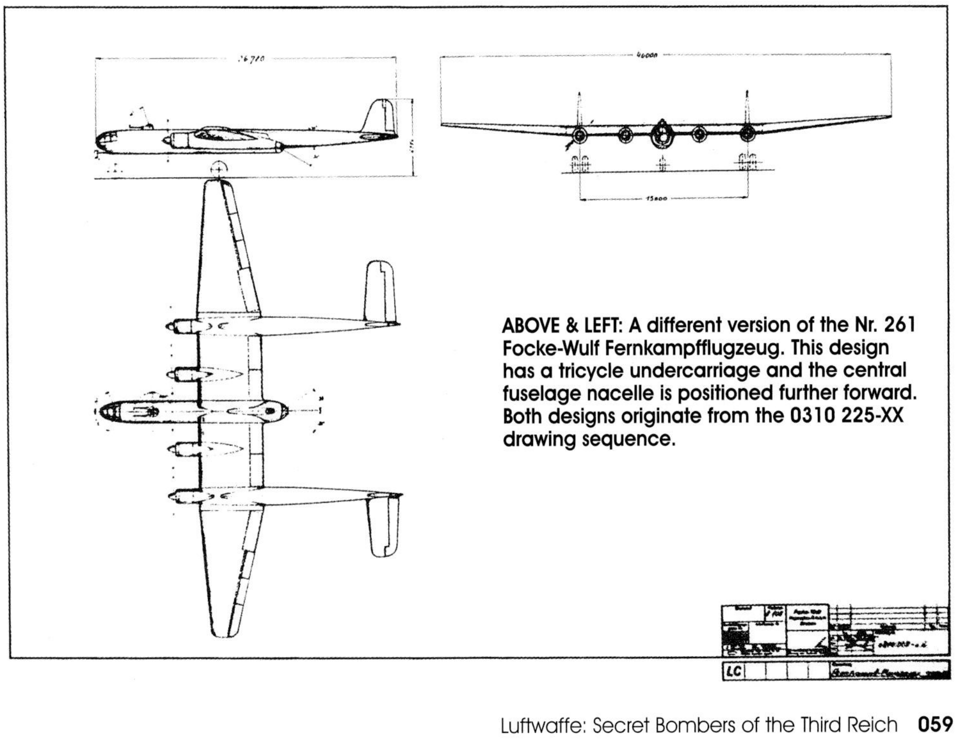

ABOVE & LEFT: A different version of the Nr. 261 Focke-Wulf Fernkampfflugzeug. This design has a tricycle undercarriage and the central fuselage nacelle is positioned further forward. Both designs originate from the 0310 225-XX drawing sequence.

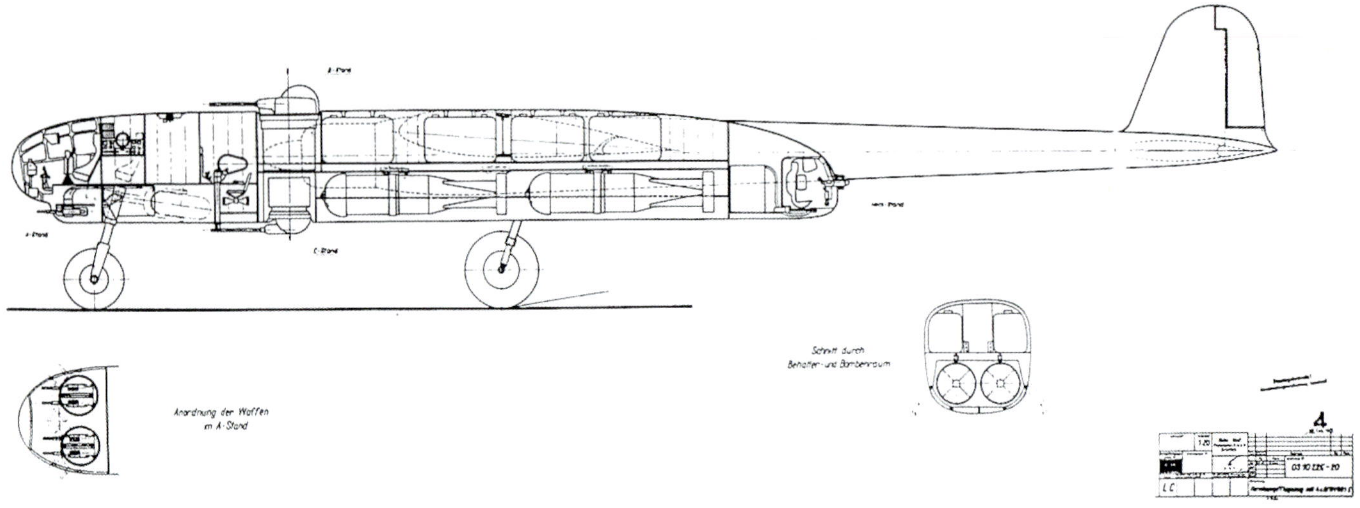

ABOVE: The Nr. 261 aircraft as seen from the side in Focke-Wulf drawing 0310 225-20.

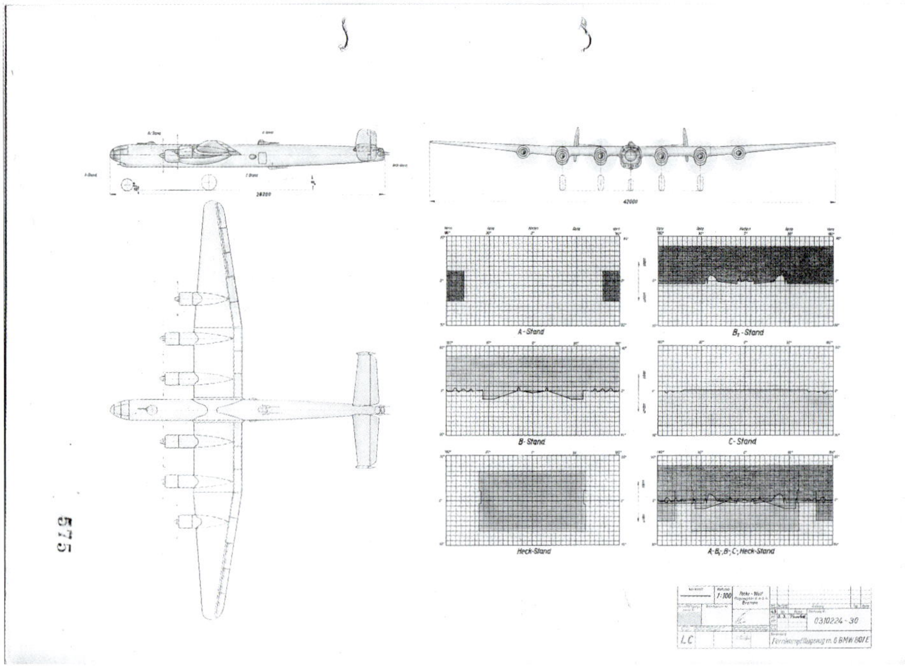

ABOVE: The definitive Ta 400 – as it appeared in Baubeschreibung Nr. 262 as Fernkampfflugzeug mit 6 x BMW 801E Motoren. The heavy armament of four MK 108s divided between two independently swivelling chin turrets was intended to allow the aircraft to operate against enemy bombers and patrol aircraft. This is Focke-Wulf drawing number 0310 224-30.

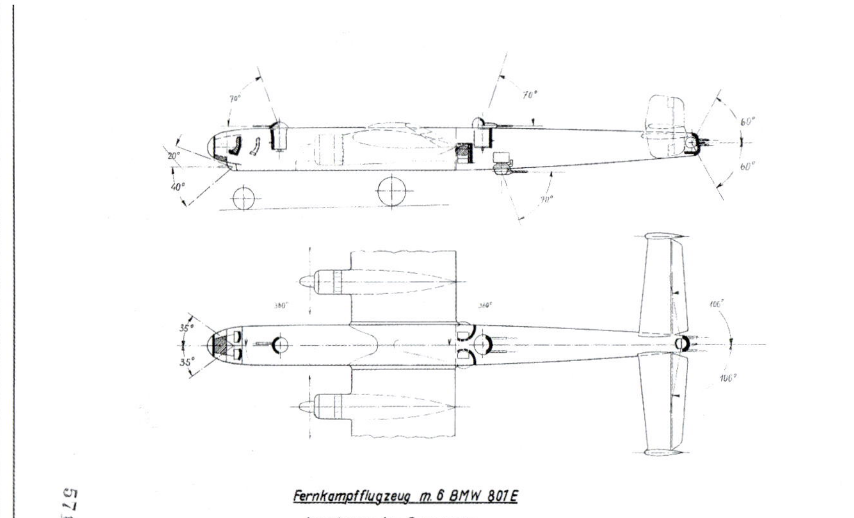

ABOVE: Fields of fire for the Nr. 262 aircraft's many turrets from drawing number 0310 224-33.

in June 1943 and not finishing until Paris was liberated on August 25, 1944. As with the Fw 300, however, they only managed to bring the job 70% of the way to completion.

The stress office spent 74,000 hours working on it during the same timescale. The jig and tool section only managed 18,900 hours, which was only 8% of the work they had been tasked with doing.

In early November 1943, Focke-Wulf put forward a newly drafted Kurzbeschreibung on the 'Fernkampfflugzeug mit 6 BMW 801 Ta 400'. This was largely a straightforward rewrite of the Nr. 262 report from March but some details had changed. Wingspan was the same but fuselage length had increased to 29.4m and height had also increased, up to 6.5m. Where the original had stipulated a crew of seven to nine, the new report gave it simply as nine. All-up weight had been 60.5 tonnes – now it was 62.5 tonnes.

There was a significant design alteration too. Where the original Nr. 262 design had pilot visibility only through the aircraft's nose, now a large glazed blister canopy was positioned above the crewmembers' heads, providing much better visibility back along the fuselage.

Work may have started in France during June 1943, but Focke-Wulf wanted to take this programme of international 'cooperation' one stage further. It had worked out a scheme in conjunction with the RLM whereby some of the French designers would be relocated to Germany.

According to British intelligence report AI 58614 of November 4, 1943: "The studies concerning the construction of this 60 ton bomber will probably be carried out partly in France and partly in Germany. Work will be divided as follows: in France, the canopy, undercarriage and the wings, and in Germany the fuselage.

"In order to carry out this work, 60 French designers are to join the 150 designers already working for Focke-Wulf in Germany, in the town of Lage (7km from Detmold) in a technical school. The work in France will be carried out by 130 designers of

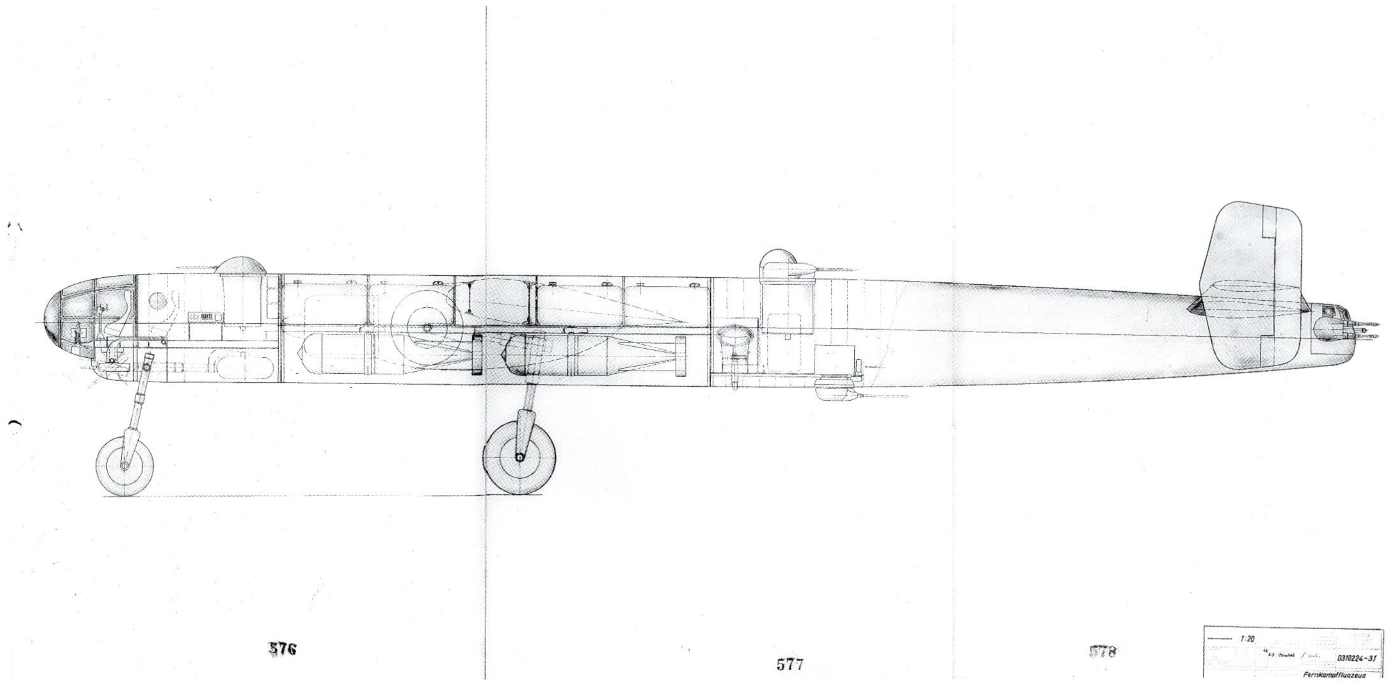

ABOVE: Side view of the Nr. 262 Fernkampfflugzeug as shown in drawing number 0310 224-31 of March 6, 1943.

ABOVE: The final version of the Ta 400 featured a redesigned cockpit structure, offering the crew a greatly increased field of vision. Art by Daniel Uhr

BELOW: Another view of the fuel tank arrangement within the Nr. 262 aircraft that would become the Ta 400.

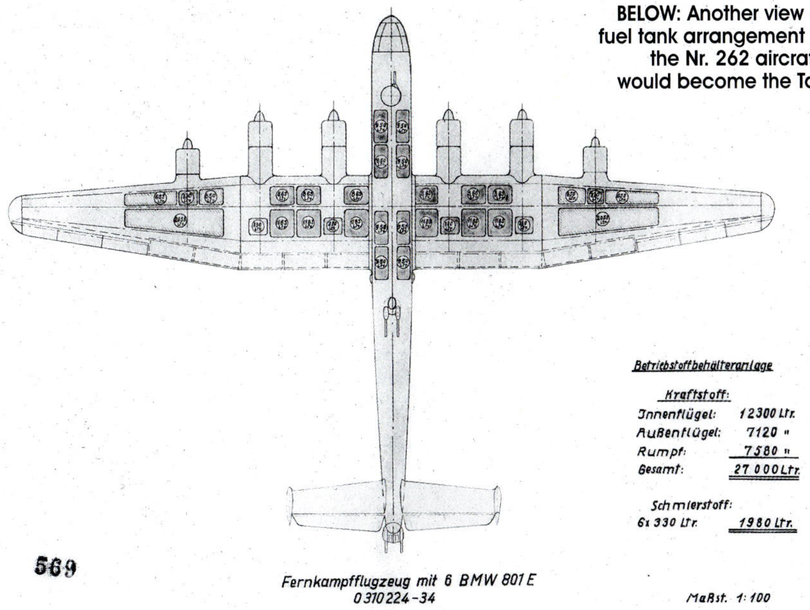

the SNCASO belonging to the Technical Group of Chatillon, which has recently been reinforced by a group of 70 technicians drawn from the SNCASE at Marignane.

"It should be noted that the 200 designers are resisting against the deportation of the group of 60 men; in spite of the financial inducement which is made more and more attractive, volunteers are not forthcoming. Even the technicians who have returned to France for leave from Germany, where they had been deported in November 1942 and February 1943, are not returning to Germany.

"The study and drawing offices for aircraft of the Focke-Wulf company consist of 1000 employees and technicians at Bad Eilsen (5km from Buckeburg). They are installed in two large hotels in the town and include 150 French designers who have been deported from France. Their living conditions are not bad but their morale is very low.

"The technicians have to obey orders given by the Germans who consider themselves far superior. As a general rule the output of the German, as of the French personnel is very bad. The work entrusted to the French is generally connected with modifications and alterations of secondary importance."

Morale was so low among the French workers designing the Ta 400 at Chatillon that they actually went on strike on December 13, 1943, demanding more pay. Within 25 minutes, a detachment of German SS officers and French police had arrived at the factory and detained 18 workers. Those who had not been detained were then forced to continue working.

It was at this point that Focke-Wulf began to reconsider its options. Another option for 'spare capacity' within the aircraft manufacturing industry was Italy. Shortly after the strike at GTC, Focke-Wulf contacted the German government's armaments liaison officer in Italy, Haberstolz, who had previously been an executive at Focke-Wulf.

Kurt Tank and technical director Willi Kaether went to meet Haberstolz personally at Como, northern Italy, on December 22, 1943, to discuss plans to have the Ta 400's fuselage built by a consortium of Italian firms.

A second meeting took place in early 1944, during which Tank discussed Ta 400 production in conjunction with the possibility of having Italian firms build jigs ▶

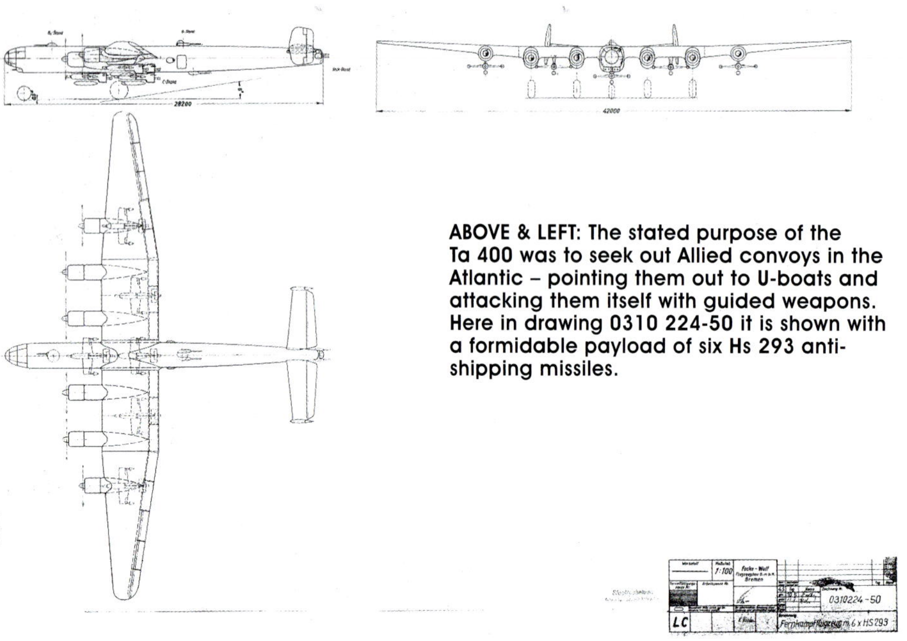

ABOVE & LEFT: The stated purpose of the Ta 400 was to seek out Allied convoys in the Atlantic – pointing them out to U-boats and attacking them itself with guided weapons. Here in drawing 0310 224-50 it is shown with a formidable payload of six Hs 293 anti-shipping missiles.

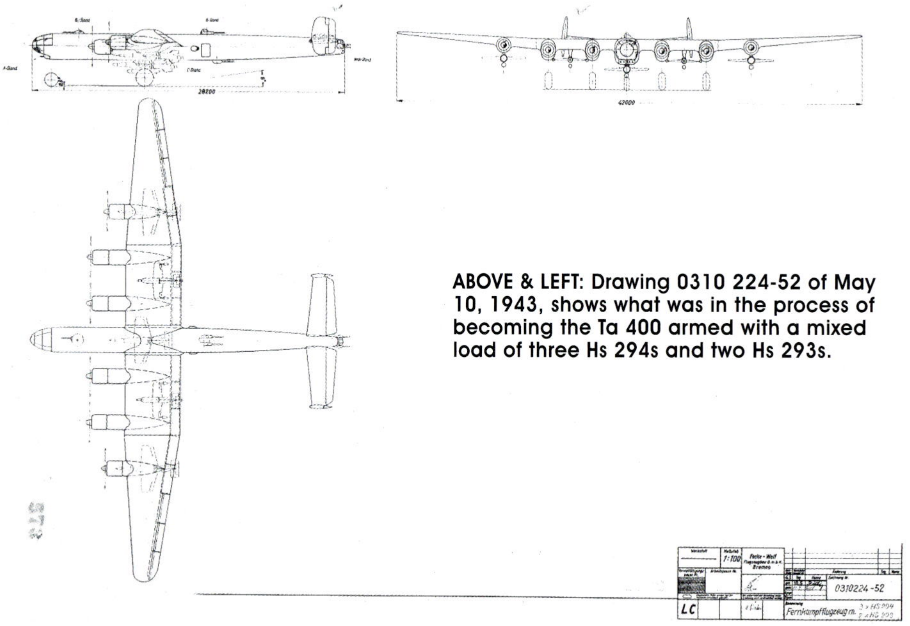

ABOVE & LEFT: Drawing 0310 224-52 of May 10, 1943, shows what was in the process of becoming the Ta 400 armed with a mixed load of three Hs 294s and two Hs 293s.

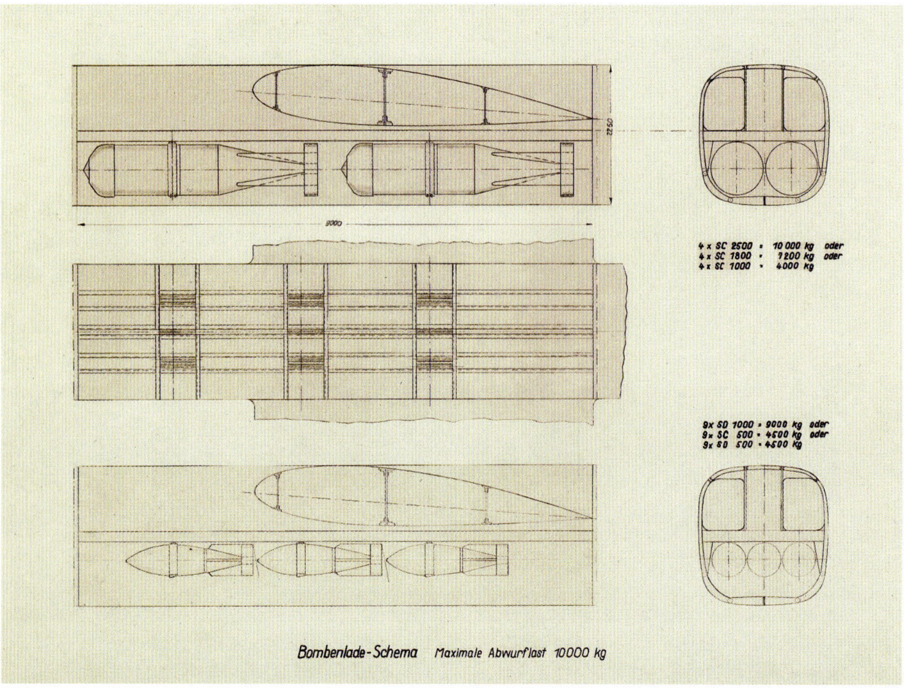

ABOVE: The Fernkampfflugzeug of Baubeschreibung Nr. 262 could carry 10 tonnes of bombs in a variety of arrangements.

for the Ta 152 as well as overhauling Fw 190s. In April 1944, Focke-Wulf opened formal negotiations with the companies themselves.

Another British intelligence report, No. 1 FIU 'A' Tech Report No. 33 of May 25, 1945, relates how Piaggio was approached first about working on the Ta 400, now using the moniker 'Ta 300A', followed by Breda. It states: "The same proposals were made about this design as to Piaggio, with the exception that Breda were to prepare detailed drawings of the centre section of the fuselage. Herr Haberstolz brought along the chief Focke-Wulf designer, Kurt Tank (the aircraft was known as the Ta 300A) and originally demanded that Ing. Filippo Zappata should take charge of an all-Italian drawing office with about 200 draughtsmen from Breda, Fiat and Piaggio to be set up at Munich.

"This was turned down and Breda was finally given the section of the fuselage mentioned above to develop in their Laveno office. Zappata was told to engage over a hundred draughtsmen, but when he was finally told what the actual job was, he said the number was ridiculous and only engaged about 20. This work was done in complete ignorance of the details of the other parts of the aircraft, and finally came the order to drop everything and send in the bill for the man-hours already spent on the job."

Meanwhile, work on the Ta 400 continued in France throughout the first half of 1944 – even after the Allies had landed at Normandy. Focke-Wulf representatives travelled to Paris for a meeting on June 10, 1944, to discuss the painfully slow progress being made on the Ta 400, particularly the design and manufacture of its fuel tanks.

According to British intelligence repot ADI(K) 603/44: "Several undercarriages for the Fw 300A were actually built in the SNCASO works at Chatillon and informant understood that one fuselage was also constructed in Germany.

"Oberingenieur Bansemir and Herr Kahrs, who had charge of Focke-Wulf research in France, both returned to Germany in June 1944, taking the blueprints with them, but it was suggested that, if anyone is interested, further information could be obtained from M de Lacjer, the former head of the SNCASO designing offices at Chatillon, who is now believed to be languishing in Fresnes prison."

It seems that Allied investigators did succeed in tracking down the unfortunate de Lacjer in his collaborator's jail cell and questioning him about the 'Fw 300A'. According to a British document entitled 'Extract from CIPC Visit to Paris – August/September, 1944, Fw 300A': "Information on this aircraft was obtained from M de Lacjer and M Legrand, and a partial mock-up seen at the factory at Chatillon-sous-Bagneux. This firm have been designing the wings, tail surfaces, and landing gear only, so know little about the fuselage, armament or equipment. A set of drawings giving the dimensions and general layout was, however, obtained.

"The Fw 300A is a six-engined bomber of maximum weight about 143,000lb, 138ft span and with a maximum wing loading of 78lb/sq ft. The landing weight was quoted as approximately 96,000lb, and a figure of 85,000lb was quoted for the weight in

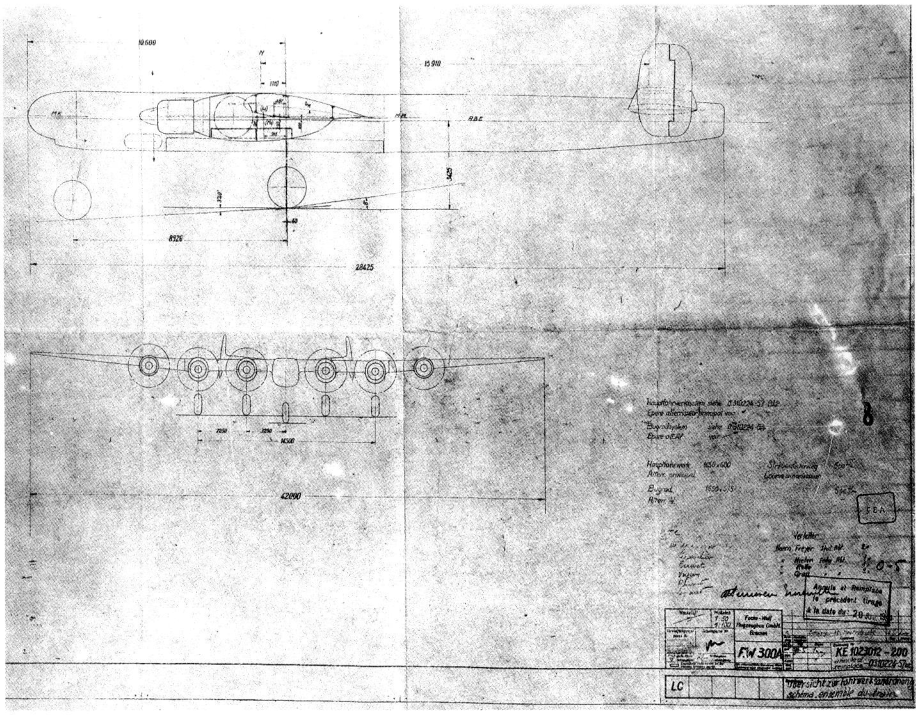

ABOVE: This drawing of the 'Fw 300A' dated May 31, 1943, bears both French and German annotations. It is numbered 0310 224-57 BIS. The image shown was clearly drawn by a French draughtsman since it lacks any form of defensive weaponry – an aspect of the design withheld from the French.

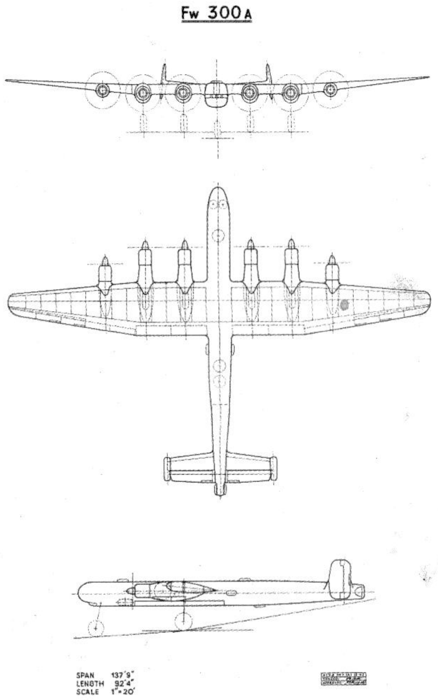

ABOVE: An odd version of the 'Fw 300A' reproduced in a British intelligence report directly from French drawings dated December 1943. The aircraft is shown with lozenge-shaped nubs where its turrets and gunnery observation windows would be.

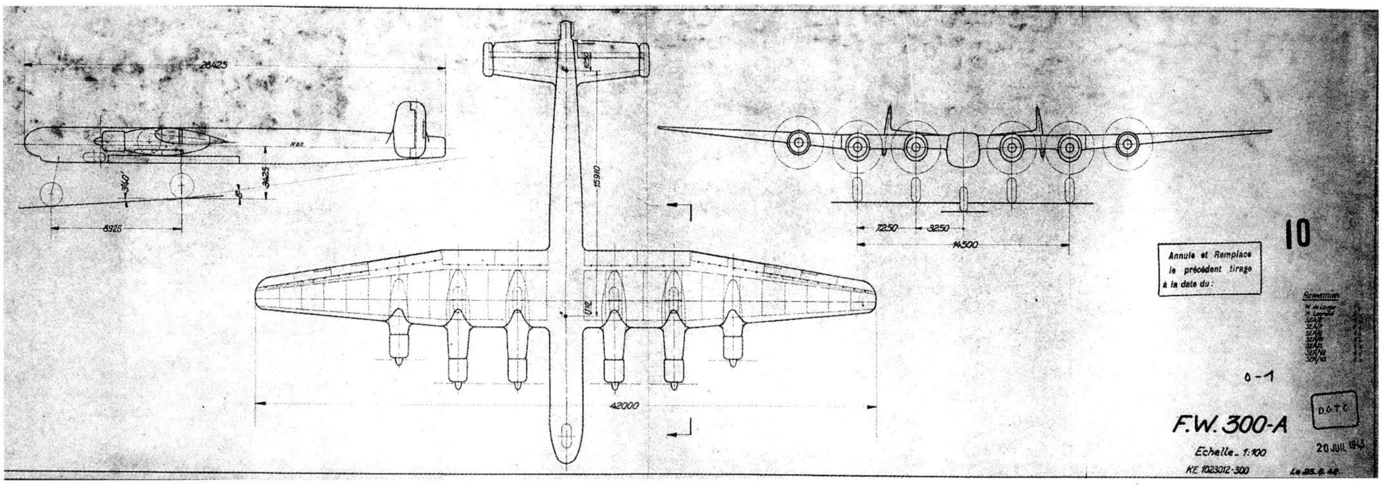

ABOVE: A French drawing of the 'Fw 300A' erroneously dated June 25, 1942. The date stamp of July 20, 1943, is closer to the truth.

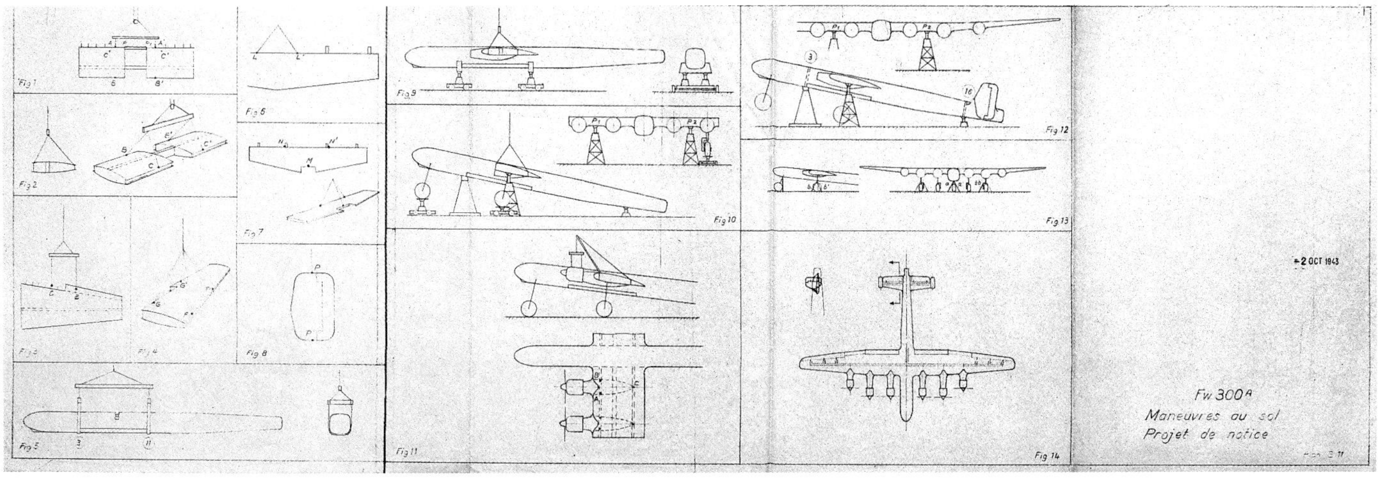

ABOVE: An instruction leaflet for handling the Ta 400 aka 'Fw 300A' on the ground. The leaflet is date-stamped October 2, 1943.

flight in its lightest possible condition (presumably, without armament, bombs or fuel). The engines were BMW 801E.

"The fuel capacity is 5950 gallons, distributed among 28 tanks, 12 in each wing, and four in the fuselage. The fuselage tanks and the eight inboard tanks in each wing are self-sealed and have provision for jettisoning fuel and for purging by inert gas. No details of the purging system were known, but a sample vent valve sent to SNCASO by Focke-Wulf was obtained and has been passed to RDT2(e).

"The landing gear consists of four main wheels (tyres 1660 x 620mm), one under each of the four inner nacelles, retracting forward, ▶

and a single retractable nose wheel. The nose wheel has no brakes nor provision for steering, but has a motor to spin it up before landing. Both the main undercarriages and tail wheel are of welded steel construction.

"The main spars are of laminated dural construction, the flanges being made up of a number of comparatively thin laminations. They were originally designed in steel but owing to the weight and difficulty in attaching fittings, they were redesigned in dural (M de Lacjer said that the difficulty was due mainly to the deterioration in quality of the German steels). The skin is of dural sheet, of thickness varying from 2-3mm, with fairly closely spaced spanwise stringers."

The French designers had been kept in the dark about important aspects of the overall design for security reasons. These included armament and engines. The report concludes with a statement at odds with the overview report on German activity in the French aircraft industry: "The design work by SNCASO has been finished, but they had no knowledge of the stage of the rest of the design, nor as to whether construction had started."

With the bulk of its designers no longer available, the Ta 400 was finally cancelled not long after the liberation of France.

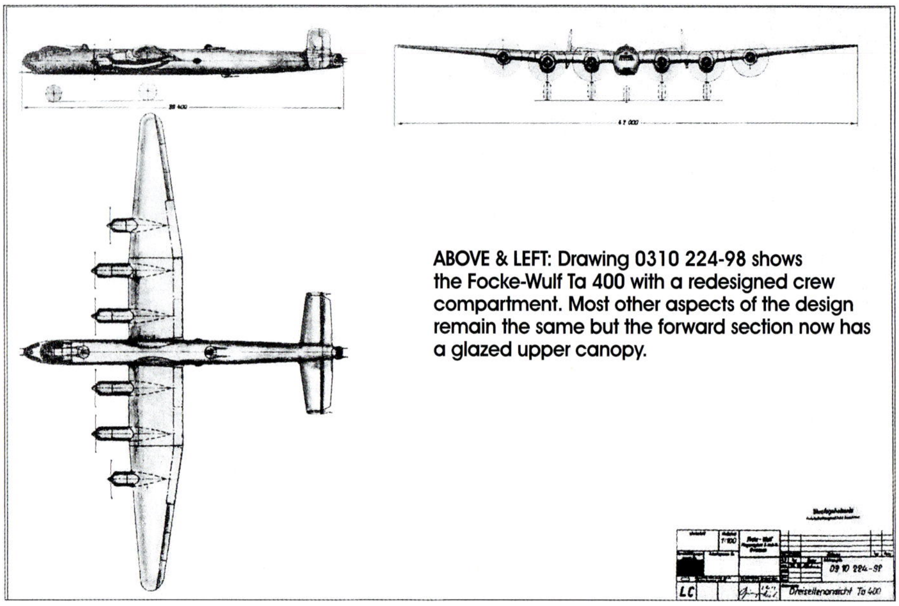

ABOVE & LEFT: Drawing 0310 224-98 shows the Focke-Wulf Ta 400 with a redesigned crew compartment. Most other aspects of the design remain the same but the forward section now has a glazed upper canopy.

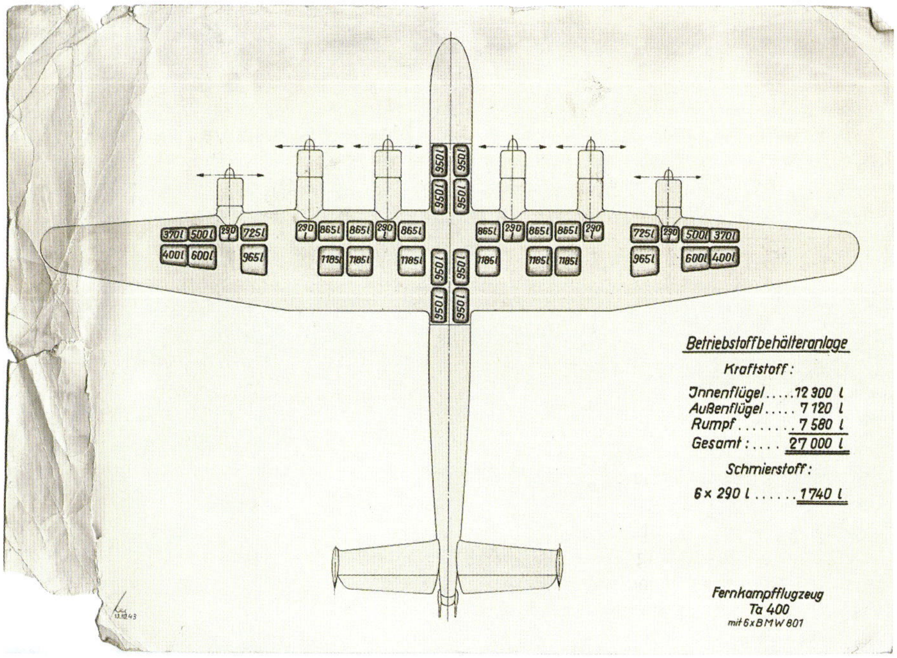

ABOVE: Similar to the earlier Fernkampfflugzeug fuel load map, this one is dated October 13, 1943, and uses the Ta 400 designation. There are minor design differences evident too, with many of the wing tanks being resized and repositioned.

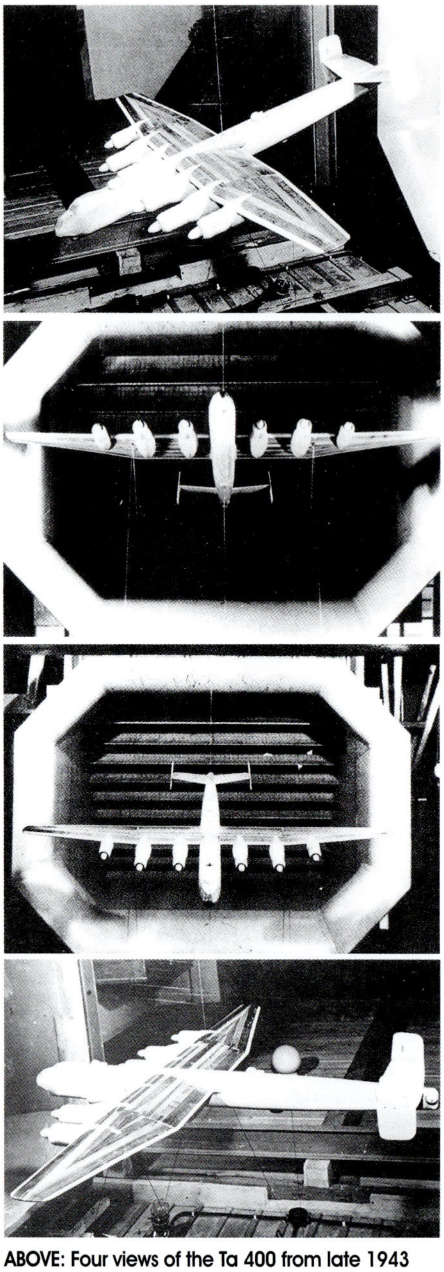

ABOVE: Four views of the Ta 400 from late 1943 undergoing wind tunnel testing. This version of the design was to have been fitted with a large glazed area above the crew cabin.

MESSERSCHMITT ME 264

It had been hoped that the first flight of the Me 264 prototype, commissioned back in 1941, would take place in October 1942 but there were problems from the outset. The undercarriage supplier VDM was unable to fulfil Messerschmitt's order on time and the aircraft's Jumo 211J-1 engines were delayed too.

The project had been given a low priority for resources so even a company as prestigious as Messerschmitt struggled to have the necessary parts manufactured. In October 1942, when the V1 was supposed to have been in the air, Milch commented that "the Me 264 is only of propaganda value". Eventually, the Me 264 V1's maiden flight took place on December 23, 1942.

In January, the RLM decided to hand the whole Me 264 project to Dornier to bring to fruition. During a meeting on February 12, 1943, Oberst Dr Georg Pasewaldt of the RLM's technical office said: "We discussed the long-range question regarding the Me 264 and gave the machine to Dornier. The Dornier company's staff were very mistrustful and in any case have such a workload that they can't handle it.

"We then took it back, because a reluctant approach is not useful. Besides, the Me 264 is so far nothing more than a flying mock-up. They still can't make anything serious out of it. What we are supposed to do next with a project like that is causing us serious problems at the moment."

On March 3, Pasewaldt reported that material for 30 Me 264s had been delivered to Messerschmitt, though this seems unlikely to have been true, since the design of the full production version had yet to be finalised. During the same meeting, while discussing air-to-air refuelling, he said: "Refuelling between two Ju 290s is better than a Ju 390 which

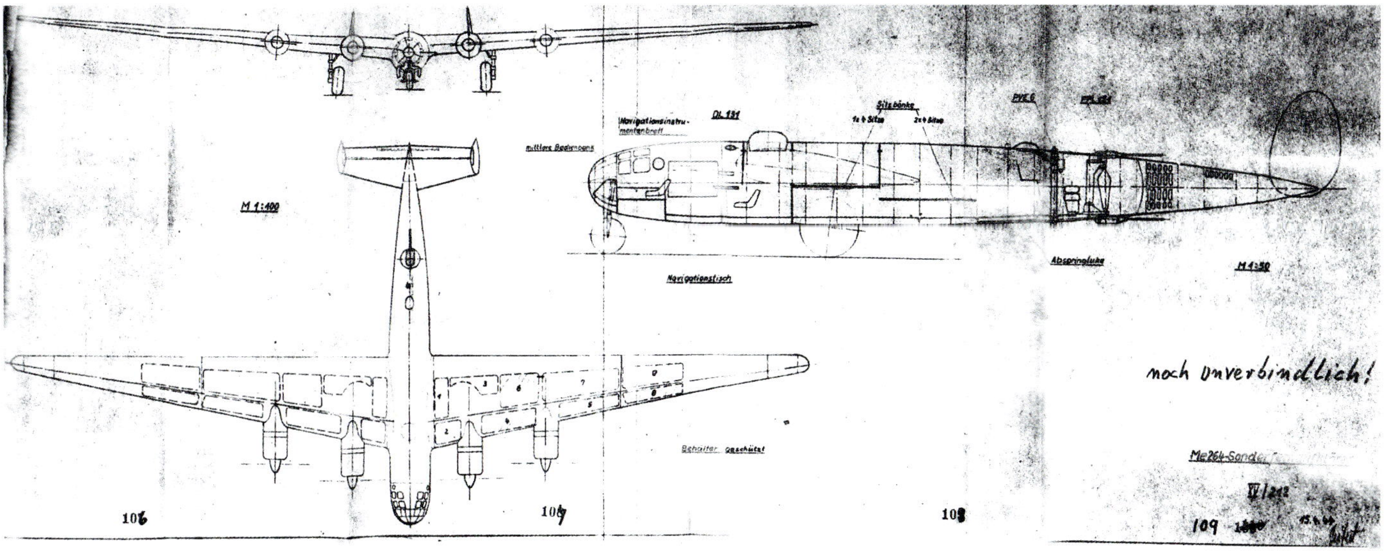

ABOVE: The Messerschmitt Me 264 as a Sonderfernaufklärer of 'special long-range reconnaissance' aircraft, as seen in drawing XV/212 of April 15, 1944. The basic form of the aircraft had changed little over the course of three years in development.

doesn't yet exist and much better than an Me 264 which will never exist".

Flight testing of the V1 continued, revealing various technical problems. The control surfaces were too powerful, the flight instruments were faulty and the undercarriage suffered repeated hydraulic failures. During a landing at Lechfeld on March 23 the left main suspension strut collapsed, forcing a halt to proceedings while repairs were carried out.

At a meeting on April 27, 1943, Erhard Milch said: "I think that there are still many obstacles and difficulties to be overcome before the four-engined Me 264 is a practical proposition. Here again we have the same construction difficulty.

"What worries me is that it can only get off the ground using rockets. I am no friend of such methods. Of course, I don't blame people for using them to break world records, but they shouldn't be for everyday use. Everything depends on good luck. If just one of the eight rocket boosters fails, the take-off will come to grief and probably leave us with a write-off. That is the spanner in the works."

Within three weeks, Milch had cancelled the Me 264 outright. The precise date of the cancellation is unclear, but it must fall between April 27, 1943, and May 13, 1943, when Messerschmitt produced a report entitled Serienablehnung der Me 264 durch das Amt or 'Series rejection of the Me 264 by the Office'. This makes it clear that the Me 264 has been cancelled in favour of the 'Focke-Wulf project'. In the introduction it says: "The rejection of the Me 264 is only due to incorrect comparisons, so below the project of Focke-Wulf and the Me 264 are juxtaposed in this detailed investigation." There then follows a report matching the characteristics of the Me 264 with the 'Focke-Wulf project', which is the Ta 400 in all but name.

A.I. (T)
17 SEP 1944
TRANSLATED

Teleprinter message

from Messerschmitt office in Paris, dated 3.2.44, to Herrn Bley, Messerschmitt office in Augsburg.

"Dr. Burckhardt and Herr Scheibe will be in Paris from 3.2.44. Negotiations regarding Caudron drawing-office staff and designers for Me.264. Presence of Herr Bley requested from 4.2.44.

Teleprinter message

from Fighter Staff, Messerschmitt in Augsburg, dated 12.7.44, to Herrn Sindern, Messerschmitt in Paris.

Presence of Herr Scherer in Augsburg on 17.7.44 absolutely essential, to deal with urgent questions connected with the beginning of production of the type in question.

Reply to previous message.

Teleprinter message

from Herr Sindern, Paris 12.7.44, to Herrn Hugo, Augsburg.

Me.264.

According to information received from the Heinkel office in Paris, presence of Herr Scherer not possible because of death in family. Herr Malsch will arrive on 16.7.44 instead of Herr Scherer.

Copy to A.I.2(g)

ABOVE: These Allied communications intercepts show efforts to transfer part of the Me 264 design work to Caudron in France. Discussions continue into July 1944 – when the Allies were close to breaking through German defences in Normandy.

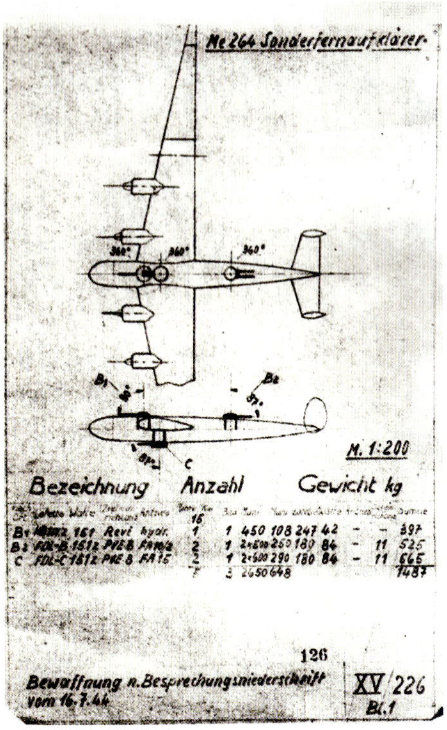

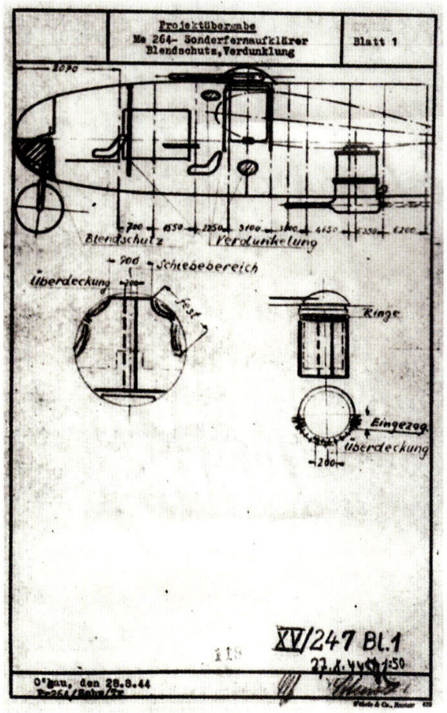

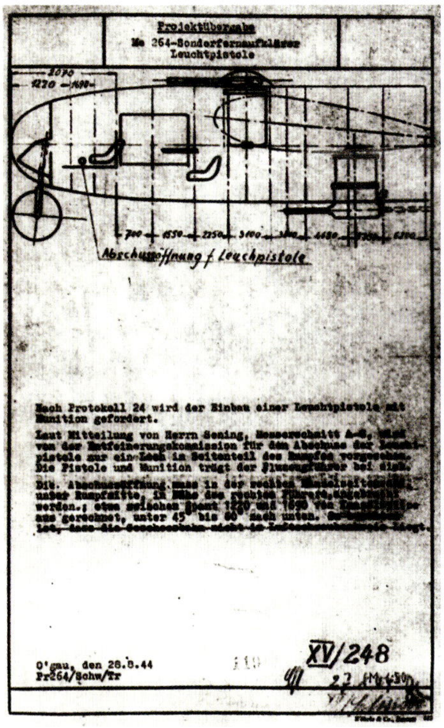

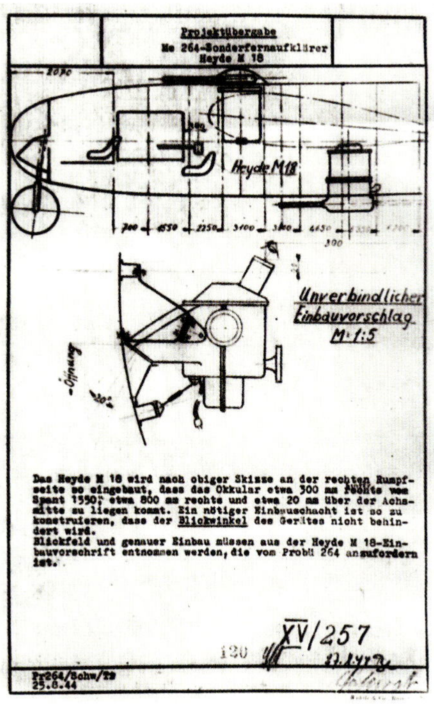

ABOVE: Messerschmitt drawings XV/226, XV/247, XV/248 and XV/257 show the design of the Me 264 Sonderfernaufklärer progressing through to the end of August 1944 – even though every effort was now being made in some quarters to have it cancelled.

At this point, the Me 264 was dead.

On June 15, 1943, the Luftwaffe General Staff engineer concluded: "What we have on hand at the moment for long-range reconnaissance are the Ju 290 and He 177 which can do the job for a while. They will be replaced by the Ta 400. Accordingly, this leaves the Me 264 in a poor position. I flew it recently and I believe it is the right thing to drop it."

Willy Messerschmitt, however, was unwilling to admit defeat and apparently went to Hitler personally to plead the case for the Me 264. On July 9, after around two months on the mortuary slab, the Me 264 was brought back to life and reinstated following the Führer's personal intervention but work continued at a snail's pace due to its low priority. At this point, Messerschmitt's resources were heavily invested in bringing the Me 262 jet fighter into production.

During a meeting on October 29, 1943, Milch said: "The Me 264 will not win the war. The Me 262 can win it. Therefore everything must be risked on the Me 262. If Messerschmitt completes the Me 262 and hasn't got anything more urgent then I would ask him to sort out the Me 264 so that we know if we should proceed with it or not.

"I do not need a machine that is able to fly 20,000km but breaks up on take-off, even if that only happens 10% of the time."

Efforts on Messerschmitt's part to continue the development of the Me 264 went on into 1944, in the face of disinterest from all other quarters. The company considered following Focke-Wulf down the road of outsourcing development to French companies, with Caudron being a possible contractor.

Further designs were drawn up during the summer for a long-range reconnaissance version of the aircraft but on July 18, 1944, the head of the Rechlin test centre, Oberst Edgar Petersen, attempted to have the type finally killed off. He reported: "The aircraft in its whole conception is not useful on the grounds of its too high wing loading, the complicated nature of its undercarriage, the exceptional length of runway required for take-off and the need for rocket boosters to assist in the endeavour, and the poor defensive armament.

"The basic idea of developing and then building the machine in a purpose-built fighter factory lacking any heavy aircraft experience is flawed and in our opinion it cannot be produced today without prejudice to the urgent Me 262 fighter production at Messerschmitt. The promised dates seem impossible to keep as still no kind of test data is available."

That same day the Me 264 V1 was wrecked in an air raid, along with the two other incomplete prototypes. But even then, Hitler himself stepped in again on August 5, 1944 and urged that production of the Me 264 should begin. Finally, work on the project was terminated on September 23, 1944.

JUNKERS JU 390

It had been resolved in May 1942 that the development of the six-engined Junkers Ju 390 would proceed but five months later, on October 20, 1942, it was decided that this work should be put on hold because of the negative impact it would have on the already painfully slow Ju 290 production line.

It had been calculated that shelving the Ju 390 would free up sufficient resources for the production of five more Ju 290s every month. Ten days later, the RLM decided that the Ju 390 should not be scrapped altogether, but instead a flying mock-up should be built using components from two Ju 290s and prepared for evaluation.

Drawings were completed by early 1943 and work then commenced on the Ju 390 V1's construction. It made its first flight on October 20, 1943, which was said to be a great success, and the type was scheduled to begin full series production in October 1944.

However, British intelligence report A.I. No. 65140 of January 10, 1944, states: "Ju 390 – Junkers transport plane with space for 120 men or equivalent in freight. It has an arrangement for carrying and catapulting a light fighter. This machine is powered by six BMW motors. It is of cheap construction, has performed badly and is very poorly regarded."

Intelligence report A.D.I. (K) 441, dated August 11, 1944, notes: "Ju 390 – six-engined. One delivered to F.A.G. 5 [Fernaufklärungsgruppe 5 or 'Long-range Reconnaissance Group 5'] for test purposes in Jan 1944. Said to have completed a reconnaissance to within 20km of American coast, north of New York, from Mont de Marsan [that unit's air base in the south-west of France]. Two of six engines (said to be BMW radials) were 'high altitude' engines. Endurance 32 hours."

A further note in the same file says: "Ju 390 (interrogation of Prof Hertel) only one of these was ever made". Hertel was Junkers' technical director Heinrich Hertel.

A.I.2 (g) report no. 2285 of November 7, 1944, states: "The Ju 390 is a six-engined aircraft which closely resembles the Ju 290 in design and general characteristics. Its intended functions are bombing and U-boat co-operation. Bomb load: the potential bomb load (for reduced range) is at least 20,000lb."

It is believed that the only completed Ju 390 was built from the extended fuselage of the Ju 90 V6, fitted with new wings, six BMW 801G-2 engines and four main undercarriage legs. Larger trapezoidal tail fins were added too, in place of the Ju 90's oval ones. Coded GH+UK, it was extensively tested until November 1944 when it was decommissioned at the Junkers company airfield at Dessau. In April 1945 it was set on fire and destroyed to prevent it from falling into the hands of the Allies. A second purpose-built Ju 390, the V2, was never completed.. ●

ABOVE: The one and only Ju 390 to be built, coded GH+UK, which first flew on October 20, 1943. Despite being chosen to enter production, the type was too time-consuming and costly by comparison to other types. Its development was initially frozen to allow for greater production capacity to be focused on the Ju 290, then the project was only worked on with very low priority.

LEFT: Essentially a grossly distended Ju 90, the only Ju 390 prototype was described as being of "cheap construction" in a 1944 British intelligence report.

BELOW: The Ju 390 V1 sits on the airfield at Dessau during the winter of 1944-45 with a tarpaulin over its windscreen, awaiting its fate – to be burned to the ground by Junkers staff.

Hitler intervenes

Heinkel He 277

With failure dogging his every step thanks to the He 177, Ernst Heinkel had abandoned plans to build a six-engined bomber and concentrated instead on fighter designs such as the He 219 and He 280. But then Adolf Hitler stepped in and the beleaguered industrialist was inspired to rejoin the fray…

At the beginning of 1943, a dispirited Heinkel could only look on while Focke-Wulf was awarded its Ta 400 development contract and the Ju 390 was finally made a reality, but around the time that a final decision on these projects was being made he was summoned, out of the blue, for a personal audience with Adolf Hitler.

On May 23, 1943, he was taken to Hitler's mountain retreat, the Berghof at Obersalzberg near Berchtesgaden, and according to his autobiography: "On my arrival, I found six of the best known German designers - Dornier, Messerschmitt, Tank, Blume of Arado, Hertel (who had left me and gone to Junkers), and Dr

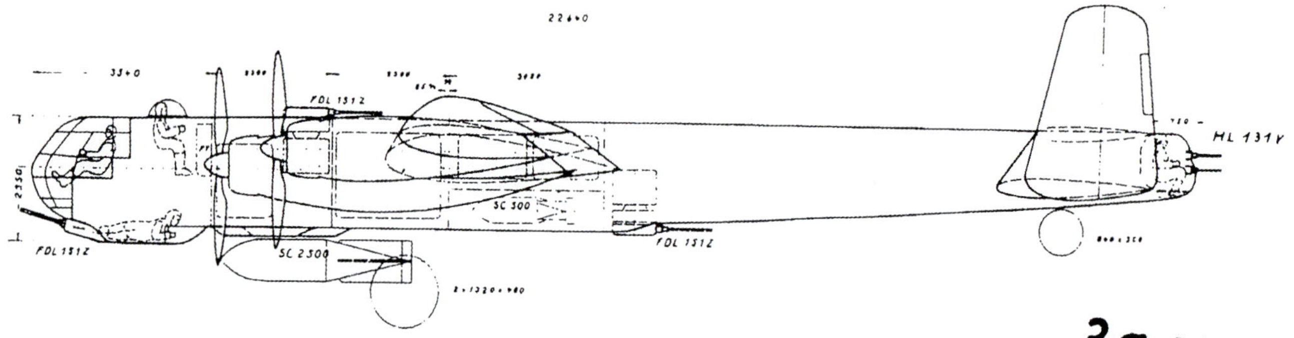

3c DB603

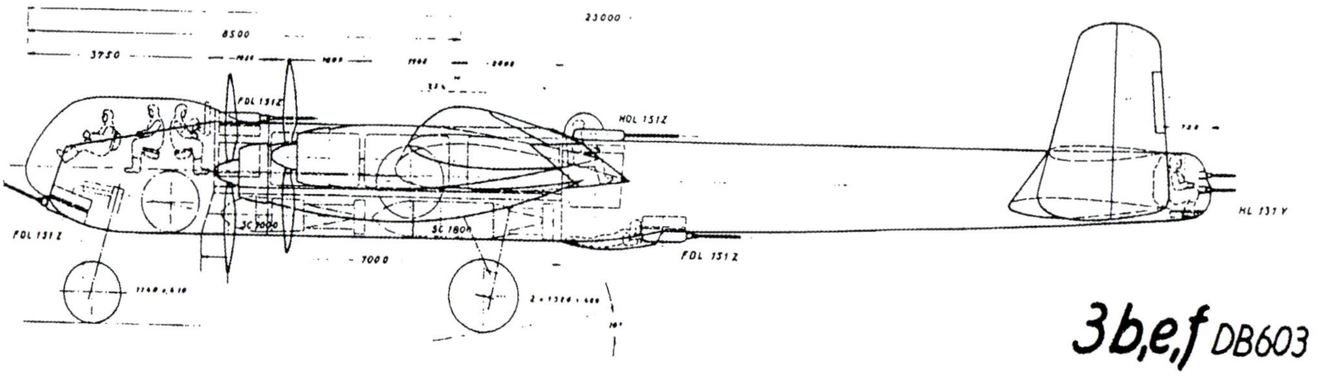

3b,e,f DB603

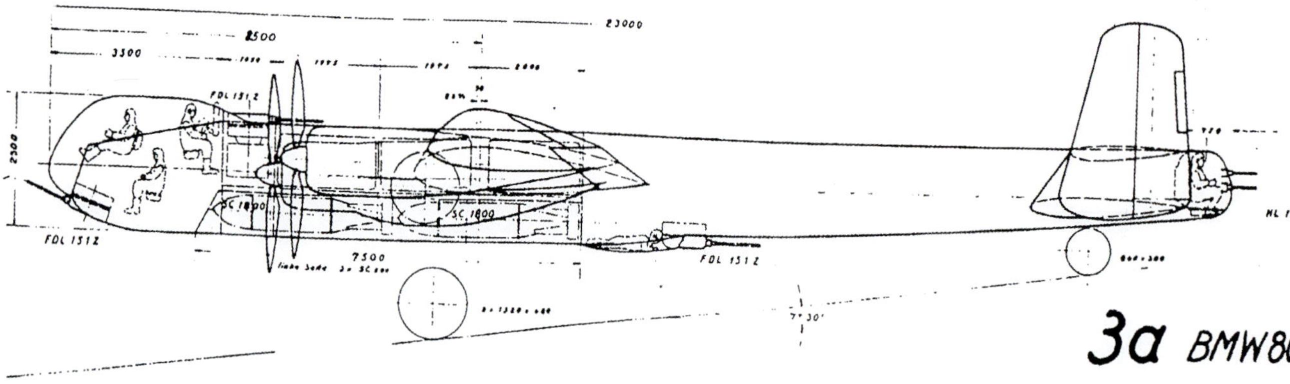

3a BMW801

ABOVE: A trio of Heinkel designs for an advanced four-engined bomber. Precisely what the final version of the He 277 was intended to look like remains a mystery, but given Ernst Heinkel's own description of it as featuring a tricycle undercarriage, it would seem that the design in the centre of these three comes closest. The only known drawings actually labelled 'He 277' show this design but with a tailwheel.

Vogt (of Blohm & Voss). I was rather surprised to see no representatives of the Luftwaffe, neither Göring, nor Milch, not even Hitler's air adjutant.

"We were called in to see Hitler one by one. I had brought [Heinkel production manager Karl] Schwärzler with me and was the first to go in. The Führer was calm and serious; he still looked in thoroughly good health. His first words cleared up the situation.

"He said with great frankness: 'The Luftwaffe knows nothing of this conference. I summoned you here so unexpectedly in order to prevent Göring or Milch putting their spoke in. I want to obtain a personal picture of the technical situation and one which is not painted in false colours by the gentlemen of the Luftwaffe. Until today, I have never interfered in Luftwaffe questions, because Göring produced the strongest air arm in the world, and for that reason I wished to demonstrate to the utmost my confidence in it. However, the terrible disappointments I have suffered during the past two years and an endless chain of information and promises which have proved to be false have compelled me to this direct approach. I require from you absolutely honest replies to the questions I'm going to ask you, and I want you to give me a ruthless, truthful picture of the situation.'

"He proceeded to ask me a number of pertinent questions, displaying a most surprising expert knowledge. In comparison with Göring, he had an astonishing grasp of air technicalities down to the smallest details. I have often thought about those 70 minutes' conversation, and I could fully understand why great technicians like Todt and Speer were strong supporters of Hitler.

"There has probably never been a politician who took such a burning interest in technical problems as he. After a short time, the conversation turned to the He 177. 'For three years this machine has been promised to me,' declared Hitler. 'For three years I've been waiting for a long-distance bomber. I can't bomb the convoys in the North Sea, nor can I bomb the Urals. The navy is screaming for air support in the Atlantic. Everything depends upon this machine. I want an absolutely direct reply to my question. When shall I get the He 177?'

"I gave him my opinion. When I mentioned the obstinate insistence upon dive-bombing performance, Hitler sprang to his feet. 'But that's madness,' he cried. 'I've heard nothing of this until today. Is it possible that there could be so many idiots?'

"Ultimately he began to develop a theme which was obviously a great favourite. He wanted 40 or 50 planes which could fly over England at 45,000ft, out of reach of enemy fighters, and appear in shifts over London to bomb it day and night. 'Such continuous bombing attacks,' he said, 'would bring life there to a standstill.' He felt a desperate need to hit back in some way at England."

Heinkel said he believed that this conversation, and what Hitler evidently told his subordinates afterwards, had been a game-changer. Suddenly the RLM became interested in a version of the He 177 with four separate engines where proposals of a similar nature had been previously been rejected.

ABOVE: Ernst Heinkel claimed that an He 277 was completed at Zwölfaxing, near Vienna, during the spring of 1944. Could this be what he meant? Certainly the He 177 V101 pictured here first flew with four separate engines on December 20, 1943, at Zwölfaxing. And the V102 and V104 were both tested with twin fins and rudders, like those intended for the He 277. However, the V101's arrangement pre-dates the He 277, based on Heinkel's account, and was in fact a prototype for the He 177B-5.

Heinkel continued: "Now, in that autumn of 1943, in view of the gloomy course the war was taking, I could easily see that this machine would come far too late to play a decisive role. Even if everything went well, mass production could not be counted on before 1945.

"Over and above that, the question would then arise as to what possible use Germany would be able to find for a plane so uncompromisingly designed for offensive warfare. Defence! Fighters! These were the only possible help for us. But as a designer I at least wanted to prove that four-engined development was the solution to all the difficulties which for years had so pointlessly kept the He 177 in pickle. We started to work."

He said that the design of the four-engined He 277 took shape very quickly. Although it was initially based on the He 177, the He 277 that emerged was an entirely new machine. Some Heinkel drawings show it as having either a 33m wingspan and 21.8m fuselage or a 40m wingspan and 23m fuselage. In either case, the four engines were to be BMW 801s. However, further proposed engine options apparently included DB 603s, Jumo 222s or Jumo 213s.

The tail was to have twin fins and rudders, while the defensive armament consisted of an FDL 151 Z on the forward upper fuselage, another on the rear upper fuselage, a third on the rear lower fuselage and an HL 131 V with a quartet of MG 131s in the tail.

Heinkel went on to recall, somewhat inaccurately with regard to the USAAF's use of Boeing B-29s, that "it corresponded in size to the 'Super Fortress', which at that time was appearing over Germany in increasing numbers. However, with a speed of 575kph (356mph) the He 277 was considerably faster. It was powered by four DB 603 engines, weighed 45 tons and was fitted with all the up-to-date equipment which had proved itself of value up to that time, including a tricycle undercarriage, which was still a novelty in Germany for machines of this size.

"The crew of six were housed in a cabin which could be pressurized for high-altitude flight. The whole of the defensive armament, forward, aft, above and below could be remote-controlled from the cabin. The minimum bomb-load was 2000kg (4400lb) and the range 6250km (3875 miles)."

Heinkel went on to say that the first He 277 had been produced during the spring of 1944 at Zwölfaxing, near Vienna, and that its performance had actually exceeded that of the He 177 "on which the old shapes had been clung to so tenaciously for reasons of speed".

He said that Hitler had continued to follow the He 277's development with interest and had continued to question Göring about it until early 1944 when he had finally been persuaded that there was no longer any real opportunity to launch bomber attacks against the Allies and that the Reich's best hope lay in a strong defensive fighter force.

"This was the situation when Göring called a meeting of industrial chiefs for May 25, 1944, in the SS Barracks at the Obersalzberg. The conference was already under the new rationalising hands of Speer and Saur. Their aim was to scrap many of the major types in service with the Luftwaffe and in future to concentrate on building only defensive weapons. On that day the Ju 390, Ju 188, Ju 288, Ju 352, Me 110 and the He 219 were shelved.

"Göring as president was, as usual, merely a façade, badly informed and as unscientific as ever. On the question of the He 277, however, probably with a view to pacifying Hitler, he was surprisingly active. He maintained that this machine should be put into production as quickly as possible to obtain an output of 200 a month.

"No one, neither Milch nor any of the authoritative officers of the Ministry, dared to contradict him. Oberst Walter Marienfeld, who was sitting next to me, whispered: 'The He 277 is the most important machine of all. The Reichsmarschall goes to bed with it every night and gets up with it every morning.'

"I made no reply. At that time what could I have replied? Göring had not once taken the trouble to be present at a test of the machine. A fortnight before we had eagerly awaited a visit from him when he had been in Vienna. The next day I learned that instead of keeping his appointment, he had spent several hours in the well-known jewellery shop of Christiane Voith on the Lobkowitzplatz."

Heinkel said that on July 3, 1944, the He 277 had been "silently removed" from the production programme, which effectively put an end to any further involvement in strategic bomber design at the Heinkel company. ●

Arrow wing and flying wing

Arado E 560 and E 555

Working on the Ar 234 jet from late 1940 onwards led Arado to assess a range of high-speed aerodynamic forms. As the projects developed, the firm compiled a research paper on how the resulting new wing shapes might be used to create a two-seater twin-engined jet bomber.

When Arado was ordered to build a straightforward reconnaissance aircraft powered by jet engines in 1940, the company had little idea of how best to approach the problem.

It therefore took the simplest route and opted for a straight fuselage and unswept wings with the engines slung beneath them in easily accessible nacelles – producing the Ar 234. But the more work was done to optimise the design, with data gathered from Germany's many experimental stations and testing sites, the more obvious it became that improved aerodynamics would deliver better performance.

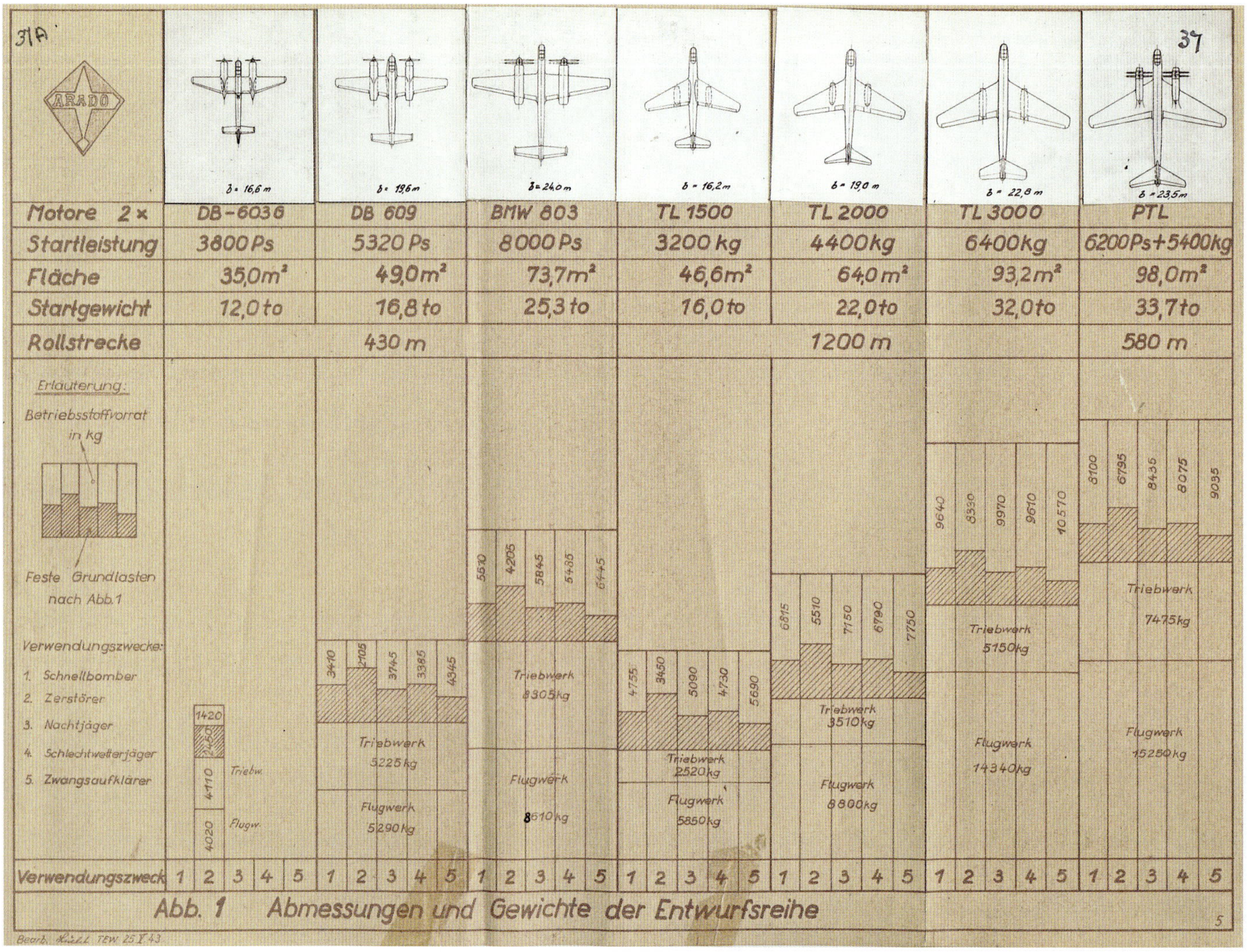

ABOVE: Seven different designs lined up for comparison in Arado's two-engined fast aircraft proposal. First is the Ar 440, next a similarly configured design but larger and powered by two DB 609s, then an even larger aircraft powered by two BMW 803s, then three jets, each with the straight-edged E 560 wing, and finally a huge turboprop-powered aircraft. Values are given for each in five different roles – fast bomber, heavy fighter, night fighter, bad weather fighter and armed reconnaissance.

ABOVE: Arado's smallest swept-wing bomber design in profile. The crew's pressure cabin is clearly derived from that of the Ar 240/440. Art by Daniel Uhr

Therefore, in November 1942, the company established a new experimental programme under the designation E 560 to assess the potential of different swept or pfeilflügel 'arrow wing' shapes. It was hoped that a swept wing form, either straight or kinked, could be developed for use with future high-speed aircraft. From the outset, it was considered that E 560 wings might well be suitable for the next stage of the Ar 234's development too.

Extensive wind tunnel testing followed which concentrated on the relationship between an aircraft's fuselage, swept wings and jet engines but because Arado lacked the necessary wind tunnels of its own, it had to rely on contractors to get the work done.

The organisations involved – first Messerschmitt, then the Luftfahrtforschungsanstalt (LFA) at Völkenrode near Brunswick in central Germany and the Flugtechniche Versuchsanstalt (FVA) at Prague in Czechoslovakia, and finally the Aerodynamische Versuchsanstalt (AVA) at Göttingen – received instructions, had test materials delivered to them and were expected to carry out the experiments before reporting back.

This indirect process resulted in delays which stretched from weeks into months but nevertheless early results were positive. After nine months, on August 11, 1943, the company produced a report entitled Vorschlag für die Weiterentwicklung schneller Zweisitzer or 'Proposal for the development of a fast two-seater'.

In its introduction, it states that the further development of piston or 'Otto' engined fast two-seater aircraft was likely to be difficult and expensive because the piston engine had reached the limits of its potential. As an example, it gave the company's own Ar 440 – a development of the earlier Ar 240 heavy fighter.

It says: "The aircraft type 'Ar 440' is at the limit and is difficult to surpass for the above reasons. Through the use of TL-engines instead of Otto engines, however, there is a reasonable prospect of skipping this boundary at a stroke and taking a big step forward on the way of further driving the flight performance.

"Due to this situation, and in view of the fact that a two-seater with a cockpit at the front has a number of uses, and provides the basis for a particularly favourable combination of aircraft performance, armament, operational capability, and is good for both its crew and for production, its future development has been investigated and we have clarified a proposal for its direction."

The basic two-engined layout of the Ar 440, with a two-seater pressure cabin right at the front of the fuselage, was used as a basis for a series of six new designs. The first was a little bigger than the Ar 440 and powered by a pair of DB 609s – a development of the DB 603 which powered the Ar 440. An even larger aircraft powered by a pair of BMW 803s driving contra-rotating propellers followed.

Next, there was an aircraft with swept wings powered by a pair of jet engines. Its wingspan was given as 16.2m and its weight was 16 tonnes. Then there was a 19m wingspan two-jet aircraft weighing 22 tonnes and then another with a 22.8m wingspan weighing 32 tonnes. Finally, there was a turboprop-powered design with a 23.5m wingspan and a weight of 33.7 tonnes.

The jet aircraft and the turboprop had the latest E 560 swept wing, but scaled up in each case to suit the application. Each of the six designs was assessed as a fast bomber, a heavy fighter, a night fighter, a bad weather fighter and an armed reconnaissance aircraft.

In particular, the report concentrated on the 16 tonne aircraft, the smallest jet-powered design. This, it was argued, represented the best possible power-to-weight ratio using a pair of Jumo 012 engines. The Jumo 012, only a drawing board project at this point, had an 11-stage axial compressor and a two-stage turbine.

The report features detailed illustrations of this aircraft design as a heavy fighter and as a heavy bomber and presents a version powered by six BMW 003s, since these engines were expected to be available sooner than the Jumo 012. Another illustration shows how the Arado design would be armed for the five different roles outlined in the report.

The report's unnamed author enthuses: "The design here revealed, under the prescribed conditions, represents a new frontier of performance improvement. Consideration of the climb performance also leads to a finding of great performance leaps by the transition to jet engines – with the prospect, also in this case to gain even more benefits by further development of the smallest design."

In concluding, the report sets out a "Proposal for the continuation of the work". This states: "In effect the investigation finally resulted in a proposal for a single development. This is shown in a short description. It builds on two components whose planned safe control is not fully guaranteed, namely the Jumo TL-109-012, which is still in development, and a wing of strong arrow shape.

"So that the objectives shown in the proposal can be reached as quickly as possible, the following is proposed: 1. Immediate start-up of an aircraft development on the type of final design shown, with an alternate solution to the Jumo motors being the use of 6 x BMW TL-109-003A engines that are also in development. 2. Accelerate the development of the necessary Jumo TL-109-012. 3. Expedite preliminary tests in order to overcome the many unfavourable expectations about the flight characteristic behaviour of the swept wing, and connected issues relating to engine exhausting." ▶

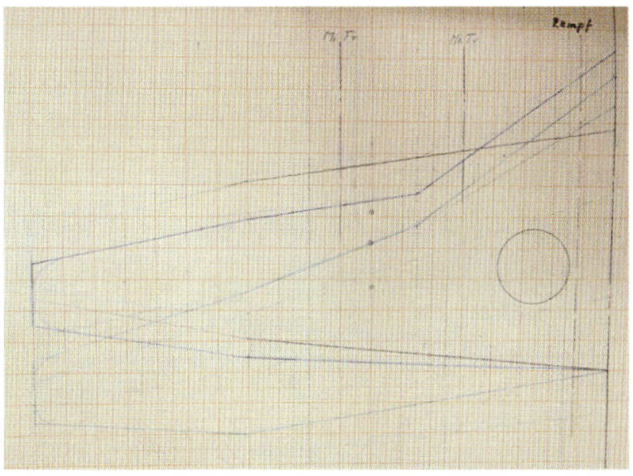

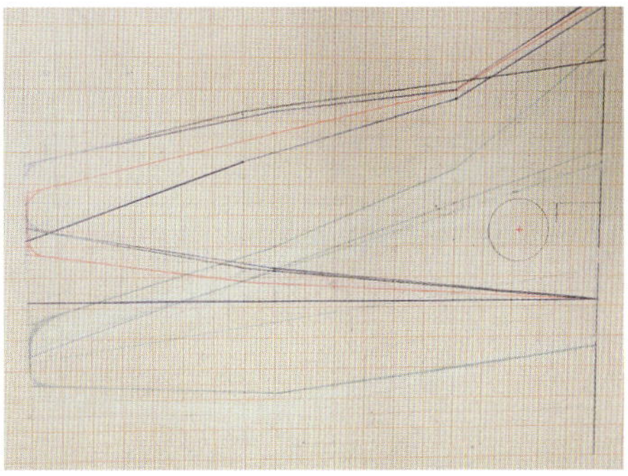

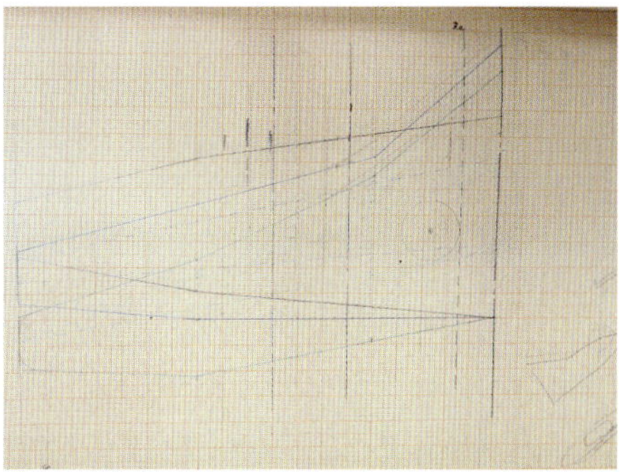

ABOVE: A variety of wing form sketches from a file of work on Arado's E 560 project. The undefined fuselage 'Rumpf' is on the right and the circle represents the positioning of the landing gear main wheel. Only one of the images bears a date – November 28, 1942.

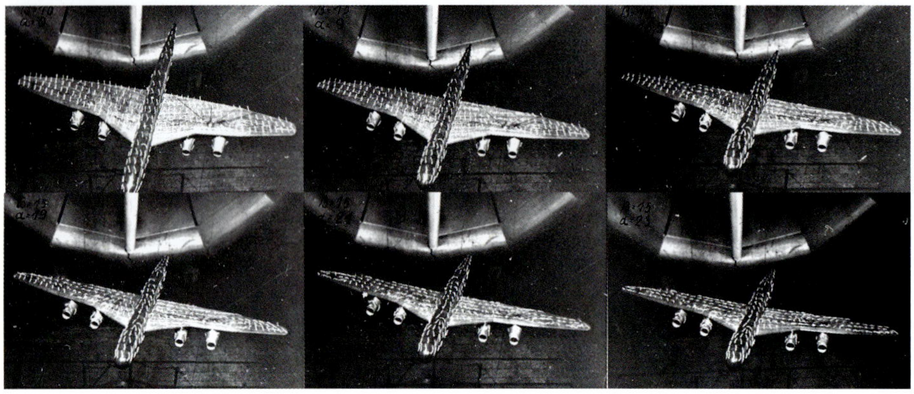

ABOVE: Six wind tunnel photos showing tests carried out on an E 560 fuselage-wing-engine nacelle form. E 560 was not intended to produce any particular sort of aircraft – only designs for swept wings which could then be applied to other configurations.

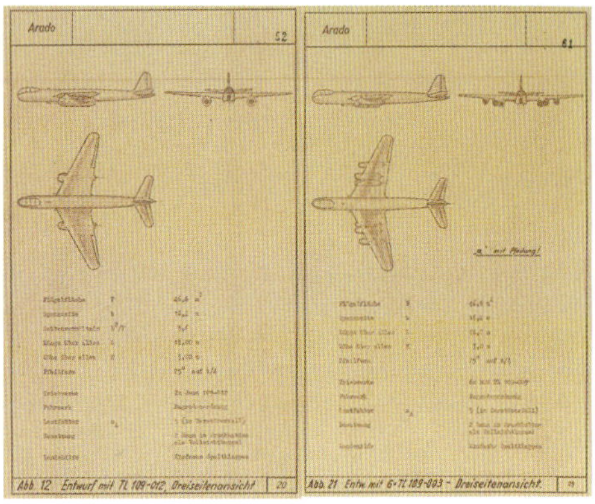

ABOVE: This configuration of a two-seater multi-purpose jet aircraft was presented by Arado in August 1943 in a proposal that it hoped would ensure funding for further development. The first design was to be powered by a pair of Jumo 012 engines and the second by six less powerful BMW 003s.

Rather than resulting in Arado being given leave to develop its two-seater jet aircraft, a design with greater multirole potential than the Ar 234, the effect of this report seems to have been to spur the RLM into commencing a new competition to find the Luftwaffe a jet bomber.

It seems likely that the lack of wind tunnel test data to support Arado's risky swept-wing design weighed against it and in September 1943, less than a month after 'Proposal for the development of a fast two-seater' had been issued, the RLM invited tenders for a new 'Strahlbomber' from Arado, Junkers and Blohm & Voss.

The Arado entry, project E 395, abandoned the straight swept leading edge version of the E 560 wing and offered instead a two-seater with a choice of either unswept wings or a less sharply swept 'crescent' version of the E 560. More detail on this project and the competition for which it was entered can be found on pages 76-77.

MOSQUITO KILLERS WITH E 560 WINGS

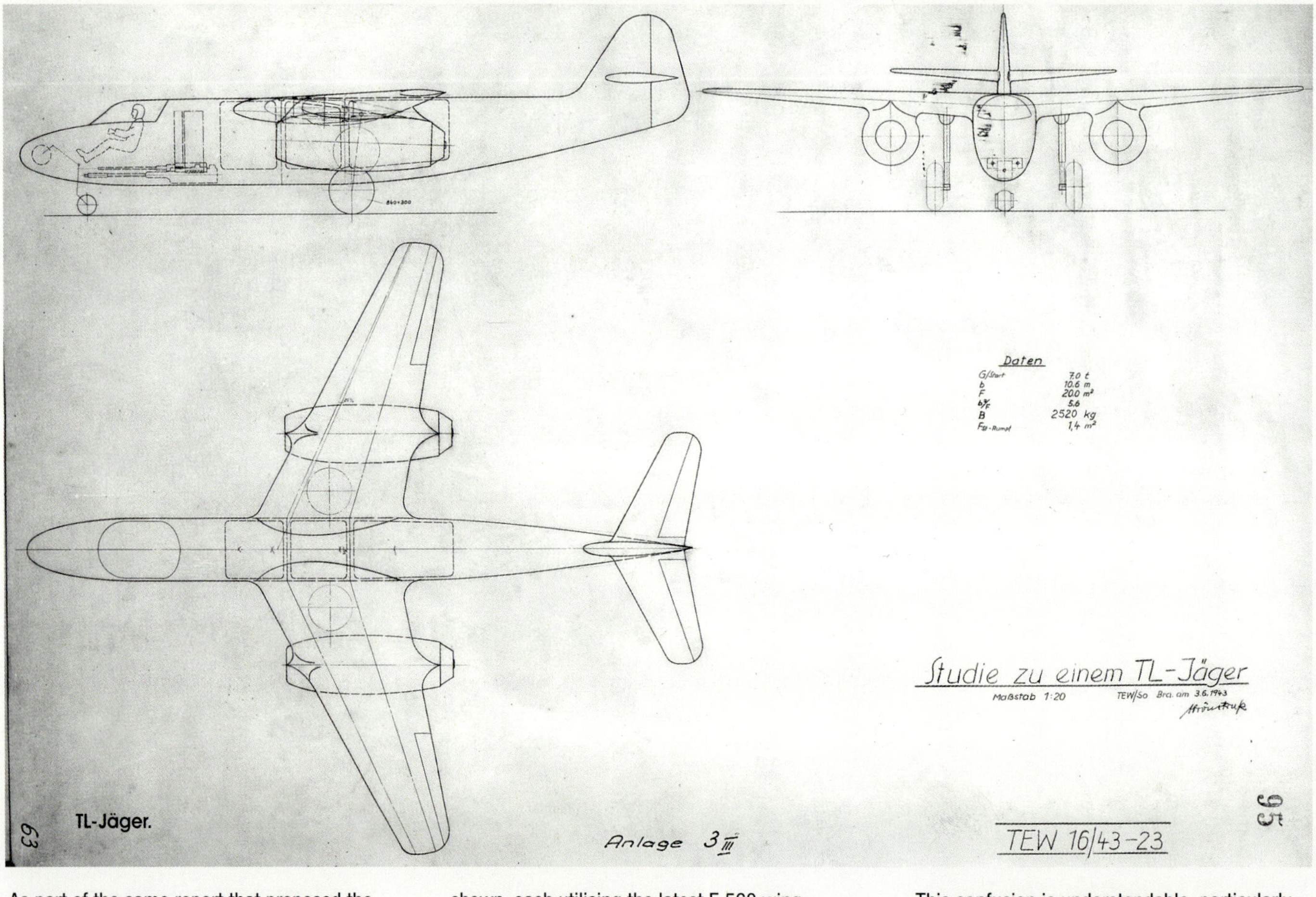

As part of the same report that proposed the building of a new two-seater fast aircraft, Arado put forward its ideas for single-seat interceptors designed to tackle high-flying Allied reconnaissance aircraft – particularly the de Havilland Mosquito.

Three different sample designs called the TL-Jäger, the R-Jäger and the K-Jäger were shown, each utilising the latest E 560 wing form. These have subsequently, and incorrectly, become known by the numbers of the drawings that depict them. The Arado TL-Jäger appears in drawing TEW 16/43-23 of June 3, 1943, the Arado R-Jäger in drawing TEW 16/43-13 of March 18, 1943, and the K-Jäger in TEW 16/43-15 of March 20, 1943.

This confusion is understandable, particularly in the latter case, since although the accompanying report makes extensive reference to the K-Jäger, short for 'Kombinationsjäger' for its mixed jet/rocket propulsion, the drawing itself does not bear this name.

The section of the Vorschlag für die Weiterentwicklung schneller Zweisitzer report

RIGHT: Arado had begun work on its Ar 240 heavy fighter project during the late 1930s and perhaps its ultimate development in that arrangement was the Ar 440 heavy fighter/bomber. Note the smoothly curving bubble design of the pressure cabin.

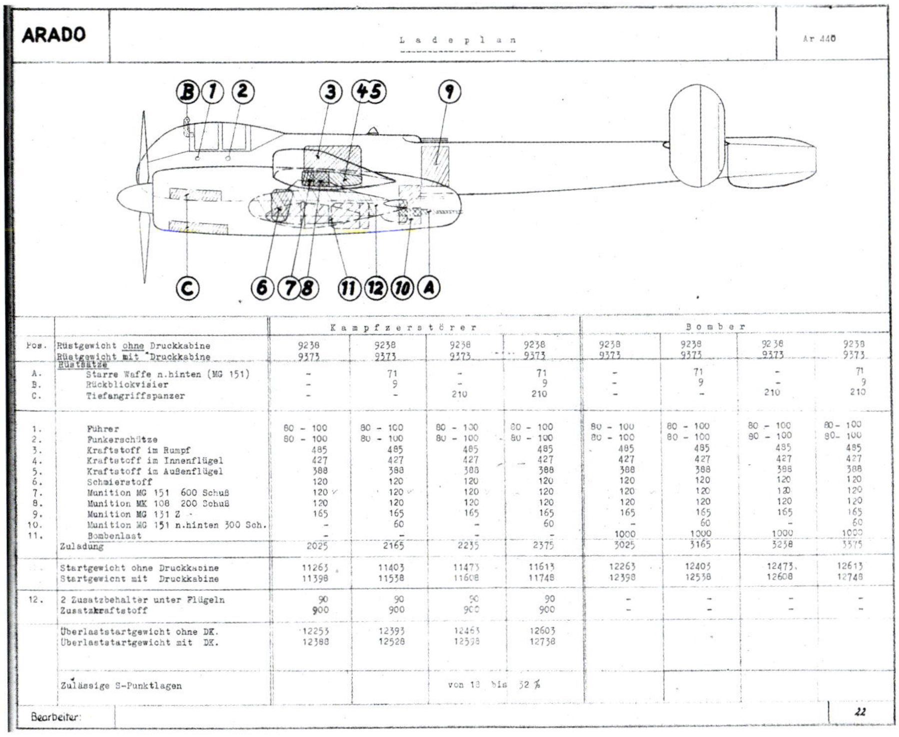

ARADO — Ladeplan — Ar 440

Pos.		Kampfzerstörer				Bomber			
	Rüstgewicht ohne Druckkabine	9238	9238	9238	9238	9238	9238	9238	9238
	Rüstgewicht mit Druckkabine	9373	9373	9373	9373	9373	9373	9373	9373
	Rüstsätze								
A.	Starre Waffe n.hinten (MG 151)	-	71	-	71	-	71	-	71
B.	Rückblickvisier	-	9	-	9	-	9	-	9
C.	Tiefangriffspanzer	-	-	210	210	-	-	210	210
1.	Führer	80 - 100	80 - 100	80 - 100	80 - 100	80 - 100	80 - 100	80 - 100	80 - 100
2.	Funkerschütze	80 - 100	80 - 100	80 - 100	80 - 100	80 - 100	80 - 100	80 - 100	80 - 100
3.	Kraftstoff im Rumpf	485	485	485	485	485	485	485	485
4.	Kraftstoff im Innenflügel	427	427	427	427	427	427	427	427
5.	Kraftstoff im Außenflügel	388	388	388	388	388	388	388	388
6.	Schmierstoff	120	120	120	120	120	120	120	120
7.	Munition MG 151 600 Schuß	120	120	120	120	120	120	120	120
8.	Munition MK 108 200 Schuß	120	120	120	120	120	120	120	120
9.	Munition MG 131 Z	165	165	165	165	165	165	165	165
10.	Munition MG 151 n.hinten 300 Sch.	-	60	-	60	-	60	-	60
11.	Bombenlast	-	-	-	-	1000	1000	1000	1000
	Zuladung	2025	2165	2235	2375	3025	3165	3238	3375
	Startgewicht ohne Druckkabine	11263	11403	11473	11613	12263	12403	12473	12613
	Startgewicht mit Druckkabine	11398	11538	11608	11748	12398	12538	12608	12748
12.	2 Zusatzbehalter unter Flügeln	90	90	90	90	-	-	-	-
	Zusatzkraftstoff	900	900	900	900	-	-	-	-
	Überlaststartgewicht ohne DK.	12253	12393	12463	12603				
	Überlaststartgewicht mit DK.	12388	12528	12598	12738				
	Zulässige S-Punktlagen			von 18 bis 32 %					

Bearbeiter: 22

FLYING WING BOMBERS

After January 1944, wind tunnel work on the E 560 wings continued but now with a firm focus on providing them for an upgraded version of the Ar 234. Meanwhile, Arado launched another experimental programme to run in parallel - E 555. This was intended to examine the nurflügel or all-wing form with little or no fuselage in between.

The earliest known document from the E 555 programme is dated July 14, 1943, and comprises a chart showing the horizontal top speeds of configurations E 555-6, -7, -8 and 10, each of which was to have been fitted with a trio of BMW 018 engines.

The last known document relating directly to the E 555 'Nurflügelprojekt' as it is entitled in Arado company documents, a handwritten sheet of calculations, is dated August 15, 1944. However, activity on the ▶

that deals with the interceptors, Appendix 2, begins: "Preview of future technical and tactical possibilities of next-step fighter aircraft. General requirements for a fighter to combat rapid aircraft.

"For rapid aircraft flying at high altitude, despite a well-organized reporting system, defensive fighters have little time to go on the attack. Therefore, a very large rate of climb is absolutely necessary and aircraft with Otto engines must be separated from those with more suitable propulsion.

"The fighter must be at least equipped with jet engines, but would not be significantly superior to the enemy in this arrangement. Above all, the rate of climb would still be regarded as insufficient, since the altitude greatly decreases the thrust of jet devices, which means a significant decrease in the rate of climb.

"By contrast, with a rocket-powered fighter (here called R-Jäger) large rates of climb and steep climb angle are possible, but due to the high specific fuel consumption has completely inadequate range, whereby the possibility of a dogfighting battle is called into question.

"If one wants to succeed with a fighter against a rapid opponent, one must combine high-altitude performance with climbing speed, long range and horizontal velocity. Even under these conditions, a successful interception will be possible only with excellent reporting and guidance to the target.

"These conditions are only applicable when the fighter is equipped both with a turbojet engine and an intermittently connectable rocket engine. This combination fighter (here called K-Jäger) alone has the potential to fight and destroy rapid opponents."

The report then goes on to outline the equipment, advantages and disadvantages of the TL-Jäger, R-Jäger and K-Jäger before concluding that the K-Jäger offers the best performance. None of these designs seems to have been intended as the basis for a real aircraft – they were simply illustrating a point.

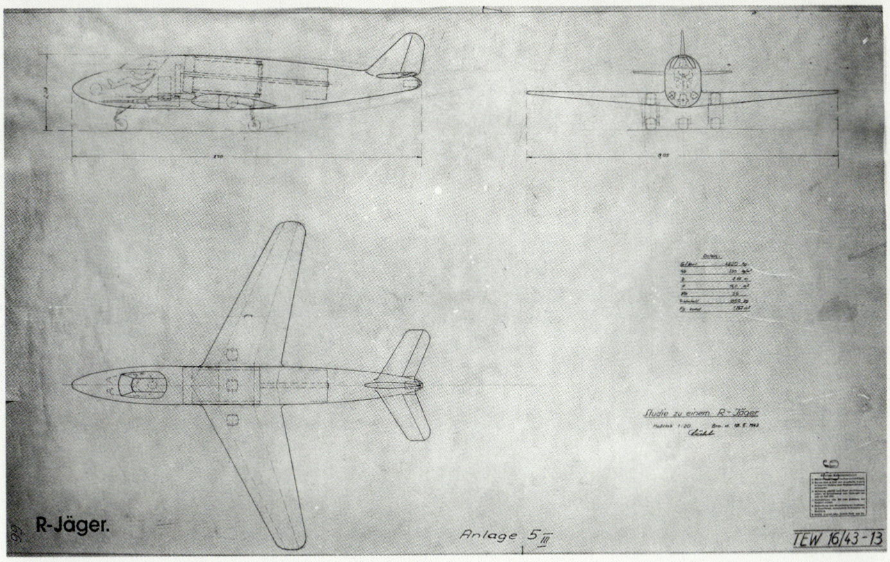

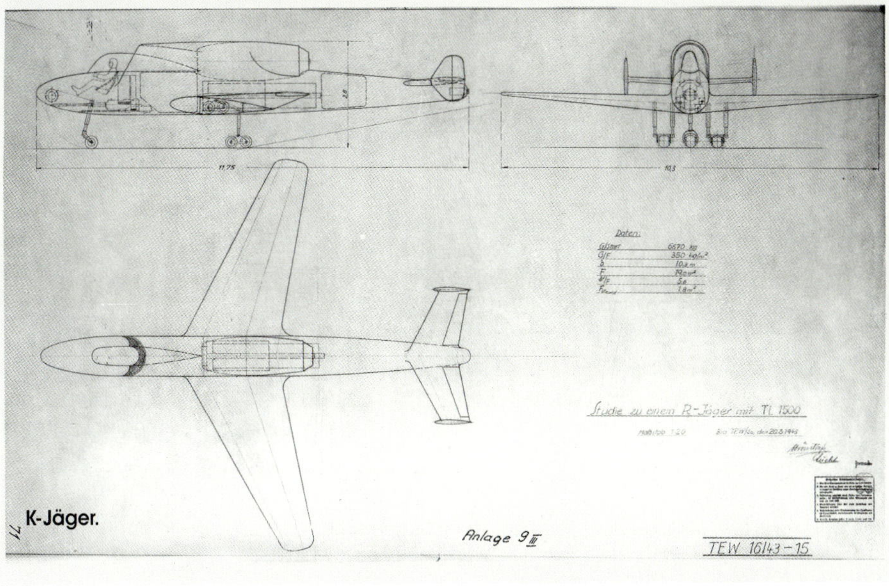

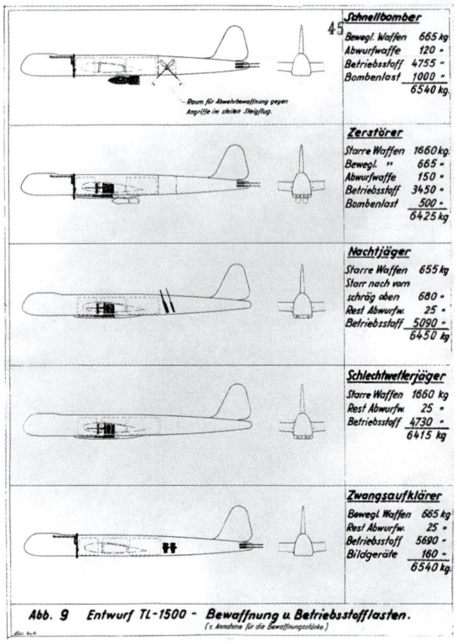

ABOVE: Weapons layouts for the five different roles envisioned for Arado's proposed fast two-seater.

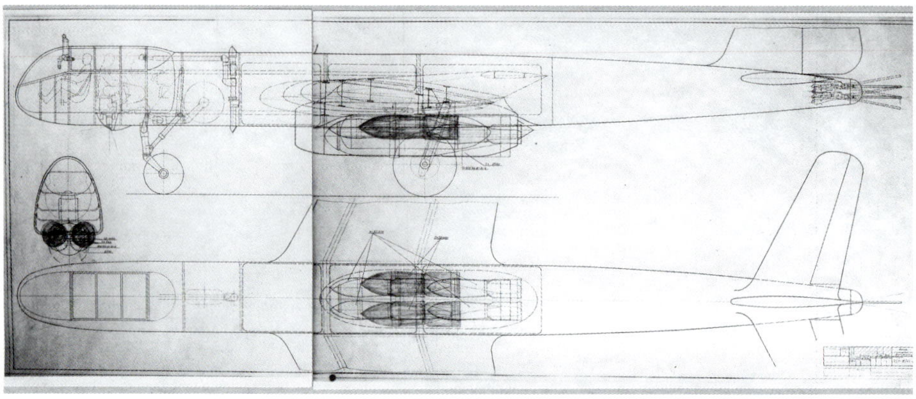

ABOVE: The Arado fast two-seater jet designed in detail as a bomber. In this drawing, TEW 16/43-26 of June 19, 1943, the payload is semi-recessed into the fuselage. Another drawing, TEW 16/43-24 of the same day, showed it as a heavy fighter.

project seems to have peaked between September 1943 and February 1944.

Then, on October 18, 1944, Arado issued a report entitled Bomber für Höhe Geschwindigkeit und Grosse Reichweite or 'A high-speed long-range bomber' which offered up the E 555 flying wing designs that had existed in one form or another since the summer of 1943 configured as a selection of bombers without using the E 555 designation, just as the fast bomber proposal had not mentioned E 560.

It seems that at least a dozen E 555 configurations existed but some were passed over in choosing 10 to present with the report. These were forms 1, 2, 3, 4, 7, 8a, 8b, 9, 10 and 11.

They varied considerably in layout, ranging from just one engine to six, depending on the powerplant. Some had tail fins on their trailing edge, three had twin-boom tails and one had a conventional fuselage but with the characteristic E 555 wing shape superimposed over it.

Mirroring what happened after Arado put forward its proposal for a new two-seat fast bomber, a new jet bomber development competition was launched around a month after the publication of 'A high-speed long-range bomber'. It was entitled Langstreckenbomber – but this time there would be no formal entry from Arado. Instead, Messerschmitt would compete against Junkers and rank outsiders the Horten brothers. Details of this competition can be found on p106-113.

While work on the Arado flying wing designs appears to have resolved itself into a report and ceased thereafter, work was continued on the E 560 shapes throughout 1944 and Arado was forced to write letters to the LFA and FVA urging them to get the work done quickly and the latest sets of results sent.

One letter from the head of the Arado projects office, Rüdiger Kosin, to the FVA, dated March 18, 1944, states: "Herewith we are sending you the measurement programme for the final measurement of the E 560 models in the Prague 3m wind tunnel that is to be carried out.

"We ask again that you perform the measurements as soon as possible, because we urgently need the measured values as a dossier for the swept-wing Ar 234 that is already under construction."

By the end of 1944, work on both E 560 and E 555 had ceased, but both research programmes would be given a new lease of life in January 1945 when they were resurrected as alternative wing layouts for Arado's entry in the night and bad weather jet fighter competition – the last such design contest of the war. They were presented simply as Arado 'Projekt 1' and 'Projekt 2' – though the former, a flying wing, had been chosen from at least seven different configurations. ●

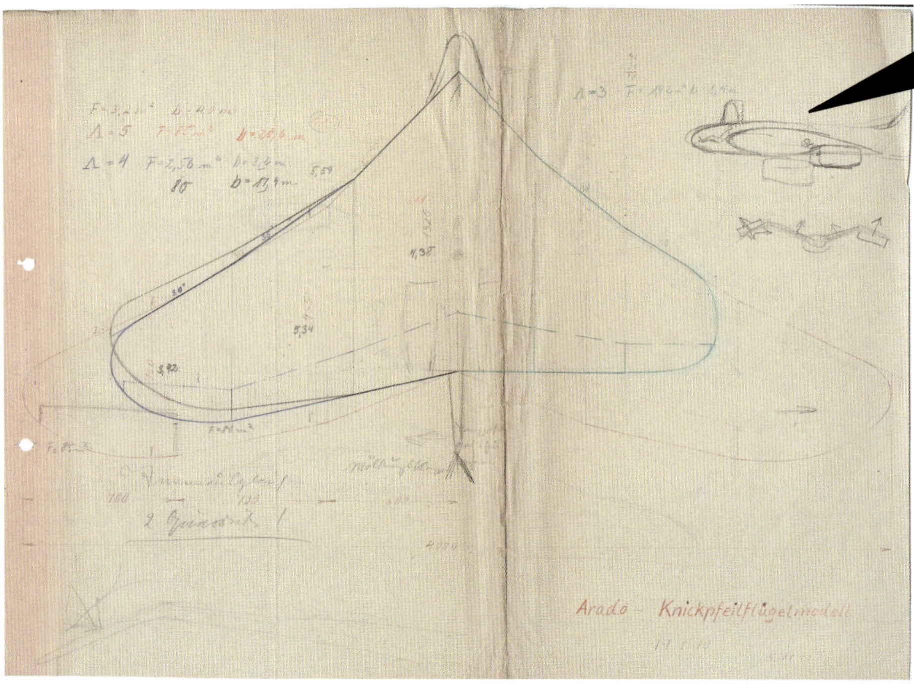

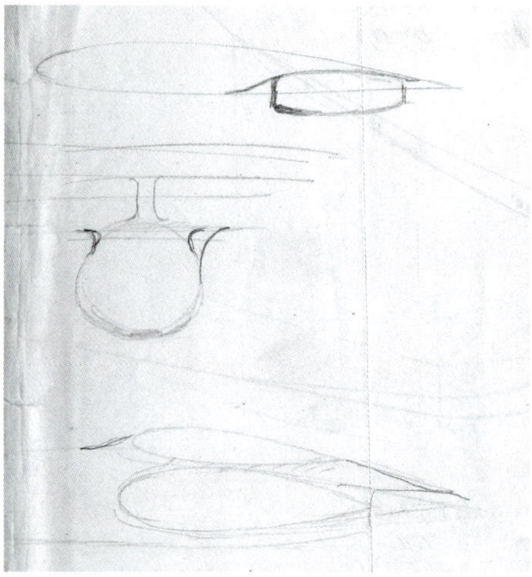

ABOVE: Hand-drawn sketch labelled "Knickpfeilflügelmodell" or 'creased arrow wing model' from the Arado E 555 project file dated November 5, 1943. This shows a range of different wing forms under consideration, along with tentative moves towards a tail. A small drawing on the same sheet (inset) shows a side view of an aircraft with one of the wings illustrated and what appears to be a very large periscope. On the reverse of the sheet are more sketches showing potential engine arrangements (pictured right).

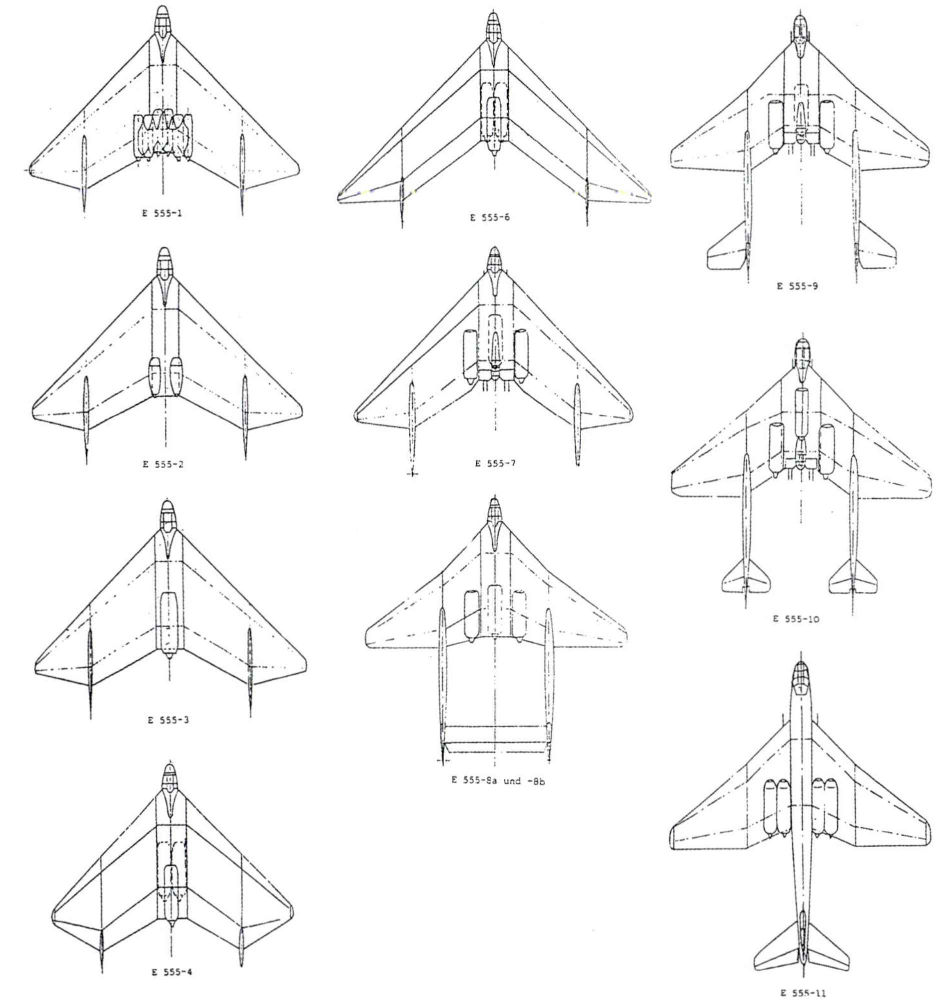

ABOVE: The culmination of the E 555 flying wing project was a report in October 1944 proposing a high-speed long-range bomber based on the wing forms that had been researched and tested. Only these 10 possible configurations were offered but no doubt many more were assessed.

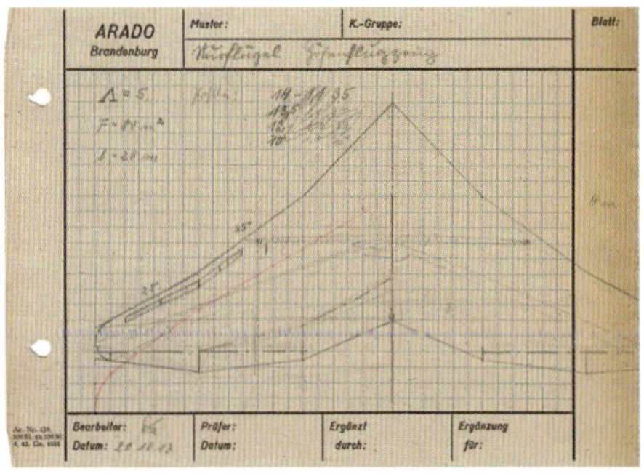

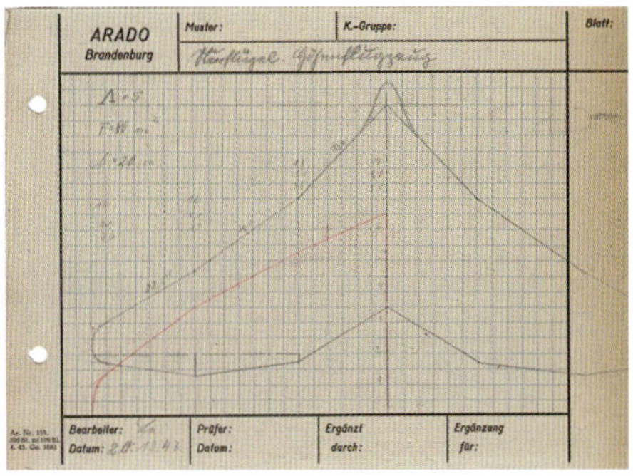

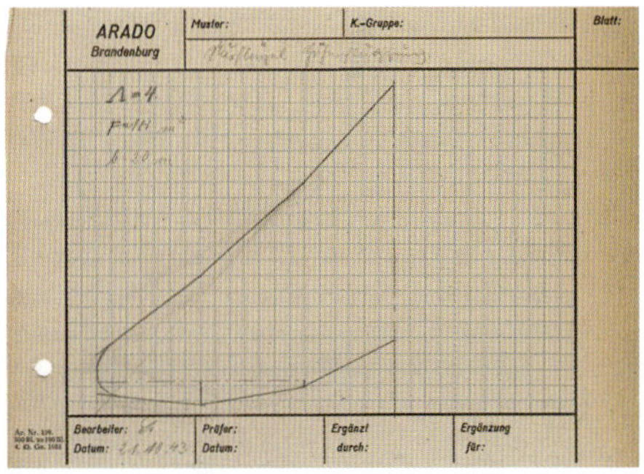

ABOVE: Three "nurflügel" sketches from the E 555 file dating from October 1943, showing more different shapes under consideration.

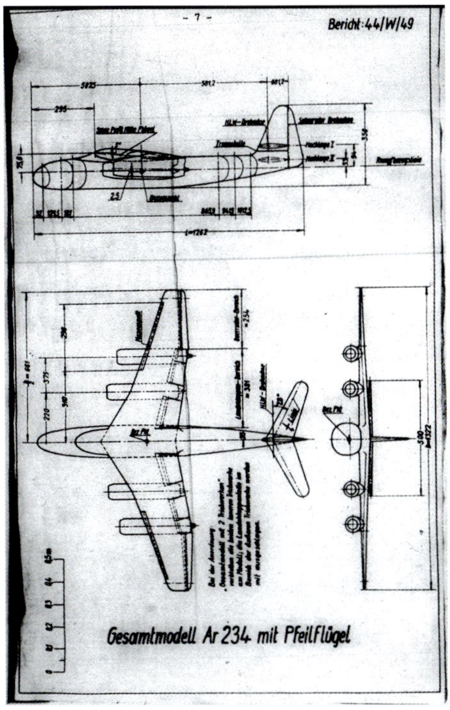

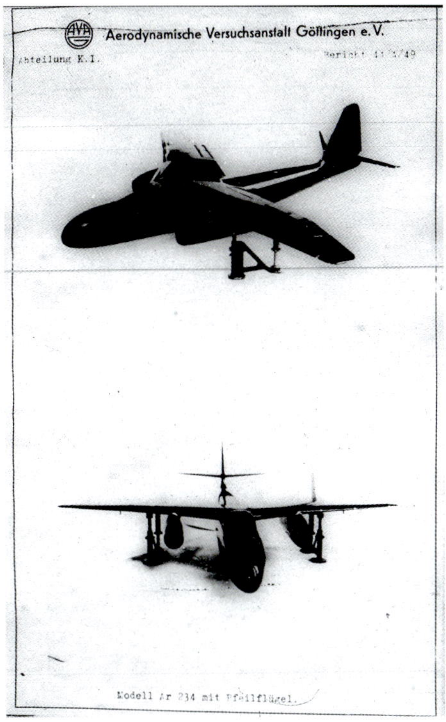

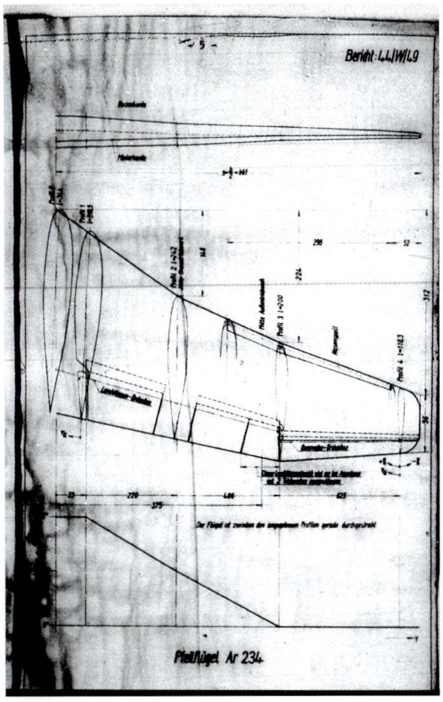

ABOVE: Even though Arado's ambition to build a jet-powered multi-purpose two-seater aircraft went unfulfilled, its research on the E 560 wing continued. Now the work was focused on providing the single-seat Ar 234 with curving swept wings or 'crescent' wings as they have come to be known. These images show work in progress on the concept at the AVA – Aerodynamische Versuchsanstalt Göttingen – one of many contractors hired to work for Arado.

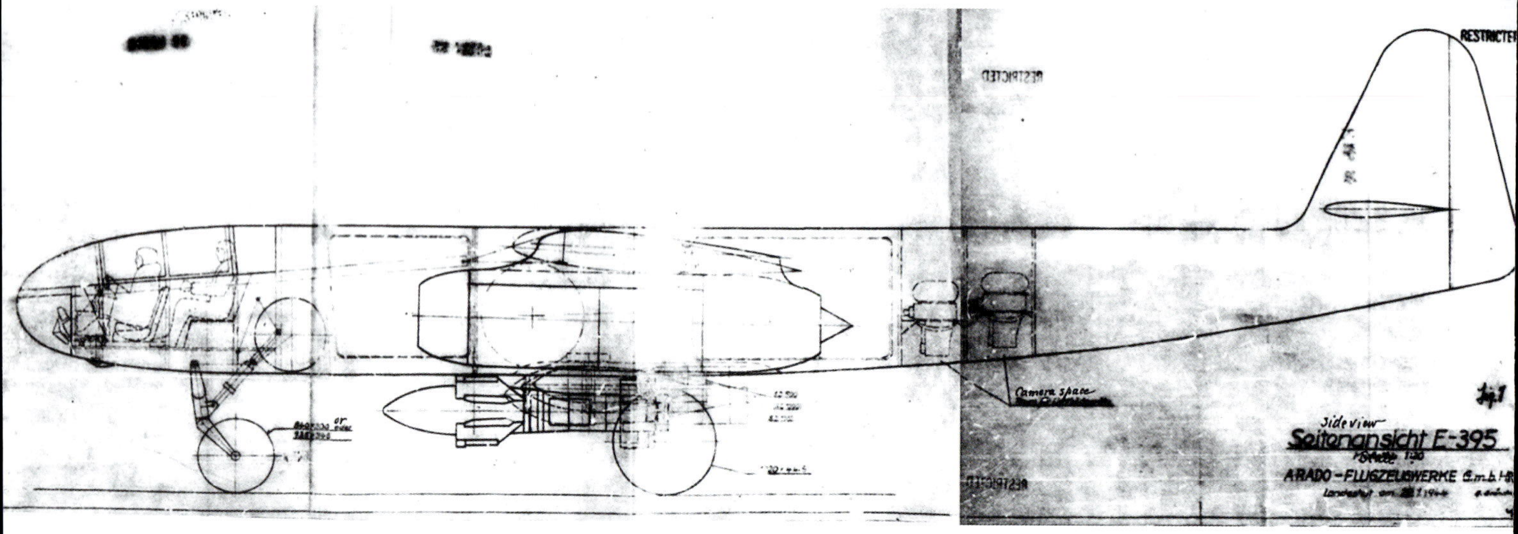

The low risk approach

ABOVE: The interior layout of the Arado E 395 shows its similarity to the Ar 234 from which it is derived. If it weren't for the two crewmen in the nose and their size relative to the aircraft in which they are seated, it would be difficult to tell the difference.

Strahlbomber – Arado E 395

Having presented a fully-formed jet bomber design and asked for permission to develop it, Arado instead found itself having to compete against two other companies. To minimise risk, its original straight leading edge swept-wing design was abandoned in favour of a less ambitious fallback – the E 395.

The first two prototypes of the Arado Ar 234 were flying by September 1943 and the V3 was being readied to join them. Everything about the project indicated that it was going to be a success.

However, the single-seater had been designed as a pure reconnaissance machine and its narrow fuselage was ill-suited to carrying anything more than cameras. Despite this handicap, Arado had already spent some time working out how the type might be made to carry cannon – either in a gondola beneath the fuselage or in the rear

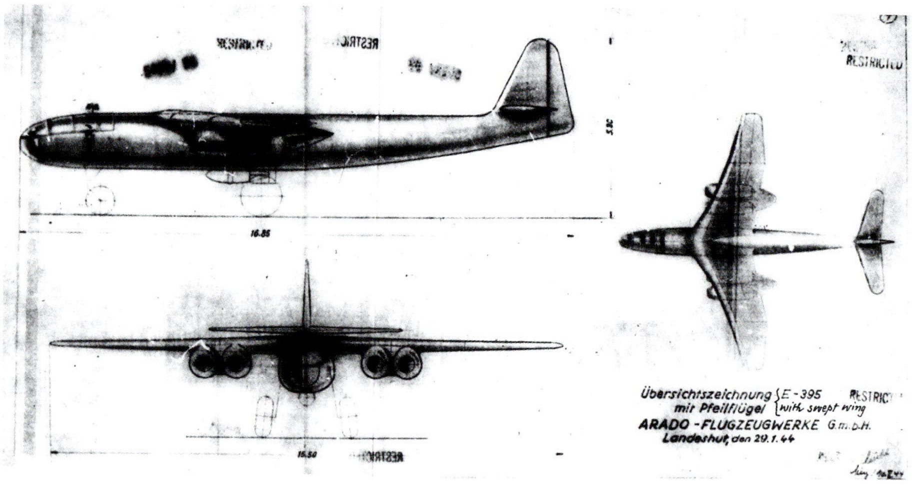

RIGHT: The 'arrow wing' E 395. A huge amount of research had already been carried out on what today is termed the 'crescent' wing form and Arado would continue this work almost to the end of 1944 with the aim of applying it to the Ar 234.

portion of the fuselage aft of the fuel tanks.

In the final equation, however, the Ar 234 was simply too small to carry a munitions payload of any significance. When the Strahlbomber competition was launched in September 1943, the firm decided to take the course of action it deemed most likely to result in success – rather than putting forward its radical swept-wing fast aircraft design, it chose instead to offer a scaled-up Ar 234 under the designation E 395.

Where the Ar 234 was 12.64m long, the E 395 was 16.85m long, and where the Ar 234's wingspan was 14.41m, the E 395's was 17.6m.

This low-risk approach seems to have been under consideration since at least August 1943, the design pre-dating the competition itself, but it had changed little even by January 1944. The slightly bulged pressure cabin of the fast-two seater proposed in the Arado report that same month was rejected in favour of a smooth bullet-shaped nose.

There is a hint of the fast two-seater in the design's four engines, however. These are given as either HeS 011s or Jumo 012s – the type intended for the design with the sharply swept wings. The aircraft offered in January 1944 was presented alongside an alternative with a "pfeilflügel". This was one of the curving E 560 shapes, rather than the straight leading edge type.

Only a very brief outline of the E 395 was given as part of Arado's final submission. It states: "Description is given of E 395 high-speed bomber equipped with HeS 011 or Jumo 012 turbojet engine. The aircraft has pressure cabin; conventional wings may be exchanged for swept-back wings.

"Slotted flaps are used for landing aids. Two fuel tanks hold a supply of 4500kg, auxiliary fuel tanks will hold a total of 7000kg. Space is provided for two MG 151 fixed machine guns, each in front and rear. Provision is made for storage of Fritz X guided missile. Extra 1500kg bomb load may be carried along."

The Arado E 395 competed against the Junkers EF 122 and Blohm & Voss P 188 – both of which relied on risky new aerodynamic forms. Yet the E 395 does not seem to have been regarded as quite the safe bet that its creators believed that it would be. It was undoubtedly a better option than that presented by Blohm & Voss, and perhaps that of Junkers, but Junkers was able to present far more evidence in support of its design.

Both Junkers and Arado were wholly owned by the German government, but where Junkers had a long history of innovation and achievement in experimental designs, not to mention an enviable reputation – it was even responsible for the engines that the winning entry would end up using – Arado had very little technological clout, lacking even its own wind tunnel facilities.

No matter how 'safe' the E 395 might have seemed superficially, without the test results and data to demonstrate its likely aerodynamic qualities and performance, Arado had to concede that there was a greater body of research data to support the Junkers design.

In addition, Junkers seems to have genuinely believed that its forward-swept EF 122 possessed the best possible configuration, whereas the Arado design was a compromise from the beginning. It was perhaps less of a surprise than it might have been, therefore, when Arado was unsuccessful. The big surprise would be later, when the E 395 concept made an unexpected comeback.

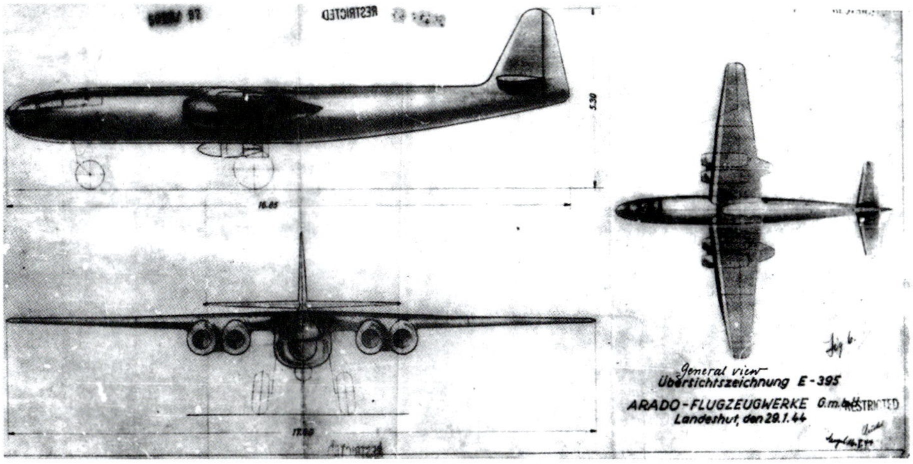

ABOVE: It looks like a safe bet – the straight wing E 395 was a scaled-up Ar 234 which traded high performance for risk-free flying.

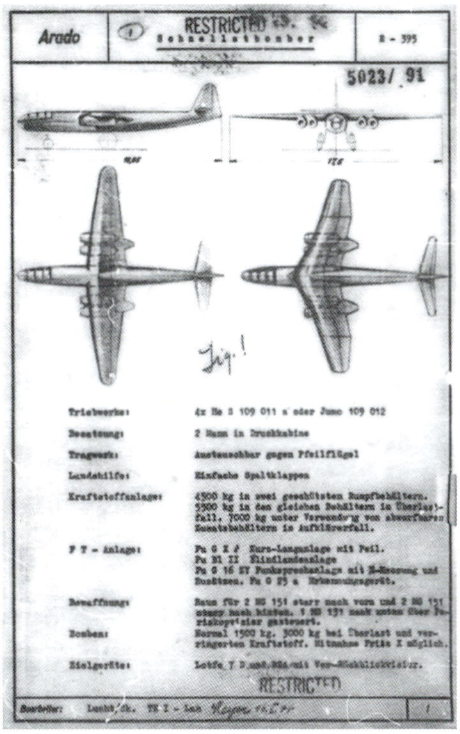

ABOVE: This direct comparison shows the difference between the straight-wing E 395 and the alternative version with Arado's E 560 'pfeilflügel' wing. In either case, the engines are fitted together in two underwing pods of two.

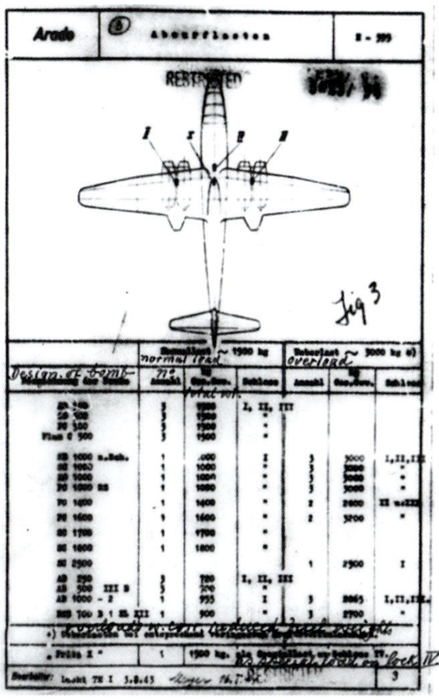

ABOVE: A data sheet on the E 395 from August 3, 1943, making it a near contemporary of the Arado fast two-seater designs outlined in the last chapter.

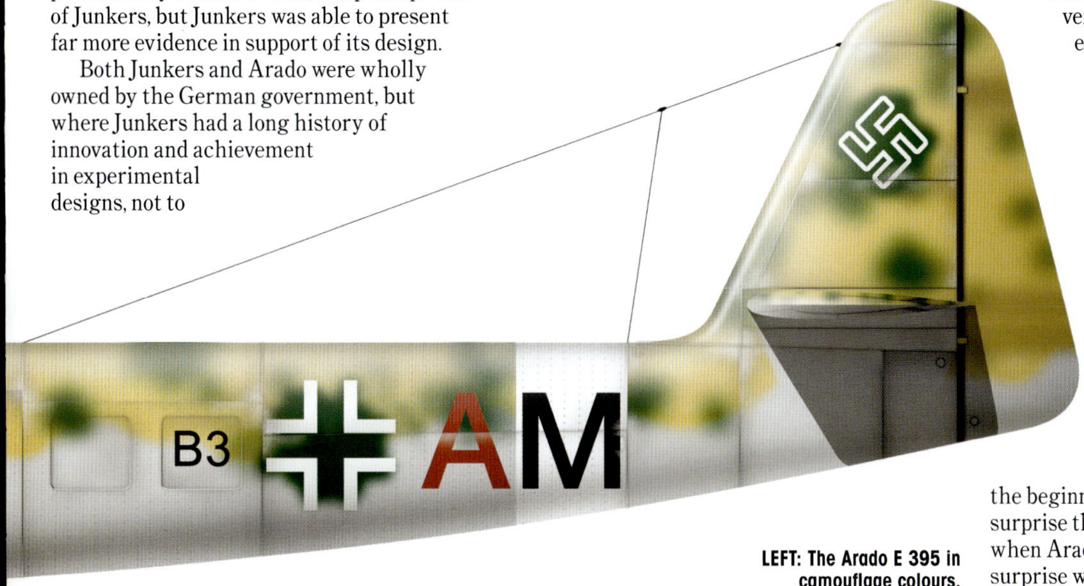

LEFT: The Arado E 395 in camouflage colours. Art by Daniel Uhr

Sweeping forwards

Strahlbomber – Junkers Ju 287

Towards the end of 1943 it was decided that the Luftwaffe needed a dedicated jet bomber – not just a Messerschmitt Me 262 fighter-bomber or an Arado Ar 234 reconnaissance aircraft converted for bombing. The result was the Junkers Ju 287.

ABOVE: A rear view of the Junkers Ju 287 V1 shows off not only its unusual swept-forward wings but also the way its broad He 177 forward fuselage was blended into its narrower Ju 188 tail unit. The fuselage and upper wings were fitted with tufts of cotton so that airflow over the aircraft could be monitored in flight.

Junkers was at the forefront of jet engine development and in 1942 had been responsible for building the first German turbojet to offer any degree of reliability - the Jumo 004.

It was with two of these engines that the Me 262 V3 prototype had managed a successful 25 minute flight on July 18, 1942, yet Junkers had yet to build an aircraft of its own that would use them.

From the late 1930s into the early 1940s the company had produced a range of experimental designs that were intended to use the turbojets produced by its engines division but none of them ended up going into production.

Nevertheless, Junkers had more wind tunnels and experimental facilities at its disposal than any other company in the world in 1943, at its Dessau headquarters and elsewhere, and used them ceaselessly to test both its own designers' work and the work of other companies. On March 19 of that year, the firm embarked on an extensive programme of tests involving swept-back and swept-forward wings in a wide variety of different configurations. From June 7 to July 15 these included comparing small wind tunnel models of both the Ar 234 and the company's own experimental design, the EF 116.

While the Ar 234 took a very conservative aerodynamic approach, with unswept wings and a straightforward tubular fuselage, the EF 116 was used to test a host of wing shapes and positions. At this time, it was unclear which configurations might offer the greatest aerodynamic benefits.

With much greater resources at its disposal, Junkers seems to have quickly surpassed the work already done by Arado on its E 560 wing and compiled a wealth of data on the characteristics, advantages and disadvantages of a wide range of different wing configurations.

Junkers' EF 116 testing came to an end on September 29, 1943, at around the same time that the RLM issued a requirement for a new Strahlbomber, or 'jet bomber'. None of the major private manufacturers - Messerschmitt, Heinkel and Focke-Wulf - was invited to tender, but minor player Blohm & Voss was offered the opportunity to join in, which it accepted.

With only the nationalised firms Junkers and Arado involved, plus the outsider Blohm & Voss, there seems to have been nothing of the bitter rivalry that could development between private firms over such a prestigious contract and the three companies enjoyed an amicable working relationship.

As previously mentioned, Arado pitched a scaled-up Ar 234, the E 395, while Blohm & Voss put forward its radical P 188. The Junkers entry was the EF 122, another unusual design but this time one based on a large amount of wind tunnel data.

Like some of the EF 116 arrangements, it featured forward-swept wings but retained a conventional tailfin and unswept horizontal tail surfaces. Wind tunnel testing of the EF 122 had actually commenced on September 30, 1943 - the day after work on the EF 116 ceased.

After a very short competition, Junkers was awarded a contract to proceed with the

'VERY CONSIDERABLE SUPERIORITY IN SPEED'

During late 1944, Deutschen Versuchsanstalt für Luftfahrt (DVL) director Günther Bock gave a lecture on the then-defunct Ju 287 which neatly summarises the goals of the project…

The desire to be able to attack very distant targets with a high-speed bomber led the Junkers concern to design the Ju 287. The work on this aircraft was commenced in summer 1943, and the conditions were that a bomb load of 3000kg should be transported for 2000km. This resulted in an aircraft having a flying weight of 23 tons.

As there were no single jet units sufficiently powerful for such a large aircraft, two sets of triple jet units were mounted one on either side of the fuselage under the wing. The calculated performance gave a top speed of 870kph [540mph] at an altitude of 6km [19,700ft]. In later models each triple unit was to be replaced by one very powerful jet unit.

In order that the navigational problems which arise during flights over long distances may be satisfactorily solved, a crew of three is provided, one being the pilot, the second bomb aimer/navigator and the third wireless operator/gunner. For defence, there is a remote-controlled gun in the tail. The large fully enclosed bomb bay will take loads up to 4500kg. When operating as a long-distance reconnaissance aircraft an additional fuel tank of 2000 litres capacity can be stowed in the bomb bay.

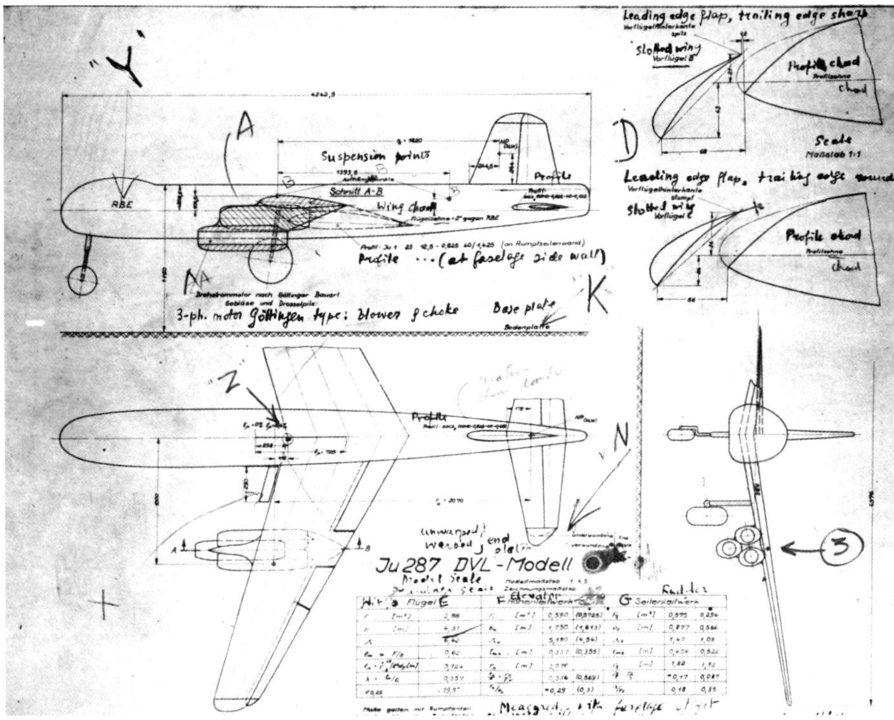

ABOVE: This drawing of a DVL wind tunnel model dates from no earlier than July 1944 and has been heavily annotated by British intelligence after the war.

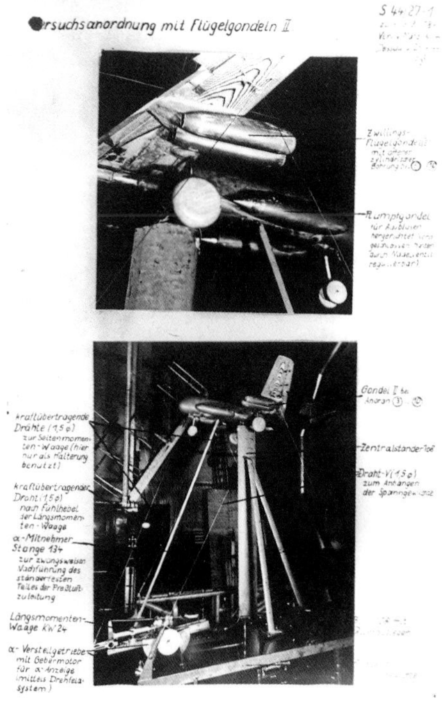

ABOVE: Models of the Ju 287 being wind tunnel-tested at Dessau on April 25, 1944.

development of the EF 122 in December 1943. At around this time the type was given the RLM designation Ju 287, although within the company the project continued to be known as EF 122.

The EF 122 design that was originally approved had four engines like its competitors, but from the outset these were to be Jumo 004Cs rather than Heinkel HeS 011s or Jumo 012s. Two were to be attached directly to the fuselage, near the nose, and another would sit atop the trailing edge of each wing.

By the end of January 1944 this arrangement had changed, with the latter engines positioned beneath the wings rather than above them. The following month, Junkers was told that it would receive a contract for a pair of flying 'mock-ups' plus 18 prototypes. And the month after that, March 1944, the Junkers design team were informed that there were going to be significant delays with the Jumo 004C – prompting another change of layout for the Ju 287, since it would now need to be powered by six BMW 003As instead. The forward fuselage engine nacelles were retained, with two more 003As being fitted under the leading edge of each wing.

Delivery of components for the first mock-up, the Ju 287 V1, began around this time at one of Junkers' testing airfields,

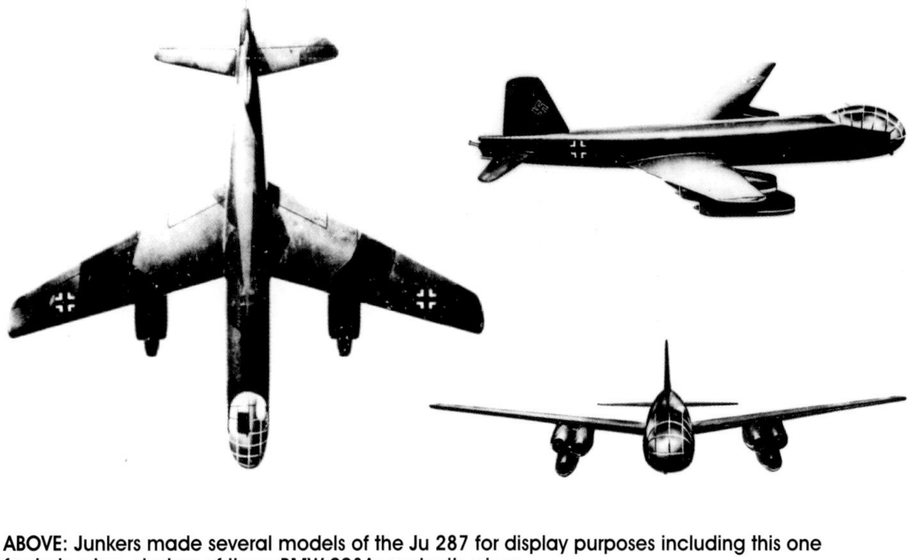

ABOVE: Junkers made several models of the Ju 287 for display purposes including this one featuring two clusters of three BMW 003As under its wings.

Flugplatz Brandis, east of Leipzig. In order to begin assessing the forward-swept wing arrangement as soon as possible, the Ju 287 V1 was to be composed largely of pre-existing parts. The fuselage came from a Heinkel He 177A-3, the rear fuselage and tail were Ju 188G-2 bits, and the fixed mainwheels and nosewheel came from a wrecked USAAF B-24 Liberator. There would be only four engines with just enough power to get it off the ground and performing a few basic manoeuvres – a quartet of Jumo 004Bs, two on the fuselage and one under each wing.

A striking feature of the aircraft is the pronounced forward sweep of the wings. This form was chosen both for aerodynamical and constructional reasons. Constructionally, the most important advantage was the possibility of providing a large continuous bomb bay immediately in front of the wing roots and approximately about the centre of gravity of the aircraft. This form also made possible the retraction rearwards and sideways of the undercarriage into a space immediately aft of the bomb bay. But apart from these general reasons, the sweep forward of the wings was most suitable for the tasks which the aircraft was to perform on account of its influence upon performance and flying characteristics, which are considerably better than those of straight or swept back wings.

However, the development of the arrow form in aircraft construction is so new and research and development still being in an elementary stage, it would seem today to be too early to pronounce a final verdict upon the advantages and disadvantages of a sweep-forward or sweep back.

The wind tunnel measurements and flight tests with the Ju 287 have shown, however, that the design chosen by Junkers which has a sweep forward of approximately 25° gives a very satisfactory compromise between the conflicting demands of flying performance and flying characteristics.

ABOVE: Ju 287 V1 takes on fuel ahead of engine tests in August 1944.

ABOVE: Installing the Ju 287 V1's engines at Flugplatz Brandis during late June or early July 1944.

ABOVE AND BELOW: Fitting the Ju 287's rocket-assisted take-off units.

ABOVE: The Ju 287's nosewheel struts now with aerodynamic fairings fitted.

Preparations were also being made for the second flying mock-up, the Ju 287 V2. This would utilise the same bits and pieces as the V1 but with the tailplane positioned 30cm lower and with six BMW 003As in place of the 004Bs - two on the fuselage and two under each wing.

A Ju 188G-2 was also going to be used to test the all-new tail section of the production model Ju 287 and a pair of He 177s would be brought in, one to test the Ju 287's bomb bay and another its bespoke retractable undercarriage.

In May, Junkers was told that the initial order had been reduced to the two mock-ups plus four prototypes, but a full production contract for 100 aircraft was also awarded. Construction of the V1 got under way with the final delivery of components being made by the end of the month. It was expected that the fully assembled V1 would be rolled out on June 16, ready for its first flight later in the month. The V2 was expected to follow in August.

In readiness for the arrival of the first production aircraft, the Luftwaffe began to draw up plans for two Gruppen to operate the Ju 287, with the first of these becoming operational in May 1945. Another engine arrangement for the Ju 287 was worked on during July 1944, where the 003As were fitted in triple-engine clusters under each wing and the fuselage positions were

The high fuel consumption of jet engines makes it particularly difficult to design jet-propelled aircraft for long-range employment in such a way that they can compete favourably with aircraft of the normal type. A careful construction, particularly as regards airframe weights, is therefore especially important for long-range jet-propelled aircraft.

The arrow-shaped wing has automatically the following disadvantages in that the wing for equal span is longer and therefore heavier than a straight wing. Junkers, therefore, made special endeavours to keep down the wing weight. A method first carried out in German aircraft construction to achieve this performance was the integral forging of the wing connections with the spar.

Normally at the separating points between wing and fuselage all the forces from the light alloy spar booms are transferred to special connecting pieces of steel whereby the transference of the forces from the spar to the connecting piece requires a considerable expenditure in weight.

This difficulty was surmounted by Junkers who forged the connections integral with the spar. This was made possible by using copper-free light alloy Hy 43 which was developed by the IG and the DVL. This alloy, while having good forging properties also has very high tensile strength. IG had planned, when the aircraft came into series production, to forge the whole spar boom, including the connecting piece, in a large press.

ABOVE AND BELOW: Stills from cine footage of one of the Ju 287 V1's final test flights during September 1944.

ABOVE AND BELOW: A testbed facility for the Ju 287's proposed three BMW 003A underwing cluster was established at Oranienbaum during August 1944 but the Ju 287 programme was suspended before they could be fitted to the V2.

deleted, and it was proposed that the V2 should be converted to this configuration.

Whether Junkers was able to hit the June 16 target rollout date for the V1 is uncertain, but on July 12, 13 and 27 it was subjected to a series of vibration tests in its hangar at Brandis. Finally, on August 8, 1944, the V1 made its first of 11 flights. Pilots reported that it was easy to control, although it was accepted that the mock-up's performance would differ from that of the Ju 287 full production version.

The V2 had almost been completed when all work on the Ju 287 was suspended – presumably because all attention and all available resources were now being focused on the rapid turnaround required for the Volksjäger, Heinkel's He 162. The V1 would never fly again and the V2 would never be finished.

The Ju 287 does not appear to have been cancelled outright, however. The British report on the Entwicklungshauptkommission (EHK) meeting of November 21-22, 1944, states: "It was clear from the minutes that the development of the Ju 287 multi-jet high-speed bomber hung in the balance."

As later events would demonstrate, the Ju 287 wasn't finished yet. ●

By adopting this principle, as well as employing other large forged parts made from Hy 43 the airframe weight of the Ju 287 was lowered by about 350kg; this reduction in weight results in a saving of fuel according to the range of up to 600kg.

It is most interesting to see how the Ju 287 as a jet-propelled bomber compares in performance with a normal high performance bomber. The Ju 288 which was designed by the Junkers at the beginning of this war, but never came to series production, has about the same flying weight as the Ju 287 and was therefore chosen for comparison.

An important standard for evaluating a bomber is its 'transport capacity', that is the product of range and bomb load. The transport capacity of the Ju 287 is considerably less than that of the Ju 288 but evaluation according to transport capacity does not take into account the flying speed. If flying speed is taken into account, at ranges of less than 2000km the jet-propelled bomber Ju 287 is superior. At greater ranges the Ju 288 is superior.

For the moment anyway, bombers with standard engines will maintain their position for long-range work. However, one must realise that with the present-day military situation, the employment of bombers over enemy territory is only possible if they have a very considerable superiority in speed.

Unfortunately, for reasons which have nothing to do with the technical possibilities of the Ju 287, development work on this type has had to be discontinued.

The best of all possible worlds

Strahlbomber – Blohm & Voss P 188

Designing a jet bomber to the RLM's exacting specification in late 1943 was a daunting prospect for Blohm & Voss. It struggled to reconcile the need to carry big loads with the aerodynamic requirements of a high-speed aircraft and as a result its Strahlbomber was an uneasy compromise with looks verging on the bizarre.

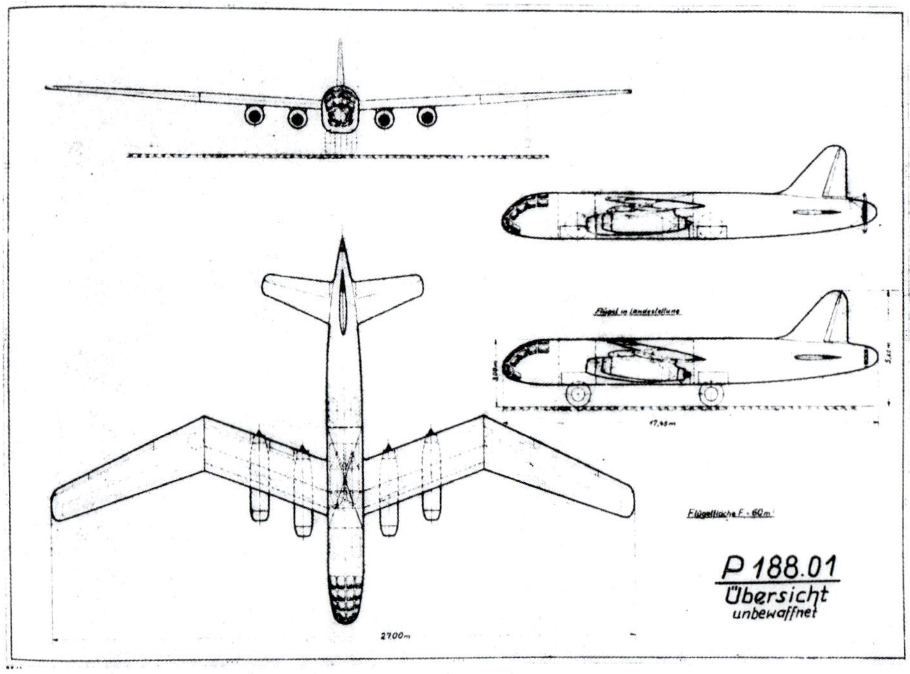

ABOVE: The Blohm & Voss P 188.01, dating from October 29, 1943. This basic version of the design lacked defensive armament and could therefore have a tailfin and streamlined pressure cabin nose. The lower of the two side views shows the type's wings tilted up in their landing position.

Attempting to come up with an aircraft design that would meet the RLM's specification, the Blohm & Voss designers encountered two seemingly intractable difficulties. The first was how to store tons of bombs and fuel and an undercarriage in an airframe aerodynamically clean enough for high-speed flight. And the second was how to build an aircraft that remained balanced enough for easy handling whether it was carrying tons of bombs and fuel or not.

The best solution seemed to come from a design they had all-but completed over a year earlier – the BV 144 passenger plane. In The Vanishing Paperclips, Blohm & Voss designer Hans H Amtmann wrote: "It was early in the war, in 1940, that the Deutsche Luft Hansa approached the aircraft division of Blohm & Voss with the request to design and, if possible, to build a twin-engine passenger aircraft which would be available right after the war. This aircraft, the BV 144, eventually was designed and built.

"Blohm & Voss was quite interested but the company could not launch a design effort of a civilian aircraft without the consent of the German Air Ministry. However, in spite of other pressing work, a brief study was made. It was clear from the beginning that it should be an advanced design in order to be competitive when the war was over.

"The preliminary design was a high-wing aircraft with a tricycle landing gear (a novelty at that time) and a variable incidence wing. These two features were thought to be advantageous for a passenger aircraft by keeping the fuselage horizontal at take-off and landing and close to the ground for easy access to the passenger compartment.

"We had tried the variable incidence wing on a twin float Ha 140 torpedo plane by varying the incidence of the large outer wing panels, and the results were so encouraging that this idea was applied to the commercial airliner."

Final design and prototype construction of the BV 144 was eventually subcontracted to French company Breguet – the Breguet design team being transferred to Blohm & Voss's Hamburg headquarters to carry out the first stage of the work. Two prototypes were built at the Breguet works in Bordeaux in southern France. According to a British report produced shortly after the liberation of France: "At the Breguet factory at Bayonne, the mission inspected two prototypes of the BV 144. The first, which had been assembled, was seen dismantled and awaiting transport to Toulouse for flight tests; the second was almost complete.

"Neither of these aircraft, however, has flown, so it is important to note that no information is available on the behavior in flight of the controls or the variable incidence gear, and with regard to the latter in particular the firm were expecting trouble due to seizing of the jacks." This latter point is of interest because it was the 'variable incidence' aspect of the BV 144 that the Strahlbomber design team applied to their project – the P 188.

Presented to the RLM in four slightly different configurations, the P 188 offered a host of novel features. The company brochure, dated December 1943, addresses the type's startling looks right at the beginning of

ABOVE AND BELOW: Two views of the French-built Blohm & Voss BV 144 airliner, the pivoting wing system of which was to be used on the P 188.

ABOVE: A photograph of the BV 144's centre wing section, showing its rotating shaft. This feature was to be carried forward onto the P 188 but the French who built the BV 144 struggled with the hydraulic actuators that were to change the angle of the wings.

ABOVE: The BV 144 brochure cover, dated July 1942.

the foreword: "For the exterior design of this project, the following sub-problems were largely responsible: the large area required for the bomb bay, the placement of large masses of fuel, the placement of the landing gear and controlling the influence of the Mach number.

"The variety of bombs required by the tender demanded a large bomb bay, but consideration was given to dividing this up to prevent centre of gravity problems when the load is released. Very similar considerations apply to the placement of the fuel. Here too, a far-reaching decentralisation with many individual tanks with a view to preventing trim problems seemed undesirable.

"Having the landing gear retract into the wings, even wide-span wings, was not readily possible due to high wing loading and for aerodynamic reasons. The usual solution, having the wheels pivot to be accommodated behind the engines, was not possible due to the use of special engines. Finally, the conditions resulting from a high Mach number call for due consideration."

In other words, the design team were worried about the aircraft being unbalanced when the large quantities of fuel required by the jet engines had all been used up and the heavy bombs had been dropped. The speed requirement meant the wings needed to be thin, so the landing gear couldn't retract into them, and the effects of flying at high speed were still very much an unknown quantity in late 1943.

The brochure continued: "Due to these four influencing factors, the project has emerged in the form presented. The two masses requiring the most space, bombs and fuel, have been consolidated in the central fuselage. In line with the prevailing development trend, we have formed a space above the bomb bay for steel containers to hold the fuel, which can be regarded as a part of the hull itself.

"The inability to simply let the wheels disappear into the wings or behind the engines has resulted in a central chassis, meaning an arrangement of the main wheels under the fuselage. Small, normal unstressed support wheels under the wings maintain the aircraft's balance."

It had been decided that in order to avoid interfering with the bomb bay, one set of wheels would be positioned directly in front of it and the other behind, at the ends of the steel fuselage centre section.

This tandem wheel configuration created further problems. Putting all the aircraft's weight onto the rear wheel during an ordinary nose-up landing would collapse it – the bomber would need to land on both its front and rear wheels at the same time, requiring it to be horizontal before it touched down.

This was where the BV 144 came in. The brochure says: "You cannot have four equal-load wheels unless you can reasonably presuppose both wheelsets striking the ground at the same time during landing. This demand, in turn, was met with the application of a rotating wing.

"We have long considered the rotating wing a means to combine the advantages of a nosewheel but with the low landing speed of an aircraft equipped with a tail wheel assembly. We recall the model under construction in France, the BV 144.

"In the present application, the flat direction of the exhaust jet during take-off is an additional advantage for maintaining the turf of the airfield." ▶

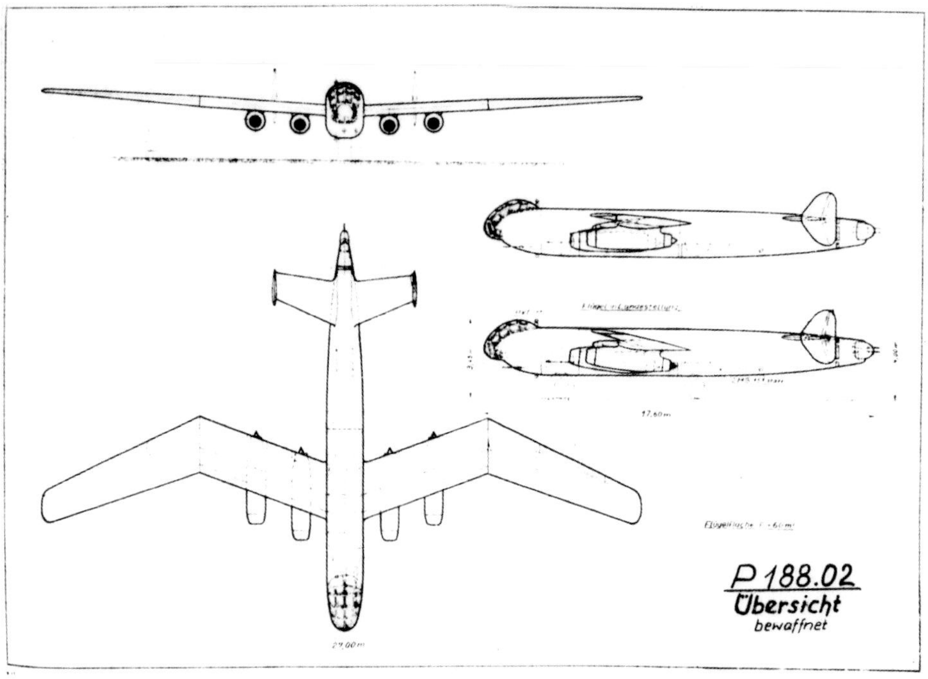

ABOVE: The armed version of the Blohm & Voss Strahlbomber, the P 188.02, had a less aerodynamically efficient high cockpit arrangement so that the gunner could look back over the fuselage to operate the remote controlled tail gun turret. The drawing is dated November 4, 1943.

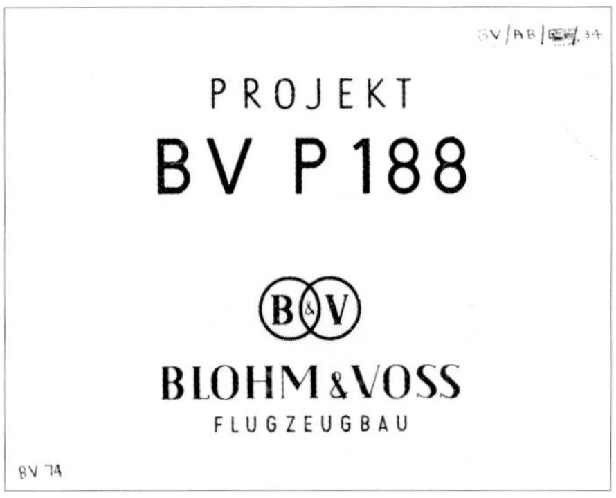

ABOVE: The cover of the P 188 brochure, which was dated 'December 1943' inside.

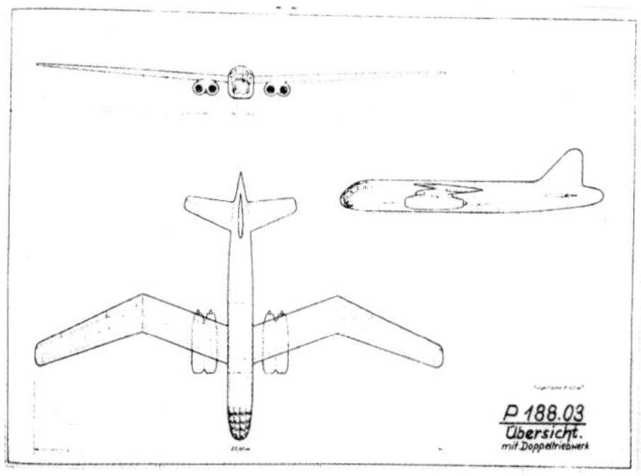

ABOVE: Otherwise similar to the P 188.01, the unarmed P 188.03 featured twin engine pods, rather than four separate installations.

Next up, the document attempts the tricky task of explaining the bomber's most striking feature – its W-shaped wing arrangement: "Considerations around the influence of the Mach number have finally led to a material distortion of the wing shape. The swept backward wing we did not like for reasons of its tendency to roll. And since we have run out of all other options, we turned to a patent application we made a long time ago for an aircraft with forward-swept wings. However, for various reasons, we could not use it."

Several reasons are then given for not using purely forward swept wings: "First, the very pronounced negative yaw behavior requires an enlarged vertical stabilizer, which we would not like to take into account for reasons of recoverable flight performance and the vibration risk."

Another reason was the negative effect of having diminishing loads – the fuel and bombs – at the centre of gravity, which made it difficult to position the engines appropriately, and there were also unanswered questions concerning flutter and "extraordinarily large torsional moments in the wing centre".

"We have extricated ourselves from this dilemma with an airfoil which is swept backwards from the hull, extending then to the outer wing, which is again swept forward. This brings the full high-speed benefit and mitigates the negative behaviour on an easily manageable mass, while avoiding the vibration risk and the large torsional moments in the wing centre."

Despite its unusual appearance, the construction and layout of the Blohm & Voss bomber was relatively simple and made good use of the space available within the fuselage.

According to the constructional description included in the brochure: "The fuselage consists of three components. In front is the crew compartment in the form of a pressure-resistant cabin. The building material is duralumin. The cabin is releasably connected to the fuselage centre section, which is constructed as a steel box and also serves as a fuel tank, under which the bomb bay located. Built from dural, the tail end is also removably attached to the centre section.

"The wing is, from the fuselage outwards, backwards swept. At the interface of the outer wing begins an equally large forward sweep. As a result of this double sweep, the twisting forces at the point where the wing joins the fuselage are anticipated to be reduced to more than half of the amount of the swept wing. In addition there will be a reduction of bending moments and a corresponding reaction to torsional moments in the inner wings."

The brochure does add a caveat by stating that further wind tunnel testing is required to determine the best possible angle for the backwards and then forwards sweep of the P 188's wings. It is also noted that the wings' chord narrows towards the tip – with a chord of 2.5m at the fuselage and 1.5m at their tips. Total wing area was 60 square metres and wingspan was 27m.

The wing rotation could be adjusted using a hydraulic piston, with a pitch range of six degrees. The central wing section was to be supported by a welded sheet steel box. This steel construction apparently had "particular advantages in terms of fire resistance". The removable outer wings were to be built from dural.

"The large proportion of the total weight made up of fuel and bomb load results in a large difference between takeoff and landing weight. The surface load is reduced from 397kg per square metre to 259kg per square metre. Any special measures to increase lift seem inappropriate therefore; normal split flaps are sufficient."

When the P 188 was being drawn up, it was uncertain whether a fast jet bomber would need to have defensive armament fitted or not. If the Allies were unlikely to field jet-propelled interceptors against it, there would be no need for it to carry cannon and machine guns to keep them at bay.

Therefore, different configurations were created: "For the unarmed machine a central rudder is intended. This is supported by the safe control of flutter risk and also the aerodynamic advantages. Since no difficulties are expected for the ailerons and elevator or the actuation of the rudder, no special devices are provided. For the armed version a division of the tail into two would be very much recommended. Accordingly, the design drawings are prepared."

It was explained that the differences between the armed and unarmed versions were not confined simply to the guns themselves: "Their difference refers not only to the armament itself but aerodynamically on the upper part of the pressure cabin. This high position depends directly on the extent to which a clear view to the rear is needed.

"If one is satisfied with a periscope sight, then also for the armed version a high position of the pressure cabin can be omitted and thus a better aerodynamic quality can be realised that is inferior only a little to that of the weapon-free machine. The range differences would then only apply due to the weight of the armament and ammunition quantity.

"But if a direct horizontal backwards line of sight is needed, then you lose speed and thus range. For the armed machine, in addition to the sufficiently high position of the pressure cabin, the following armament system is provided: forward – under the cabin two MG 151 with 300 rounds of ammunition; the hull sidewalls two MG 151 with 250 rounds or two MG 213 with 250 rounds, in the tail one FPL 131 Z with 500 rounds or earlier on or under the fuselage one FPL 131 Z with 500 rounds."

The two main undercarriage wheelsets had tyres measuring 1140mm by 410mm and "the retraction of the rear set is designed so that the wheel can be held in any position. Under the wings, support wheels in the dimensions of 740 x 210 are fitted. They do not reach quite to the ground and are therefore landing shock free. They are laterally pivoted into the wing".

Power for all four versions of the P 188 would come from a quartet of Jumo 004Cs, although other engine types were not ruled out. The brochure says: "For the first designs, and for the benefit of the calculations, Junkers' special engines have been adopted."

However, the design team regarded all projected jet engine types as likely to be problematic: "For reasons of simple manufacturing and low expenditure on construction work for their accommodation, none of the engine types seemed desirable."

Early tests with the P 188's backwards and forwards swept wings had demonstrated that positioning the engines would cause "substantial difficulties".

It had not yet been decided whether keeping the engines together in two pods of two or separating them into individual pods would be best. The brochure states that the Blohm & Voss design team had halted an investigation into this problem at an early stage because it raised too many theoretical considerations to allow for an accurate estimate. Instead, the two key designs presented – P 188.01-01 and P 188.02-01 – each had four separate engine pods.

The largest proportion of the P 188's fuel, 6800 litres, would be housed in the steel fuselage container. This was to be 8mm thick on its rear side, 3mm thick at the front and 5mm thick on its outward facing sides. "Here, the main protection is designed for attack from behind". The front was thinner because "the attack from the front endangers the crew to a much greater extent" – incoming rounds would hit the pressure cabin before they could reach the tanks.

The inner wings would, between them, house an additional 3000 litres of fuel because their "construction as a steel shell is particularly suitable for this".

The bomb bay was part of the same steel fuselage centre section that housed the main fuel tanks and measured 4.6m long by 1.7m wide and 1.05m high. Its doors on the left and right were to be opened hydraulically and on one side a portion of the bomb bay door could be folded "to allow unobstructed loading with normal bomb carriage. The horizontal position of the fuselage is advantageous for the loading process".

Bomb load options for the P 188 included one 2000kg bomb, three 1000kg bombs, four 500kg bombs or eight 250kg bombs.

Despite its constructional simplicity, the P 188 seems to have offered few advantages and some serious potential risks arising from its unusual configuration. As a result, it was dropped and the Ju 287 went forward. Yet the Ju 287 would not go entirely unchallenged as the RLM felt that a more conventional design ought to be put into development. The result was the Heinkel He 343. ●

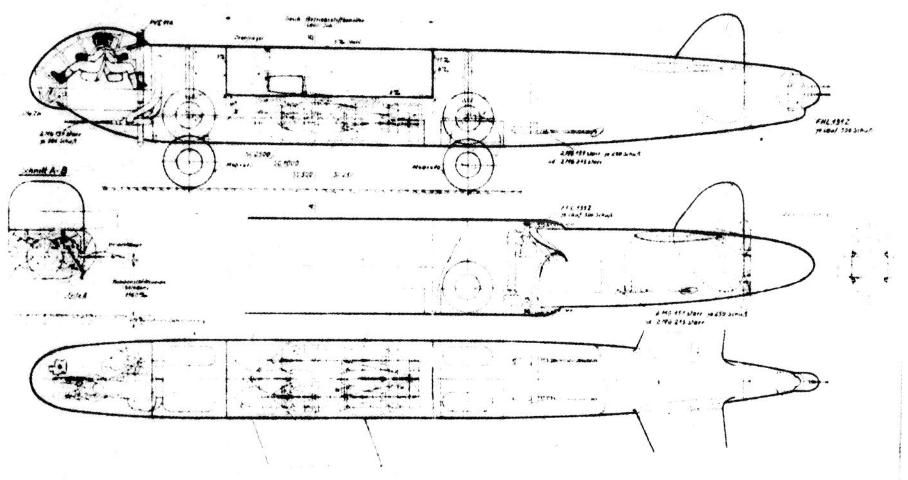

ABOVE: An interior view of the P 188.02 showings its cramped pressure cabin with good visibility for the gunner, tandem undercarriage and centrally positioned steel fuel tanks/bomb bay. In addition to the remote controlled rear turret, there are a pair of fixed rearward-firing cannon under the fuselage and two more in the 'chin' position.

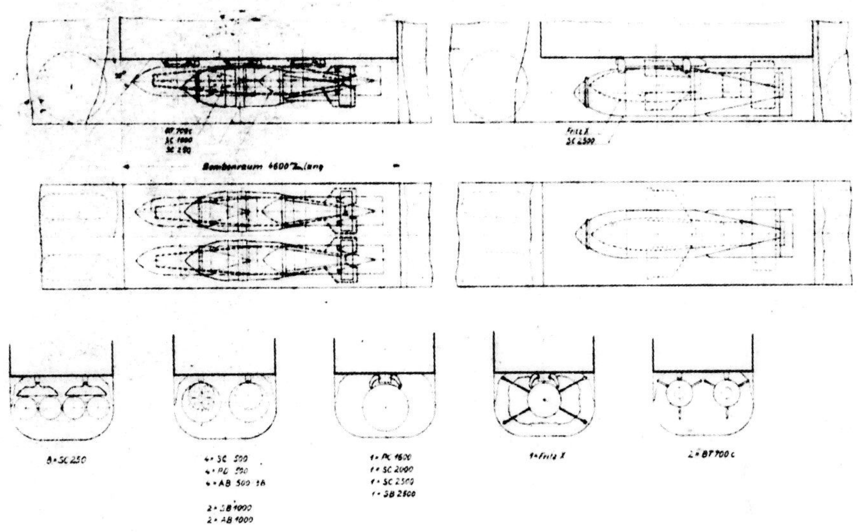

ABOVE: One of the chief difficulties Blohm & Voss encountered in designing the P 188 was in providing a sufficiently roomy bomb bay. Some of the many possible bomb load configurations are presented in this brochure drawing.

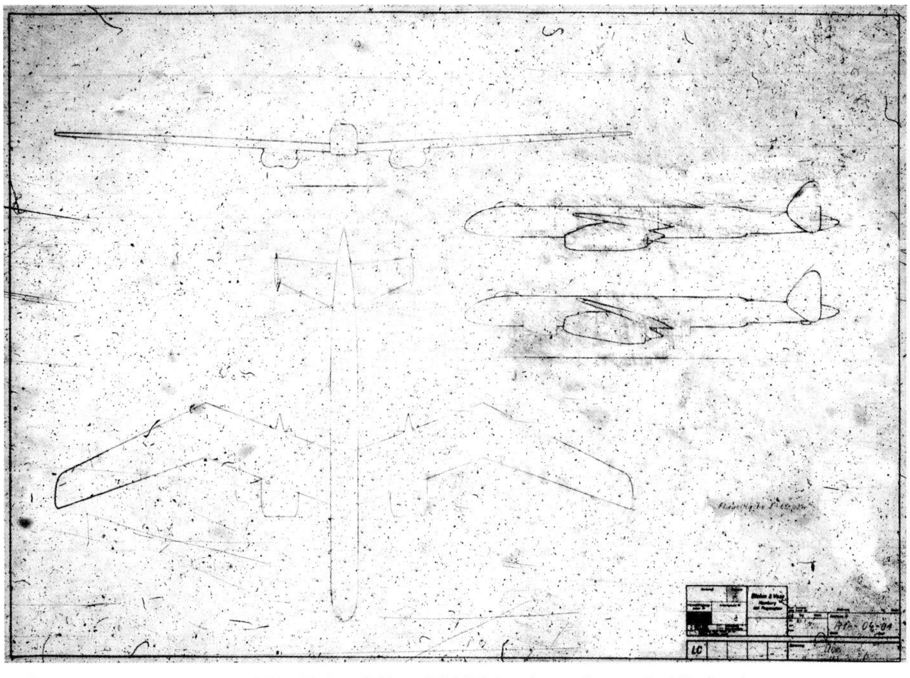

ABOVE: Little is known about the Blohm & Voss P 188.04 – shown here – but its fuselage seems narrower than that of the other three designs, leading to speculation that it was to have been larger in scale. An attempt is made to combine the benefits of the streamlined 'low' pressure cabin nose with a high up gunnery position by including a Perspex bubble on top of the fuselage.

The special task

Strahlbomber – Heinkel He 343

With the complex Ju 287 chosen to proceed as the Luftwaffe's new jet bomber, the RLM decided that a simpler design based on tried and trusted technology was needed as a failsafe. Having already rejected the Arado E 395, it turned to Heinkel and ordered it to design a new bomber based on a scaled up Ar 234 with the utmost urgency.

When Heinkel was approached by the RLM in January 1944 and told to design a new jet bomber, the urgent nature of the job was made clear.

The basic premise was straightforward and sounded rather familiar - take the Arado Ar 234 with its straight wings, clean fuselage and brief but relatively successful test flight record and scale it up. The result would no doubt be a larger more capable machine, designed and built in record time.

Naturally, the RLM told Heinkel that Arado itself had already done much of the legwork on this front by designing the E 395 and would be happy to hand over all of the relevant project documents. Not that it would have any choice in the matter.

ABOVE: A 1944 model of the Heinkel 'Strabo 16 to' used to show how the type might look in flight. The four-engined jet bomber would go on to receive the RLM designation He 343.

Heinkel chief designer Siegfried Günther went to collect the documents personally from Rüdiger Kosin at Arado's offices in Landeshut, Silesia, eastern Germany, on January 24, 1944. Just over a week later, on February 1, a report was produced by Heinkel entitled 'Strabo 16 to' which further emphasised the haste with which the bomber was to be rushed through to full production. Indeed, the tone is strongly reminiscent of that used during the Volksjäger competition some seven months later.

The report begins: "Summary. The task is to create a four-engined two-seater jet bomber with good flight characteristics and minimal time spent on design and construction. To this end, the V-patterns of an existing single-seat, twin-engine aircraft of 10 tonnes is used as a model.

"It is to be a 1.55 times enlarged version, in particular the wing is replicated with almost every detail. The fuselage, compared to the model, is changed insofar as it receives a two-seat cockpit and a bomb bay. The fuselage cross-section with 1.8m width is determined by the placement of the Fritz X and by the simplified landing gear system. The bomb loads are as far as possible moved backward to obtain a not too large change in the centre of gravity.

"The undercarriage system, with simple pivot action, is similar to that of the model, but retracts not into the side but into the bottom of the fuselage. The track width of 2.7m is

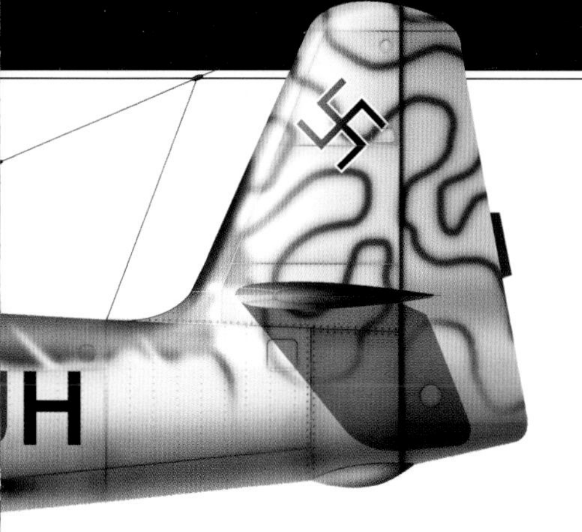

ABOVE LEFT: The simple design of the Heinkel He 343 was meant to speed up its development. Its origins as a scaled-up Ar 234 are evident. Art by Daniel Uhr

200mm larger than that of the model. The aircraft has a starting load of 16.5 tons.

"For the Jumo engines, a single assembly under the wing was chosen for each. This individual arrangement increases operational reliability in case of failure of a single engine, compared to the twin arrangement, and interchangeability. In addition, the twin arrangement produces too much resistance and too great a change in the centre of gravity."

From the overall aircraft weight, 1050kg had been set aside for equipment such as defensive weapons, ammunition, armour and a brake parachute. There was also the option of reducing the bomb load to free up more weight if the 'Strabo 16 to' needed to be fitted out for reconnaissance or as a heavy fighter.

Top speed, assuming Jumo 004C engines with a predicted thrust of 1015kg each, was 534mph and range was 870 miles carrying 1.5 tonnes of bombs.

The report continues: "This aircraft can with the greatest effort and as on industrial object (given the highest priority classification for material supply, quartering, personnel protection, and – help) go into large scale series production in January 1945, so that by the end of July 1945 about 200 aircraft have been delivered.

"Since neither material nor prototype testing can be carried out in time, we are conscious that this is a risk and that there is a possibility errors may occur in the first aircraft to be delivered. This must be taken into account."

It seems Heinkel had been told that a special team was to be formed to design and produce the 'Strabo 16 to' away from existing facilities, with staff Heinkel employees being set up in hotels and given conference centre-like facilities in which to get their work done away from all distractions.

The second-to-last page of the 'Strabo 16 to' report is entitled 'Personnel for quartering' and lists the number of men needed for each part of the process – a total of 430 from Heinkel, 70 from subcontractor Rotan and 130 from the RLM, making a total of 630.

The final page of the report is entitled Strabo 16 to Erforderliche RLM – Entscheide or 'Strabo 16 to Necessary RLM – Decisions'.

Nine points then follow, including the need for the Reichsminister RuK (Rüstung und Kriegsproduktion) or Minister for Equipment and War Production, Hans Kehrl, to classify the project as 'urgent', thereby giving it an overriding claim on materials and other resources; provision of rooms for Heinkel staff at three locations near Vienna – the School of Engineering in Mödling, the Napola (Nationalpolitische Lehranstalt or 'National Political School of Teaching', a boarding school) at Traiskirchen, and the Hotel Panhans at Semmering, and provision of a camp for labourers with food provided.

The last two points were: "8. Issuing a command that [subcontractor] Fa. Rotan-Wien, which works at the moment to 80% for Ernst Heinkel AG, can be used 100% for the special task. About 30 designers currently work at Rotan for Focke-Wulf and Junkers and there are 20 engineers for other tasks. 9. Provision of a Fieseler Storch as liaison aircraft."

The 'Strabo 16 to' report includes drawings showing how the Ar 234 at 155% compared to the original Heinkel jet bomber project, P 1068, and then to the 'Strabo 16 to' itself. Once the report had been submitted, the RLM issued the designation He 343 and the name 'Strabo 16 to' disappeared for good.

The He 343 had a wingspan of 18m and was 16.5m long. By comparison, the Arado E 395 had a wingspan of 17.6m and was 16.85m long. The Ar 234's wingspan was 14.41m and it was 12.64m long.

Expecting that the RLM would set the wheels in motion for the He 343 immediately, Ernst Heinkel was dismayed when first weeks and then months passed without the necessary action being taken.

By July 1944, he had had enough and personally wrote an angry letter to the head of technical development at the RLM, Siegfried Knemeyer.

Dated July 8, 1944, it begins: "Definition of problem. When in January of this year (1944) we were ordered to design a jet-bomber with characteristics similar to the jet fighter Ar 234, to construct 20 experimental aircraft, and simultaneously to prepare its mass production, the following considerations were basic to our problems: 1) It is necessary to provide the Luftwaffe as soon as possible with a jet bomber ready for combat operations. 2) The construction is to follow already tested principles in order to avoid any obstacles to speedy mass production.

"3) Also the selection of the engine should be based on the same viewpoint, therefore only actually available and tested jet engines should be considered for installation, however propulsion units of higher power output, but still in state of development and not sufficiently tested, should be kept in mind for the further development of the model.

"4) Simultaneously with this order, Junkers was asked to design and to construct experimental models, and to prepare for mass production of a jet bomber, in which a number of risks were taken into consideration. The hazards of a forward-swept wing could be compensated for at best by a gain of 30kph; this does not seem to be worthwhile for a model suitable for mass production."

It is telling that the fact of the Ju 287's existence is identified by Heinkel as a "problem". The letter goes on: "He 343. During our work on the P 1068 we did some valuable preparatory work on the field of jet propelled bombers. The design was based on a 150% magnification of Ar 234, in order to avoid hazards in speedy mass production.

"Four Jumo 004C engines were chosen as propulsion units, each providing 1000kg of static thrust. This propulsion unit has already proven itself in operation. The design data for the aircraft (size, weight, area, etc.) were determined by the tactical requirements for jet bombers."

He then goes on to make a comparison between the He 343 and the Ju 287. The two types were based on a similar specification, but where everything about the He 343 had been intended from the outset to emphasise speed and ease of production, the Ju 287 had been designed with the long term in mind, as a fully developed new aircraft. Heinkel, however, seems not to have made this distinction, or to have deliberately ignored it.

He noted that the He 343 airframe weighed 5260kg compared to 7070kg for the Ju 287, meaning that "therefore the Ju 287 requires 1.8 more tons of materials. This higher expenditure of material can only be justified in view of the shortage of materials, if a substantially higher power output were reached in comparison with He 343."

Then there was the maximum payload. On the He 343 it was 2000kg but on the Ju 287 it was 3000kg. However, carrying three tonnes of bombs, Heinkel argued, the Ju 287 would need some serious assistance to get airborne and even if it did, it would struggle to gain altitude fast enough for a minimum margin of safety to be observed: "The carrying of a 3000kg bomb load raises the take-off weight of Ju 287 to 23,555kg. With such a weight, ▶

ABOVE: Another view of the 'Strabo 16 to' model, this time from the side. The aircraft was to be rushed through production, with designers put up in hotels until the work was completed. This intensive development programme never happened for the 'Strabo 16 to' but Heinkel would use the process to good effect more than seven months later while working on the He 162.

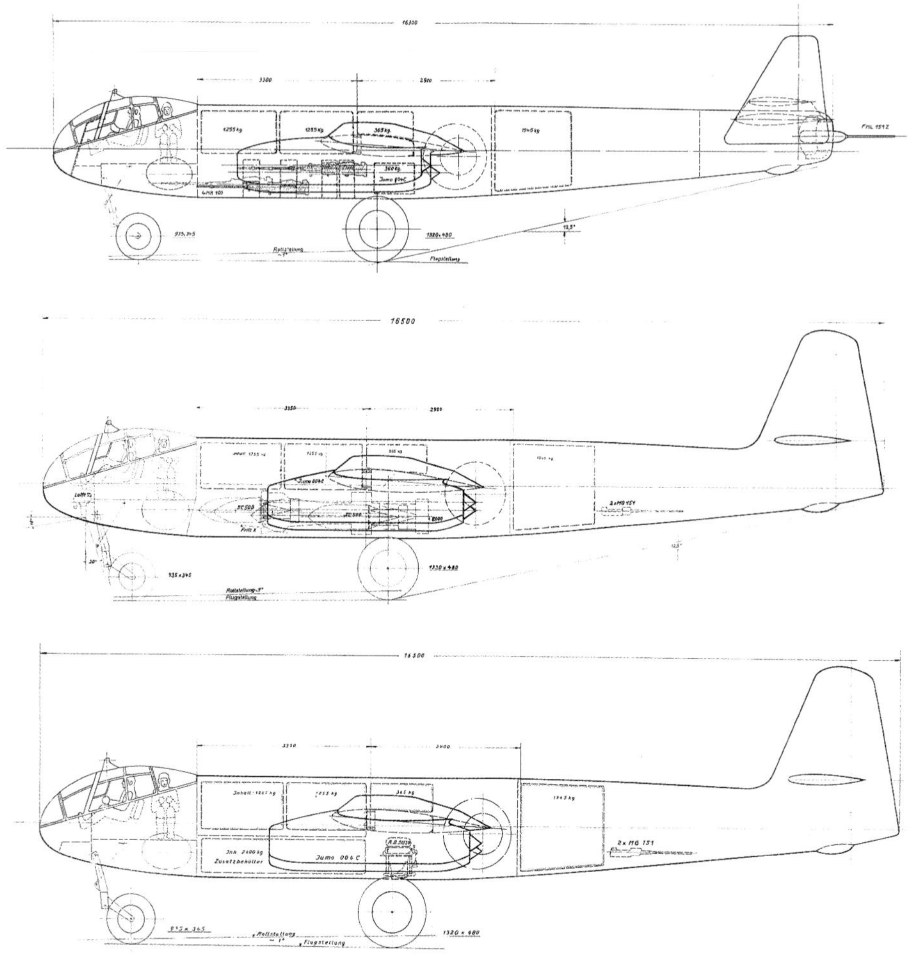

ABOVE: Three versions of the Heinkel He 343 were proposed – the heavy fighter or 'destroyer' pictured at the top, the bomber in the middle, and the reconnaissance machine at the bottom. The heavy fighter version required an entirely different tail section, with two fins to provide better rearward visibility via the pilot's periscope.

the aircraft can take off only with the aid of a take-off assist.

"For an angle of climb of 3^0 after take-off, necessary for flying safety, the take-off weight of Ju 287 without assist has to be limited to 21.5 tons. In the case of jet propulsion, small reserves in take-off are particularly questionable, because with rising air temperatures the take-off capacity of these engines decreases more than in the case of Otto-engines.

"We consider this unsatisfactory take-off as a most considerable part of the risks involved with the Ju 287. For a take-off weight of 21.5 tons, the bomb load should be reduced to 2000kg and the fuel to 6000kg. This reduction equalizes the practical bomb load capacity of both aircraft. The longest cruising range for equal bomb load and equal armour to 1500km for the Ju 287 as compared to 1600km for the He 343."

Not satisfied with this, he went on: "The greater expenditure for Ju 287 does not bring comparable advantages in bomb load capacity and range. The maximum speed is approximately the same for both types." Next, he offered some questionable assertions about the BMW 003 jet engine, which was at that time the power plant most likely to be fitted to the Ju 287.

In conclusion, he wrote: "The greater load space of Ju 287 gives no advantage. The power output of Ju 287 is also reached by He 343, but with considerably lower material expenditure and with four instead of six engines.

"The He 343 can be successfully used as reconnaissance aircraft and bomber. The heavy Ju 287 does not possess this versatility. The flight test of He 343 should not create any new problems. The test should be performed in shorter time, than that of Ju 287, whose many new features, such as e.g. the forward swept arrow-shaped wing, did not yet prove their operational safety. Therefore the He 343 could be ready for mass production at an earlier date than the Ju 287."

Far from being given top priority, it seemed to Heinkel as though his 'special task' was simply being ignored in favour of a rival: "During the conference at Berchtesgaden on May 25, 1944, the Ju 287 was favourably commented upon, while the He 343 was not even mentioned at all. It is proved in the above statements, that the performance of the Ju 287 can be obtained at lower cost by the He 343 (production time, fuel) and without involving the risks of the latter.

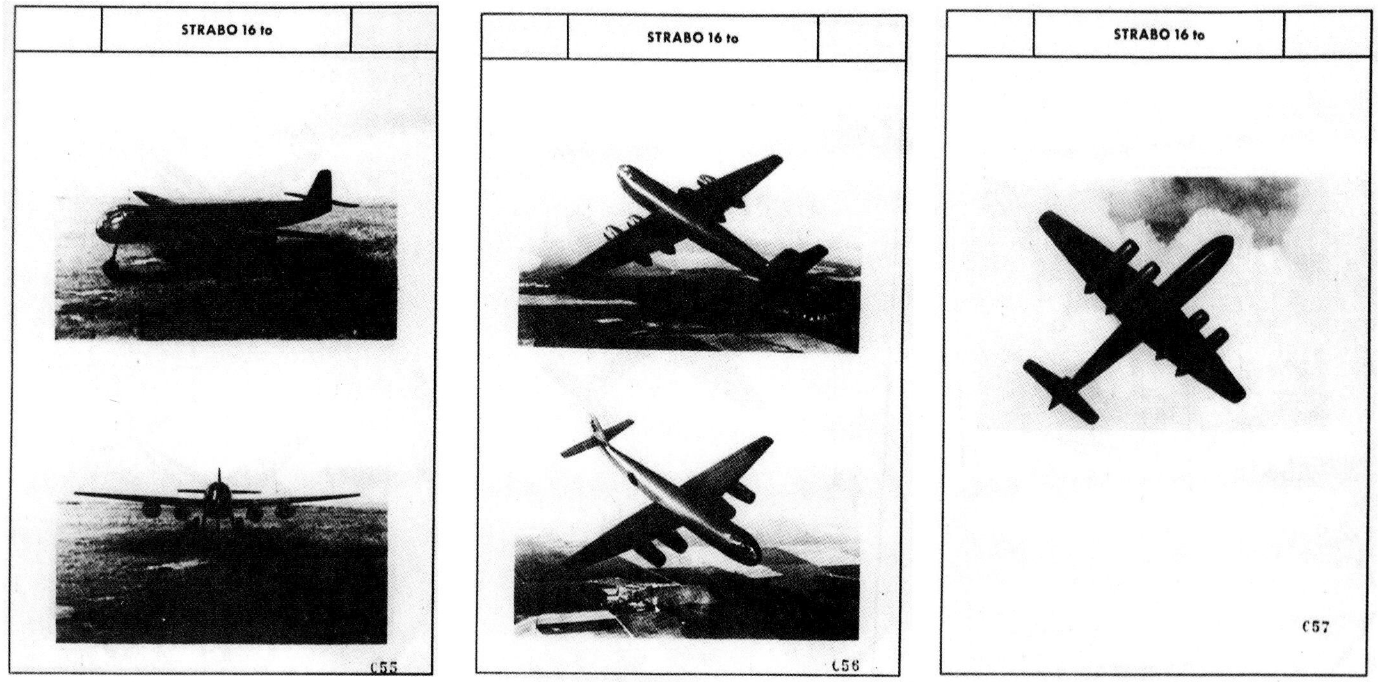

ABOVE: Three pages from a microfilmed print of the 'Strabo 16 to' report, dated February 1, 1944, which show photographs of the Heinkel model staged against various different backdrops to give an idea of how it would look in flight.

"Therefore, in the interest of the national defence, at least a parallel order for mass production of He 343 should be issued simultaneously with the order for mass production of the Ju 287. This order would also fulfil the original demands, expressed in the beginning as definition of problem, i.e. to deliver to the front line as soon as possible a jet bomber ready for combat, with lowest material output, and with least risk."

Taken aback by the letter's vitriolic content, Knemeyer forwarded it on to Heinrich Hertel, technical director at Junkers, for his comments. Hertel wrote back to Knemeyer, then sent a copy of Heinkel's letter on to Walter Cambeis, Otto Mader and Dr Rothe at Jumo and his colleague Richard Thiedemann at Junkers Aircraft. Attached was a note which read: "The Heinkel 'statement' belonging to the proceedings I received from Oberst Knemeyer strictly confidentially and exclusively for my personal use. I therefore first had to send my viewpoint directly to Obert Knemeyer. I request that you use the Heinkel documents exclusively for your personal guidance, these being confidential even with respect to administrative offices."

The letter Hertel wrote back to Knemeyer began: "The statements by Professor Heinkel lead to a grossly mistaken conclusion due to three fundamental misconceptions in his estimations."

Firstly, he said, a Heinkel data sheet dated May 24, 1944, gave the He 343's engine as the underpowered Jumo 004B, whereas Heinkel had calculated the type's performance based on the use of the more powerful Jumo 004C.

Given that the surviving documents, including the original 'Strabo 16 to' report from February 1944 all give the He 343's power plant as the Jumo 004C, this claim does not seem to be entirely credible.

Hertel then went on to argue that Heinkel had given a lower thrust rating for the BMW 003 engine when used in the He 343 compared to when it was used in the Ju 287

Also "in his survey Mr Heinkel compiles data on the Ju 287 which correspond perhaps to some projected design, but not to the results obtained in construction; thus Mr Heinkel estimates the weight of Ju 287 too high and the performance too low".

Evidently Heinkel did not have access to the very latest test results on the Ju 287, unlike Hertel himself. Hertel went on to argue that the Ju 287 had a greater bomb load, though he fails to address Heinkel's argument that this would result in more starting aids such as rockets being required.

Furthermore: "Despite its considerably lower speed the He 343 does not possess a flexible defence armament. The rigid rear guns are considered unsatisfactory. Hr Heinkel apparently admits the necessity of flexible tail armament, because he himself plans in his blueprints (343.01-11B dated May 24, 1944) a solution with twin rudders and rear turret for the fighter-bomber version.

"The design of two completely different fuselages, including tail assembly, seems hardly logical. We still support the viewpoint that it is important in this case to plan and to construct the turret in advance and to manufacture it as standard equipment, ready to be installed at any time."

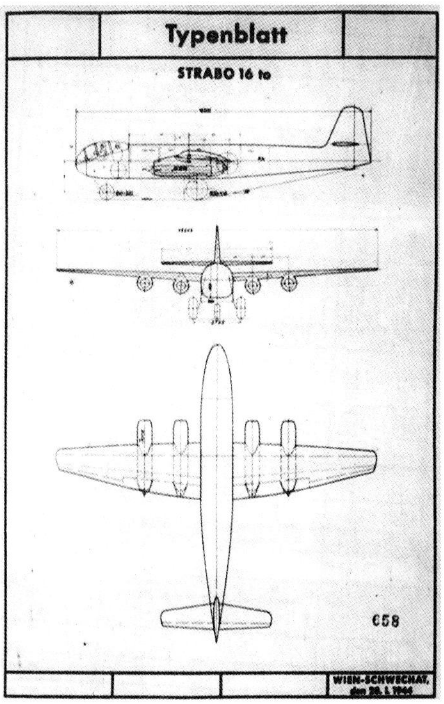

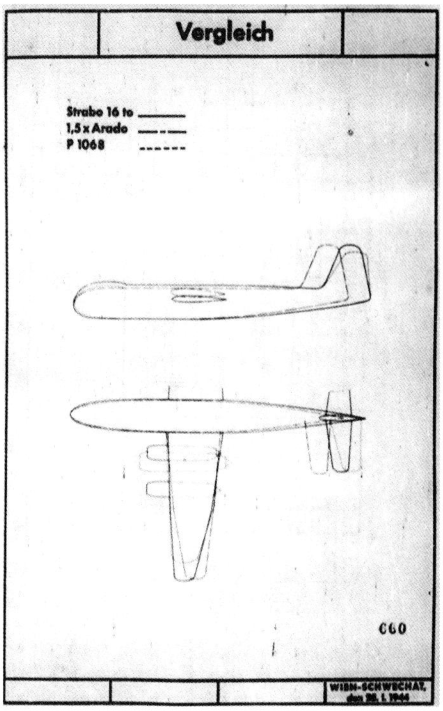

ABOVE LEFT: A basic three-view of the 'Strabo 16 to' bomber from the report. At this stage, only a bomber version was being considered. ABOVE RIGHT: Outlines of the 'Strabo 16 to', scaled up Arado Ar 234 and Heinkel P 1068 set against one another. It is evident that the 'Strabo' has the longer tail of the P 1068 but the fin form of the enlarged Ar 234. The Strabo's wings are almost identical to those of the bigger Ar 234 but with their tips extended a little. In the side view, it can be seen that the Strabo has a more pronounced cabin 'bulge' than either of the others.

Regarding the forward-swept wings of the Ju 287, Hertel wrote: "The continuous reference to the hazards of an arrow-type wing is misleading, since extensive tests in the wind tunnel proved that this problem will be solved in a short period of time."

And finally: "Contrary to the conclusions of the 'statement', attempting to equalise the performance of the two types by misconceived comparisons, it is proven clearly that the performance of the Ju 287 is definitely superior when the same engine is used (Jumo 004C). For equal cruising range, it has double bomb load, 70kph higher speed, flexible defensive armament and pressurised cabin.

"In the design of Ju 287 we have always kept in mind the possible installation of Jumo engines. The basic layout of Ju 287 anticipates the greater overall flight weight in excess of 25 tons, required for the installation of Jumo 004C. Therefore the delivery of an airframe for this type does not create any difficulty (besides some setback in the delivery date, because the blueprints were prepared for the BMW engines).

"The constant fluctuation of plans with various data on performance and delivery of propulsion units can no longer be justified. In order to eliminate this state of precariousness in aircraft development and to stop the juggling with engine data, which unfortunately is beyond our control.

"I did all I could to keep the development of propulsion units BMW 003 and Jumo 004C at the same level thus assuring a similar installation. The industry should of course be promptly and fully informed on the engines to be installed since every change in plans delays production.

"No comment can be made, due to lack of time, on the other arguments advanced in the statement."

Hertel seems to have viewed Heinkel's letter, which was never intended for him, as a direct attack on the Ju 287, rather than the letter of someone attempting to gain redress for a broken promise that it was.

In any case, the He 343 was discontinued and development work on the Ju 287 carried on until the end of September 1944, when it was suspended. Just like the Ju 287 however, this was not quite the end for the He 343. The project number, P 1068, appears to have been resurrected. According to the minutes of a meeting of the EHK 'Flugzeuge' or chief development commission for aircraft, dated November 21-22, 1944, discussed in British report German Aircraft: New and Projected Types: "Work on the '1068' piloted flying model with rocket propulsion was to continue as planned (N.B. This appears to have been a flying scale model of the He 343)."

Further on in the same report, there is a note about 'DFS 1068 research aircraft'. It says: "This experimental high-speed aircraft was reported to have been under construction at Ainring. Trials were to have been made with wings of 0, 25 and 35 degrees sweep-back in order to determine the most suitable angle for both low and high-speed flight.

"The design is very clean and speeds of the order of Mach 1.0 (700 to 660mph) were expected at altitudes of 23,000 to 39,000ft. Propulsion was to be provided by four turbo-jet units (either BMW 003 or HeS 011).

"One proposal called for the mounting of two jet units under each wing. As an alternative it was suggested that one unit should be slung under each wing and the remaining two units mounted in the upper rear portion of the fuselage."

No further detail on the DFS 1068 has surfaced and it is presumed that both the model and the data relating to it were destroyed. ●

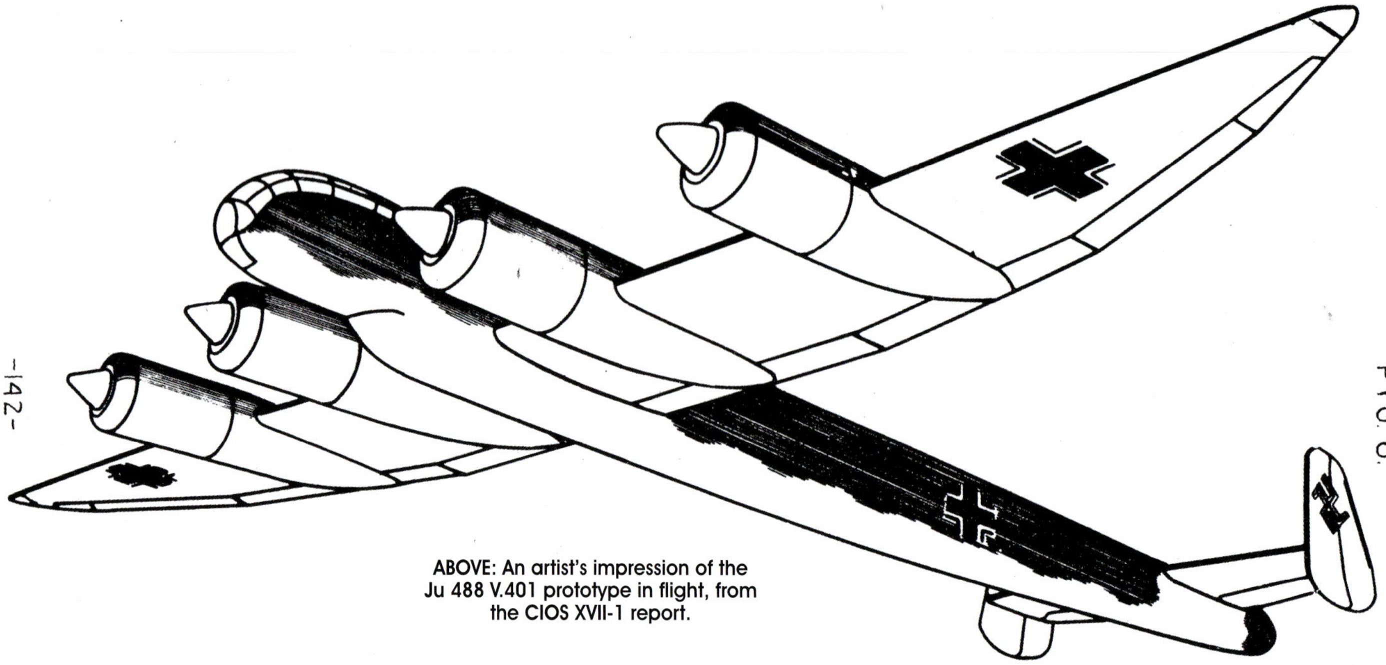

ABOVE: An artist's impression of the Ju 488 V.401 prototype in flight, from the CIOS XVII-1 report.

Frankenstein's bomber

Junkers Ju 488

When Focke-Wulf was awarded a contract to build the Ta 400 it was accepted that the aircraft would not be ready before the end of 1945 at the earliest. In the meantime, there remained an urgent need for a long-range bomber that was simple and cheap to build. Junkers had the answer…

The last German piston-engined bomber project of the war was the Junkers Ju 488. The Fernkampfflugzeug competition had petered out in May 1943 with the RLM choosing a design that would not be ready for two and a half years at best.

The Focke-Wulf Ta 400 would provide not only the bombing power needed to strike at Britain, but also the ability to fly lengthy missions over the Atlantic looking for convoys and attacking them with guided anti-shipping missiles.

But it was a plan for the long-term. An aircraft that could perform these duties even moderately well was urgently needed and in July 1943 Junkers offered a radical solution – why not put one together using readily available bits and pieces from the adaptable Ju 88 series?

A contract was awarded but Junkers, being at maximum capacity just like every other German manufacturer, followed the example set by Focke-Wulf, Heinkel, Blohm & Voss and Messerschmitt by sub-contracting the work to French companies.

The best surviving source on the Ju 488 is probably CIOS XVII-1 German Activities in the French Aircraft Industry, dated January 1945. This was based on a combination of French and German documents, together with information supplied first hand by the French workers concerned.

It states: "At Toulouse the three firms of Latécoère, Breguet and SNCASE had been working jointly on the design and manufacture of this aircraft. Junkers had ordered 10 prototypes, of which the first, known as V.401 (also referred to as V.4010 or V.401C) and intended merely as a flying model without any operational equipment, was almost complete when it was wrecked by an explosion in July 1944."

The actual construction of the Ju 488 took place at Breguet's Montaudran Works, at the Montaudran Airfield south-east of Toulouse. The explosion was caused by a cell of French Resistance saboteurs, led by Léon Elissalde, on the night of July 16-17. They apparently used Sten guns to drive out the German guards before throwing grenades to destroy the V.401.

The report continues: "Some design work has also been done on the operational version, numbers V.403 to V.406 inclusive. It should be noted that this aircraft was known to the French as the Ju 188, derived from the Ju 88, but is in fact the Ju 488, derived from the Ju 188.

"The Ju 488 is derived from the Ju 188 by making the following modifications: a) A new wing centre section with engine and undercarriage leg is inserted between the fuselage and each existing wing, so that the aircraft becomes a four-engined type with a wheel under each nacelle. b) A new section of fuselage about 3m (9ft 9in) long is inserted between frames 12 and 13 just aft of the

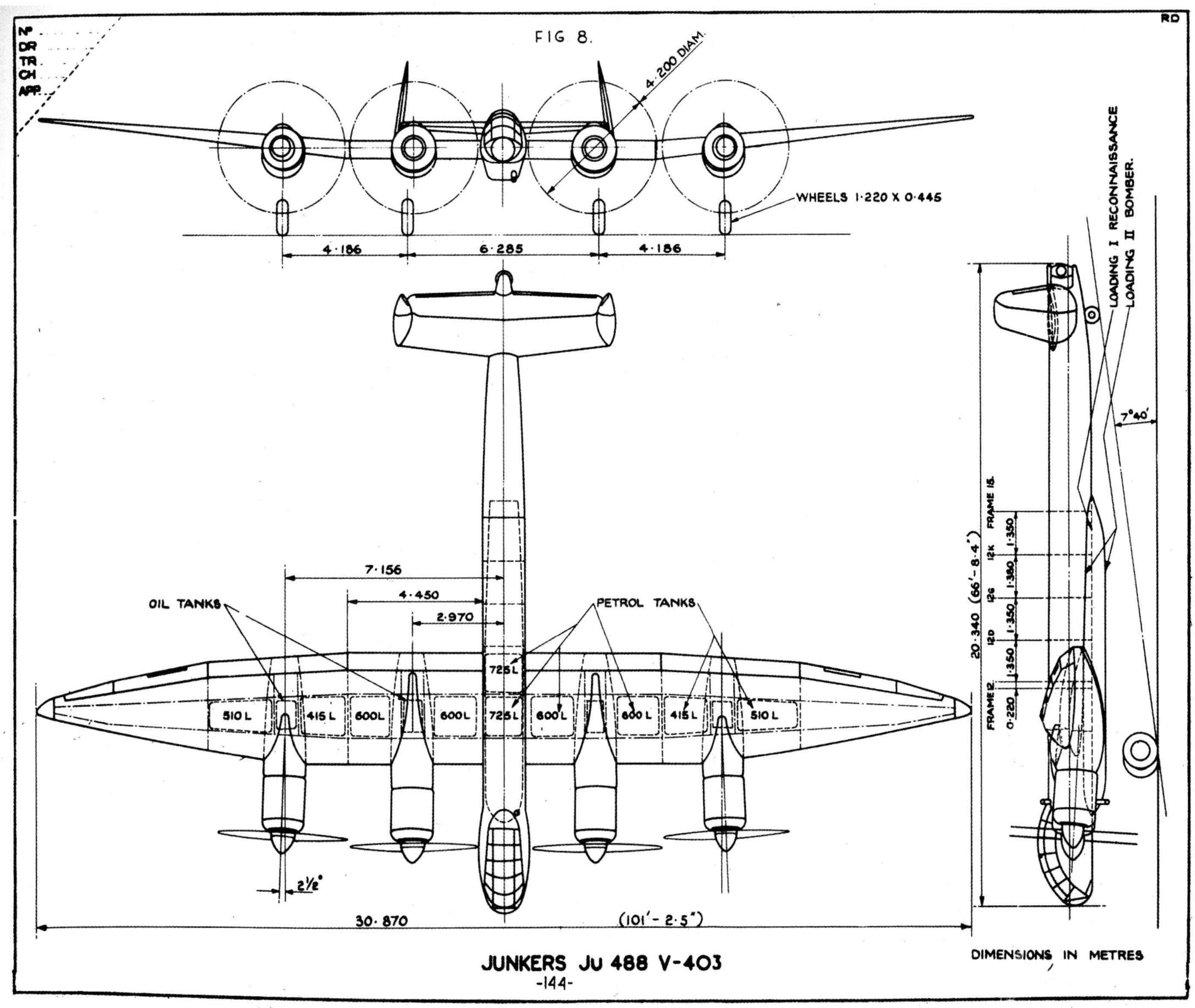

ABOVE: Representing the production model, the Ju 488 V.403 features main landing gear wheels of uniform size, larger propellers and the option to either have a protruding bomb bay or not, if the aircraft in question was to be built for reconnaissance. It was to have a single remotely controlled barbette turret on the end of its tail. During the 1960s, a drawing of the Ju 488 circulated showing a dorsal turret – but no evidence for this exists in contemporary documents.

mainplane. c) The existing tail unit is replaced by a Ju 288 tail unit.

"The first aircraft was constructed using a fuselage, and outer wings supplied from Germany and a tail unit from Holland. All the other parts required were made in France. The engines were said to be 18-cylinder, air-cooled direct injection BMW 802 developing 2000bhp."

Precisely which engines were intended for the Ju 488 has been the subject of some controversy. While the CIOS report XVII-1 clearly states that BMW 802 were to be fitted, information given elsewhere has suggested that Jumo 222 units were to be used in the eventual production version of the Ju 488.

The historical account that included this information, which also suggested that the Ju 488 was to have a dorsal gun turret, was written during the 1960s at a time when most ▶

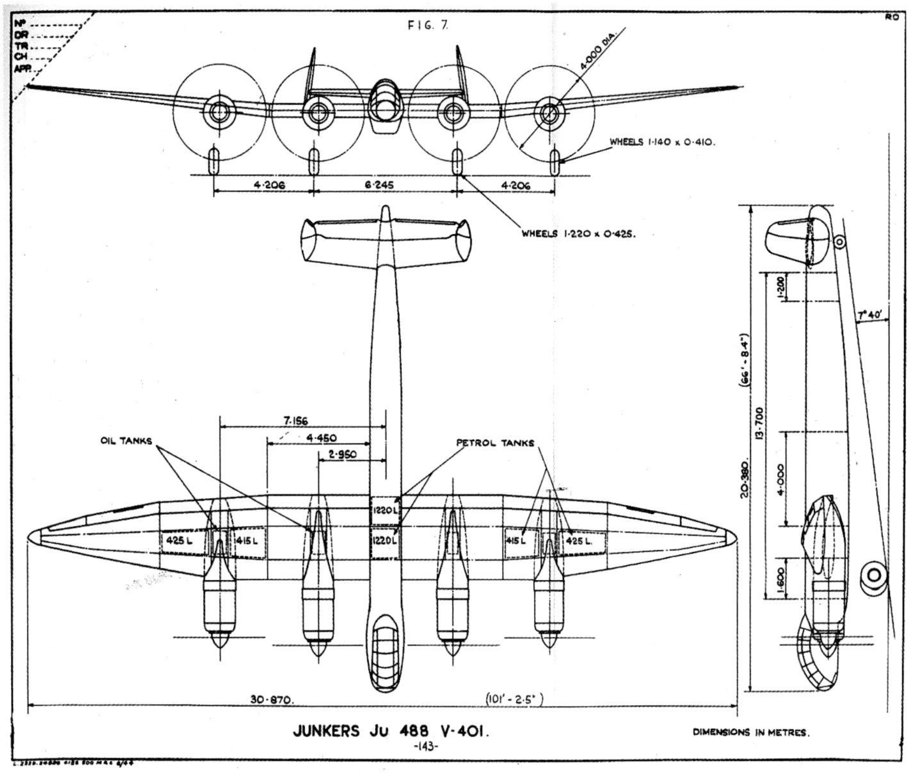

RIGHT: The Ju 488 V.401 was intended only as an experimental aircraft and would have lacked most of the equipment and many of the fittings seen on the production model. Its engine positioning was also slightly different, it had smaller propellers, a protruding bomb bay and larger inboard landing gear wheels than outboard.

ABOVE: A view of the Ju 488 V.401 under construction at Breguet's factory south-east of Toulouse. The bulbous cockpit is furthest away from the camera, near the large shed door, while the port wing has been attached and the starboard wing sits on a frame a few metres away from the fuselage. The horizontal tail surfaces have also been fitted.

intelligence reports on German wartime projects was still classified as top secret. It ought now to be treated with a degree of caution, if not outright scepticism.

The report goes on to note the differences between the bare bones "flying model" V.401 and the more complete V.403 to V.406 aircraft that had not been built: "In addition to the different arrangement of fuel tanks, the following differences are visible on the drawings of the two models: on V.403-6, the inboard engines are set slightly further out from the fuselage than on V.401 (2.97m against 2.95m), while the position of the outboard engines is the same (7.156m).

"A larger propeller (4.2m against 4m) is fitted. In order to avoid the propeller discs of the inboard and outboard engines from overlapping, the axes of the outboard engines on V.403-6 have been set out two and a half degrees in plan view.

"In side view also, the axes of the four engines on V.401 are parallel to the fuselage datum while on V.403-6 the axis is set up three and a half degrees to the fuselage datum, presumably in order to give ground clearance for the increased diameter propellers.

"On the underneath of the fuselage V.401 has a bomb bay extending a little way below the line of the original fuselage structure, while at the tail the taper of the fuselage is reversed to lead up to the larger sized tail unit of the Ju 288. On V.403-6 two versions are possible – 'bomber' with a fairly deep bomb bay, or 'reconnaissance' with no excrescences on the fuselage lower surface.

"V.403-6 have a remotely controlled barbette in the extreme tail, said to be fitted with two 20mm or 30mm guns. The main wheel types on V.401 are 1.14m by 0.41m for the outboard pair, and 1.22m by 0.445m for the inboard pair. This was said to have arisen because the original idea of distributing the load equally to the four wheels would have necessitated considerable strengthening of the outboard undercarriage structure, and the solution adopted was to put large tyres on the inboard wheels so that they took a greater share of the load. On V.403-6 however, all four wheels appear to have tyres 1.22m by 0.445m.

"V.403-6 is shown fitted with a pole projecting above and below the fuselage on the starboard side just aft of the cockpit. This might represent a periscopic sight for the tail guns. The French stated that a small group of Germans was working on the design of a catapulting seat for ejecting the pilot. All the drawings of this were removed when the Germans left. The French thought the aircraft was a good one for series production. All the sub-assemblies could be transported by rail."

The V.403 and later versions were expected to be able to carry 3000kg of bombs up to 1500 miles before turning round and doing the same distance back, for a 3000 mile 'radius of action'. This was with engines at 90% power, doing 367mph at 13,000ft. Flown at the most economical speed of 263mph, range could be increased to 1750 miles each way.

This was sufficient for bombing any part of Britain from bases in France or covering a limited area of the Atlantic on anti-shipping missions but was far short of making the Ju 488 capable of any sort of attack on the United States.

In addition to the CIOS report, there is another brief note on the Ju 488 in German Aircraft: New and Projected Types, published almost exactly a year later, which states: "The Ju 488 is a high altitude long-range bomber and reconnaissance aircraft powered by 4 x BMW 801 TJ engines. It is derived from the Ju 188 by fitting a new wing centre-section to carry two additional engines and a modified undercarriage incorporating one retractable wheel under each engine nacelle.

"Other innovations are a longer fuselage and the fitting of a Ju 288 tail. The aircraft carries a crew of three, with armament of twin MG 131 in a remotely controlled tail turret.

"Two prototypes were intended, the first, known as the V.401, a flying model without any operation equipment was destroyed in France by Allied bombing. Design work had been done on equipped versions V.403-V.406 inclusive. The main difference between the

ABOVE: A side view across the factory at the incomplete Ju 488 V.401. The detached cockpit unit can be seen on the centre right of the image.

V.401 and V.403-6 is in the fuel stowage and capacity, the V401 having 900 gallons and V403-6 1250 gallons."

It is worthy of note that this summary gives the aircraft's engines as BMW 801 TJs, however, neither account mentions the Ju 488 having a pressure cabin. Nor do they state that the 488 was composed primarily of parts from the Ju 388 – as most modern accounts insist. What Junkers' ultimate plans for the makeup of the Ju 488 production model were and what its powerplant was to be may never be known.

Toulouse was liberated on August 19, 1944, effectively bringing the Ju 488 project to an end. ●

ABOVE: Another view of the Ju 488 V.401, this time from the side but also more to the rear. The cockpit is on the right while the fuselage is clearly still a work in progress.

Death from (ve

Sänger Raketenbomber

By far the most ambitious German bomber project of the Second World War was proposed by rocket scientist Eugen Sänger in August 1944. Flying at uncatchable speeds and unassailable altitudes, his vehicle was designed to strike at targets anywhere in the world.

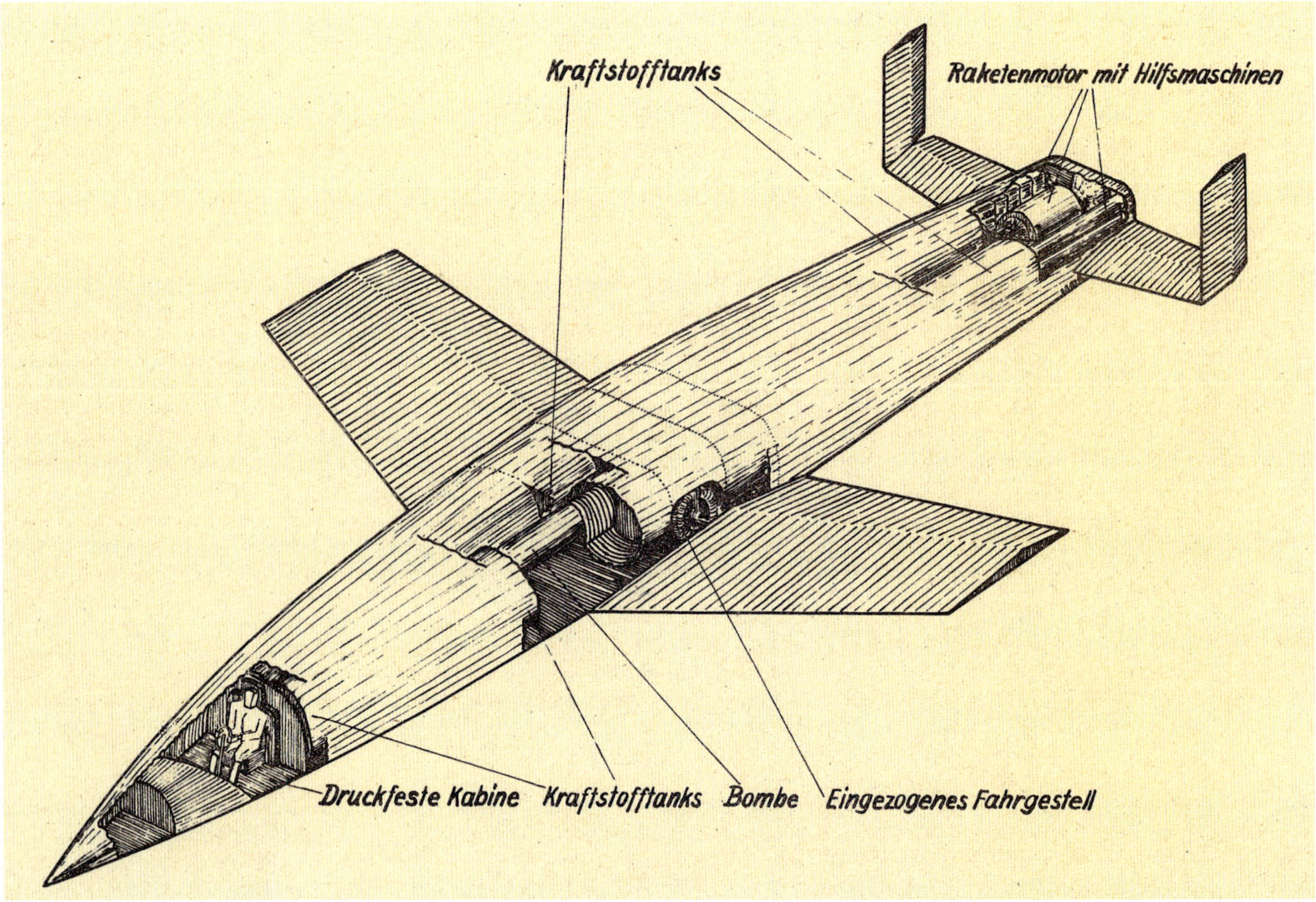

ABOVE: A drawing of the 10 tonne rocket bomber proposed by Eugen Sänger in August 1944 from the original project report. Sänger stated that a 100-strong rocket bomber fleet would be able to level a large city anywhere on earth in a few days.

Building a spacecraft had been the dream of Austrian Eugen Sänger since his student days in the 1920s and in 1933 he published a research paper on rocket flight engineering. Later that year, he took steps to construct a rocket motor at the Technical University in Vienna.

Starting out with small models, he used a combination of oxygen and gas-oil fuels and created a small engine capable of producing a controllable 30kg of thrust. This attracted research funding which he used to pay for purpose-built rocket engine testing installations.

Working with fellow pioneers Count Helmut Zborowski and Irene Brendt at Trauen Aeronautical Testing Station during the late 1930s, he experimented with liquid-fuelled motors and gradually developed plans for a revolutionary new type of rocket-propelled bomber.

During the early part of the war, he worked on ramjet designs for fighter aircraft before returning to his original rocket bomber idea. The latter was summarised in a report he produced in August 1944 while based at the Deutsche Forschungsanstalt für Segelflug EV 'Ernst Udet' at Ainring in Upper Bavaria. It was called Über einen Raketenantrieb für Fernbomber or 'About a rocket engine for long-range bombers'.

He wrote: "The rocket bomber will differ from the present-day propeller-driven bombing aircraft in the following essential points: in place of the propeller propulsion from the fuselage front it has the rocket propulsion in the fuselage stern; the fuselage is in the shape of a bullet with tapered hind part, the wings have a thin wedge-shaped profile with sharp leading and trailing edges and high wing loading at the start of the flight; the cabin is constructed as an airtight stratosphere chamber."

He had considered whether the rocket bomber could be made to take off under its own power but concluded that it would be too heavy and would need wings that were too big. Therefore, he believed, it would be best if the bomber was launched on the back of a high-speed catapult.

"Catapult-starting on a horizontal take-off track until the speed of sound is reached

ry high) above

appears most favourable and is assumed here," he wrote. This meant the aircraft could be launched at supersonic speed without burning any of its own fuel and without suffering the effects of breaking the sound barrier in the air.

Two different sorts of flight plan were considered – one where the bomber accelerated up to top speed then remained at that speed, and another where it accelerated up to a speed so high that the rest of its flight could be a steadily decelerating glide. It was decided that the latter was best.

"The whole procedure for use takes place somewhat as follows: the rocket bomber at the surface of the earth is brought to a speed of about 500m/sec by a ground-fixed rocket drive in a period of 11 seconds over a 3km starting path; then climbs at full motor drive to a height of 50-150km along a path which is inclined at 30° to the horizon at first, but later becomes flatter.

"The duration of the climb is four to eight minutes; usually during this time all the fuel supply on board will be consumed. At the end of the climb the rocket motor is turned off, and the aircraft, because of its kinetic and potential energy, continues on its path in a sort of oscillating gliding flight with steadily decreasing amplitude of oscillation. This type of motion is similar to the path of a long-range projectile which from similar heights follows a descending glide-path.

"Because of its wings the aircraft descending its ballistic curve bounces on the lower layers of the atmosphere and is again kicked upwards, like a flat stone ricocheting on a water surface, though during the entrance into the dense air each time a fraction of the kinetic energy is consumed, so that the initially big jumps steadily become smaller and finally go over into a steady gliding flight."

Sänger described his vehicle's rocket engine in great detail, outlining precisely how it would be built – based on his own experience of constructing experimental engines – and how it would function.

The bomber itself was to be of a somewhat simpler construction, with a curved upper side and a flat underside. It was pointed at the front end and "the large blunt end surface at the stern of the fuselage is necessitated by the size of the mouth of the jet of the rocket motor. The relatively small wing stumps serve mainly for stabilization in flight, and for landing; the wing cross-section is the well-known triangular wedge profile.

"The size of the rocket bomber was chosen as a compromise between a series of contradictory requirements. The idea of making the aircraft as large as possible is suggested by the fact that then the ratio of additional load to weight when empty is generally more favourable, the construction of larger rocket motors is simpler, and with increased size of aircraft the military strength of a rocket bomber group increases while the number of capable pilots required per unit of load transported decreases."

In Sänger's view, the ideal starting weight was about 100 tons – the vehicle itself weighing 10 tons and its fuel, contained in 76 cubic metres of tank space, weighing 90 tons.

On this basis, at the end of its mission the empty vehicle with all of its fuel gone could glide in to land at a relatively sedate 93mph. Landing gear would consist of a retractable nosewheel and a pair of retractable skids – all of which would be housed in the fuselage between the wings. According to Sänger's report: "The front wheel serves to prevent dangerous contact with the ground of the bow end during the bouncing motion of the aircraft during landing, and to slow down (with the aid of the landing gear) the aircraft as quickly as possible.

"Behind the bow is the pressure tight cabin, in which the single pilot sits. It is tight for inside pressure of 0.4 to 0.5 atmospheres, with vacuum outside, and should permit rapid exit of the pilot in case of danger (e.g. after take-off).

"Because of the smooth external shape, visibility from the cabin is very poor. In free flight at high velocity, side view slits and optical aids are sufficient. For landing a ▶

ABOVE: Sänger's purpose-built experimental rocket engine installation in action. The test in progress involved a one tonne high pressure combustion chamber using cooling by evaporation. The engine's fuel tanks are above the roof to the left. The cloud is actually cooling agent. Note the observer on the right.

ABOVE: Another Sänger rocket motor on test. This one produced one tonne of thrust for five minutes.

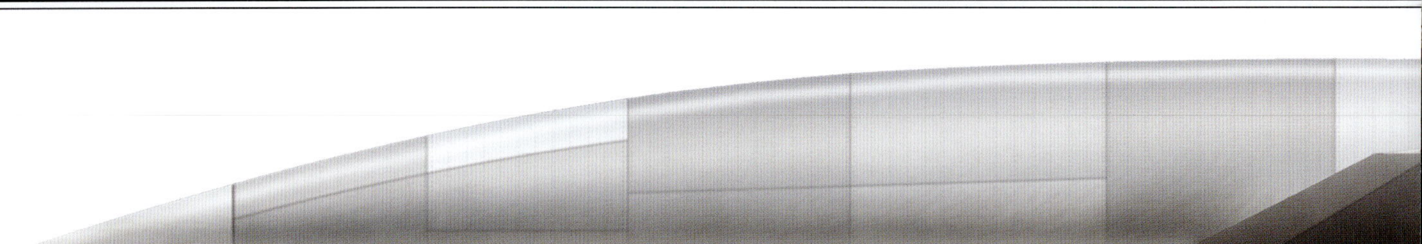

kind of detachable windscreen can be used, since then the pressurisation of the cabin and maintenance of the bullet shape are unimportant.

"A further essential arrangement for the cabin is that the pilot's seat be so arranged that the pilot can take up the high accelerations along the aircraft axis in the best possible position, so that not only body and head but also feet and arms have good supporting surfaces, and at the same position can be shifted.

"The remaining equipment of the pilot's cabin - instruments and radio equipment, ventilation etc. is not considered further. At the back of the pressurised cabin are the tank installations which consist of two large tubes 20.5m long and with maximum diameter 1.9m; these constitute the main part of the fuselage. The upper fourth of the tubes' circumference forms the skin of the aircraft, while the lower half and the space between the tubes is covered so that the required shape is obtained."

The vehicle's bomb bay was positioned "between the wings and the tanks" and it would be able to hold weapons up to 30 tons in weight.

Sänger wrote that he had considered making the rocket bomber entirely automated or remote controlled because "one must admit that an unmanned rocket aircraft can be driven at somewhat higher accelerations than a manned craft; nevertheless, the unmanned craft also soon reaches the point where greater accelerations are compensated for by the greater construction weight necessary for craft capable of undergoing large accelerations. In addition the rocket bomber, because of its long range and the accurate navigation necessary for the bomb release cannot do without a pilot on board.

"Thus the permissible accelerations are limited to values that can be withstood by trained flyers."

The reasons for the careful positioning of the pilot, based on data derived from medical studies, were explained in detail: "In the sitting position the limit is determined by disturbance of the circulatory system, especially caused by loss of blood from the brain or heart due to differences in the hydrostatic level inside the circulatory system. This danger decreases in the lying position, and the limit then seems to be set by difficulties in breathing as a result of greatly increased weight of the thorax.

"This more favourable lying position is directly achieved in a laid back seating arrangement since the accelerations due to the engine are taken up by the pilot in directions perpendicular to the axis of his body. In the lying position in centrifuge tests accelerations of 20g for more than a minute have been withstood by drugged apes, and accelerations of 17g for more than 180 seconds by men."

For its catapult launch, the bomber would be positioned on a rocket-powered take-off sled. The sled would require a perfectly straight, perfectly horizontal track several kilometres in length, and because the bomber and sled together would weigh some 150 tons, the slide rails would need to be very precisely installed and the road-bed beneath them would need to be made out of reinforced concrete. Furthermore, the kilometres-long tracks would need to be covered with lubricants so that the sled could "glide on them with little friction".

Once the bomber had successfully gained the upper atmosphere and was travelling at a speed of between 3000 and 4000m/sec (between 6710mph and 8947mph), it would be able to perform one of two different forms of attack - point and area. For the former, the bomb would be precisely aimed at an individual target "and released at moderate altitude and velocity under the same conditions as for ordinary bombers.

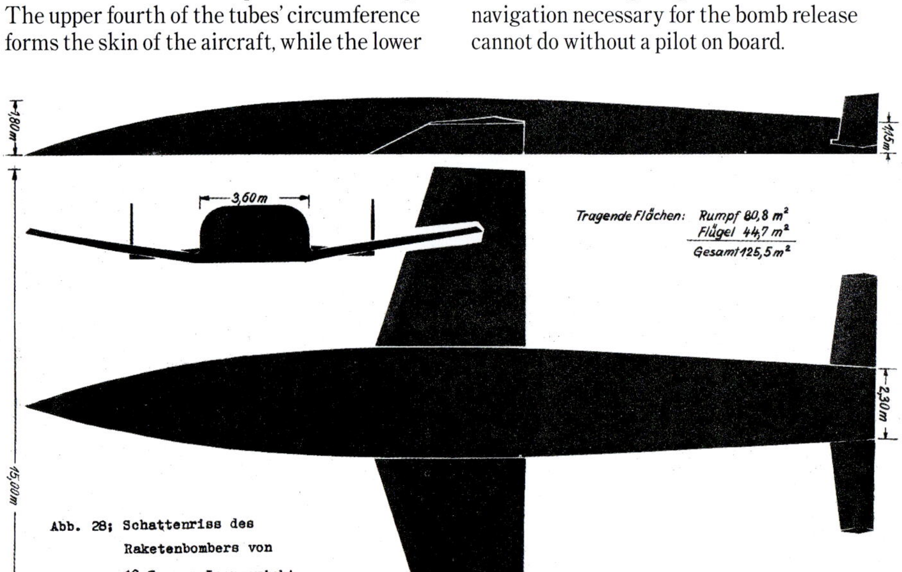

ABOVE: A three-view of Sänger's rocket bomber from the original report.

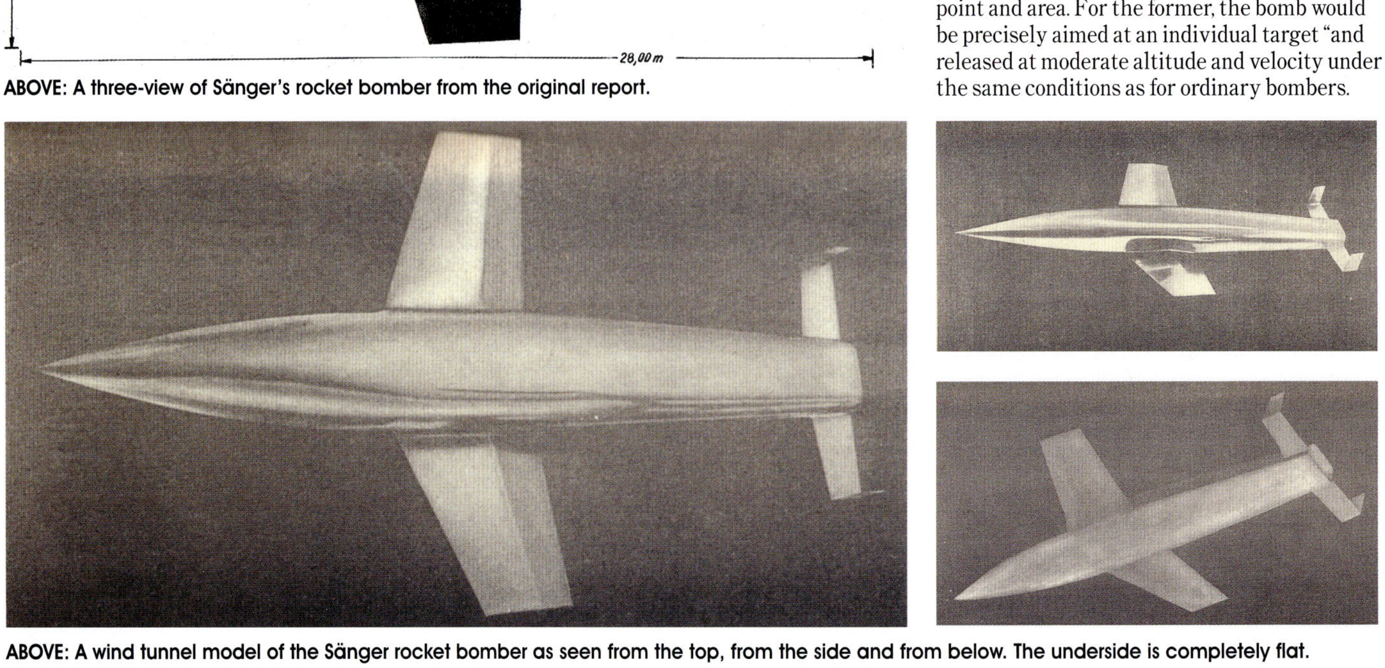
ABOVE: A wind tunnel model of the Sänger rocket bomber as seen from the top, from the side and from below. The underside is completely flat.

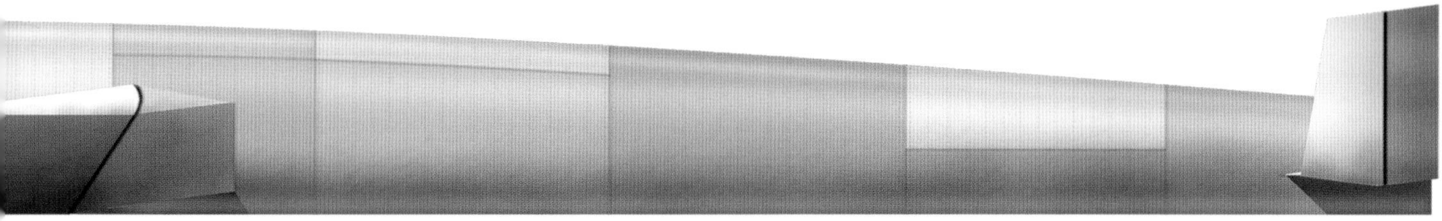

ABOVE: Eugen Sänger's proposed sub-orbital rocket-propelled bomber presented a very slender profile. Art by Daniel Uhr

In practice the same sub-types of bomb release are available to the rocket bomber as for other bombing aircraft, e g. bomb release during horizontal flight, dive-bomb attack, bomb release during climb, low-altitude bombing, etc.

"The well-known conditions and difficulties of these types of release apply practically unaltered to the rocket bomber, especially as regards the accuracy attainable and the need for adequate visibility at the target, so nothing new can be said about these types."

Area bombing was a different story: "Here the bomb is thrown from great altitudes (50-150km) and at very high velocities of flight (up to 8000m/sec), i.e. under conditions far beyond those of long-range artillery fire.

"Since the target, for the distances involved, will not be visible, the release on an area will be aimed indirectly, e.g. by celestial navigation. Thus it is independent of weather and visibility at the target. Because of this, it does not reach the accuracy of release on a point, and we must expect spreads of several kilometres. So with area bombing one cannot hit particular points, but rather a correspondingly large area, with sufficient probability.

"To achieve an anticipated effect on this whole surface, a single drop will not suffice, rather we will have to project several bombs toward the same target; these will distribute themselves over the surrounding surface according to the laws of chance.

"The distribution of hits inside the area will not be uniform; the bombs will strike more frequently in the neighbourhood of the target than far away; there will also be unavoidable bomb-hits far outside the area being attacked. However, on the basis of laws of probability, the bomb distribution can be predicted well enough so that the goal of the attack can be achieved with the same or even greater accuracy than for point attack."

The penetrating power of bombs released at a single target at a dive speed of 500m/sec would be 100m through the earth's crust, 10m through reinforced concrete or 2m through armour plate, "in other words greater than the strength of all known ships' armour".

"Entirely new conditions occur for the area bomb, which has a velocity of impact 10 times as great. The energy of impact is much greater than the energy content of the explosives in the bomb. The strength of the material of the bomb itself will permit it to penetrate a structure, or even to go through a city with numerous buildings, because of the small angle of impact."

Sänger went on to paint a graphic picture of the destruction his rocket bomber would be capable of wrecking if it could be built and used as he intended: "From the mechanics of the explosion process we can get a clear picture of the effect of high impact velocity of an area bomb on the explosive effect.

"In the following consideration we shall assume an impact velocity of 8000m/sec, which we would get if the aircraft descended to the earth's surface at 8000m/sec and released the projectile at short range. After detonation of the area bomb on or above the earth's surface the mass of the resultant ball of fire has not only a radial velocity of 2400m/sec, but also the forward speed of 8000m/sec. The front face of the explosion sphere collides with the air and excites a shock wave as if the explosive had 18.7 times as much energy content.

"The intensity of the explosion wave there is 18 times as great as for a bomb exploding at rest. The intensity drops rapidly for the sideward directions and disappears completely at the rear."

For all its destructive potential, actually carrying out an area attack would be relatively straightforward - and the further away the target the better.

"For procedures of attack on an area the need to fly slowly over the target disappears, so that one has more freedom in carrying out the procedure. The most obvious procedure for area attack with single propulsive period and return home, consists in the bomber being catapulted from its home base, and then driven until it gets sufficient energy to get to the vicinity of the target, turn and get back home. The turn path uses up very large amounts of energy, so that this attack procedure remains limited to small distances and bomb loads.

"Area attack over great distances is very much simplified, if an auxiliary field exists not too far from the target, so that the bomber can land and take on new fuel for the return trip. In this case the area attack goes as follows: after release the bomber makes a partial turn through an angle less than 180 degrees (this requires smaller energy consumption than for a complete turn) then flies to the auxiliary field on its residual energy.

"This area attack with single propulsion, partial turn and auxiliary field is applicable to all distances on the earth; it assumes, however, that within at most a few thousand kilometres from the target there is a suitable auxiliary field for landing and which has a take-off apparatus. In view of the large number of possible targets for area attack, this requirement can be fulfilled only in exceptional cases."

If no auxiliary base was available, the bomber would fly a straight course all the way around the earth - circumnavigating the globe - until it reached its home base.

"As an example of an area attack with single propulsion period and circumnavigation, we shall use the attack on the city with a million population most distant from Germany - Sydney in Australia. In this case the range of attack is 16,500km, the possible bomb load is three tons.

"The flight goes as follows; take-off and motion after take-off do not differ from the same phases of previous examples - 36 seconds after take-off the motor begins to operate and consumes the 87 tons of fuel on board over the next 5.8 minutes. At the end of this climbing process the velocity is 7200m/sec, the altitude 101km, distance from take-off point is 815km and weight is 13 tons.

"This very high initial speed drops to 300m/sec in the course of the supersonic descent which is 39,185km long. After a 10,000km journey, the strongly oscillating descent must be damped sufficiently so that at the release point, 15,400km from take-off, it runs smoothly enough at the stationary altitude to enable accurate aiming for the bomb release.

"At the release point the altitude is 49km, the velocity is 6400m/sec, and the range of projection of the bombs is 1100km. After release the bomber starts its supersonic glide with only 10 tons weight, during which the course which was previously in a plane has ▶

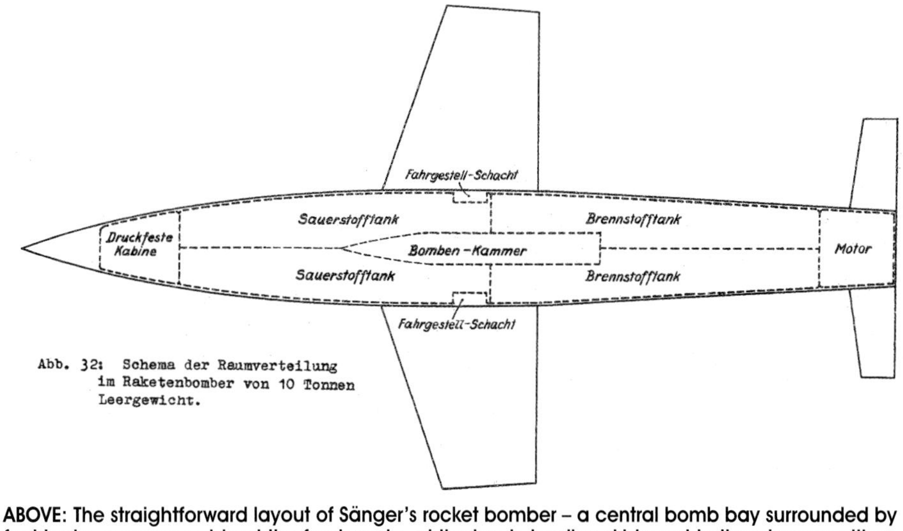

ABOVE: The straightforward layout of Sänger's rocket bomber – a central bomb bay surrounded by fuel tanks, pressure cabin at the front, motor at the back, landing skids next to the wings on either side. The nosewheel installation is not pictured.

ABOVE: A Karabiner 98K bolt-action rifle, shown in the foreground, was used to fire a bullet around an 8m radius track during high speed friction testing at Sänger's experimental facility.

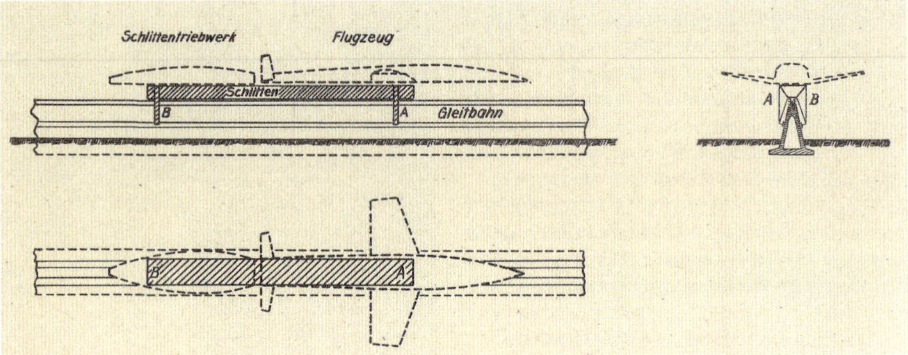

ABOVE: One of the hardest parts of building the rocket bomber in the Germany of 1944 would have been building its 3km take-off track and rocket-powered launch sled. These would have made an inviting target for Allied bombers. This diagram from the report shows how the sled would have been locked onto the rail to prevent high speed accidents.

to be altered slightly in order to lead back to the home base. There the bomber lands 13,060 seconds - just over three and a half hours - after take-off, having travelled 40,000km."

Suggested targets for point attacks by the rocket bomber included individual houses, railway stations, tunnel entrances, streets, bridges, dams, single ships, canals, dikes, breakwaters, gas tanks, water tanks, oil tanks, munitions depots, magazines, power stations, transformer stations, airdromes, harbours, factories and troop concentrations. If the Luftwaffe was willing to sacrifice the bomber itself - not killing the pilot but simply being unable to get the bomber airframe back - then the range of attack could "extend over the whole of the earth's surface".

Area attacks could "be directed against the entire earth's surface. The probable scatter of bombs over several kilometres limits them to target areas of this magnitude, e.g. cities with over a million population, large industries, fleets etc."

Sänger was emphatic that his rocket bomber was not a development of any existing military craft and was not intended to replace any existing type "but rather, a problem has been solved for which no solution existed up to now, namely, bombardment and bombing over distances of 1000 to 20,000km.

"With a single rocket bomber point attacks can be made, e.g. from Central Europe, on distant point targets like a warship on the high seas, a canal lock; even a single man in the other hemisphere can be fired upon.

"With a group of 100 rocket bombers, surfaces of the size of a large city at arbitrary places on the earth's surface can be completely destroyed in a few days."

A 12-step development process for bringing the rocket bomber into service was offered - first the engine combustion chamber would be developed, then the fuels, then the auxiliary engines, then a model of the rocket motor would need to be tested. Next, wind tunnel and tow tests could be carried out on a model of the airframe, then the airframe could be built, then its full scale motor could be bench tested, then the take-off sled could be developed, followed by take-off and landing tests using the completed bomber. Then there would be flight tests, navigation tests and finally bomb release tests.

Despite the huge amount of research that went into his design - resulting in a report the size and weight of an old-style telephone directory - Sänger had seriously underestimated the difficulties inherent in his proposal and the problems that attempting to build his rocket bomber would face.

The bomber was meant to operate at altitudes of between 164,000ft and 492,000ft but this high up none of its control surfaces would work since there would be no air flowing over them. Without advanced alloys to form a heat shield, the bomber would suffer intolerable heat build-up during re-entry and be destroyed.

Other problems were likely to arise from the aerodynamic form of the vehicle too - but Sänger's fundamental idea was no mere fantasy and the American space programme would eventually demonstrate that the basic principles of his idea did have a basis in scientific reality. In 1944 however, it was just an idea. ●

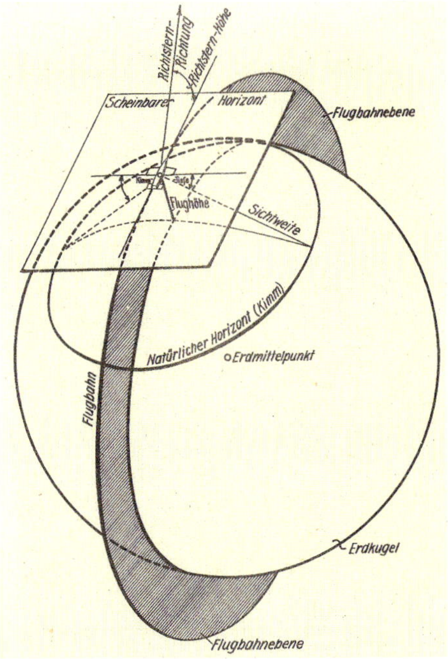

ABOVE: The rocket bomber during the aiming phase of its flight plan while circling the globe towards its target.

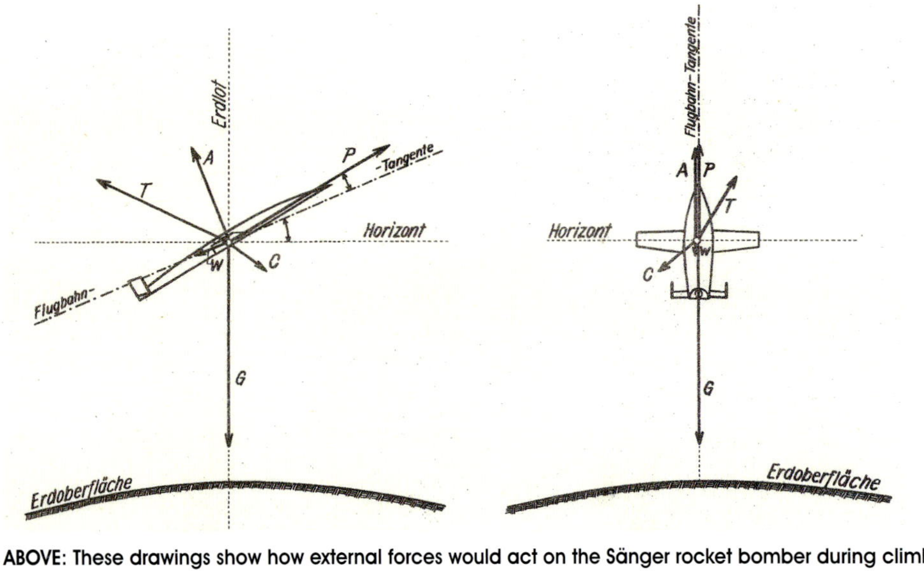

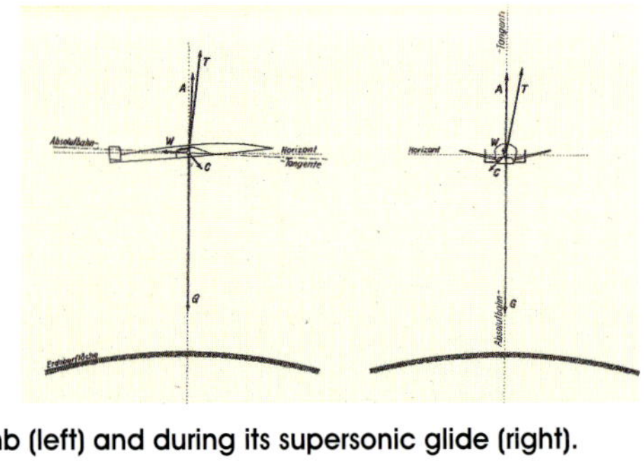

ABOVE: These drawings show how external forces would act on the Sänger rocket bomber during climb (left) and during its supersonic glide (right).

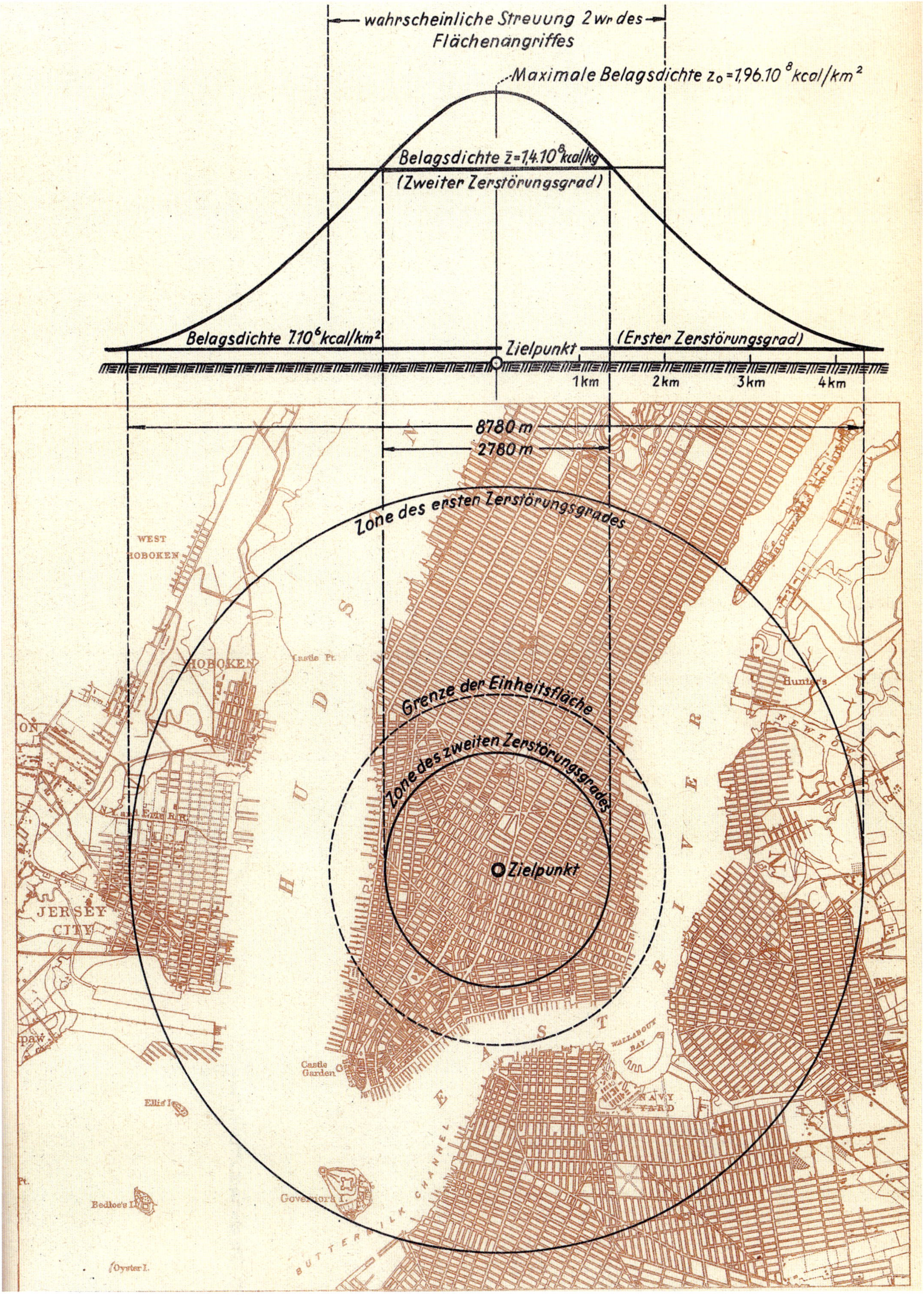

ABOVE: A map of late 1930s New York from page 339 of Sänger's report, showing what the report itself describes as "a distribution curve of bomb hits" from the rocket bomber. This map has been appropriated for use in numerous other contexts to illustrate numerous theories concerning a German attack on New York but it properly belongs here as part of an examination of Eugen Sänger's rocket bomber project.

The best form of defence

Daimler-Benz Schnellstbombenträger, Trägerflugzeug and Selbstvernichter (SV) aircraft

With Allied bombers pounding German industry and infrastructure on an almost daily basis by late 1944, and with efforts to create an effective interceptor fighter apparently getting nowhere, thoughts turned to another way of stopping them – destroying them at source.

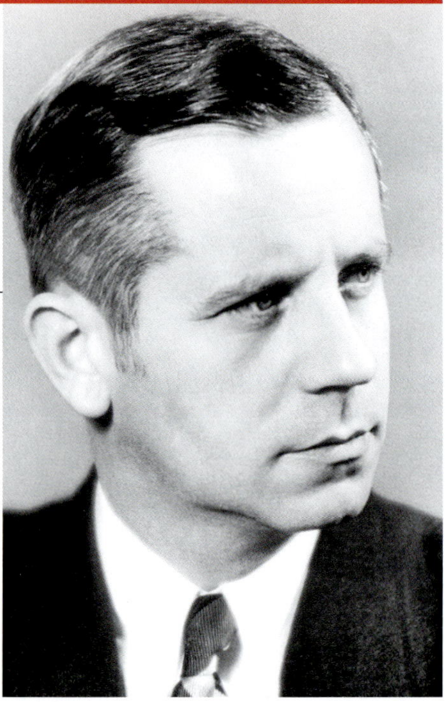

ABOVE: Daimler-Benz technical director Fritz Nallinger conceived the Schnellstbombenträger and Trägerflugzeug as a solution to the problem of getting a heavily laden jet bomber off the ground.

Willy Messerschmitt instigated the last bomber competition of the war in November 1944 by offering the EHK his P 1107 project. His proposal was simple - build a fast four-engined jet bomber that could bypass Allied defences and deliver a heavy payload. The Arado Ar 234 had proven that a jet could easily evade piston-engined interceptors but having been designed as a reconnaissance aircraft it was incapable of carrying enough bombs to make any real difference.

The P 1107 bomber, he argued, would be similarly unassailable but much more effective and the EHK agreed that the idea needed to be explored. As Messerschmitt set to work on developing this idea and his designers began sketching it out, Focke-Wulf chief engineer Herbert Wolff started to draw up a rival design. But by December he had encountered a seemingly insurmountable problem.

While it was possible to design a fast swept-wing bomber and give it sufficient range to reach England with a decent load of bombs, getting it off the ground in the first place was very difficult. Swept wings generate less lift and given the sheer weight of the necessary payload the bomber would need a very long concrete runway - exactly the sort of runway that was proving to be such an easy and attractive target for the Allied bomber formations.

Focke-Wulf chief designer Kurt Tank himself evidently mentioned this problem to Daimler-Benz director Fritz Nallinger, who went away and gave it some serious thought. From this brief exchange, Nallinger and his colleague Erich Übelacker formulated a

LEFT: The revised single fuselage version of the Trägerflugzeug with V-tail version of the fast bomber loaded beneath it, ready for take-off. Once the carrier had taken the bomber up to launch altitude, not far from its base, it would fly back down to pick up the next one. Art by Daniel Uhr

proposal which could not only solve Tank's problem but also help to solve the much wider problem of the Allied bomber streams which at that time were inflicting severe damage on German industry and infrastructure.

A short while later, Nallinger came back to Tank and presented him with the idea – a second aircraft specifically designed for heavy lifting which could get the fast bomber off the ground and carry it up to an altitude from which it could be launched. Fitted with rugged fixed landing gear, powerful engines and large wings, the carrier would be able to operate from rough landing strips and could be moved easily from one area to another. Only a handful of these would be necessary, since each one would only fly short distances before turning round, landing and repeating the process.

Daimler-Benz as a company then commissioned Focke-Wulf to carry out the detailed design work and crunch the necessary numbers to turn the proposal into a seemingly viable prospect for production. In the meantime, Nallinger and Übelacker co-authored an outline proposal entitled 'Reflections on the development of a fast bomber'. Written in the first person, apparently by Nallinger, it seems to have been written to be delivered as a speech.

The proposal begins: "In the current air war, the enemy power ranged against Germany compels us to speculate on the various points of view regarding what can be done against it.

"The most obvious solution is the construction of fighters and destroyers that can fight the enemy bombers and their fighter escort in direct attack. Such measures, however, at this stage of the war, can only be partially successful. This is because a large number of aircraft are necessary to effectively tackle the large masses of bombers and escort fighters.

"It is understood that in spite of all that, this path must be followed and that as much as possible fighters of technical quality superior to that of the enemy must be provided. However, one must consider the combat of such bombers also from the point of view of attacking the bases and the supplies that are an absolute prerequisite for the bombers to fight.

"My colleague, Mr Übelacker, and I have especially thought about how the bases of the enemy bombers, the airfields, hangars and supplies can be effectively combated. It is reasonable and extremely effective to launch the largest possible surprise attack and bombard these airfields and hangars. If it were possible to destroy these bases in one day or over several consecutive days, including the aircraft located there, then it would at least for a time, allow us to recover from the bombing of the enemy that is paralysing us.

"Our industry and our transport network could make a reasonable recovery during this time, which would in turn create the opportunity for us to build the fighters we need for the defence of our homeland and to make fuel available for them. Such a surprise attack against the enemy could not be carried out by German bombers of the normal type, such as the enemy use themselves, not even a bomber of a more modern design with a speed of 372-434mph. Such an attack, even started with a great company of bombers, would miserably expire when faced with the exceptionally strong opposing fighter force."

Nallinger and Übelacker argued that it would not be possible for German industry to build enough bombers for such an attack anyway. But "from these existing facts we made considerations about how a successful attack, as described above, could be achieve despite a not too big industrial capacity. We came to the conclusion that only a fast bomber can solve this problem".

The fast bomber they were thinking of needed to meet three requirements – it had to fly at close to the speed of sound so that it could not be intercepted by the enemy, it had to be cheap, and it had to be able to carry a bomb load larger than that of conventional bombers despite being smaller than them in order to save materials.

If the first requirement could be met, there was no way even an Allied jet fighter could catch the German jet bomber unless it happened to randomly cross paths with it – and even then it would be very difficult to hit with conventional weapons.

Furthermore: "At the altitude at which the fast bomber would be travelling, the flak is also powerless; only the anti-aircraft missile could be used as a defense, but the accuracy due to the high airspeed of the fast bomber would be very uncertain here." ▶

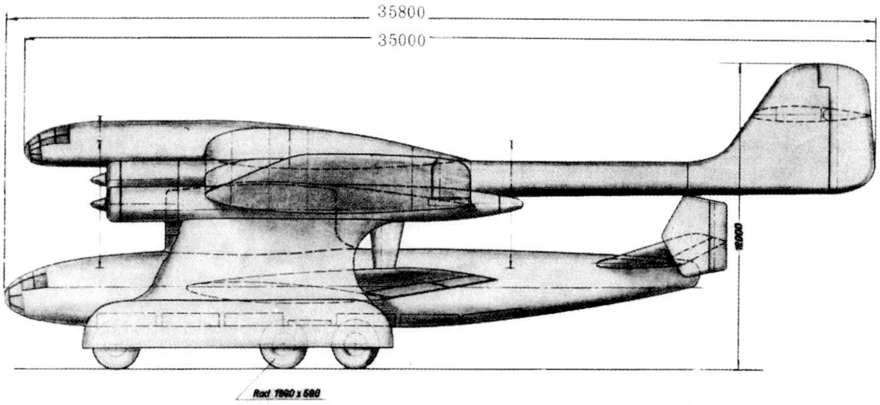

ABOVE: The fast bomber and carrier combination as envisioned in February 1945. The twin-boom carrier was powered by six Daimler-Benz DB 603Ns, while the bomber had a single Daimler-Benz turbojet of unspecified type.

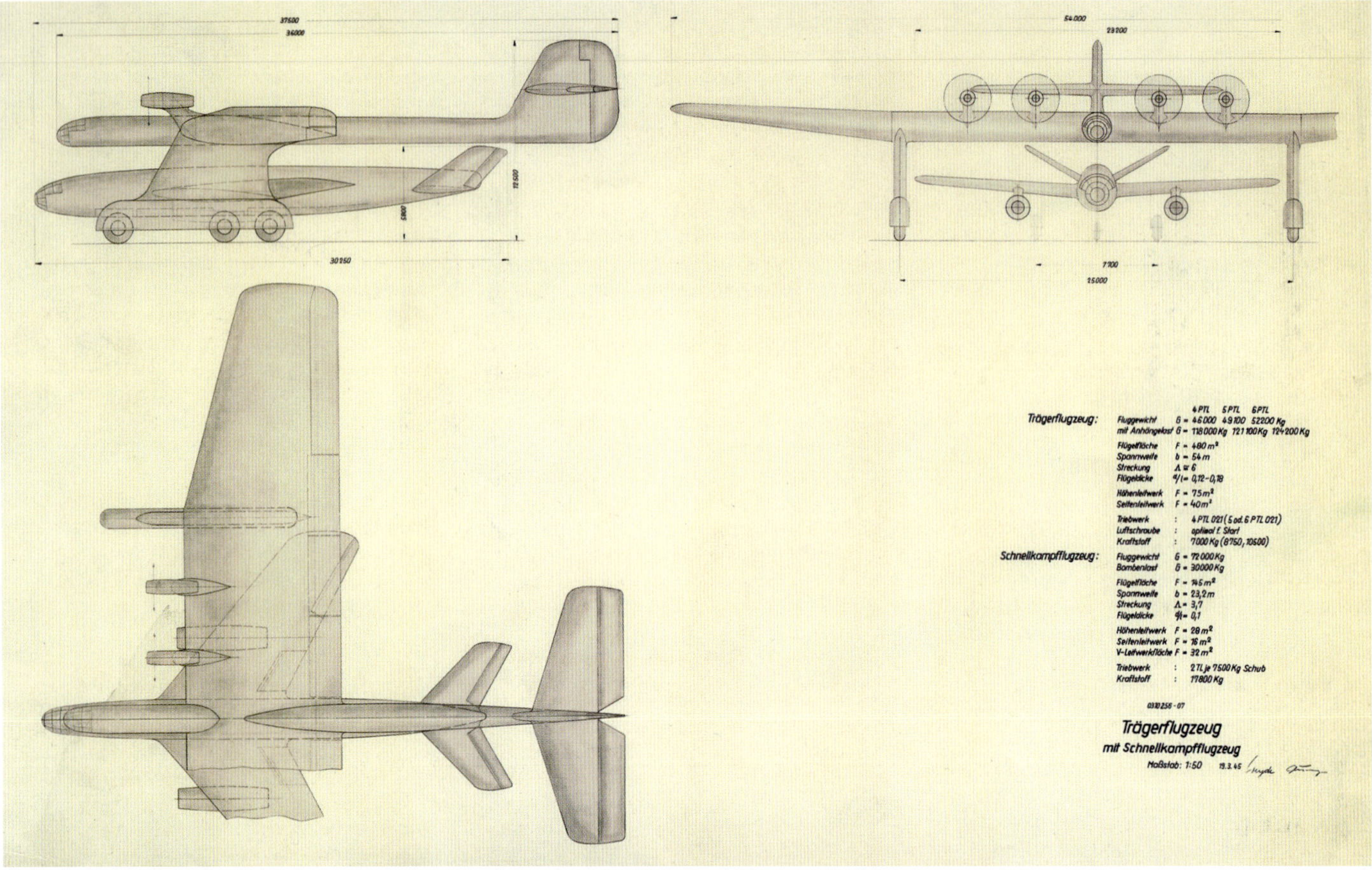

ABOVE: The fast bomber and carrier combination as it appeared in Focke-Wulf drawing 0310 256-07. This design was produced more than a month after the first reports describing the project had been published. The carrier's layout had been substantially altered and it was now to be powered by Daimler-Benz turboprops.

Even detecting the fast bomber's approach would be tricky, because of the short time it would take to reach its target and the fact that people on the ground would not be able to hear it either. Although the bomber would be built to attack Allied bases, it could also be used as a reconnaissance machine: "Here, the bomb bays are equipped with auxiliary fuel tanks. In order to achieve the maximum speed, the aircraft carries no offensive or defensive weaponry. Its defence is secured only by its high speed." Fitted out for the reconnaissance role, the fast bomber's range would be increased to between 4970 miles and 5600 miles – a vast improvement on its range with 30 tons of bombs, which was just 1240 miles.

Now the Daimler-Benz executives came to the key part of their proposition, and the part that was supposed to be of interest to Focke-Wulf: the "help agent". The proposal states: "In order to achieve this speed and at the same time carry a large bomb load with the smallest construction cost, we have to turn to a help agent. The bomber aircraft is designed with a very high wing loading of 500kg per square metre, with the extraordinarily high payload of 30,000kg, a combat radius of 620 miles and a cruising speed of 620mph. Launching an aircraft with such high wing loading on its own would entail a take-off speed of about 310mph.

"The chassis and the tyres would need to be designed for 70 tonnes total load and in this dimension they would be too large to be retractable into the aircraft. Starting with 310mph would probably not only make concrete runways, but a start cart necessary also any starting aids such as powder rockets, a Walter device or the like, using both necessary and today hardly procurable fuels.

"Such ground facilities would certainly also lead to false starts and therefore to the destruction of the aircraft. In addition, such activities would be highly visible from the air, and we have already seen that the enemy bombers prefer attacking and destroying those runways. Thus, the starting of such an aircraft would be quite impossible. So one has to be freed from such dependencies, and able to launch from any ordinary airfield or area of land.

"And based on the above considerations, in my view, the chassis, the tyres and all the components that need to be used during the landing impact must be designed for only the landing weight of the empty aircraft so that when the aircraft is fully laden, the landing gear is not used at all but remains retracted. Thus, these components are very light in relation to the fully laden vehicle."

The answer was the carrier aircraft, one of which would be needed for every three fast bombers. Attaching the bomber to the carrier would be much easier than was the case with other 'piggyback' composites because the process would be more like loading bombs, with the bomber manoeuvred into position underneath the very tall carrier.

"Borrowing the large wing area and the strong landing gear of the carrier, the bomber can start on any normal airfield. The take-off run can be very short, less than 500m, so that even small airports can be used. The carrier aircraft makes possible further rapid deployment of the composite from one place to another because it can also be used to some extent as a large van within which the entire entourage can be transported. With the carrier aircraft, it is possible not only to launch fast bombers but also other high wing loading special aircraft.

"So you can see that such a team, even though it may seem at first sight to be cumbersome, has many advantages, so that on closer inspection it is nevertheless worthwhile to formalise this idea, and it should again be emphasized that the actual bomber can be kept very lightweight in its construction, because a large part of the components need to be designed only for the landing weight of the empty aircraft.

"Professor Tank of the Focke-Wulf has taken an active interest in our proposal, and he has taken our proposal and had it checked by his company, who have drawn it up in the form of a project. I would like to thank Professor Tank for his responding to this proposal. In cooperation with Professor Tank and his staff we have calculated the proper values for this project. Details I will show later in the summary. More detailed information can be found in the Kurzbeschreibung Nr. 28 brought out by the Focke-Wulf company. From this, it is apparent that the objectives of this proposal can be achieved."

The proposal briefly outlines the fast bomber's empty weight as 22 tonnes and the bomb load of up to 30 tonnes. Potential targets for a single fast bomber would include airfields, major rail systems, factories, ports and shipping; and "in a surprise assault with relatively few aircraft, all important airfields of the enemy and the aircraft parked on them could be destroyed". The fast bomber would require fewer crewmen than an ordinary bomber and fewer trained pilots and radio operators would be required.

SUICIDE ATTACKERS

Hauling heavily laden bombers into the air and transporting men and materials from airfield to airfield were not the only uses to which the carrier aircraft could be put, however. In addition to the joint Nallinger-Übelacker proposal, Erich Übelacker had come up with his own idea – using the carrier as a launch platform for suicide attack aircraft.

The document continues: "I want to present this complementary proposal by my colleague, Mr. Übelacker. He suggests the extension of the fight against the enemy bomber force through the building of manned self-destructing aircraft, each with a 2.5 tonne explosive charge which is housed in the fuselage nose. Such aircraft can of course also be unoccupied and equipped with remote control.

"This aircraft also has the high wing loading of about 500kg per square metre and is as fast as the bomber previously described. It would start from the same carrier aircraft as a team. Here, however, the carrier aircraft can launch anything from a single aircraft up to six of them."

Rather than being launched directly against Allied bomber formations however, this explosives-packed suicide attacker was to be used primarily against ships. The importance that the Germans attached to sinking Allied shipping has seldom been so clearly put: "It is proposed that these aircraft will be used for fighting ships, in this case in particular to combat tankers. The destruction of a tanker of 15,000 tonnes means the loss of fuel for three major attacks on Germany by the enemy.

"The idea here with the sacrifice of a man and an aircraft, or using remote control only an aircraft, to prevent three large attacks is, in my view, significant. Of course, this aircraft can also be used for attacking different shipping targets, i.e. warships.

"The bombing and torpedo bombing of ship targets is generally of poor efficiency and tankers are particularly hard to sink, whereas the correct application of a 2.5 tonne shaped explosive charge is the fastest way to get the job done. Besides the carrier aircraft, which can be used here in the same design as for the fast bomber, also the fast bomber itself can now be used as reconnaissance for this self-destructing aircraft. Thanks to its high range as a scout it will be able to locate ships early enough before they dock. As a result of its high speed, the fast bomber cannot be attacked as a single machine.

"Furthermore, the self-destructors can optionally be guided to their target under the leadership of the fast bomber. Work on the self-destructor aircraft has also been commissioned from Professor Tank by my staff."

Finally, the proposal turned to the thorny issue of actually making the fast bomber/carrier/self-destructor a reality. The first problem identified was simply finding sufficient production capacity for it but the hardest task would be building engines that were sufficiently powerful for the fast bomber: "The greatest difficulties are likely to lie with the development of the jet unit necessary for the fast bomber with 13,000kg of takeoff thrust. This device must have 10 times the thrust of the strongest unit available today.

"To solve such a problem in a short time, given war events, would be extraordinary. However, thinking very positively and with the benefit of our experience we believe this problem could be solved both on the engine side and on the side of the fuselage in such a short time that these two projects could be employed in a reasonable time.

"However, the decision to proceed would have to be taken immediately, and every possible measure must be taken to aid development in the shortest possible time. This proposal should not be placed with those other prospective projects for warfare but, in my view, must be initiated at once." ▶

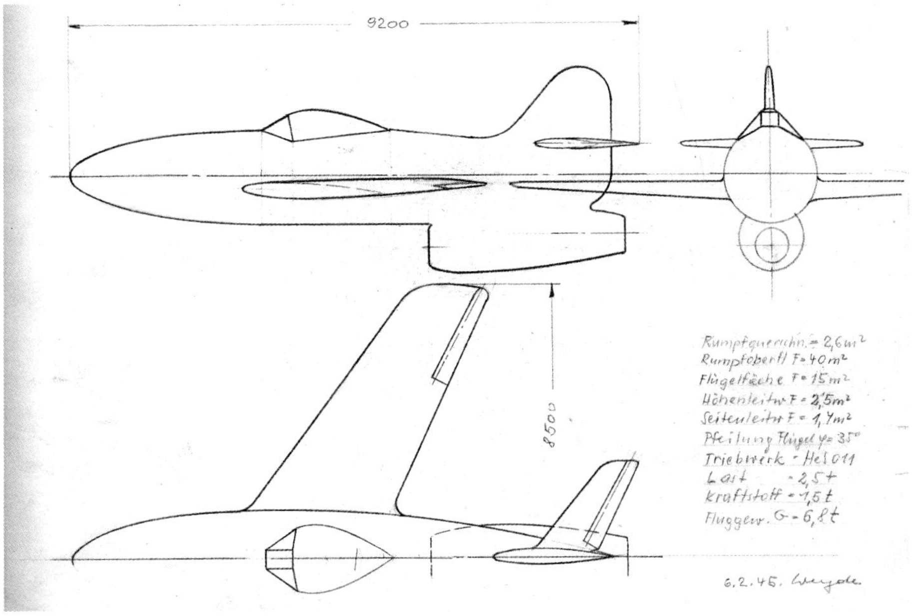

ABOVE: An early pencil sketch of Focke-Wulf's SO Flugzeug, dated February 6, 1945 – the day before the report containing the finished drawing was completed.

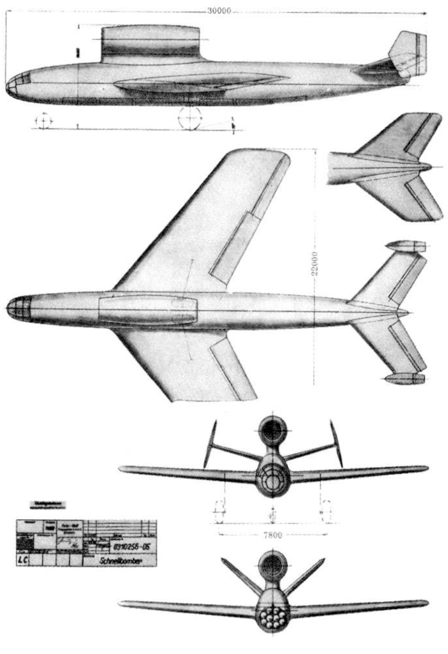

ABOVE: The Daimler-Benz fast bomber as it appears in Focke-Wulf drawing 0310 256-05.

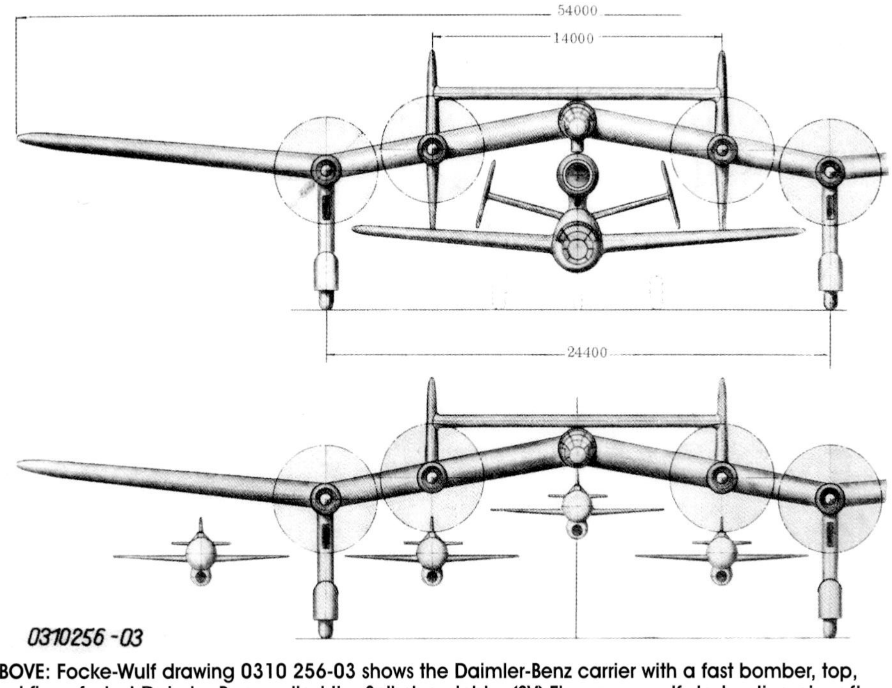

ABOVE: Focke-Wulf drawing 0310 256-03 shows the Daimler-Benz carrier with a fast bomber, top, and five of what Daimler-Benz called the Selbstvernichter (SV) Flugzeug – self-destructing aircraft. Focke-Wulf called it a Selbstopfer (SO) Flugzeug – self-sacrifice aircraft.

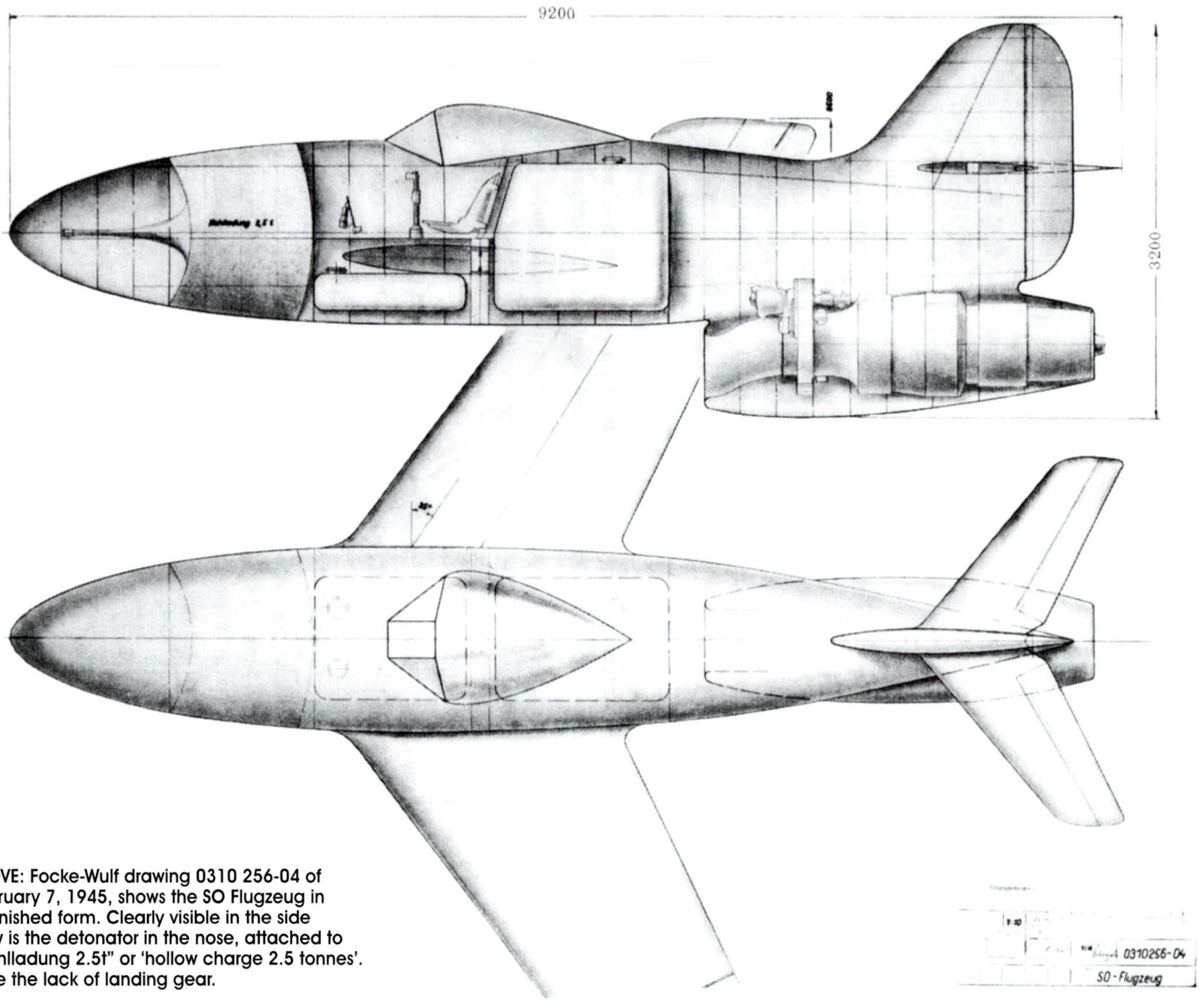

ABOVE: Focke-Wulf drawing 0310 256-04 of February 7, 1945, shows the SO Flugzeug in its finished form. Clearly visible in the side view is the detonator in the nose, attached to "Hohlladung 2.5t" or 'hollow charge 2.5 tonnes'. Note the lack of landing gear.

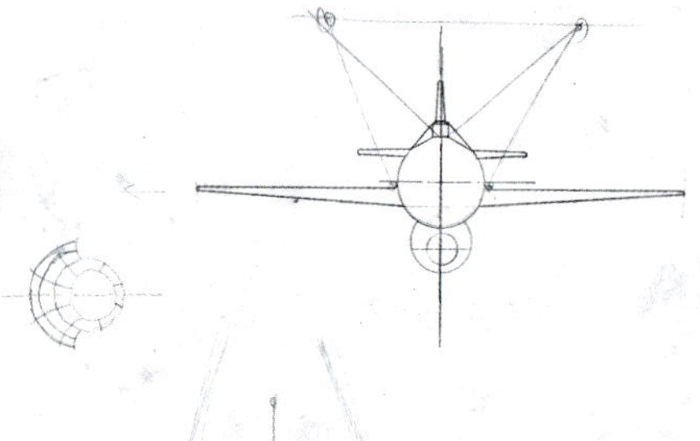

ABOVE: Another Focke-Wulf pencil sketch showing a forward view of the SO Flugzeug with what appears to be an attempt to show how it might have been attached to its carrier aircraft.

FOCKE-WULF'S OUTLINE

In contrast to the long and somewhat rambling Daimler-Benz fast bomber proposal, the Focke-Wulf report it references, Kurzbeschreibung Nr. 28, cuts straight to the chase. The document is dated February 10, 1945, but each individual page also has its own date and roughly half of them are dated February 17, 1945. Presumably, as was the usual practice at Focke-Wulf, pages containing outdated information were removed and updated ones inserted as the project progressed.

It begins: "Preliminary remarks: the present description deals with a fast bomber aircraft that can carry a load of 30,000kg about 1000km far into enemy air space, the journey is achieved at a speed of about 1000kph. This performance is possible only at extremely high wing loading, which was chosen in the present case with 500kg per square metre at maximum flight weight.

"As a take-off with such high surface stresses is not possible without help, the fast bomber aircraft is connected at the start with a large carrier aircraft of low power and wing loading and lifted by this to some extent in the air. This starting method requires probably some effort, but promises the following decisive advantages: first, the roll distance can be kept very small – less than 500m – so that even small airports can be required to make use of this fast bomber.

"Second, the landing gear of the fast bomber only needs to be designed for the maximum landing weight. Third, the launch of the bomber and carrier combination is independent of the supply of special starting means such as powder rockets, Walter devices and the fuel they need etc. Fourth, only one launch aircraft is needed for every three fast bombers. The carrier also enables the rapid deployment of the combination from one place to another and can be used as a large van to carry the entire entourage.

"Fifth, with the launch aircraft, not only the fast bomber can be carried but also other more highly loaded special aircraft, such as the SO Flugzeug described later, which can be used with a pilot or unmanned via remote control."

Following this short outline of the project, which more or less summarised the Daimler-Benz proposal, each of the three aircraft concerned – the fast bomber, the carrier and the self-destructor – was examined more closely in turn.

First up was the Schnellbomber, which Daimler-Benz itself referred to as the Schnellstbombenträger. Kurzbeschreibung Nr. 28 notes that the aircraft design to which its data refers is shown in drawing number 0310 256-05. The two crewmen would be accommodated at the front of the 30m fuselage where "the glazing gives good visibility in all directions. Entry and exit and emergency exit is done through the opening of the nosewheel bay".

The bomb bay in the central portion of the fuselage would "consist of six equal areas with six pairs of folding flaps". Fuel tanks in the fuselage could hold 17.8 tonnes but the bomb bays could accommodate another 20 tonnes if necessary. Otherwise, each bomb bay could hold either five SB 1000s or 10 SC 500s, making a total bomb load of 30 tonnes.

A tricycle undercarriage was to be fitted and in order to keep the wheels small, it was designed for a maximum landing weight of between 28 and 30 tonnes – the weight of the aircraft in an almost empty state. The report states: "The nose wheel is the size of 1015 x 380mm and each main landing gear wheel is 1550 x 575mm. Prior to loading the aircraft, an additional wheel of the 1550 x 575mm size is plugged onto each main landing gear. These are removed after the fast bomber has been attached to the carrier aircraft".

The 22m span wings had a 38 degree sweepback and the tail was either a "two side-piece tail or V-tail". There was little to be said about the 13,000kg starting thrust engine except that "Daimler-Benz will construct the jet engine. The mounting of the device is arranged on top of the fuselage with a narrow base".

Regarding the aircraft's equipment, engine, navigational and radio gear were to be housed in the cockpit. The oxygen system and the hydraulic system for landing gear doors, landing gear mechanisms and the system for the bomb bay doors would be located in the rear fuselage.

Rather than next looking at the carrier aircraft, Focke-Wulf chose instead to present what it called the SO Flugzeug and Daimler-Benz called the SV Flugzeug – the self-destructing suicide attack aircraft.

In fact it was a simple aircraft which lacked both weapons and undercarriage and there was little to be said about it either' other than "fuselage: the fuselage has a circular cross section and in the bow is the explosive charge of 1.5m diameter. Wing structural: the wings are swept to 30 degree; they join the fuselage in the middle. Engine: the engine is suspended under the fuselage and arranged accordingly. The fuel is in two containers of 1500kg and is behind the pilot".

In a data chart, Focke-Wulf gave the relevant drawing number as 0310 256-04, stated that the single jet engine intended to power the SO Flugzeug was an HeS 011 with 1500kg starting thrust and gave wingspan as 8.5m while length was 9.2m. The explosive in the nose was a 2500kg hollow charge.

The aircraft's purpose was given as "ship-targeted destruction".

The carrier aircraft, known to both Daimler-Benz and Focke-Wulf as the Trägerflugzeug, shown in drawing 0310 256-03, came last but some interesting details were given. Regarding the fuselage, the report says: "The partially glazed forward fuselage is used to accommodate the crew. All of the equipment is located central hull. Landing gear: fixed undercarriage with six wheels of size 1880 x 680mm. The front pair of wheels is steerable. In the chassis panel is the entrance for the crew. From here a passage leads through the wing to the fuselage and onto the flight deck."

The carrier's wing area was to be 500 square metres with a wingspan of 54m. The aircraft was to be 35m long and 12m tall. As far as the engine was concerned: "The propulsion system consists of six engines with DB 603N motors. Four-blade propellers would be used which were 5m in diameter.

"Four engines of normal type with annular radiator are attached to the front spar, while two engine in the wings are installed (behind the main spar). For both of these motors, the cooling system is in the chassis fairing. The propellers of the two motors work as pressure screws. Fuel is accommodated in the box beam, the lubricant container being arranged in each case in the motors."

When it came to loading, the carrier would simply be moved into position over the static bomber and once it was attached the bomber's undercarriage would be retracted "and the system is ready".

This was not quite the last word from Focke-Wulf however, since a drawing not included in Kurzbeschreibung Nr. 28 was appended to the file. Drawing number 0310 256-07, dated March 19, 1945, shows a dramatically redesigned carrier with only a single fuselage compared to the earlier design's twin-boom. As a result, its length was increased from 35m to 36m and height was up from 12m to 12.5m. Wingspan remained the same however.

This new design was to be propelled by four Daimler-Benz PTL 021 turboprops. Values are also given for a carrier powered by five or even six PTL 021s.

As well as alterations to the carrier, the SO/SV Flugzeug also seems to have been revised. A drawing appears in German Aircraft: New and Projected Types which shows it reconfigured with its jet engine on top of its fuselage rather than underneath, and the pilot is seated much further back with only a tiny window to look out of between the engine above his head and the fuselage below.

With the naming conventions of this Daimler-Benz project already confused by its association with Focke-Wulf, shortly after the war the British muddled matters still further by giving the different designs arbitrary letters from the alphabet.

So in German Aircraft: New and Projected Types, the revised carrier shown in drawing 0310 256-07 became 'Daimler-Benz Project A', the version of the fast bomber without the V-tail, shown in drawing 0310 256-05, became 'Project B', the original carrier design of drawing 0310 256-03 became 'Project C', the fast bomber paired with the original carrier became 'Project D', the original carrier paired with the revised SO/SV Flugzeug became 'Project E' and the revised SO/SV Flugzeug on its own became 'Project F'. The original SO/SV Flugzeug was missing altogether but might otherwise have ended up as 'Project G'.

It is highly doubtful that the Germans ever used these designations and they were simply applied to make referring to one configuration or another easier.

Quite what the German government actually made of Daimler-Benz's highly-unlikely-to-succeed proposal is unknown but it can be safely assumed that it met with a firm rejection. ●

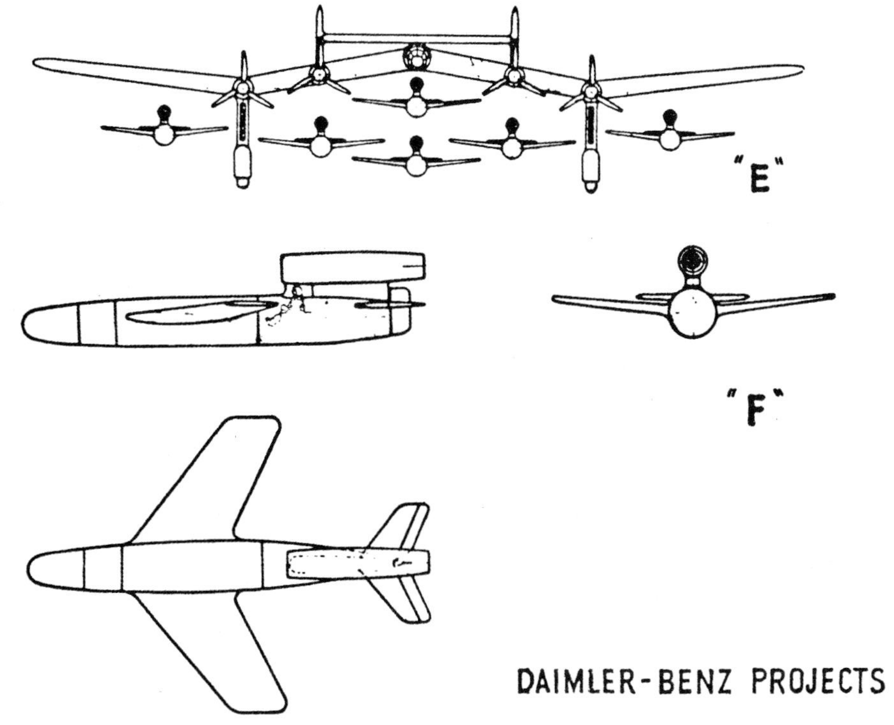

ABOVE: The original drawings appear not to have survived but this illustration from British intelligence report German Aircraft: New and Projected Types of January 1946 shows what appears to be a revised form of the Focke-Wulf SO Flugzeug, with the single HeS 011 turbojet repositioned above the fuselage. Now the carrier was to lift six 'self-sacrifice' aircraft – presumably being able to do so because of the repositioning of the turbojet. The project letters were arbitrarily added by the British.

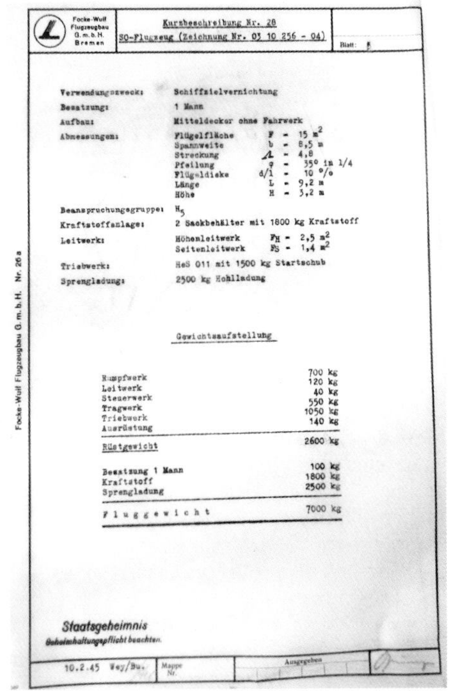
Focke-Wulf Flugzeugbau G.m.b.H. Bremen

Kurzbeschreibung Nr. 28

SO-Flugzeug (Zeichnung Nr. 03 10 256 - 04)

Blatt: 5

Verwendungszweck:	Schiffzielvernichtung
Besatzung:	1 Mann
Aufbau:	Mitteldecker ohne Fahrwerk
Abmessungen:	Flügelfläche F = 15 m²
	Spannweite b = 8,5 m
	Streckung Λ = 4,8
	Pfeilung φ = 35° in 1/4
	Flügeldicke d/l = 10 °/o
	Länge L = 9,2 m
	Höhe H = 3,2 m
Beanspruchungsgruppe:	H_5
Kraftstoffanlage:	2 Sackbehälter mit 1800 kg Kraftstoff
Leitwerk:	Höhenleitwerk F_H = 2,5 m²
	Seitenleitwerk F_S = 1,4 m²
Triebwerk:	HeS 011 mit 1500 kg Startschub
Sprengladung:	2500 kg Hohlladung

Gewichtsaufstellung

Rumpfwerk	700 kg
Leitwerk	120 kg
Steuerwerk	40 kg
Tragwerk	550 kg
Triebwerk	1050 kg
Ausrüstung	140 kg
Rüstgewicht	2600 kg
Besatzung 1 Mann	100 kg
Kraftstoff	1800 kg
Sprengladung	2500 kg
Fluggewicht	7000 kg

Staatsgeheimnis
Geheimhaltungspflicht beachten.

10.2.45 Wey/Bu. Mappe Nr. Ausgegeben

Focke-Wulf Flugzeugbau G.m.b.H. Nr. 26a

ABOVE: One of two pages in Focke-Wulf's Kurzbaubeschreibung Nr. 28 to provide outline information on the projected SO Flugzeug, shown in drawing number 0310 256-04.

The last chance

Langstreckenbomber – Messerschmitt P 1107, Junkers Ju 287 and Horten XVIII

Messerschmitt's P 1107 resurrected interest in a jet bomber months after work on the Ju 287 was suspended. Now the Ju 287 was brought back to stand against it and at the eleventh hour it was "decreed" that a third competitor should join the fray – the Horten XVIII flying wing.

After presenting a four-engined jet bomber idea to the German government in November 1944, Willy Messerschmitt was given two months to work up a firm proposal, with a deadline of the end of January 1945.

The result was a brochure dated January 26, 1945. This very brief document outlined the project as a two-stage development but neither stage was fully illustrated and only scant data was offered. Despite the date on the cover, the committee tasked with assessing the proposal did not receive it until some days later.

In the meantime, on January 27, Junkers issued its own report document, also brief, comparing the P 1107 to the Ju 287 and emphasising their similarities. At around this time, a date was set for a formal conference to fully examine the two designs and a third design was added, the Horten XVIII.

The mammoth four-day event was to take place from February 20-23 at Junkers' Dessau headquarters and would involve both the Sonderkommission 'Flugzeugzellenbau' or Special Commission for Airframe Construction and the EHK 'Flugzeuge', the latter chaired by Junkers director Heinrich Hertel.

A panel of interested parties and independent experts was assembled to go over the designs, establish their relative merits and identify their flaws. These included Ludwig Bölkow, representing Messerschmitt; Hans Gropler, head of Junkers' project office; Reimar and Walter Horten, representing themselves; Rüdiger Kosin of Arado, production

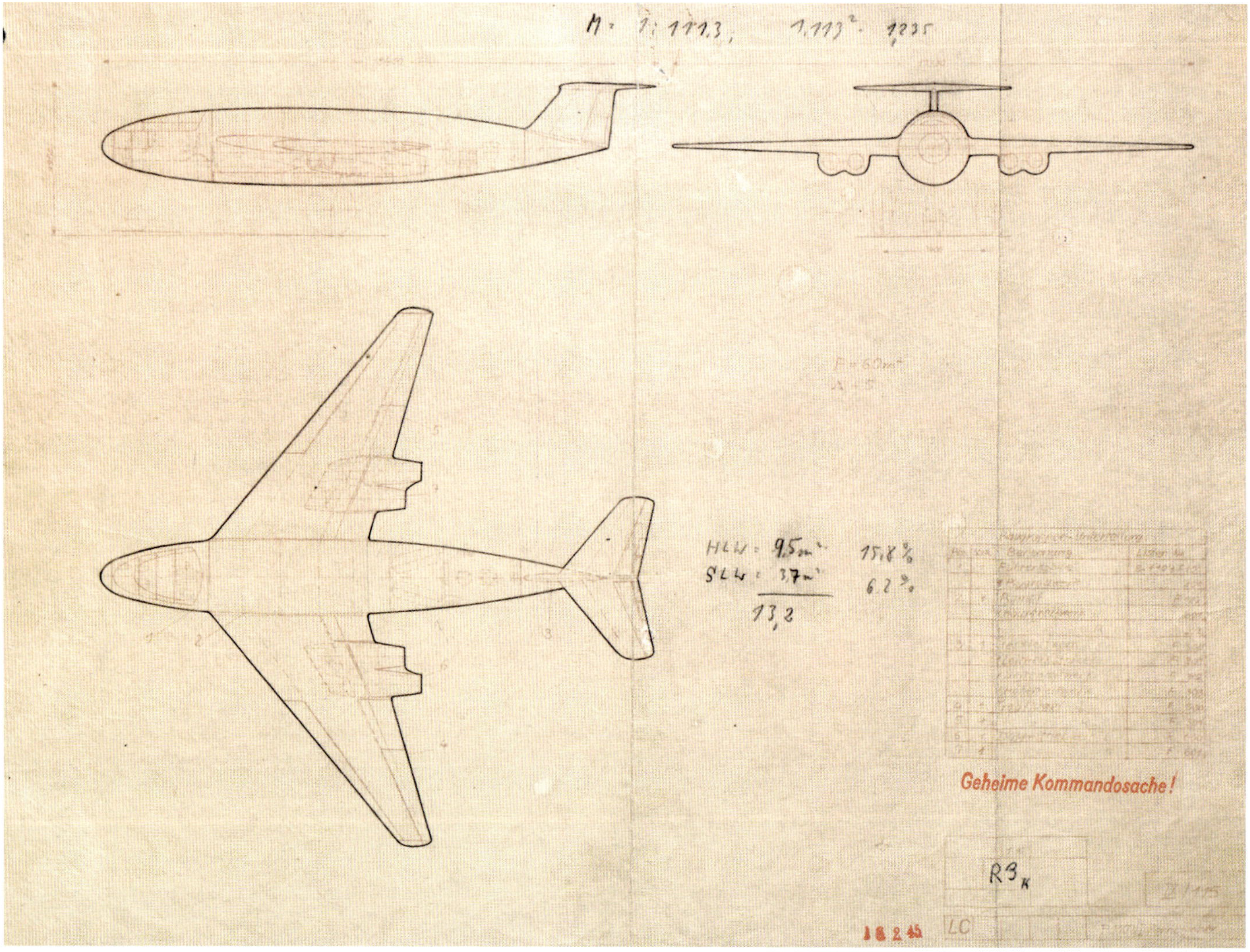

ABOVE: Willy Messerschmitt's jet bomber proposal to the RLM in November 1944 prompted renewed interest in such a machine. However, the Messerschmitt design office struggled to come up with drawings showing the design until the last minute. This Messerschmitt drawing, IX/115, P 1107/I Fernbomber is date-stamped February 16 – four days before the meeting at which it was due to be discussed.

management specialist Senior Staff Engineer Kohl and Professor August Quick of the Deutsche Versuchsanstalt für Luftfahrt (DVL).

It is worth pointing out that of these eight men, only Bölkow and the Hortens were not government aviation industry employees – Junkers, Arado and DVL staff were effectively all working for the same 'firm'.

By the time of the event, drawings of the P 1107 still had not been submitted and Bölkow was left attempting to outline his company's project with just the performance predictions and a description for his fellow delegates to go on.

The first stage "vorläufige Lösung" or 'temporary solution' P 1107 was a bomber with a smooth cigar-shaped fuselage and swept wings with a 17.3m span. Its engines were to be grouped into two pairs of two and attached to the underside of its wings and its horizontal tail surfaces would be positioned at the top of its fin in a T-tail configuration.

Its tricycle undercarriage would consist of a double nosewheel and two very large mainwheels – all of them retracting into the 18.4m long fuselage – and within the tail was room for a large reconnaissance camera. It would be unarmed save for its bomb load.

The second stage "endgültige Lösung" or 'final solution' as Messerschmitt put it, would utilise the same fuselage and undercarriage but with the engines now submerged into the wing roots and the T-tail replaced with a V-tail. Wingspan remained the same but the nature of the V-tail meant the overall length was slightly reduced, to 18m.

Little time was spent outlining the Ju 287's features at the beginning of the conference since most of those present were already intimately familiar with its design but the Hortens' XVIII was largely an unknown quantity.

The flying wing had been designed by Reimar Horten only a few months earlier, while he and his brother Walter were working on their large flying wing transport, the Horten VIII. Speaking to historian David Myhra in 1980, Reimar explained that the design submitted to the RLM for examination – known simply as the 'Horten XVIII' throughout the post-conference report – was actually the second version of the aircraft.

An earlier version that Reimar referred to as the 'Ho XVIIIA' had been worked on, but it was the 'Ho XVIIIB' that had been put forward. Consequently, the conference report makes reference to the Ho XVIIIB's unique features, such as its fixed undercarriage and use of four HeS 011 turbojets rather than the six Jumo 004Cs apparently planned for the Ho XVIIIA.

From the post-conference report itself, issued by the DVL at Berlin-Adlershof on February 25, 1945, it is clear that all the delegates were fascinated by the Horten XVIII's layout and were keen to explore its potential through detailed engineering calculations.

It was required that each of the three designs should be assessed with a fuel load of 33,000lb and a payload of four tons of bombs. After a brief preamble and under the heading of 'formulation of the task and its execution' the report states: "In a report of January 27, 1945, a comparison was drawn between the 8-287 and an 'optimum design'; which in the absence of the original material was based on the Messerschmitt design. In the meantime the drawings of the Messerschmitt P 1107 arrived which were used as a basis for the following enquiry. It was further decreed to include the Horten preliminary project XVIII in the comparison.

"The Junkers 8-287 was examined in its thin form, and was only adjusted to new conditions as regards equipment, number of crew, bomb and fuel loads. According to the abbreviated description issued on January 26, 1945, by Messerschmitt, provision was made for a temporary and a final solution for the Messerschmitt project P 1107.

"The final solution agrees in all material points with the 'optimum design' of the first report; differing from the latter principally in the sharper tapering of the wings and in a shorter fuselage. In the case of the temporary solution, Messerschmitt have avoided certain ▶

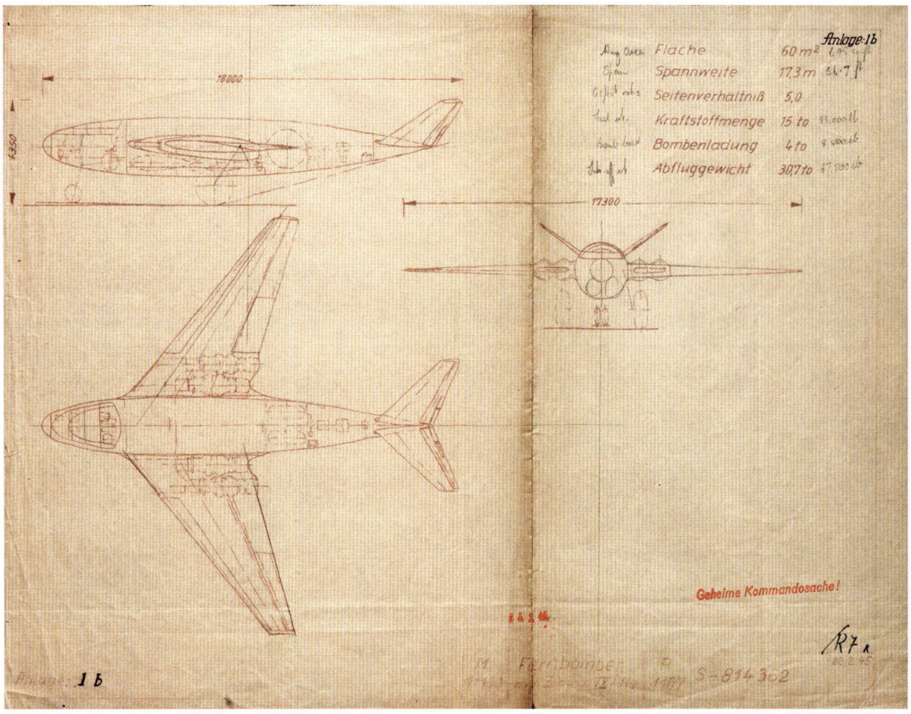

ABOVE: The advanced version of Messerschmitt's P 1107 – shown here in drawing IX/114. The main differences were the engines which are integrated into the wings rather than being partially slung under them, and a V-tail in place of the preliminary design's more conventional T-tail.

ABOVE: Concept art for the P 1107 preliminary design. The bomber's strongly swept wings and flying T-tail would have made it a formidable sight when viewed from below.

ABOVE: The final version of the P 1107 envisioned by Messerschmitt, as seen in this concept artwork reproduced from an original microfilmed report produced after the Lackstreckenbomber conference.

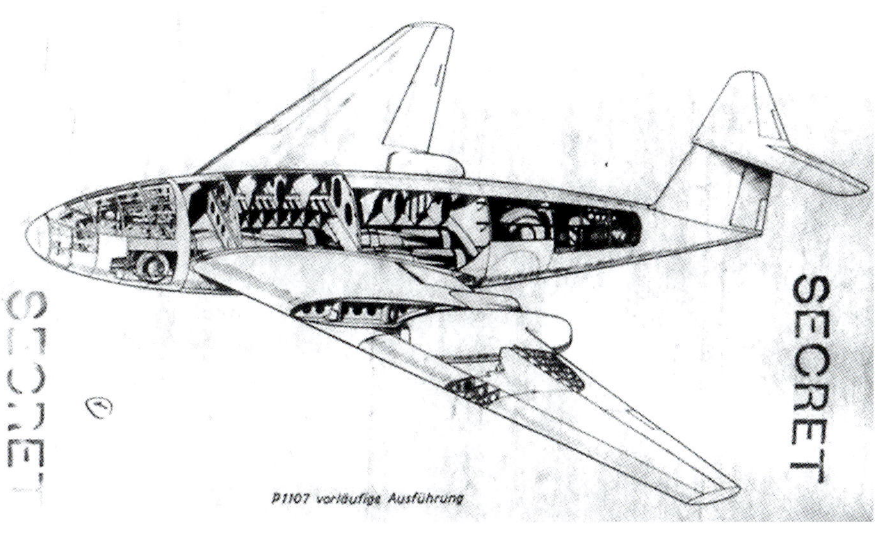

ABOVE: A cut-through drawing of the Messerschmitt P 1107 preliminary or temporary design. The unusual greenhouse glazing above the roomy cockpit, the capacious bomb bay and enormous mainwheels tucked into the fuselage are evident.

risks involved in the final solution which lead to expectations of an improvement in performance on the one hand, but a longer time for development on the other (installation, in the case of the temporary solution, of the power unit under instead of on the wing, standard tail plane instead of a V-tail plane).

"The Horten XVIII preliminary project differs from the other two types above all in its 'flying wing' type of construction and its by far greater wing surface area (1680sq ft instead of 646sq ft). It is therefore as regards disposable load not fully exploited with the present power units."

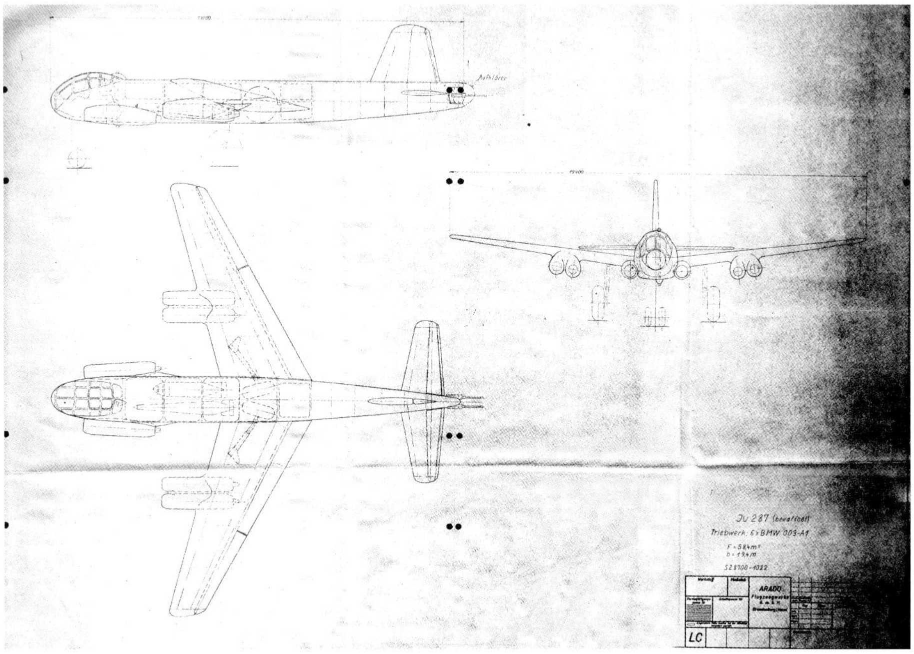

ABOVE: A late period drawing of the Junkers Ju 287, as furnished by Arado. Arado seems to have routinely made its own copies of rivals' late period jet aircraft designs. Note the unusual periscope arrangement.

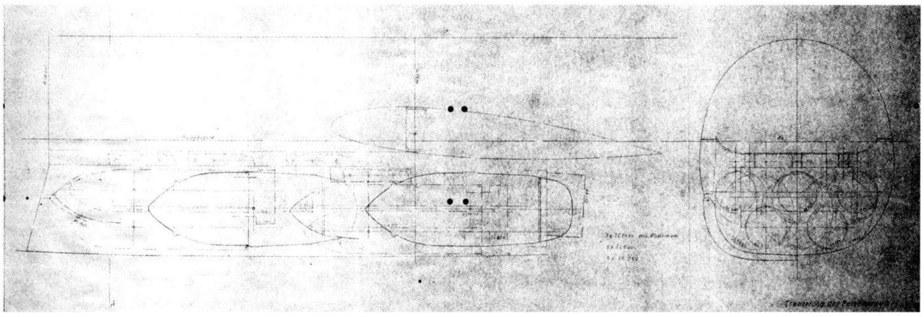

ABOVE AND BELOW: Arado copies of Junkers drawing showing the different combinations of bombs that could be fitted into the Ju 287's capacious bomb bay.

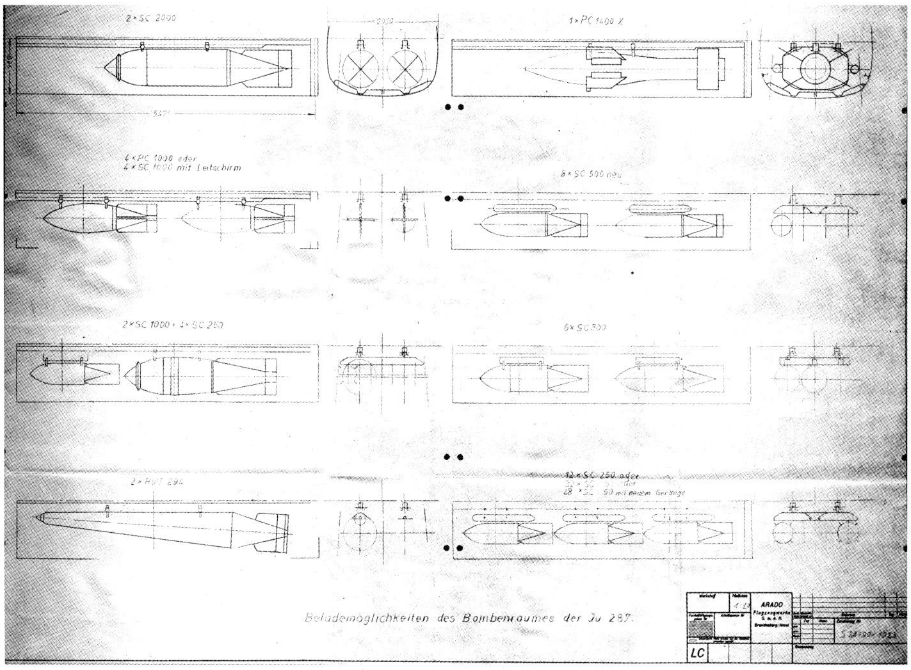

Some comments were then made about the relative weight of each design. During the course of the conference, the panel of experts estimated their different weights based on the use of standard construction materials: "In the case of the 8-287, of aluminium construction, the estimate was based on the actual weight with allowance for alterations necessary to meet the demand for longer range.

"The weights in the case of the P 1107 and the Horten XVIII were adjusted to those given in the material furnished by the Junkers project office. The structural weight of the Messerschmitt project thus estimated about 3380lb higher than that stated in the description furnished by Messerschmitt."

This was a recurring theme for Messerschmitt. As with the Me 264, it seems that Messerschmitt's numbers were routinely over-optimistic – sometimes to a degree which might have tipped the scales in the company's favour if the 'error' went undiscovered. Quite why the firm persisted with this strategy, or if it was not a strategy, quite how the company managed to get away with such embarrassingly poor calculations is uncertain.

In any case, Bölkow seems to have gamely tried to salvage something from the latest mess: "In the opinion of Messerschmitt's representative 660lb can be saved by lightening the wing and fuselage."

Surprisingly, given the Horten brothers' uncanny ability to acquire men, materials and whatever other resources they happened to require through unconventional and irregular ways and means, "the construction weights in the case of the Horten XVIII are about 2200lb lower than those originally estimated by Horten.

"Wood is laid down as the material for the outer main wings of both the P 1107 and the Horten XVIII while the remainder of the structure groups are to be made from metal. About 660lb to 1320lb can be saved in construction weight by substituting an aluminium wing for the wooden type."

The next factor to be considered was top speed. This was an area in which Messerschmitt traditionally excelled, or at least aimed to excel, and this competition was no exception. The report makes it clear that in this case Messerschmitt outstripped the others: "From the thrust of the power unit, taking into consideration the reduced drag, the following flying speeds resulted at an altitude of 23,000ft – 8-287 550mph, P 1107 580mph, Horten XVIII 535mph. The maximum speed of the P 1107 is about 31.2mph higher than that of the 8-287 (temporary solution about 15.6mph higher).

"A study shows that at that speed the P 1107 enters a range in which the drag slopes up sharply as the speed of sound is approached. As a result possible disturbance in the flying characteristics appears which render it impossible to exploit this speed.

"The Horten XVIII is slightly slower than the 8-287, a fact attributable in the main to its larger wing surface. On the other hand its speed is within a range probably free from disturbances caused by approaching the speed of sound."

Range was apparently a contentious issue, particularly for the Horten brothers. Some 35 years after the conference, Reimar told Myhra that Junkers had presented a design with a 5000-6000km range, that Messerschmitt's range was

ABOVE: The last configuration of the Ju 287, though not necessarily intended to be its final form, featured three engines under each wing. Art by Daniel Uhr

7000-8000km and his own design could manage 9000km. However, he said he and his brother actually believed that the XVIII could stretch to 11,000km but did not tell "the people there at the conference".

In fact, the conference-calculated ranges were: 8-287 4430km at a cruising speed of 488mph and altitude 23,000ft, P 1107 4850km at 548mph and Horten XVIII 5350km at 486mph. According to the report: "Optimum range was calculated on the assumption that the entire fuel load of 33,000lb (except for a residue of 572lb) was consumed and that an additional supply of fuel is used for warming up and take-off run, which is not included in the take-off weight. The altitude was so chosen that at full thrust there remained a reserved climbing speed of 394ft/min and the flight itself was carried out at that height, with full thrust.

"The range in the case of the Horten XVIII in spite of its higher drag, is the highest, because owing to its lower surface load, it possesses a higher ceiling, especially at the commencement of flight, and also owing to the performance characteristic of the jet power unit flight at high altitude is especially economical.

"As the Horten was originally designed for a larger fuel load than that indicated for the other types (33,000lb) its load for the purpose of this comparison was taken at 41,800lb and the airframe weight taken at 1102lb higher in order to take into consideration the necessary reinforcement etc. The optimum range then obtained rose from 5350km to 6500km."

This is a fairly substantial shortfall from the numbers Reimar would later relate to Myhra. The figure of 11,000km range was used by Reimar to justify his assertion that the Horten XVIII was not only nicknamed the "Amerika-Bomber" but also that it was ordered into production by Hermann Göring on April 1, 1945, primarily on the basis of its stupendous range.

It is worth noting that the round-trip distance from Cologne on the Rhine in far western Germany to New York, by air, is 12,000km. And Cologne would fall to the American First Army just over a week after the Langstreckenbomber conference, in early March 1945.

It seems highly unlikely that anyone present at the conference was thinking of using the winning design, assuming it could be designed and built in time, against the United States. Even if they had been aware there was an outside chance that the Horten XVIII's range might be stretched to 1000km short of New York on the American east coast, hitting targets in liberated Europe or Britain, or shipping, would still have been the intended goal.

There were deductions to be made against the calculated ranges too: "In the case of the ranges mentioned above it was assumed that bombs would be dropped from the height of the economical flight. This in the case of the three aircraft under consideration lies between 36,100ft and 42,600ft.

"When operating against naval targets however it will be possible to drop bombs from these altitudes only in exceptional circumstances, rather it will be necessary for the aircraft to descend to a lower altitude. Owing to the climb which would have to follow the release of bombs, the range would of necessity be shortened and this has not been taken into account in the foregoing calculations. Such reduction in range may amount to about 186 miles."

It was here apparently, once again, that Messerschmitt had got its sums wrong, leaving Bölkow to carry the can: "In the short description of the P 1107 an optimum range with 33,000lb of fuel is given as 7400km, for which 1452lb of the fuel load was assumed for supplementary use for warming up, take-off run etc. and non-usable residue was put down as 572lb.

"Although the amount of fuel available for the flight was less than that mentioned in the above description the range was calculated to be greater than that given in the report. The cause of this divergence could not be explained by Herr Bölkow, Messerschmitt's representative, as he had no access to the necessary data and the technical adviser on performance calculations from Messerschmitt had not arrived in Dessau.

"On page 3 of the short description issued by Messerschmitt on January 26, 1945, the P 1107 project is compared with the Me 264 which according to the particulars given has a range of 7480 miles with a bomb load of 6600lb. It is also mentioned in that description that further systematic development of the P 1107 would lead to the attainment of ranges superior to those of the Me 264.

"Such statements can lead to misunderstandings inasmuch as a further development of the P 1107 over a long period of time is obviously envisaged whereby after several intermediate steps it is thought to obtain a completely new aircraft with correspondingly improved power units."

When it came to the take-off run, none of the three contending designs did particularly well. The Horten XVIII "owing to its smaller surface load is materially superior to the other aircraft" but like the other two it still required starting rockets to help it get off the ground.

It must hardly have come as a shock that "the take-off runs given by Messerschmitt in their short descriptive treatise are materially more favourable than those we have obtained; and we cannot see prospects of their being realised". ▶

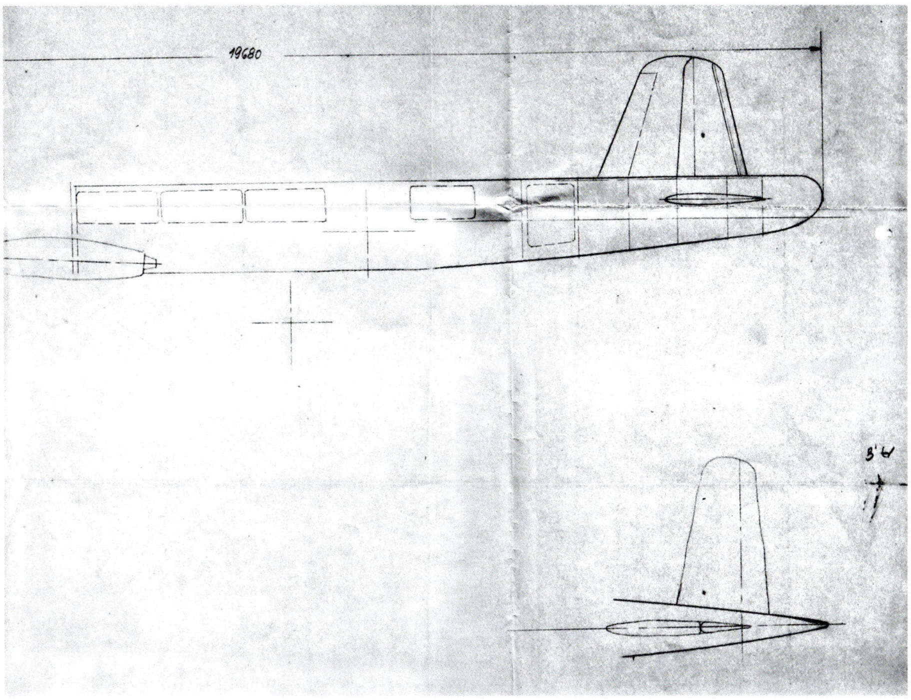

ABOVE: This drawing shows an alternative tail arrangement for the Ju 287 – presumably to be used if no defensive armament was required.

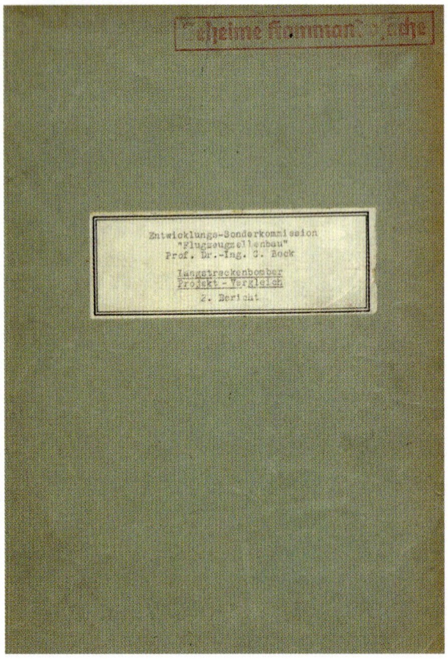

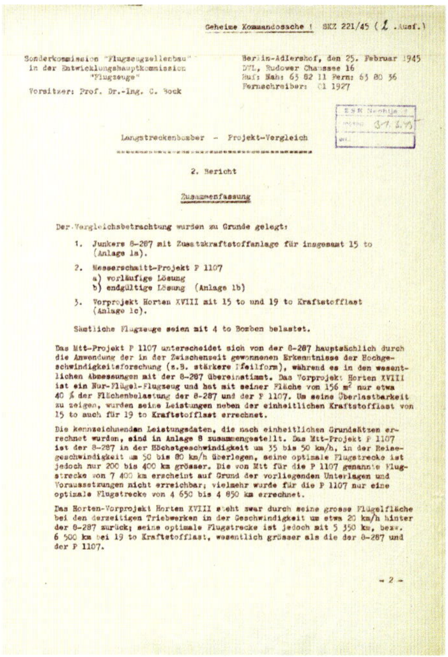

Geheime Kommandosache ! SKZ 221/45 (2 .Ausf.)

Sonderkommission "Flugzeugzellenbau"
in der Entwicklungshauptkommission
"Flugzeuge"

Vorsitzer: Prof. Dr.-Ing. G. Bock

Berlin-Adlershof, den 25. Februar 1945
DVL, Rudower Chaussee 16
Ruf: Nah: 63 82 11 Fern: 63 80 36
Fernschreiber: 01 1927

Langstreckenbomber – Projekt-Vergleich

2. Bericht

Zusammenfassung

Der Vergleichsbetrachtung wurden zu Grunde gelegt:

1. Junkers 8-287 mit Zusatzkraftstoffanlage für insgesamt 15 to (Anlage 1a).
2. Messerschmitt-Projekt P 1107
   a) vorläufige Lösung
   b) endgültige Lösung (Anlage 1b)
3. Vorprojekt Horten XVIII mit 15 to und 19 to Kraftstofflast (Anlage 1c).

Sämtliche Flugzeuge seien mit 4 to Bomben belastet.

Das Mtt-Projekt P 1107 unterscheidet sich von der 8-287 hauptsächlich durch die Anwendung der in der Zwischenzeit gewonnenen Erkenntnisse der Hochgeschwindigkeitsforschung (z.B. stärkere Pfeilform), während es in den wesentlichen Abmessungen mit der 8-287 übereinstimmt. Das Vorprojekt Horten XVIII ist ein Nur-Flügel-Flugzeug und hat mit seiner Fläche von 156 m² nur etwa 40 % der Flächenbelastung der 8-287 und der P 1107. Um seine Überlastbarkeit zu zeigen, wurden seine Leistungen neben der einheitlichen Kraftstofflast von 15 to auch für 19 to Kraftstofflast errechnet.

Die kennzeichnenden Leistungsdaten, die nach einheitlichen Grundsätzen errechnet wurden, sind in Anlage 8 zusammengestellt. Das Mtt-Projekt P 1107 ist der 8-287 in der Höchstgeschwindigkeit um 35 bis 50 km/h, in der Reisegeschwindigkeit um 50 bis 80 km/h überlegen, seine optimale Flugstrecke ist jedoch nur 200 bis 400 km grösser. Die von Mtt für die P 1107 genannte Flugstrecke von 7 400 km erscheint auf Grund der vorliegenden Unterlagen und Voraussetzungen nicht erreichbar; vielmehr wurde für die P 1107 nur eine optimale Flugstrecke von 4 650 bis 4 850 km errechnet.

Das Horten-Vorprojekt Horten XVIII steht zwar durch seine grosse Flügelfläche bei den derzeitigen Triebwerken in der Geschwindigkeit um etwa 20 km/h hinter der 8-287 zurück; seine optimale Flugstrecke ist jedoch mit 5 350 km, bezw. 6 500 km bei 19 to Kraftstofflast, wesentlich grösser als die der 8-287 und der P 1107.

– 2 –

ABOVE: The cover and first page of the project comparison report from the Langstreckenbomber conference. The report itself was issued by the DVL in Berlin on February 25, 1945, two days after the event. The first page states the three projects in contention.

The panel raised some concerns about the pronounced sweepback of the P 1107 and Horten XVIII's wings - the feature which enabled each of them to achieve their outstanding maximum speeds. The lack of test data concerning strong sweepback on very large 'flying wing' aircraft was particularly troublesome: "Up to now, apart from single small experimental aircraft, no experiences as to the practicability of sweepbacks of this size are available. Surprises are therefore to be expected, the overcoming of which will present new problems.

"The question of the probable flying characteristics of the Horten XVIII and the open questions arising therefrom are discussed later in this report. As a special point of some importance it may be here mentioned that the 'flying wing' aircraft of this size and shape have not hitherto been built for high speeds and that therefore difficulties of the most diverse character may be expected during development until personnel are fully trained.

"While we today have ample experience to draw upon when it is a question of eliminating unpleasant flying characteristics in aircraft of normal design and faults, for example, regarding stability, can usually be corrected by small alterations in design, this fund of experience is not yet available to us in the case of the 'flying wing' aircraft.

"Moreover, undesirable points in the flying characteristics of flying wing aircraft can often only be removed after alterations to the wing itself which in the majority of cases would involve considerable constructional outlay. For these reasons the time required for development and testing of a flying wing aircraft is even today greater than that in the case of an aircraft of normal type."

BUILDING THE BOMBER

Some considerable effort was put into working out exactly how long it would take to build each of the three designs. Following the usual production processes, the first prototype would take a long time to complete, with the second taking less time and the third less still and so on.

At a rate of 25 aircraft per month, it would take around 28,000 man hours to build a single 8-287 from the 200th aircraft onwards. If production could be ramped up to 100 aircraft per month, each one could be expected to take 19,000 hours to make.

The report states: "Precise information from Messerschmitt regarding the P 1107 is not to hand, the data however should not differ materially from that given in the first for the 'optimum design'. On that basis, the productional outlay for the P 1107 may be about 10% lower than for the 8-287."

Untrustworthy though it may have been, Messerschmitt and its factories were at least a known quantity. Similarly, alongside Arado, Junkers was the German government's 'in-house' manufacturer and could therefore count on vast production resources if it was deemed necessary that they should be expended.

It is only a slight exaggeration, however, to say that the Horten brothers were just two men working in a shed. Therefore, the conference's production man, Kohl, was given the task of interrogating the brothers closely about their production capabilities and reporting back on them.

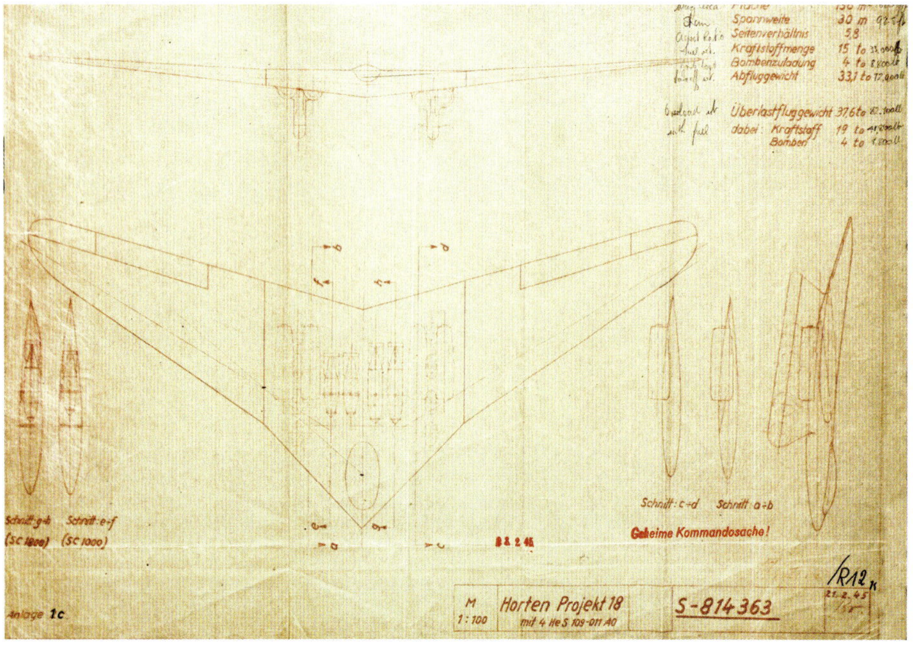

ABOVE: The Horten XVIII design submitted for the February 20-23 conference. Unusually, it is labelled Horten Projekt 18, whereas Horten projects were usually known by their number as a Roman numeral – e.g. Horten III or Horten IX. Equally strangely, the drawing is dated February 21, 1945 – the second day of the conference. Later in life, designer Reimar Horten would identify this design as the 'Ho XVIIIb'. But as far as the delegates at Dessau were concerned, this was the only design they had been asked to consider.

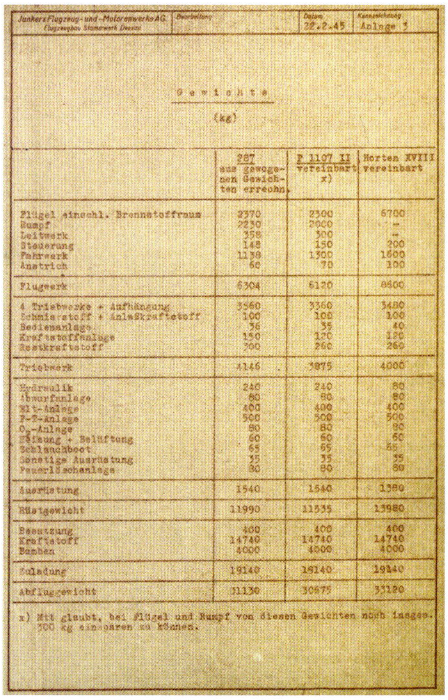

Junkers Flugzeug- und -Motorenwerke AG. Flugzeugbau Stammwerk Dessau | Datum 22.2.45 | Kennzeichnung Anlage 3

Gewichte

(kg)

	287 aus gewogenen Gewichten errechn.	P 1107 II vereinbart x)	Horten XVIII vereinbart
Flügel einschl. Brennstoffraum	2370	2300	6700
Rumpf	2230	2000	–
Leitwerk	358	300	–
Steuerung	148	150	200
Fahrwerk	1138	1300	1600
Anstrich	60	70	100
Flugwerk	6304	6120	8600
4 Triebwerke + Aufhängung	3560	3360	3480
Schmierstoff + Anlaßkraftstoff	100	100	100
Bedienanlage	36	35	40
Kraftstoffanlage	150	120	120
Restkraftstoff	300	260	260
Triebwerk	4146	3875	4000
Hydraulik	240	240	80
Abwurfanlage	80	80	80
El.-Anlage	400	400	400
F-T-Anlage	500	500	500
O_2-Anlage	80	80	80
Heizung + Belüftung	60	60	60
Schlauchboot	65	65	65
Sonstige Ausrüstung	35	35	35
Feuerlöschanlage	80	80	80
Ausrüstung	1540	1540	1380
Rüstgewicht	11990	11535	13980
Besatzung	400	400	400
Kraftstoff	14740	14740	14740
Bomben	4000	4000	4000
Zuladung	19140	19140	19140
Abfluggewicht	31130	30675	33120

x) Mtt glaubt, bei Flügel und Rumpf von diesen Gewichten noch insges. 300 kg einsparen zu können.

ABOVE: Another page from the Langstreckenbomber projects comparison report, showing the relative weights of the three competing designs.

LEFT: The Horten XVIII of the Dessau conference as it might have looked when built. Immediately obvious is the huge faired-in undercarriage. Art by Daniel Uhr

His memo begins: "Re: Production outlay on Horten project. The figures given at the end of this report have been ascertained with due regard to the flying wing form and the following assumption in comparison with present outlays on bombers in the equivalent size range.

"The Horten XVIII project consists of a right and a left outer wing made of wood and a centre section with supports the pressure cabin, undercarriage, turbojet unit and also presumably the landing flaps. In the outer wing, which is about 32.8ft long, are housed the rudder units such as outer flaps, tin foil flaps and the spoiler.

"These control surfaces are made of aluminium. The centre section is a mixed construction of steel, wood or steel/aluminium. Both the outer wings are identically alike and have a box form main and auxiliary spar. The covering is said to be comparatively thick (0.59-0.79in). For the construction of this outer wing an auxiliary jig for the sub-divided leading edge will be required in addition to that for the spars. The framework must be glued to the covering in a jig which must have pressure irons for fixing the clamps.

"A jig will also have to be made for the centre section, so that the symmetry of position for the pressure, the mechanism for the remote-controlled weapons, the power units, the unretractable undercarriage and also the connection for the outer wing may be preserved.

"The pressure cabin will have to be built in a special jig so constructed that it can also be used for pressure testing. Auxiliary jigs will also have to be made for the main and auxiliary supports, irrespective of whether these are of steel tube construction or Wagner supports. The transverse joining elements in the centre section as well as their sections require simple jigs."

Kohl had asked the Hortens how long they thought it would take to build one example of their machine. They had replied: 12,000 man hours. In his memo, Kohl matter-of-factly states that just designing and drawing the prototype would take 120,000 hours, while designing the jigs to build it would take another 300,000 hours, the necessary tools another 60,000 hours. Then actually building the Horten XVIII V1 would take another 80,000 hours, and the same again for the V2.

The construction crew would then be able to refine their processes a little and the V3 and V4 would only take 60,000 hours each, the V5 and V6 50,000 hours each. Once 20 machines had been built, the team might be expected to turn one out in 30,000 hours. Once 100 had been made, another round of intensive work would be needed - getting material ready for series production, 75,000 hours, overhauling the jigs for series production 100,000 hours, making more jigs another 400,000 hours.

The next machine in the series, No. 101, might then take 25,000 hours to build.

Kohl wrote: "The figure of 12,000 hours given by Horten will at best only be obtainable after the 500th machine. The comparatively low figure of 25,000 hours for the 100th machine is attributable to the flying wing shape with its comparative roominess and easy accessibility.

"Also the basic demands of the project - no retractable undercarriage, turbojets placed on wing, unprotected tanks, no de-icing equipment."

HORTEN'S REMARKS

After being subjected to Kohl's and the expert panels' enquiries, Reimar Horten was given the opportunity to make his own statement, in writing, about the Horten XVIII. In it, he complains that the capabilities of the Horten XVIII have been artificially retarded for the competition: "For the purposes of comparison with the 8-287 and the P 1107 the Horten XVIII project was put back to 8800lb of bombs and 33,000lb of fuel. By so doing the weight reserves of 15,400lb were left out of considerations.

"The highest speed was attained with the current model of the HeS 011 power unit. It was not assumed that an improvement in thrust could be achieved by further development of the power unit. With 20% higher thrust output however the design with 88,000lb take-off weight is still just below the Mach number-drag slope. At maximum speed below this value the flying characteristics of the aircraft do not give cause for any apprehensions.

"The maximum speed does not provide any criterion for comparison between the 'flying wing' type of construction and normal types, as the sizes of the aircraft must be taken into consideration. To do justice to the aircraft being compared to the Horten, the wing surface of the latter should be reduced to such an extent that by raising the wing load the take-off run would be made equal."

Another complaint was that the experimental station at Rechlin had required turbojets to be positioned in nacelles, he wrote, rather than being installed internally. He now ▶

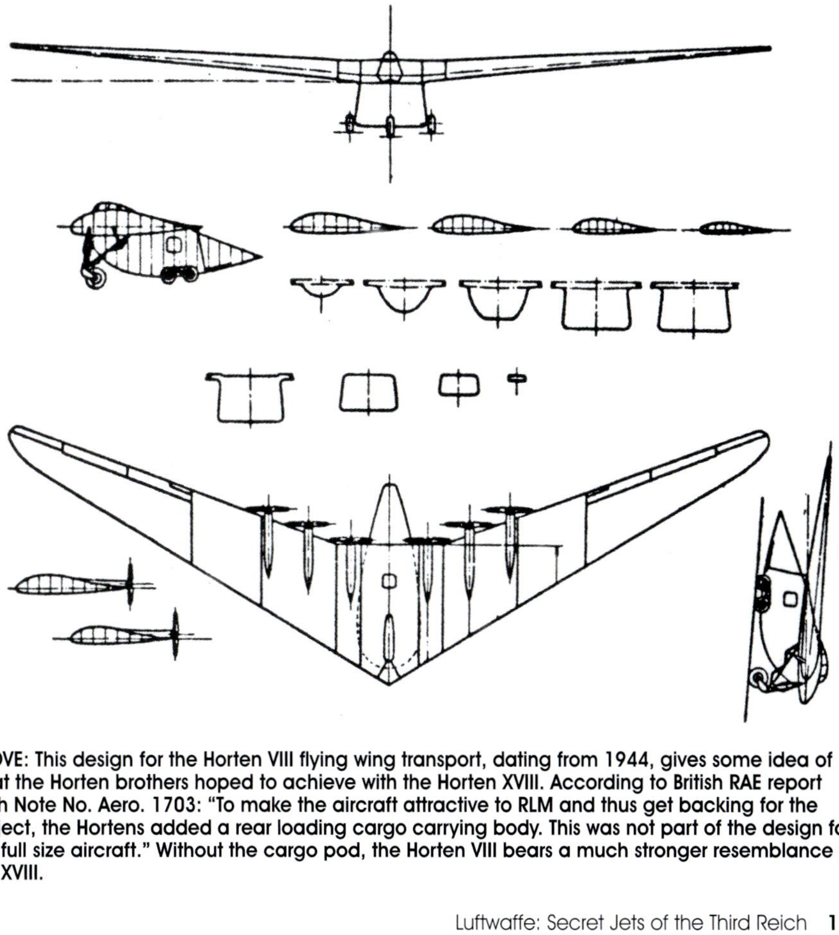

ABOVE: This design for the Horten VIII flying wing transport, dating from 1944, gives some idea of what the Horten brothers hoped to achieve with the Horten XVIII. According to British RAE report Tech Note No. Aero. 1703: "To make the aircraft attractive to RLM and thus get backing for the project, the Hortens added a rear loading cargo carrying body. This was not part of the design for the full size aircraft." Without the cargo pod, the Horten VIII bears a much stronger resemblance to the XVIII.

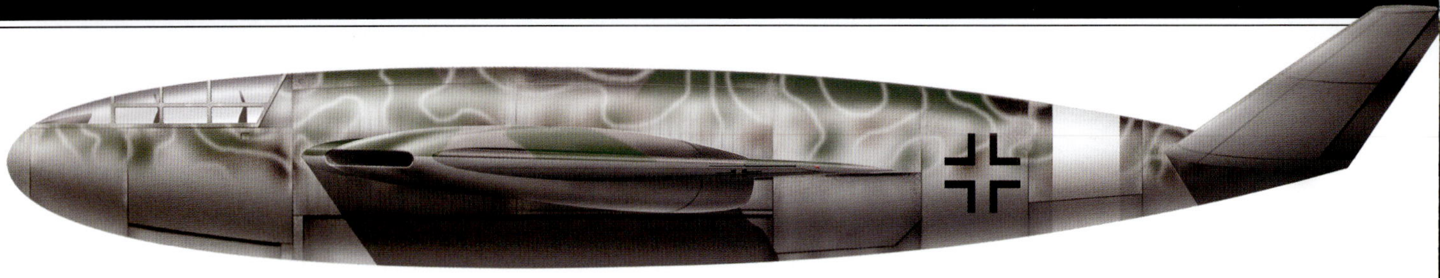

ABOVE: Messerschmitt's ambitious P 1107 design in its 'final' form, with its engines inside its wings and a V-tail. Art by Daniel Uhr

found that Messerschmitt with its P 1107 had "provided for partial internal installation of the power unit, for which the 'flying wing' owing to its larger wing chord incidence is better suited. This method of arranging the power unit displaces the Mach number-drag slope so that the maximum speed in inclined flight or in horizontal flight with increased output is considerably better".

THE EXPERTS' VIEW

In what would seem to be a rather unfair move, a sub-committee of the experts present at the conference – comprising Kosin, Gropler, Quick and Bölkow – was appointed to provide a counter view, in writing, to Horten's statement.

They examined "flying characteristics and risks", controllability, arrangement of engines and the characteristics of the undercarriage. Under the first category, they decided that the aircraft was likely to stall slowly but problems might occur if the pilot had to manoeuvre sharply, particularly when putting the nose down during banking. However, they accepted that these sorts of manoeuvres would be less common with a heavy bomber than they were with a fighter.

Nevertheless "careful tests are necessary especially for high speed flying at low altitudes" and "lateral stability (blind flying, high altitude flying etc.) in the case of tailless aircraft is a subject upon which really little is known" and "special attention must be given to this question". Then again, they said that they expected "that no insurmountable difficulties" would arise in this regard with the Horten XVIII.

Under the heading on 'controllability' they concluded: "Controllability about the longitudinal and transverse axes appears to be satisfactory. On the other hand, it is questionable whether the available lateral control will satisfy requirements.

"Adjustment of control seems difficult with regard to very small directional stability, the unusually high slip-roll moment and the disturbances appearing from engine failure etc. Great attention must be paid to these questions."

The sub-committee actually agreed with Reimar that the positioning of the engines in nacelles under the wing, rather than installing them inside it, was less than ideal. There would be particular problems arising from boundary layer air at the engine intakes which would require "careful and exhaustive preliminary experiments either in the wind tunnel or during actual flight as on the basic experiences gained up to now they cannot be estimated and involve great uncertainties".

Similarly, no one liked the fixed undercarriage. Even Reimar himself was unhappy with it. He later told Myhra he had thought about landing the Horten XVIII on a landing skid rather than a wheeled undercarriage, but did not mention this at Dessau because "there must have been between 30 and 40 individuals from many different aircraft companies. So you see, I did not want to give them all my ideas".

The sub-committee wrote: "The unusual arrangement of the undercarriage may give rise to several difficulties in actual operation, especially taxying in curves and manoeuvring on the ground do not at first sight appear to have been satisfactorily solved.

"The experiences gained with the Arado 232 however appear to be relevant here. The wear on the wheels will be greater than normal."

Finally, under "general observations", they wrote: "It must be pointed out that present experiences with tailless aircraft, especially with aircraft of this size, are very small. Even though there are no great fundamental doubts regarding this project, one must reckon with the fact that time required for testing will be less favourable than in the case of normal aircraft."

WHO WON?

When it came to picking a winner, the conference was torn between the great advantages and great risks embodied by the Horten XVIII and the ease with which the Ju 287, an also-ran by comparison, could be put into series production.

The report summary states: "As the design of the 8-287 is complete and the technical risks involved have already been greatly reduced by extensive experiments of the most diverse types, difficulties in the commencement of series production are less to be anticipated in the case of the aircraft.

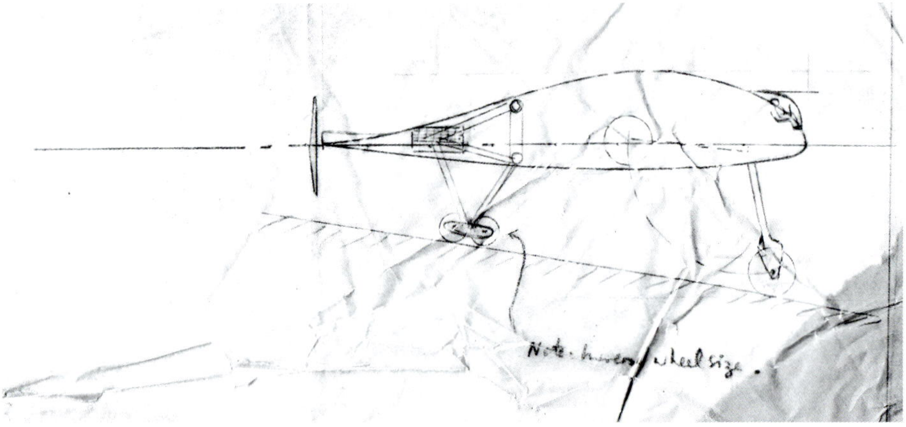

ABOVE: Side view of a different version of the Horten VIII large flying wing transport from an original pencil sketch, with English annotations added later. The very capacious interior of the wing/fuselage is clear.

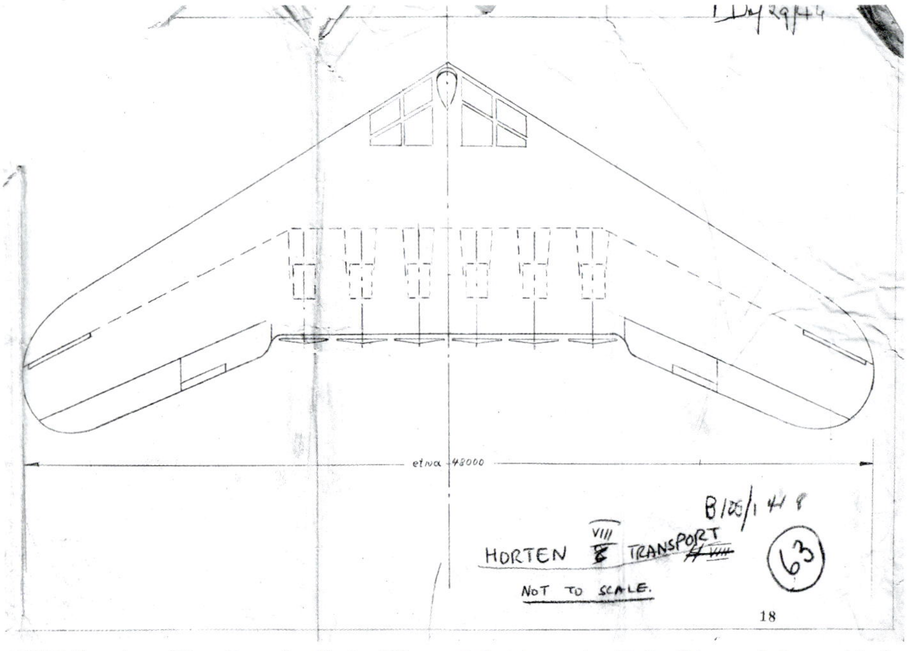

ABOVE: Top view of the alternative Horten VIII pencil sketch, again with English annotations added later. One original German word is visible however – 'etwa' – showing that the wingspan was 'about' 48m.

"As regards the P 1107 and the Horten XVIII we have up to now only preliminary projects which still require thorough working out on the part of the manufacturers. It follows from this that it will be at least seven months before the first experimental aircraft of the P 1107 and Horten XVIII are ready so that under the most favourable circumstances we may reckon on one and a half to one and three quarter years before a quota of 25 (or 100) aircraft per month is available.

"As the new projects utilise, in part, constructional forms hitherto not employed in aircraft construction (for example pronounced sweepback), unexpected difficulties in development and testing must be anticipated. It is therefore highly probable that the difference in schedule between the 8-287 and the two new projects is displaced at the expense of the latter.

"This might be the case especially as regards the Horten XVIII with its flying wing type of construction hitherto not used in similar types of aircraft. For this reason we make the following proposals: Should the rapid production of a long-range bomber be deemed necessary, we recommend the adoption of the 8-287 in its present form with slight alterations.

"As however on the basis of present knowledge the 8-287 certainly does not represent the final word in high speed long-range bombers, it is advisable to institute exhaustive studies based on the P 1107 and Horten XVIII projects with the object of attaining useful technical progress regarding the 8-287 on the one hand and on the other to reduce as far as possible by thorough preliminary work the risks always entailed with jumps in development of this kind."

Lastly, the conference delegates were particularly keen to avoid a re-run of the development nightmare that they were just now beginning to extricate themselves from - the Heinkel He 162, which had gone from drawing board to full production in around eight months: "We strongly advise against the enforced working out of these new projects at the same time as starting series production as was the case with the 8-162, as the technical risks are materially greater in the case of these new projects and setbacks in the development of such large aircraft types must have a greater effect on production than in the case of the 8-162."

Was the main recommendation of the conference, "the adoption of the 8-287 in its present form with slight alterations" acted on? Independent sources suggest that it was.

USAAF Technical Intelligence Report No. A-481 of June 5, 1945, says: "The Junkers concern started work on a fast jet-propelled bomber, Ju 287, in June 1943, and a prototype was flown in the summer of 1944. The design was supposed to be ready for mass production in the fall of 1944; but work on the project was stopped by the Air Ministry in the fall of 1944 and was not re-established until March 1945, at which time work on plans for mass production was again started."

BIOS evaluation repot No. 13 of September 22, 1945, says regarding the Ju 287: "At the end of September [1944] all work on this aircraft was stopped by the RLM because of the fighter programme. In January 1945 Junkers received orders to start work once again on the Ju 287 on the highest priority." ●

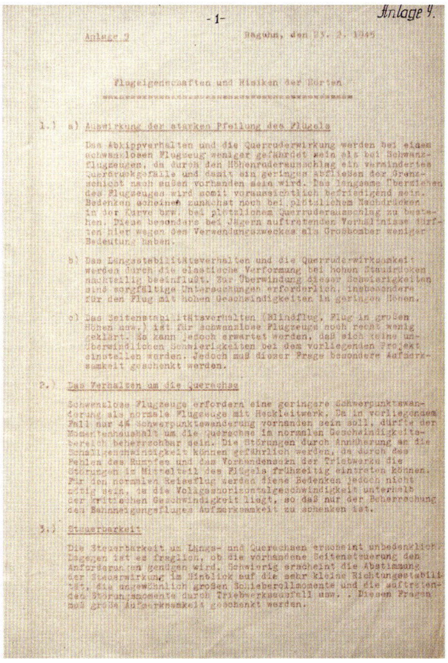
-1- Anlage 4.

Anlage 2

Flugeigenschaften und Risiken der Horten

1.) a) Auswirkung der starken Pfeilung des Flügels

b)

c)

2.) Das Verhalten um die Querachse

3.) Steuerbarkeit

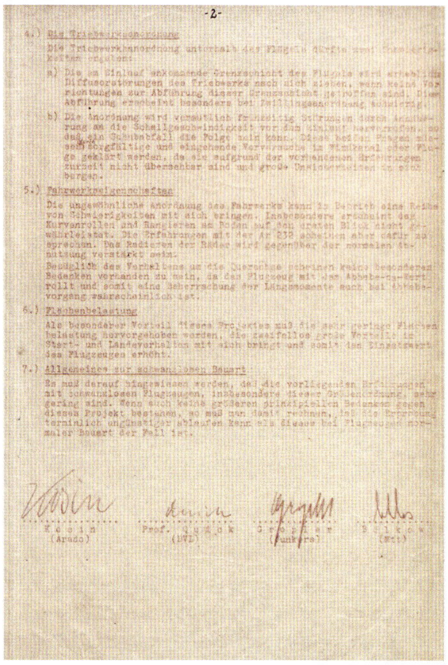
-2-

4.) Die Triebwerksanordnung

5.) Fahrwerkseigenschaften

6.) Flächenbelastung

7.) Allgemeines zur schwanzlosen Bauart

Kosin (Arado) Prof. Quick (DVL) Gropler (Junkers) Bölkow (Mtt.)

ABOVE: A subcommittee was established during the February meeting with a panel of experts specifically tasked with assessing the Horten XVIII in detail. Their signatures appear at the bottom – Rüdiger Kosin from Arado, Professor August Quick from the DVL, Hans Gropler from Junkers and Ludwig Bölkow from Messerschmitt.

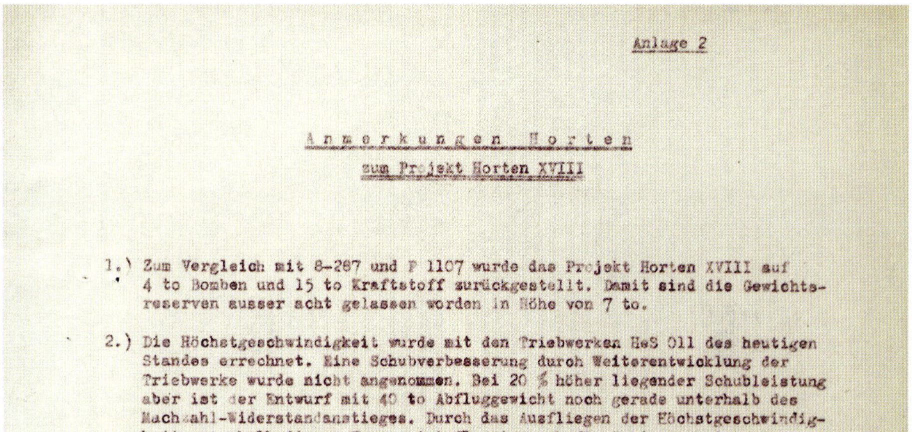
Anlage 2

Anmerkungen Horten
zum Projekt Horten XVIII

1.) Zum Vergleich mit 8-287 und P 1107 wurde das Projekt Horten XVIII auf 4 to Bomben und 15 to Kraftstoff zurückgestellt. Damit sind die Gewichtsreserven ausser acht gelassen worden in Höhe von 7 to.

2.) Die Höchstgeschwindigkeit wurde mit den Triebwerken HeS 011 des heutigen Standes errechnet. Eine Schubverbesserung durch Weiterentwicklung der Triebwerke wurde nicht angenommen. Bei 20 % höher liegender Schubleistung aber ist der Entwurf mit 40 to Abfluggewicht noch gerade unterhalb des Machzahl-Widerstandsanstieges. Durch das Ausfliegen der Höchstgeschwindigkeit unterhalb dieses Wertes ist flugeigenschaftsmässig zu keinen Befürchtungen Anlass gegeben.

3.) Die Höchstgeschwindigkeit gibt kein Werturteil über die Bauart Nur-Flügel-Flugzeug / Normal-Flugzeug ab, da hierfür die Flugzeuggrösse angerechnet werden muss. Um der Aufgabenstellung der Vergleichsflugzeuge gerecht zu werden, müsste die Flügelfläche in dem Masse verkleinert werden, dass durch die Erhöhung der Flächenbelastung gleiche Startwege entstehen. Bei entsprechender Flugzeuggrösse mit gleichem Fertigungsaufwand (Metallbauweise, Inneneinbau der Triebwerke, Einziehfahrwerk) liegen voraussichtlich dann die Höchstgeschwindigkeiten oberhalb derjenigen der Vergleichsflugzeuge. Der Betrag von 860 km/h wird nach der Vergleichsrechnung mit festem Fahrwerk und gondelartiger Aufhängung der Triebwerke erreicht.

4.) Die Raumverhältnisse gestatten mit der gegebenen Auslegung die Innenaufhängung von 4 x SC 1000. Die Grössenanpassung des Projektes, wie in Punkt 3 gefordert, würde den Raum für 4 x SC 1000 im Flügel beibehalten.

5.) Die Triebwerksanordnung ist entsprechend der Forderung der E'Stelle Rechling als Gondel vorgesehen worden. Auf diese Ausführung beziehen sich die Vergleichsrechnungen. Das Projekt P 1107 hat jedoch den "Teil-Innen-Einbau" der Triebwerke vorgesehen, zu dem das Nur-Flügel-Flugzeug durch die grösseren Flügelschnitte besser geeignet ist. Diese Triebwerksanordnung verschiebt den Machzahl-Widerstandsanstieg, so dass die Höchstgeschwindigkeit im Bahnneigungsflug oder bei Triebwerksleistungserhöhung auch im Horizontalflug wesentlich besser wird.

6.) Sämtliche Daten zur Leistungsberechnung können naturgemäss nur geschätzt werden. Windkanalmessungen an den Projekten sind erforderlich, um genaue Leistungsvergleiche zu erhalten.

gez. Horten

ABOVE: In contrast to the adjudicators' statement, Reimar Horten's signature does not appear at the bottom of his statement to the conference about the Horten XVIII. Reimar and his brother were certainly not made to feel welcome at the event but do seem to have won respect for their design.

Ultimate flying win

Messerschmitt P 1108

While the relatively conventional P 1107 had been Messerschmitt's chosen contender for the Langstreckenbomber requirement, the firm's design department had worked in parallel on a flying wing design – the P 1108 – but despite the promise of better performance, the likelihood of long production delays meant it was never put forward.

ABOVE: Contemporary concept drawing showing Messerschmitt 'Fernbomber' powered by four HeS 011s. Here the engine intakes are to the rear of the upper fuselage.

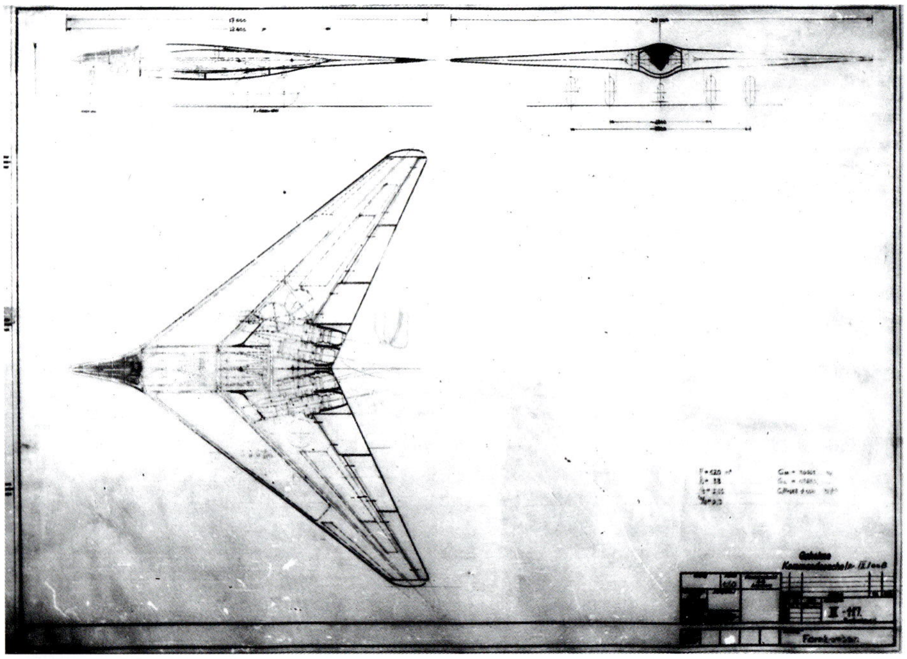

ABOVE: Messerschmitt drawing IX 117 shows a highly unusual Fernbomber – a true flying wing without a tail fin or fuselage. The engine intakes are on the upper surface of the aircraft but of extremely low profile and the turbojets are positioned at an angle. The five-wheel undercarriage is also unique, with the outer wheels retracting sideways and to the rear, while the inner wheels go straight up. The nosewheel tucks up into the aircraft's pointed beak-like nose.

When the Americans overran the Messerschmitt design facility at Oberammergau in April 1945, they were interested to discover that one of the last projects worked on by the company involved designs for a large flying wing bomber.

Most of the drawings were examined and copies were made before they were parcelled up ready for shipping back to the United States. The French then arrived and collected as much data as they could relating to the project before loading it onto lorries bound for Paris.

By the time a team representing the British Ministry of Aircraft Production, led by de Havilland Mosquito designer Richard Clarkson, arrived at Oberammergau on June 18, much of the data had gone.

Nevertheless, Clarkson diligently set about gathering what information he could about Messerschmitt's end of war designs - including the P 1107 and P 1108. An interview with project leader Ludwig Bölkow on Saturday, June 23, proved to be particularly revealing.

Clarkson wrote: "All the calculations on this project had been removed to Paris by the French, only general arrangement drawings and Herr Bölkow's memory were available. All figures quoted should therefore be regarded as approximate.

"In November 1944, Professor Messerschmitt suggested to the German government that it might be possible to carry 8800lb of bombs for 4350 miles range at 500mph with jets.

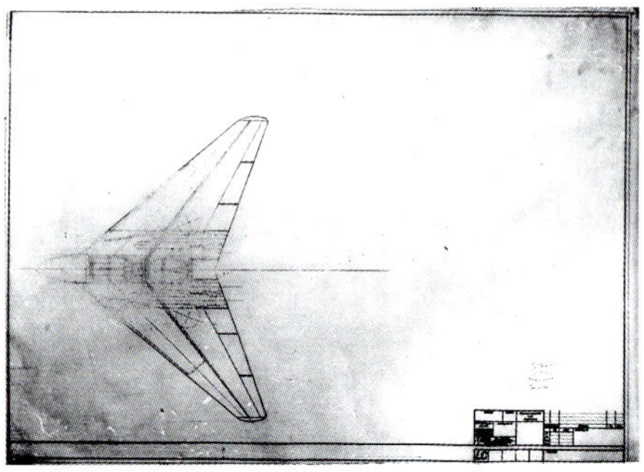

ABOVE: This unnumbered Messerschmitt drawing shows a halfway point between the extreme features of the IX 117 design and the more moderated approach of the one shown in IX 118. The engines have been realigned but still appear to be fed from upper surface intakes, while the cockpit has assumed a more rounded aspect. There is no rear fuselage overhang, however.

gs of the Luftwaffe

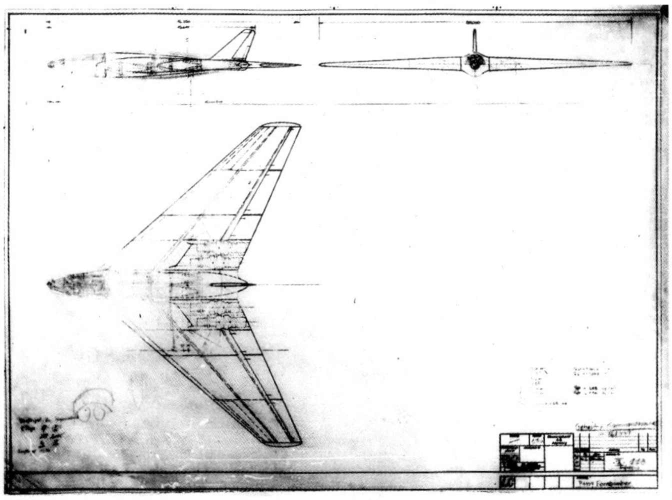

ABOVE: Apparently a simplification of the aircraft shown in drawing IX 117, the flying wing shown in IX 118 is labelled P 1107 Fernbomber suggesting that at this point the P 1108 had yet to become a distinct project in its own right. The IX 118 design now boasts a sharply swept tailfin, a more conventional bullet-shaped cockpit and a regular tricycle undercarriage. The engine intakes remain on the upper surface.

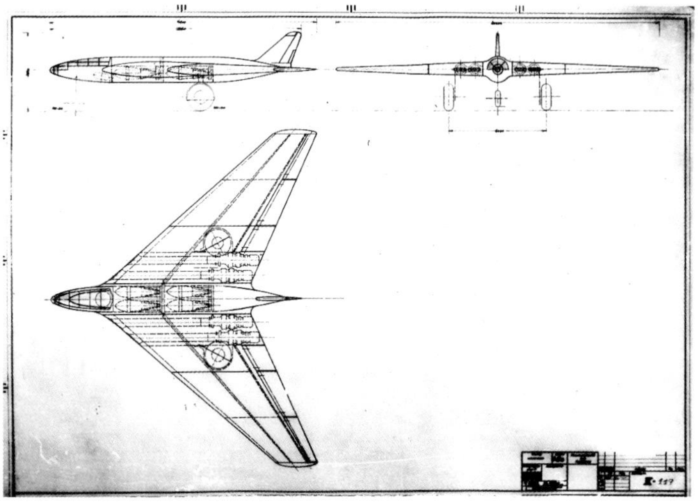

ABOVE: The design most commonly thought of as being the P 1108 – depicted here in drawing IX 119 – sees the unusual intakes of the two earlier designs replaced with four slot intakes on the wing leading edge. Rather than a teardrop-shaped profile, the fuselage is now more tubular and the tailfin sits on an extension which protrudes from the trailing edge.

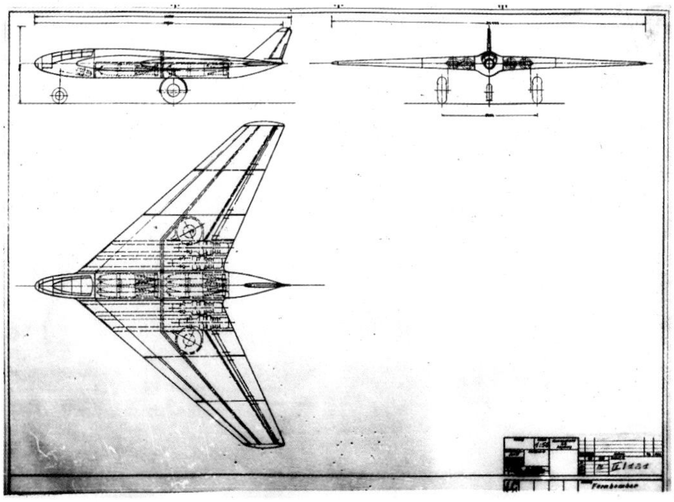

ABOVE: Drawing IX 121, labelled simply 'Fernbomber' sees the bomber's cockpit canopy given a curved rather than straight sill and the fuselage has once again been re-profiled to have a gently curving back. The entire central section has been repositioned to give a longer overhang to the rear and a shorter nose at the front.

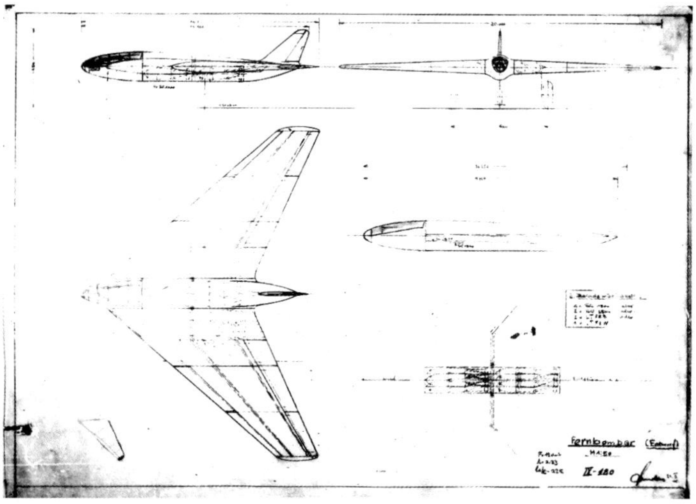

ABOVE: The key features of drawing IX 121 survive into Fernbomber drawing IX 180 – shown here – such as the curved cockpit sill and fuselage profile, although another cockpit form is suggested. The chief difference now is the shortening of the nose still further. It is unclear from this design exactly where its engine intakes are meant to be positioned.

The Government were interested in the possibilities of the project for convoy raiding and strategic bombing of Russia.

"An analysis of a conventional layout with tail showed that with four Heinkel 011 engines of 2860lb thrust each it might be possible to do 3100 miles range with 8800lb of bombs, but that a tailless layout had better promise of realising the desired figures.

"A number of tailless layouts were examined between November 1944 and February 1945 and these were all available at the plant.

"In the meantime, the Government decided that Messerschmitt's had no available design and production capacity for tackling the job and gave it to Junkers and the Horten brothers. The latest of the Messerschmitt general arrangement drawings therefore does not represent the final solution.

"Herr Bölkow stated that the figures given corresponded to a range of 3100 miles and that the subsequent proposal was to load the aeroplane up to about 77,000lb to get the 4350 miles range.

"Take-off would be by rockets or catapult on a trolley, the aeroplane to be cruised throughout at its operational ceiling which would be about 18,500ft initially and 29,500-33,000ft finally, the undercarriage only being used for landing."

He said that one of the key issues that had occupied the Messerschmitt team had been where to put the engine intakes and what shape they should take.

"The best location of entry ducts was under discussion and undecided, i.e. whether above, below or in the leading edge of the wing. Considerable wind tunnelling would be needed. It was noted that as with the P 1101-1111 fighters the question of entry duct position and losses played a very important part in the settling of the layout.

"Some inconclusive tests, marred by engine and aeroplane variations, had been attempted on a Me 262 to get information on the effect of entry duct length on losses. Wing section – not laminar flow. Messerschmitt's have no time for making accurate laminar flow wings in wartime, and in any case their value at high Mach number is doubtful, and furthermore the presence of leading edge slots renders them ineffective."

The P 1108 was to have metal wings but the option of using wood for the section outboard of the engines had been investigated and was thought to be a "promising development, cheaper than the metal wing". Some highly unusual configurations had been examined ▶

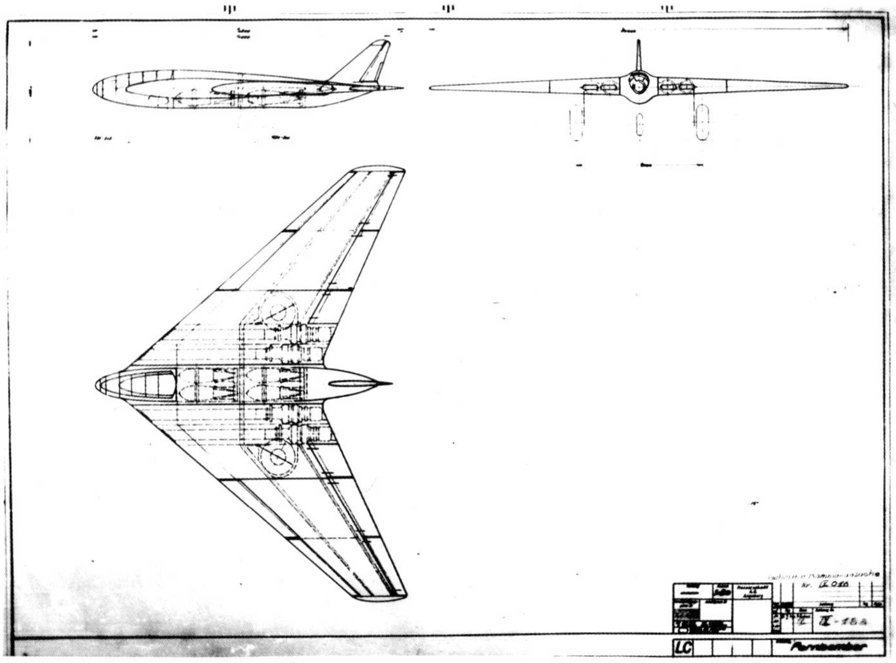

ABOVE: Apparently a redraw of IX 180, drawing IX 188 now shows the aircraft's intakes once again positioned in the wing leading edge.

ABOVE: The drawing number of this P 1108 design has been obliterated by the microfilming process but it would appear to be the first to be labelled 'P 1108' rather than simply 'Fernbomber' or even 'P 1107'. Indeed, the design appears to be a halfway house between the more radical flying wings and the conventional P 1107. It features the shorter nose and longer tail of the IX 188 design but with the more prominent fuselage and features of the P 1107.

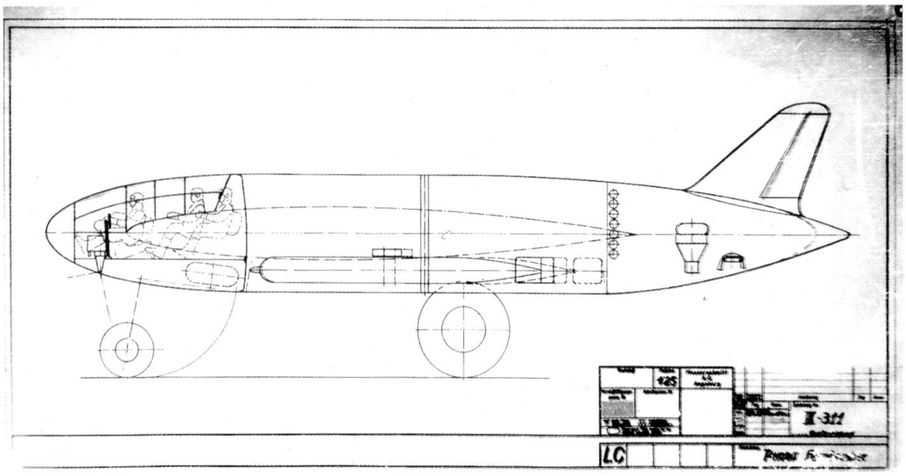

ABOVE: A different version of the IX 310 drawing, this time showing a torpedo in place of bombs, since one of the aircraft's most important duties would have been to continue the destruction of Allied convoys at sea.

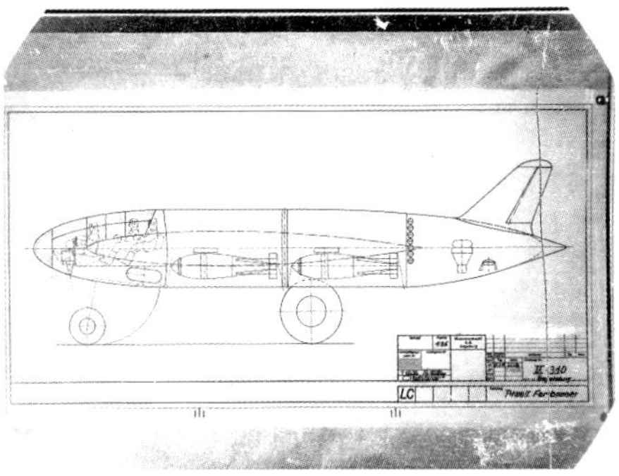

ABOVE: This profile drawing, labelled P 1108/I has a clear date on it – February 22, 1945 – making it a fairly late addition to the series. The similarities to the P 1107 are clear, as is the fact that it lacks any form of horizontal tail surfaces. A camera is visible towards the rear of the fuselage to make clear the P 1108's dual role as a reconnaissance aircraft.

- some of which are unknown today.

"Swept forward and swept back wings had been considered," wrote Clarkson. Bölkow had said that "with a swept forward wing there is a cross flow in the boundary layer towards the root which causes the root to stall before the tip, leaving a peak load at the tip which results in a heavier wing structure.

"The bombs are in the fuselage and it is believed that the bulk of the 4400 gallons of fuel could be stored in the wing outboard of the engines and wheels, the remainder in the fuselage above the bomb cell.

"The fuel tanks were unprotected, the fuel being heavy oil (melting point about 0°C) and relatively non-inflammable. It

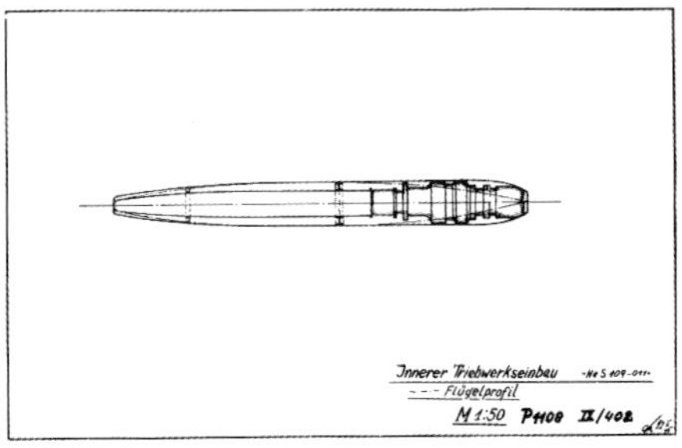

ABOVE: Drawing IX 402, dated February 22, 1945, shows the P 1108's inner engine installation in profile.

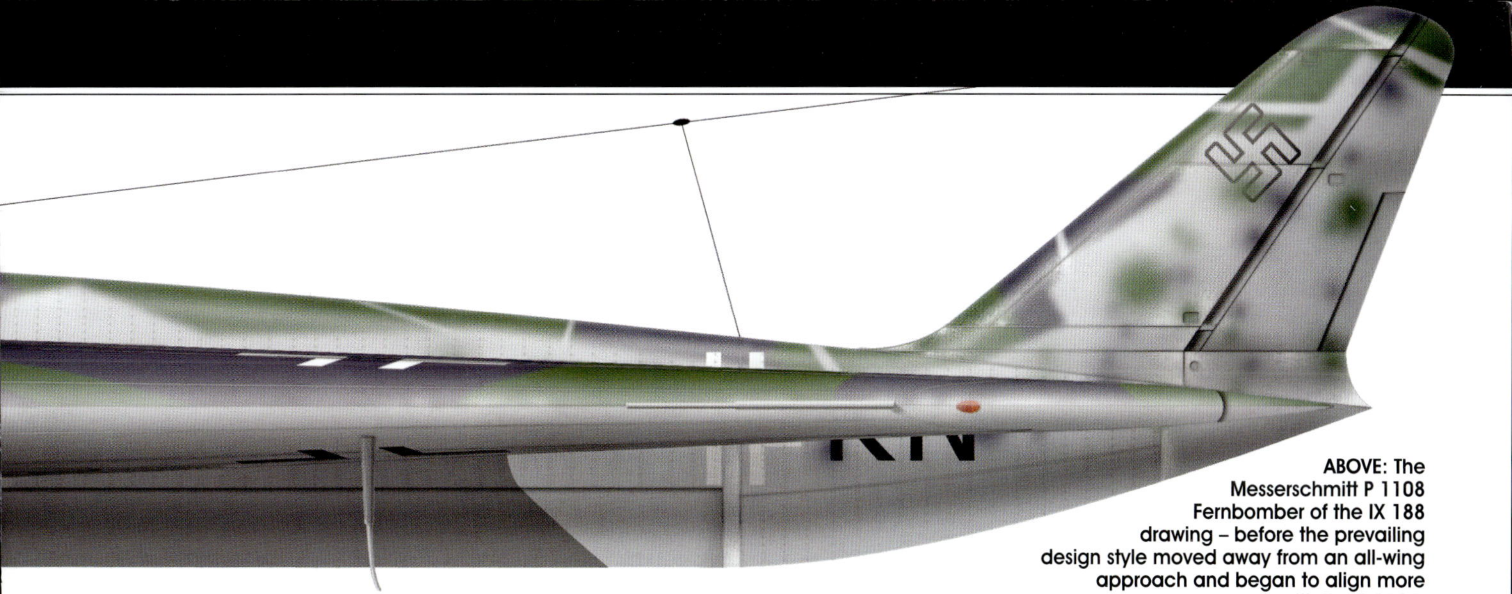

ABOVE: The Messerschmitt P 1108 Fernbomber of the IX 188 drawing – before the prevailing design style moved away from an all-wing approach and began to align more with the P 1107.

would be kept fluid by means of immersion heaters; work on this had been done and an experimental Me 262 installation was due to fly in June-July 1945. The reason for this choice of fuel was availability and cheapness - it is available in the Vienna region."

Bölkow also suggested that the P 1108 might be put to good use by the victorious Allies. Clarkson wrote: "It was mentioned that a civil version would be a good economic prospect.

"As mentioned earlier in these notes the final general arrangement and the above notes do not represent Messerschmitt's considered and final thoughts on the project, the design was still fluid and the size and number of engines were undecided."

A little more information about the P 1108 can be gleaned from examining the drawings themselves. As Clarkson recorded, they include a wide range of different configurations. ●

ABOVE: Period concept art showing the short nose, long tail version of the Messerschmitt P 1108 Fernbomber.

JUNKERS' LAST GASP

While some of Junkers' design team would continue their work for the Soviets after the war, their last project for the Nazi regime in Germany was the EF 130.

Little is known about this four-jet bomber, except what is recorded in German Aircraft: New and Projected Types: "Of the flying-wing type, this project has stabilising fins and rudders mounted on the trailing edge of the wing approximately mid-way between the wing tips and the fuselage.

"Landing flaps are fitted inboard of the stabilisers with ailerons outboard. The wing is of wood and the fuselage of metal. The power plant is 4 x HeS 011 jet units installed centrally. Several different designs were submitted for the EF 130 project and it was the subject of considerable controversy, particularly the positioning of the four jet units.

"A retractable tricycle undercarriage is fitted. Fuel tanks are located in the wings and centre section. The design had a wingspan of 78.8ft, a wing area of 1290sq ft, all-up weight of 77,000lb to 84,000lb, top speed of 620mph and a range of 3700 miles."

Only one period drawing of the EF 130 is known to exist – the one that accompanies the above report – and it has been suggested that even this may be either a very basic preliminary layout or a sketch drawn from someone's memory because the original documents were not available. Certainly, nothing else is known about the "considerable controversy" regarding the several different designs, nor what those designs actually looked like.

ABOVE: The Junkers EF 130 as it might have looked – with a Ju 388 cabin to make construction quicker and cheaper. Art by Daniel Uhr

ABOVE: The only known contemporary drawing of the EF 130 – though many modern day artists' impressions have been created to fill in the blanks.

Red bombers

P 1107, Horten XVIII and Ju 287 in Russian hands

The Germans had put a great deal of effort into their Langstreckenbomber plans, only to run out of time. But if the Soviets now held copies of those plans, how might they choose to use them? During 1946 British intelligence began to consider the uncomfortable possibility that the P 1107, Horten XVIII and Ju 287 might get a fresh lease of life under new ownership...

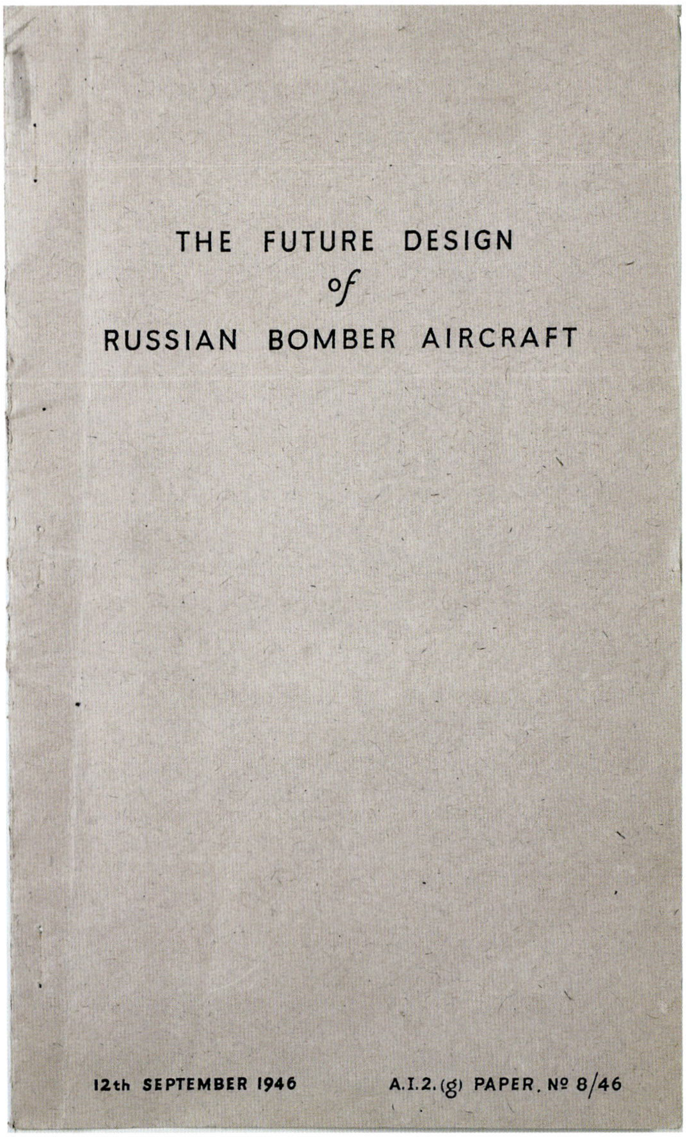
THE FUTURE DESIGN
of
RUSSIAN BOMBER AIRCRAFT

12th SEPTEMBER 1946 A.I.2.(g) PAPER. Nº 8/46

ABOVE: Relations between the Western Allies and the Soviet Union cooled rapidly once the Second World War was over. By the summer of 1946, the thoughts of British intelligence had turned to German aircraft engineers known to be working for the Russians and the wartime bomber designs they might be developing. This speculative report was the result.

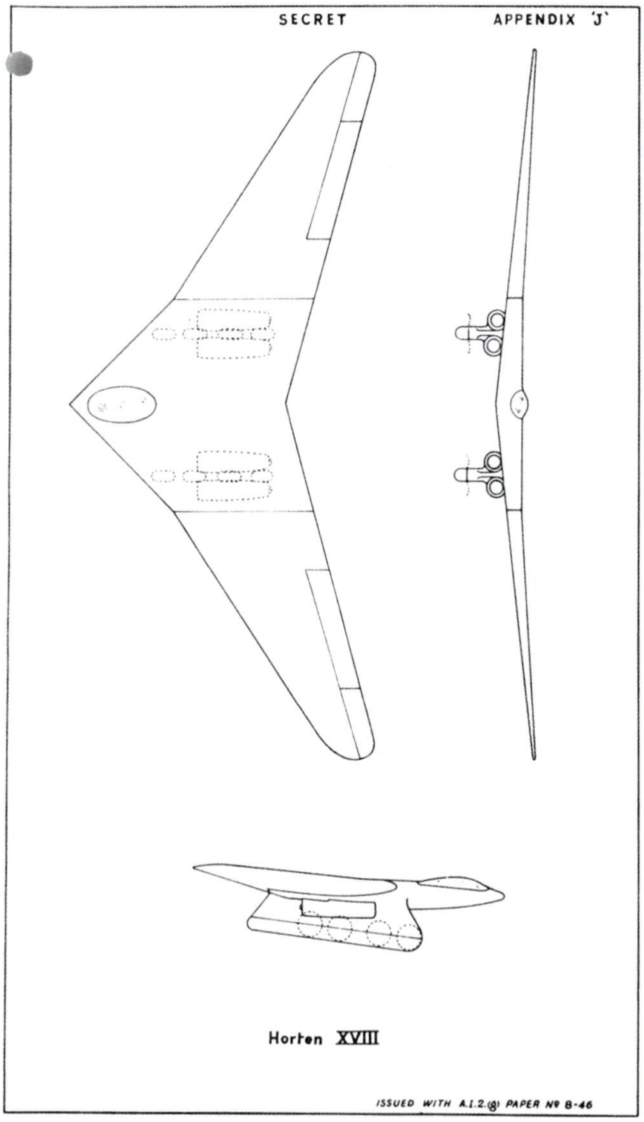

ABOVE: It was believed that of all the bomber designs likely to have been captured and examined by the Soviets, the Horten XVIII was the most likely to be taken on and developed to provide the Soviets with a fleet of fast, long-range, high altitude bombers perfect for striking at targets in Western Europe.

The war in Europe had ended on May 8, 1945, and during the months that followed Germany was occupied by the victorious Allies while the Third Reich was systematically dismantled.

Four zones of occupation were set up, with the Soviet Union naturally taking the easternmost portion. It also gained effective control of the countries through which its forces had fought the retreating German armies - Poland, Czechoslovakia, Hungary, Romania, Bulgaria and the Baltic States.

Relations between the Western Allies and the Soviets, which had always been strained at best, now cooled significantly. It became clear to Britain and America that the Russians, their vast army now occupying all of Eastern Europe, had little interest in

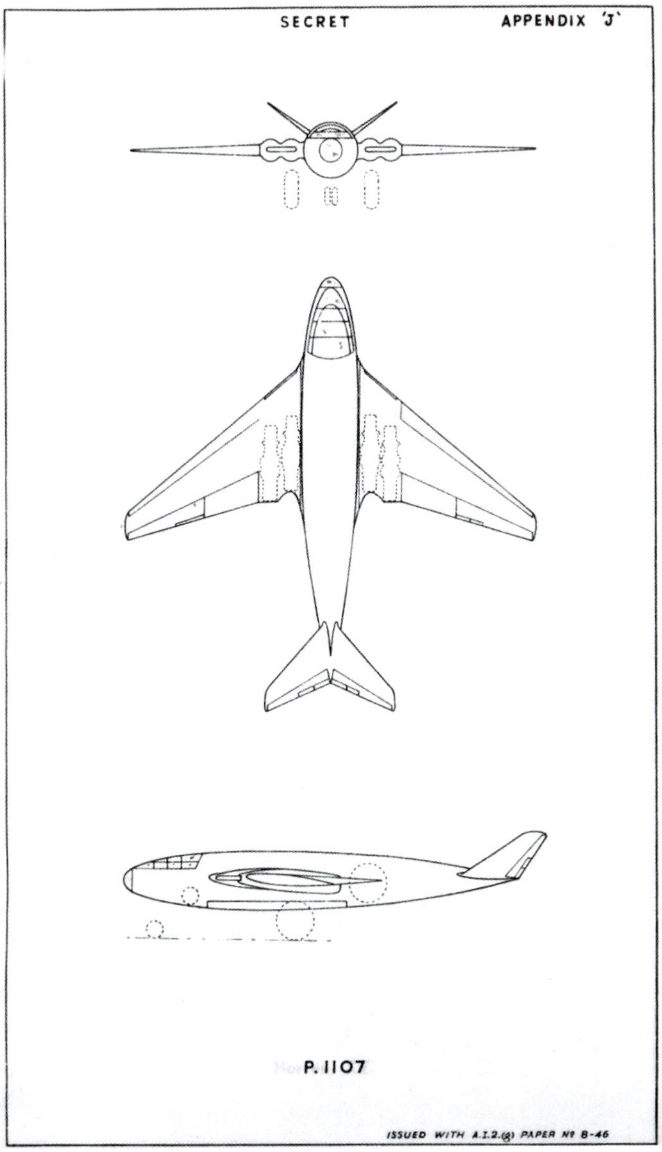

ABOVE: The British believed it was highly unlikely that the Soviets would choose to develop the Messerschmitt P 1107 fast bomber design. Even though it was the fastest of the three late-war Langstreckenbombers, Messerschmitt had designed it in such a way that several stages of time-consuming and expensive development would be required – only to obtain an overall performance worse than that of the Horten XVIII.

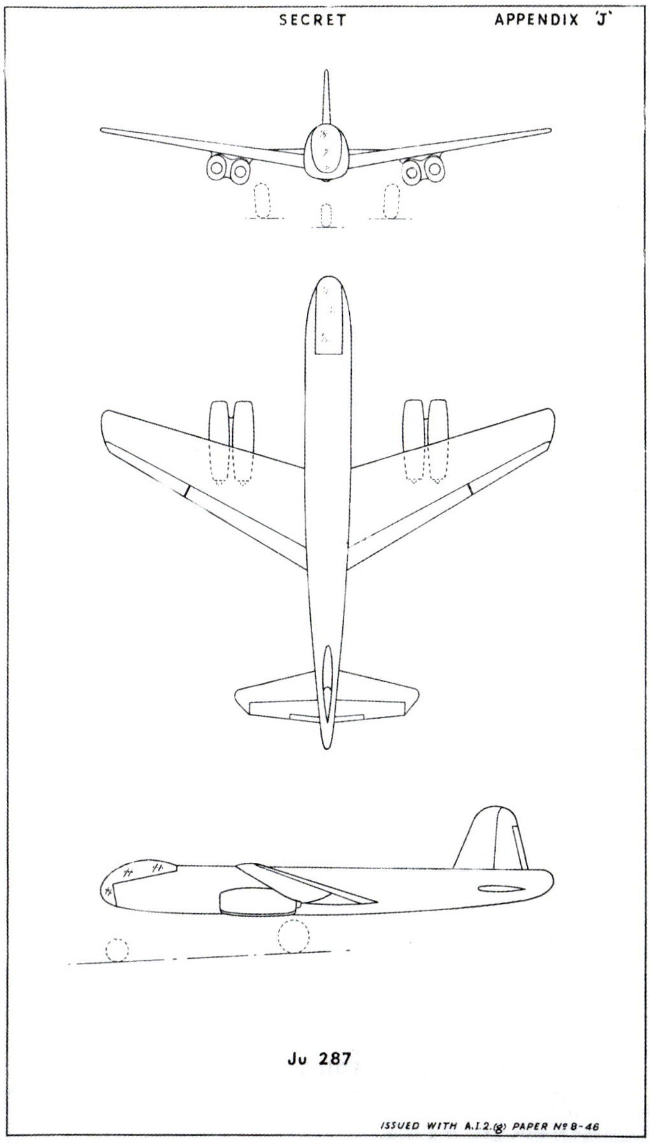

ABOVE: It was evident to the British that Junkers had laid detailed plans for the ongoing future development of the Ju 287 even before the war ended. Projections included the fitment of advanced BMW 028 turboprop engines by 1948.

friendly cooperation and reconciliation.

With this in mind, British intelligence was asked to consider what weapons the Soviets already had and what weapons - particularly what bombers - they might soon be able to develop given the wealth of German aeronautical know-how they had undoubtedly captured during the closing stages of the war.

The result, published on September 12, 1946, was a report entitled The Future Design of Russian Bomber Aircraft.

It explains how, during the war, the Russians had put all of their effort into producing aircraft, tanks and artillery in large numbers - all of it intended to provide close support for the Red Army. Little had been done to create even a small strategic bomber force.

But with the war over "the effect of strategic bombing on both Germany and Japan is too obvious to be ignored. Least vulnerable to strategic bombing attack herself, Russia cannot afford to overlook the vulnerability of possible enemies and there is evidence that this problem is receiving full attention.

"Despite the security measures taken some information comes through from her zone in Germany and although this information is not plentiful it is all highly significant.

"Considerable activity is reported in all of the former German aircraft factories in the Russian zone, the largest and the one receiving the most attention, being the Junkers works at Dessau. The main activity is centred on jet propelled bombers and fighters and in improving the high altitude performance and thrust of German gas turbines."

It appeared as though the worst fears of the British and Americans were coming true. The Russians, regarded as technologically less advanced, were attempting to catch up rapidly through the use of captured German engineering data. Their goal, it seemed, was to quickly build a fleet of bombers capable of exploiting the "vulnerability of possible enemies," such as Western Europe, to aerial bombardment.

The report goes on: "The great interest shown by Russia in the more advanced types of German aircraft and engines is not comparable with our own. Flying trials and test results have not shown the aircraft or engines to be so good that the results will influence British airframe or engine design.

"The low maximum thrust and short life between overhauls, although largely due to a lack of heat resisting steels, shows the basic design of the engines is not up to British standards. We were anxious to know the state of technical development and finding that the lead was held by Germany in relatively few fields we have centred our interests, notably on guided projectiles and rocket units.

"But Russia has found a state of technical development far in advance of anything she has herself achieved and is now endeavouring to exploit the whole field of aeronautics. The conquest of Germany placed the possibility of rapid technical development within her grasp, a technical advance that could not be achieved in under 10 years of solely Russian effort."

CALL IN THE BLACKSMITH

The report next examines the state of Russian-made aircraft during the closing stages of the war - before any captured material could be exploited. And the description given is unflattering to say the least: "From Russian aircraft which we have examined, ▶

ABOVE: The Soviet EF 140 bomber – created by German ex-Junkers designers working for the Russians.

it is apparent that there is a shortage of skilled workers. The fighter aircraft are well finished externally and the machining and finish has been of a high order where efficient functioning of the equipment has demanded it. But where roughness of finish cannot affect efficiency it is as though the village blacksmith had been called in to help.

"Welding is crude, large pieces of metal adhering to the weld which are quite unessential to strength and there is a casualness about loose nuts, missing cowling buttons and faulty ammunition belt links that would not be tolerated by the RAF.

"Machine tool output creates a bottleneck, for too few special machines and skilled workers are available to increase the production of high precision equipment and the light metal industries are not yet fully developed, so wooden construction of aircraft parts still prevails.

"Russia is well aware of this deficiency in men and materials and is making every effort to counteract it. An organisation exists to decide on the allocation of skilled labour according to the most essential features of each aircraft type: skilled labour and material is allocated to those parts requiring a high degree of finish and the remainder of the aircraft constructed and assembled by unskilled labour probably of very low intelligence."

Existing Soviet heavy bombers, primarily the Petlyakov Pe-8, are described as "backward" and "all inferior to modern British types," particularly given their "lack of operational equipment (blind flying techniques, navigational aids and blind flying instruments of reliability). By no stretch of the imagination, can the present Soviet heavy bomber force be considered a serious threat to other world powers".

Aero engine development similarly lagged far behind the pace set by Britain and the US, with the Soviets unable to build a single engine capable of operating at high altitude. It was known that the Soviets had been working on turbojets however: "Some research and development on gas turbines was undertaken by Soviet engineers during the war but little is known about this activity. To judge by the lack of success achieved in the building of turbo-superchargers it is unlikely that Soviet jet engine design is very advanced."

All this was about to change however.

The report paints a worrying picture: "Conquest of Germany placed a very large number of skilled aeronautical workers at the control of Russia and it is natural that she should now attempt to make up her deficiencies by employing German engineers, technicians, and skilled and semi-skilled workers to carry on the research and development which capitulation brought to a halt.

"Here is the skilled labour so badly needed to raise the quality that has handicapped Russian design. But more than that, there is the designing and engineering skill which far surpasses anything in Russia. There are the factories and the workers who produced jet aircraft in quantity; multi-engined bombers of advanced design and of proven reliability are ready for quantity production; also delivered into their hands is the first jet propelled bomber ever to fly.

"It is an opportunity that Russia is determined to use to the full and this is emphasised in all reports. Whether exploitation is intended only to carry on research and development or quantity production is not material to the future of Russian technical development. What is material is that Russian advance will now be so much more rapid than a solely Russian effort could hope to be."

ADVANCED JET BOMBERS

With all this engineering skills, test data and hardware in hand, what would the Russians choose to build? The British report examines the possibilities: "It is generally believed that Germany did not and could not produce a multi-engined heavy bomber. This belief is quite unfounded in fact, for despite the poor record of the He 177, due to a sweeping specification that designated to the aircraft too many roles, there were other multi-engined aircraft with creditable performances, namely the Ju 290 and Ju 390.

"Although not built by Germany in sufficient quantities to form a strategic bomber force there is no reason why this should not be done by Russia. Reports indicate that this is the intention, to produce both these aircraft in quantity in Russian factories, either in the Odessa region or behind the Urals using an element of German skilled labour.

"This, however, would be no more than an interim measure. The future lies in gas turbine and rocket propulsion. That Russia is well aware of this and is anxious to be to the fore is evident by the interest shown in German gas turbine and rocket engine development. It is not surprising therefore that considerable urgency is apparent in this development work being pressed forward on the jet-propelled types."

Details of the Langstreckenbomber conference of February 1945 are then given – including the three competitors which "represent the most advanced stage of jet bomber design at present available to the Russians".

A FORCE OF 1500 JU 287S

A brief description of the Ju 287 is given, which provides a useful insight into how the British saw the type's development: "Germany's desire to be able to attack very distant targets by means of a high speed bomber resulted in the designing by Junkers of the Ju 287, and work on the project commenced in the summer of 1943. The original specification called for a bomber capable of carrying a bomb load of 6600lb to a range of 1240 miles; the resulting all-up weight was 50,600lb.

"Although no jet unit sufficiently powerful to permit a twin jet installation was available, it was expected that when they were available, high speed at altitude could be attained, and to delay the effect of the critical Mach number, the wing was to be swept forward approximately 25 degrees. The effect of sweep forward is similar to that of sweep back, with the additional advantage of better control at low speeds.

"A further advantage was the long length of fuselage forward of the leading edge, which, free of obstructions, permitted a bomb bay length of over 17ft. The critical Mach number for the Ju 287 wing was claimed, by wind tunnel tests, to be 0.83 but the RLM refused to accept this figure and it was reduced to 0.8.

"It was realised that the high fuel consumption of jet engines make it extremely difficult to compete with aircraft of the normal type, therefore careful construction of the aircraft was planned, in order to reduce airframe weight to a minimum. When compared with a piston-engined bomber, in this case the Ju 288, the higher flying speed of the jet aircraft must be taken into account, and in this respect comparison between the Ju 288 and Ju 287 found the latter superior for ranges up to 1240 miles.

"Development of the project was stopped by the RLM in the middle of 1944, and on resumption of work in March 1945, an increase in performance was demanded. The long range bomber programme called for an aircraft with a fuel capacity of 4000 gallons; this increase the range to 2900 miles and reduced cruising speed to 488mph. In addition, the bomb load was increased to 8800lb."

Few of the Junkers documents known to exist today given much insight into how the Ju 287 was eventually to be developed, had the war continued, but the British report on future Soviet bombers was evidently based on German wartime documents that no longer survive.

It states: "By the time of the collapse in May 1945, one of two prototypes built had been flown, using a Heinkel 177 fuselage and a fixed undercarriage. With four Jumo 004 jet engines the aircraft was grossly underpowered, the purpose of the tests being to provide information on the swept forward wing. The calculated performance at an altitude of 20,000ft was 540mph. In later versions each double unit was to be replaced by one very powerful unit.

"The Jumo 004B is an engine of low thrust output, and several stages of development were planned to increase this output. Experience gained on the 004B was to be used as the basis for a new series, the 004 H4, a thrust of nearly 4000lb making this engine comparable with the Derwent V. Another engine on which work had been done, and which is likely to receive high priority from the Russians is the BMW 018, with a static thrust of 7700lb. Two of these units installed in the Ju 287 were calculated to give a top speed of 560mph at 25,000ft.

"It will be remembered that the critical Mach number of the Ju 287 wing was 0.8, at which speed the rise in the drag coefficient is so steep that a big increase in thrust results in a disproportionately small increase in speed. This speed, 560mph at 25,000ft, represents the ultimate development of the Ju 287, without major airframe redesign, since fuel consumption drastically reduces range.

"Production. The BMW 018 is estimated to be in production by the end of 1947, so during 1948, a jet bomber force composed of Ju 287s could be in service in the Soviet Air Force. Within two years a total of 1500 Ju 287s could be produced. This is based on a German estimate of 25 aircraft a month during 1947 and 100 a month during 1948."

Accompanying the report is an appendix with specifications for the Ju 287 if it were to be equipped with four HeS 011 A-0s or six BMW 003As in 1946, six BMW 003Ds or two Jumo 012s in 1947, or in 1948, four Jumo 004 H-4s, two BMW 018s or two BMW 028 turboprops.

THE UNLIKELY P 1107

The British lacked even the Germans' limited faith in either Messerschmitt the designer or Messerschmitt the company, and predicted that the Russians would follow suit in rejecting the P 1107 as too difficult and time-consuming to build.

Its design was "typical of Messerschmitt's approach to aeronautical problems. The pronounced sweepback, the V-type tail unit, the high wing loading and the calculated optimum range of 4560 miles shows the same bold approach to the problems of high speed bombers that characterised the radical design of the Me 262 jet fighter.

"With the first few aircraft, Messerschmitt proposed to avoid development difficulties by fitting a standard tail unit and installing engines under, instead of submerged in the wing. Then sufficient experience had been gained the necessary modifications were to have been made and the P.1107 would emerge as the fastest jet bomber in the world.

"Top speed of the P.1107 was calculated at 580mph when fitted with four HeS 011 jet units and flying at 23,000ft. At this speed the drag coefficient begins to rise at a steep angle and more powerful jet units, e.g. BMW 018s would have a disproportionately small effect in increasing the maximum speed. An increased thrust of 4000lb was ▶

ABOVE: Despite embodying the state-of-the-art in jet bomber design in 1945, the basic Ju 287 design was already beginning to show its age by 1948, when work on the EF 140 was begun.

calculated to raise the top speed to 610mph at 23,000ft and 615mph at sea level.

"To obtain the maximum range the cruising speed would have to drop to 548mph and correspondingly less at greater heights. The service ceiling was calculated at 42,500ft when fitted with BMW 018 jet units.

"Assisted take-off was necessary as with the other projects, a thrust of between 2640 and 4400lb being required during the last 10 seconds of the take-off run, depending on take-off weight and runway available.

"Messerschmitt claimed that systematic development of the P.1107 would lead to a range greater than 7500 miles with a bomb load of 6600lb but this proposal involved so many changes by intermediate steps that a completely new aircraft would evolve. It would resemble the P.1107 in so few features that it could be treated as an entirely new design based on the experience of the P.1107."

Despite the somewhat more realistic British approach to the P 1107's prospects, it is clear that the report's unnamed author harbours more than a little respect for the attitude of Germany's aircraft designers, if not their actual work.

He states: "Considering that the P.1107 is not yet built it may seem premature to consider an even more advanced design. But such statements indicate the progressive attitude of German designers and their determination to overcome the difficulties of high speed flight and the limits of range set by the high fuel consumption of jet engines."

Yet this would cut little ice with the pragmatic Russians. Indeed, intelligence reports seemed to suggest that the Russians had already rejected the P 1107: "Production: Under the most favourable circumstances four years would be the least requirement for the production of the P 1107 at a rate of 100 aircraft a month.

"A year has already been lost, as there is at present no indication of Russian interest in this project, so this aircraft is unlikely to be produced in sufficient quantity to form a strategic bomber force before 1952. Development work during the period 1947-1950 may affect the eventual design but such changes are likely only to extend the range without alteration of speed."

Engine options for the P 1107 were seen as four HeS 011s, two Jumo 012s, two BMW 018s or two BMW 028 turboprops.

THE SOVIET HORTEN XVIII FLEET

Britain's aeronautical engineers were very interested in the wartime work of the Horten brothers and rated it highly, though they had little interest in replicating it directly and still less interest in working with the designers themselves.

Given the choice between the three types, it seemed to the British that the Soviets would quickly recognise the inherent benefits of the Horten XVIII for the task at hand – bombing Britain and her allies. The design, "of the 'flying wing' type, had a wing area of 1680sq ft, as compared with the 646sq ft demanded by the RLM specification. It was, consequently, of a much lower wing loading than the other projects, the Ju 287 and P 1107, and due to this, the drag figures for the Horten XVIII were higher, and maximum speed the lowest of the three projects.

"But, due also to the lower wing loading, the operational ceiling is higher, and the range extended for the same fuel capacity by the ability to fly higher and thus make more efficient use of the jet propulsion. By using the designed fuel capacity of the Horten XVIII a range of 4050 miles was possible although at this loading assisted take-off of between 2650lb and 4400lb thrust, depending on the length of runway available, was required."

So far so good, but there were challenging design problems to be overcome: "The Horten brothers, designers of this project, pointed out the present difficulties with tailless aircraft, despite their having more experience of this type than any other designer (their research work, however, has since been interrupted). This meant that development time would be longer than for the Ju 287 or P 1107. Centre of gravity shift is more severely limited, and changes of stability when approaching the speed of sound can be more dangerous than in conventional aircraft."

Yet these did not seem to be unsurmountable obstacles and the Horten XVIII's performance would make it ideal for any future attack on the West – the distance from London to Moscow being some 1500 miles.

"The aircraft is an attractive proposition for the Russians for several reasons. As a long range bomber, the radius of action is 2000 miles (take off and climbing consumption plus a residue of 70 gallons are allowed for in this calculation), with a full bomb load of 8800lb.

"The wood and metal construction is a method in which Russian workers are experienced. In the man-hours involved in production this aircraft was expected to score heavily over the other projects. By the 500th aircraft, 12,000 man-hours was the estimated requirement, compared with 19,000 for the Ju 287 and 17,000 for the P 1107.

"These figures indicate the intense work German production engineers had put into reducing labour costs – equivalent man-hours for the Lancaster were 40,000. The Hortens' low figure was attributed to the comparative roominess of the flying wing shape, and easy accessibility for installation of internal equipment.

"Performance: Despite the advanced design of this flying wing project an increase in the maximum speed at altitude is limited

ABOVE: A side view of the Soviet EF 140 bomber, complete with red under-wing stars.

by the comparatively low critical Mach number of 0.77. Designed to take the HeS 011 jet unit with a static thrust of 2860lb the maximum speed was estimated as 500mph at 35,000ft. Any increase in engine power would result in such a small increase in speed as to render it uneconomical, in addition to the difficulties that would be met so close to the critical Mach number. At 25,000ft the absolute maximum speed was 534mph.

"Production: It was estimated by RLM that one and a half to two years was necessary to reach a production of 25 aircraft per month. This is under the stimulus of war and a 100% increase of this figure, at least seems necessary under present conditions, so in about four years, that is 1950, the Horten XVIII may be coming into service and by 1952 a fleet of 1000 front line bombers is a possibility."

A Soviet Horten XVIII might be powered, the report states, by four HeS 011 turbojets, two BMW 018s or two BMW 028s - the best performance being provided by the latter.

ENGINES AND AERODYNAMICS

German jet engines at the end of the war, the British concluded, were hampered by a lack of experience with superchargers but with access to better materials, and given a little more time, rapid development was possible.

The report notes: "The projected programme of jet engine development was ambitious and if successful would have been equal to the most advanced stage of British development. Capitulation in 1945, however, found the Germans limited to the 2000lb thrust of the Jumo 004 and the 1760lb thrust of the BMW 003.

"If development continues with success under the Russians, jet engines of high thrust will undoubtedly be in service in the near future. The time from the design stage to production is only two to three years for gas turbines compared with five to six years for piston engines of high output. Design is, in general, complete for gas turbines and pure jet engines of German origin, so that one to two years may see engines of 7000lb static thrust in production."

Having carefully examined the three German bomber designs, the British calculated their most economical cruising speed and the optimum altitude at which to achieve it. For the Ju 287, it was 490mph at 23,000ft and for the P 1107, it was 530mph at 25,000ft.

The Horten XVIII was different, however, with its most economical performance being achieved travelling at 500mph at 37,000ft due mainly to its lower wing loading.

"The trend becomes clear from these considerations," the report states. "To make interception difficult, high altitude and high cruising speed are essential. These characteristics belong to the Horten XVIII. Low wing loading simplifies aerodrome requirements and decreases the length of pilot training time. A flying wing design lends itself most readily to large surface area for low wing loading yet allows thickness to chord ratio to delay the approach of the critical Mach number.

"So it is apparent that Russian jet bomber design will be in step with British and American trend if the Horten XVIII eventually becomes the standard aircraft of the Soviet strategic bomber force."

The report gives a table showing a "summary of production" with only the Ju 290 available in 1947 at "estimated production 150 per month". The Ju 390 could provide a "bomber force of 1200 aircraft possible by end of 1948", while the Ju 287 could come into service in 1949 at a "max production of 100 per month from 1948. Bomber force of 1200 aircraft estimated by end of 1949".

Then for 1950-52, the P 1107 and Horten XVIII are given as "max production of 100 per month. Bomber force of 1800 aircraft estimated by end of 1952".

NOT SO ROSY AFTER ALL

The British believed that the Germans working for the Russians, particularly if they did so under duress, would probably not provide their best work.

Under a heading of "factors which limit rate of development", the report notes: "Russia must feel intensely pleased with her prospects in advanced bomber types. The future is not, however, as rosy in hue as may first appear. An advanced design does not become an operational aircraft, quantity produced, until many essential requirements are satisfied.

"Occupation by Russia was looked on as a far more frightful consequence of war than occupation by Britain or America. Many who were able to make their way westwards did so, including most of the leading figures in the aeronautical industry. The bulk of the workers were unable to leave the area but designers, engineers and technicians used what transport was available and escaped to the Western zones; movement of key personnel to the 'Redoubt' in Bavaria also depleted what is now the Russian zone.

"A recruiting campaign has since been in progress to attract technicians over to the Russian zone. Excellent prospects are offered such as a house, state appointed servants and the ration scale of a Russian general; wives and families will be cared for, and permanent work is offered to those willing to make their homes in Russia. Many who were captured in the Eastern zone have gone to Russia but there is no evidence of anyone of repute having gone from the British or American zones. A large number of men, contacted by the Russians, have disclosed these invitations to the British in the hope of an equally enticing offer to remain, but although few German aeronautical workers have found employment with the British there have so far been no cases of desertion to the Russian zone; there have been cases of desertion away from the Russian zone."

Then, under a heading of "mistrust of Russian intentions" it is stated: "German technicians are in the unenviable position of having to earn a living under a master they are not anxious to serve and for this reason alone they are unlikely to give of their best. Under the stimulus of war, progress was rapid, but under peace conditions and working for a conqueror there will naturally be a drastic reduction in enthusiasm and volume of work.

"Work already in hand will continue but when new approaches must be made to difficult development problems the Germans will control the rate at which development proceeds.

"Mistrust exists between Russian and German. Where helpful suggestions have been made by German technicians to improve equipment scheduled for early production, the Russians have refused to allow alteration. Design is frozen in the stage reached when the war ended.

"Suggestions for improvement prompted by Germans are regarded as attempted sabotage and firmly forbidden. Such an element of mistrust stifles invention and soon the Germans will realise that exploitation is the programme, not use of German skill. New ideas will be held back under the hope of eventual freedom to work for a new Germany."

WHAT ACTUALLY HAPPENED

When the war ended, the Soviet Union tried to recruit German aircraft engineers and designers - some of whom were given little choice but to agree. Among those who joined the Soviets' ranks were Heinkel chief designer Siegfried Günter, Junkers engine specialist Alfred Scheibe, Junkers engine factory technical director Ferdinand Brandner, Junkers' head of aerodynamics Georg Backhaus and the head of the Ju 287 programme at Junkers, Hans Wocke.

Rather than integrate the Germans into existing Soviet design teams, it was decided that they should be formed into separate units known as OTBs or 'special technical bureaus'. These would have Soviet supervisors and would be directed by representatives of Soviet aircraft factories. A reorganisation followed which saw them re-designated as OKBs or 'design bureaus'.

As the British knew, most of the activity was centred on the captured Junkers facility at Dessau, which had fallen inside the Soviet zone when Germany had been partitioned by the Allies. There were also groups of German designers working at Berlin, Halle and Stassfurt. In April 1946, it was decided that the Dessau team, OKB-1, should continue the development of the Ju 287 bomber.

The work was given a new project number, EF 131, which followed on directly in sequence after the final wartime Junkers project - the EF 130. The first prototype was built out of what Junkers had been working on as the Ju 287 V2. Apparently completed in late 1946, it was test flown in the Soviet sector of Germany before being dismantled and taken by land into the Soviet Union.

Further tests commenced during the spring of 1947 but it was found that the fuselage was insufficiently strong for high-speed flight and had to be strengthened. In August of the following year all further work on the EF 131 was cancelled. However, the Ju 287 V2/EF 131 had always been compromised by its engines - six Jumo 004Bs - so it was now decided to build a new bomber based on the EF 131 but with only two, much more powerful, engines.

This was designated the EF 140 and had a fully retractable undercarriage, bespoke crew cabin and even a dorsal gun turret. It was the Ju 287 as it might have been had the war continued. The British had backed entirely the wrong contender for the "future design of Russian bomber aircraft" by believing that the Horten XVIII would be developed. In fact, even the EF 140's days were numbered, since the Russians ultimately went on to develop bomber designs that were entirely their own. ●

Unknown!

Postwar 'discoveries', new discoveries and mysteries

Inconsistencies and oddities from among the documents allegedly produced by the Germans during the Second World War were detailed in this volume's predecessor, Luftwaffe: Secret Jets of the Third Reich. Further research has uncovered still more examples – alongside genuine new discoveries…

Vast sums were spent on aeronautical research by Germany during the Second World War, resulting in a whole host of unusual and innovative aircraft designs. Focke-Wulf's Triebflügel Flugzeug – a vertical take-off fighter that used ramjets to power a trio of spinning wings epitomises the creativity that flourished, particularly as the war was drawing to an end.

It was no surprise, therefore, that Allied engineers and designers were fascinated, bewildered and even amused by the strange designs they discovered when every last scrap of documentation relating to unbuilt German aircraft projects was rounded up and examined following Germany's defeat.

In Britain and the United States copies of these designs and the calculations, test results and drawings that accompanied them were widely distributed to interested parties within the aviation industry and further afield. As previously related, representatives from various prominent British manufacturers had actually gone into Germany as part of the intelligence gathering operation and learned about some projects first hand.

The situation in America was documented by C Lester Walker in an article for the October 1946 edition of Harper's magazine entitled 'Secrets by the Thousands': "Someone wrote to Wright Field recently, saying he understood this country had got together quite a collection of enemy war secrets, that many were now on public sale, and could he, please, be sent everything on German jet engines. The Air Documents Division of the Army Air Forces answered: 'Sorry – but that would be 50 tons.'

"Moreover, that 50 tons was just a small portion of what is today undoubtedly the biggest collection of captured enemy war secrets ever assembled. If you always thought of war secrets – and who hasn't? – as coming in sixes and sevens, as a few items of information readily handed on to the properly interested authorities, it may interest you to learn that the war secrets in this collection run into the thousands, that the mass of documents is mountainous, and that there has never before been anything quite comparable to it.

"The collection is today chiefly in three places: Wright Field (Ohio), the Library of Congress, and the Department of Commerce.

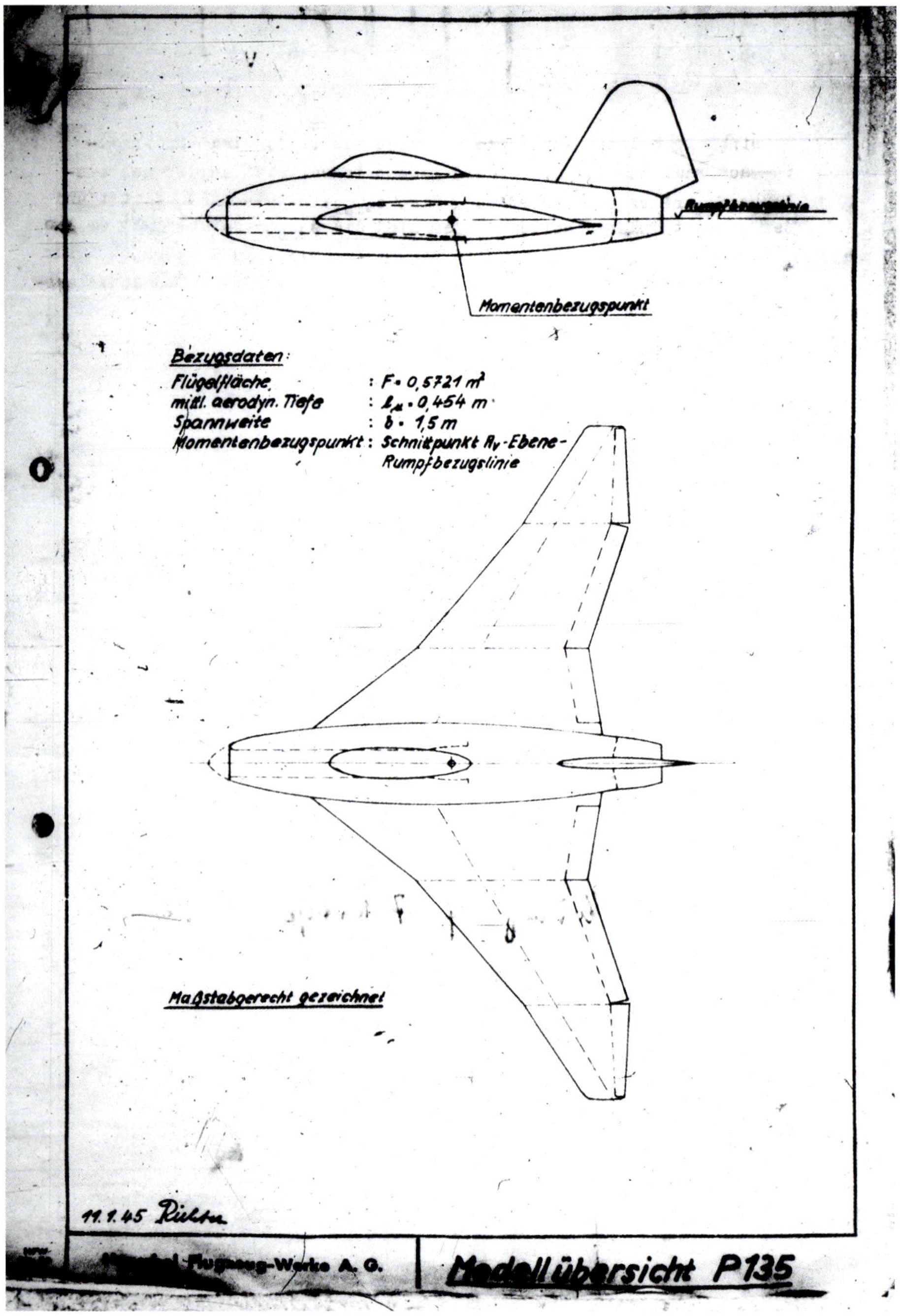

ABOVE: Original drawing of the Henschel P 135 as a wind tunnel model dated January 11, 1945.

BELOW: The Henschel P 135 as it might have looked in service as Red 26 with JG 1. Art by Chris Sandham-Bailey

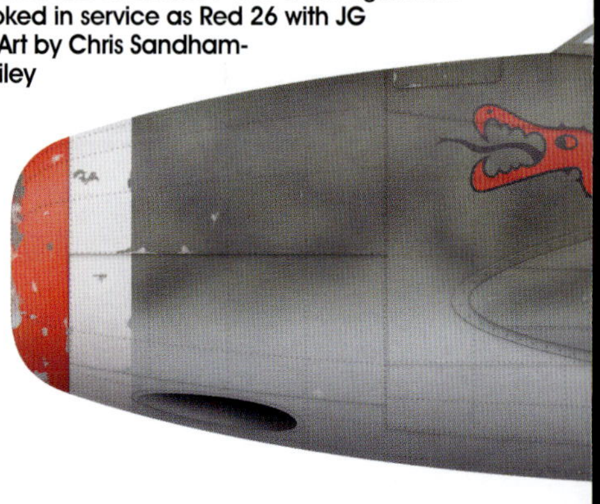

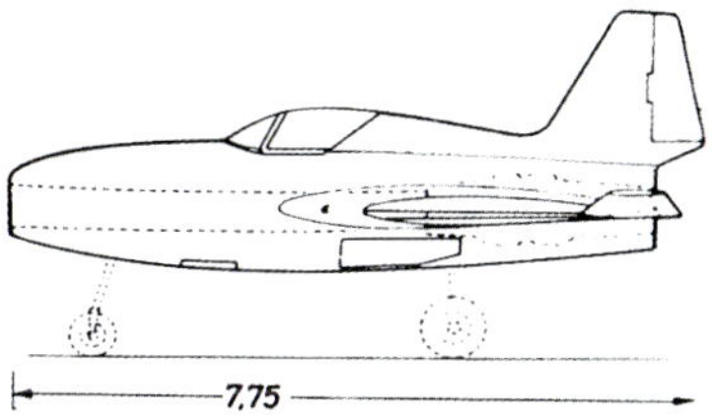

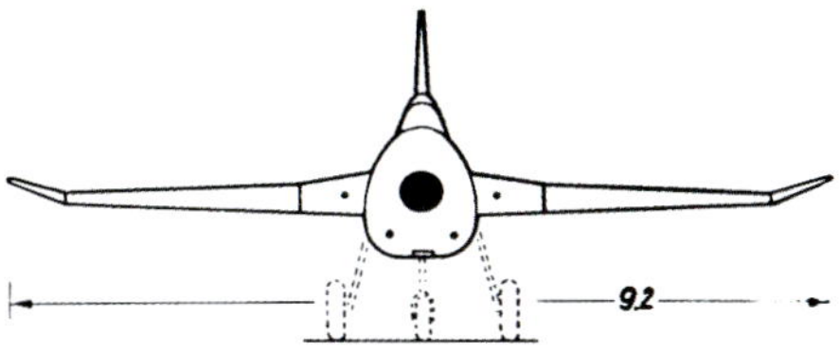

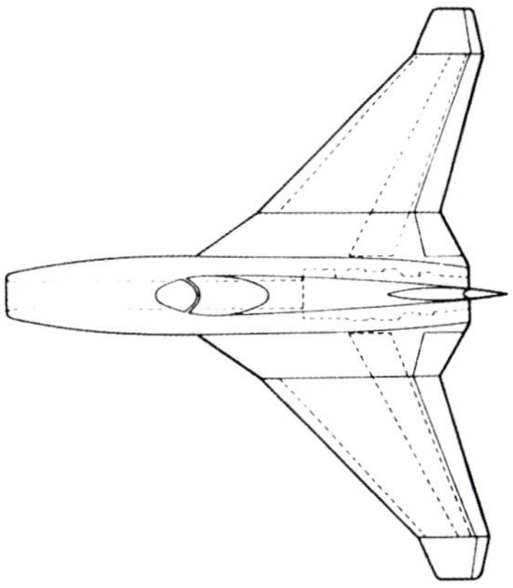

ABOVE & LEFT: Drawing of the Henschel P 135 as it was previously thought to look – with a prominent 'spine'. No original drawing of it looking this way has ever been published. It is possible that the design of January 11, 1945, was later amended but there is no hard evidence to support that idea.

Wright Field is working from a documents 'mother lode' of 1500 tons. In Washington, the Office of Technical Services (which has absorbed the Office of the Publication Board, the government agency originally set up to handle the collection) reports that tens of thousands of tons of material are involved.

"It is estimated that over a million separate items must be handled, and that they are, very likely, practically all the scientific, industrial and military secrets of Nazi Germany. One Washington official has called it 'the greatest single source of this type of material in the world, the first orderly exploitation of an entire country's brain-power."

Copies of many of these previously top secret documents, though not all of them, were made available for the American public to buy.

Walker wrote: "And is the public doing anything with these one-time war secrets? It is – it is eating them up. As many as 20,000 orders have been filled in a month, and the order rate is now a thousand items a day. Scientists and engineers declare that the information is 'cutting years from the time we would devote to problems already scientifically investigated'." The biggest customer was reportedly Amtorg, the Soviet Union's foreign trade organisation.

"One of its representatives walked into the Publication Board office with the bibliography in hand and said 'I want copies of everything'," Walker noted. "The Russians sent one order in May for $5594 worth – 2000 war secrets reports. In general, they buy every report issued."

As a result, with copies of German documents spread far and wide, the appetite for yet more secrets continued to grow. When there were no more secrets readily available to learn, there was a strong impetus to go out and find more. Researchers ploughed through the German documents on aircraft projects available in archives, particularly those in the US, and made fresh 'discoveries' throughout the 1960s and 1970s. Standards of image reproduction in print during this period were low and often original drawings were redrawn for the benefit of readers.

This resulted in some designs being misinterpreted by inexpert artists or so far separated from their original source material that they became either unrecognisable or inexplicable. Dimensions were erased, annotations removed or replaced with typed text for easier reading, and other data such as signatures and dates erased.

HENSCHEL P 135

A good example of the confusion surrounding some German 'secret projects' designs is the Henschel P 135. Next to nothing is known about it – even what it looked like is uncertain since no original drawings of it were known to exist. This is largely down to the fact that Henschel's design facility at Berlin-Schönefeld was captured by the Russians when they took the city and all the documents held there were either destroyed or removed to the Soviet Union, perhaps never to be seen again.

Henschel was investigating numerous advanced aerodynamic forms towards the end of the war, contracting at least some of its wind tunnel testing to organisations such as the Deutsche Versuchsanstalt für Luftfahrt (DVL) – and it is through this work that its late-war designs are chiefly known. A small number of DVL documents have survived and with them evidence of Henschel's designs.

Until recently, the only known drawing of the P 135 was an obvious redrawing. Whether it was based on an original or drawn from memory after all the originals were removed or destroyed is unknown. However, an original Henschel company drawing of a wind tunnel model has now come to light which shows a somewhat different version of the design.

Rather than having a cockpit canopy which blends into the fuselage, the P 135 of January 11, 1945, had a bubble canopy rather like that of North American P-51D Mustang. Its double-cranked wing was of a very different form to that shown in the previously known drawing and its fuselage was of a cleaner and more conventional shape.

It has been suggested that the P 135 was presented to the RLM in February 1945, and if that is the case then it is likely that the presented design would have looked more like the wind tunnel design than that of the previously known drawing. However, there is no evidence that Henschel presented the P 135 for the 1-TL-Jäger competition at that time. Neither is there any evidence regarding the engine proposed for it, nor its armament.

Elsewhere, the design has been attributed to the head of Henschel's design department, Friedrich Nicolaus, but the wind tunnel model drawing is signed 'Richter'. Hard evidence concerning the background of the P 135 remains elusive.

MESSERSCHMITT P 20

More is known about Messerschmitt somewhat portly P 20 fighter design. It was one of three single-jet fighter projects considered for development by the company in 1943 – the others being the P 1092/a and P 1092/b.

The closest Messerschmitt ever came to a turbojet-powered Me 163, the P 20 was far slower – certainly slower than its competitors, with a top speed of 905kph (562mph) at 6km altitude, compared to 931kph (578mph) for the P 1092/a and 914kph (567mph) for the P 1092/b.

Despite its claimed superior manoeuvrability a lack of pace was an unforgivable flaw where Messerschmitt was concerned.

Ultimately none of the three were successful and fresh designs were prepared when the RLM decided to issue an official specification for a single-jet fighter in July 1944.

Nevertheless, the P 20 is an interesting design that has received little

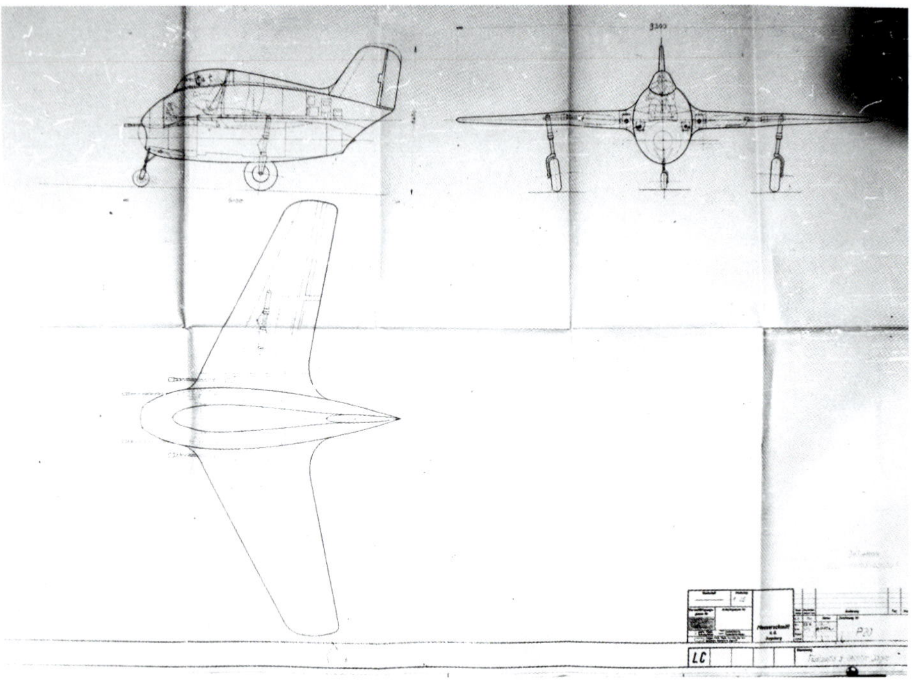

ABOVE: The stubby little Messerschmitt P 20 was one of the company's earliest single-jet designs and sought to take advantage of the aerodynamic lessons learned from the Me 163. It was, however, too slow for a company that prided itself on being all about speed.

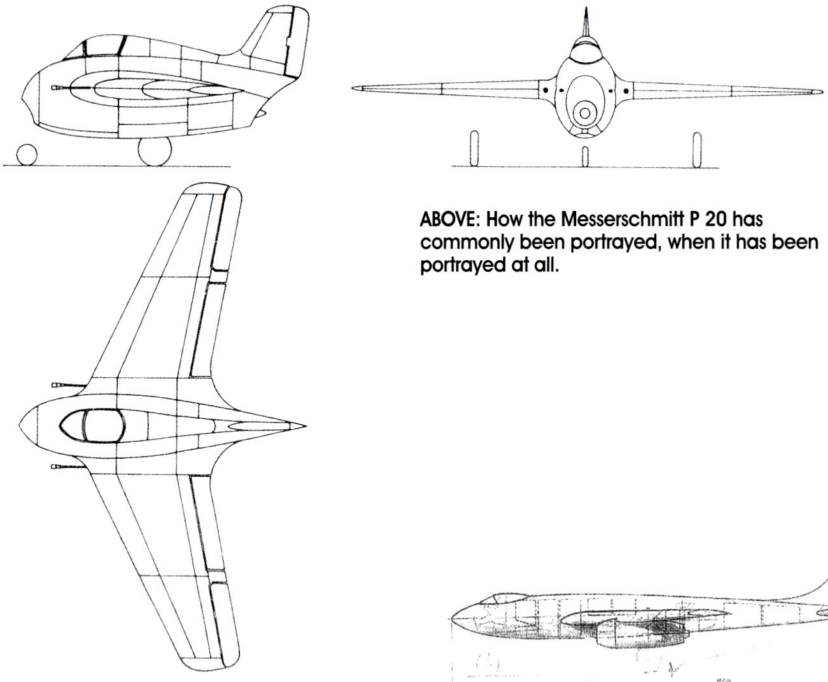

ABOVE: How the Messerschmitt P 20 has commonly been portrayed, when it has been portrayed at all.

attention over the years. As with the P 135, until recently the only known drawing of it was clearly a redrawing. However, when a period drawing of it did surface it was evident that the redrawing, though imperfect, was much closer in detail than had apparently been the case with the P 135.

Subtle errors in the shape of the canopy, tail, armament and engine exhaust are evident, and the lack of undercarriage detail makes the design seem insubstantial and unreal. The detail available in the original drawing brings the design to life in a way that was previously impossible.

FOCKE-WULF BOMBER MIT 2 HES 011

During early 1944, Focke-Wulf produced drawings for a pair of fast single-seat bombers powered by a pair of HeS 011 engines. This placed them in roughly the same category as the Arado Ar 234B but beyond that almost nothing is known about them for certain.

All sorts of information has been applied to them – the names of their designers, the idea that they were designed to carry 1000kg of bombs 1000km at a speed of 1000kph, their designations as 'Focke-Wulf 1000 x 1000 x 1000 Projekt A' and 'Focke-Wulf 1000 x 1000 x 1000 Projekt B', even a third design is offered as 'Projekt C' but none of this makes much sense.

The only drawing with any information attached to it gives a glimpse of the truth. It is labelled simply 'Bomber mit 2 HeS 011' and a drawing number, 0310 239-01 is given along with a date in April 1944. It depicts a slender aircraft with all-swept wing and tail surfaces and its engines underslung beneath its wings in pods.

The other drawing attributed to the same 'series' has no associated drawing number, although 0310 239-10 has been suggested. It shows an all-wing bomber with the cockpit protruding from the leading edge. The engines are entirely buried in the wing-fuselage and control surfaces exist only as a pair of inverted fins, one at either wingtip. This aircraft design has no title and no other information is apparently available beyond what can be gleaned from the drawing itself.

What is most striking about the designs is that, assuming they were genuinely associated with one another, they represent entirely different design philosophies applied as a solution to the same problem. One has a broadly conventional layout – wings, tail and podded engines, but with a highly advanced aerodynamic form – while the other has an unconventional layout – with all of the aforementioned features being now wrapped up in a single form.

It may be the case that Focke-Wulf took these two very different approaches. The company tended to take one design and vary it this way or that to offer different permutations on a theme. However, the difference between its two contenders for the 1-TL Jäger competition, one a twin boom

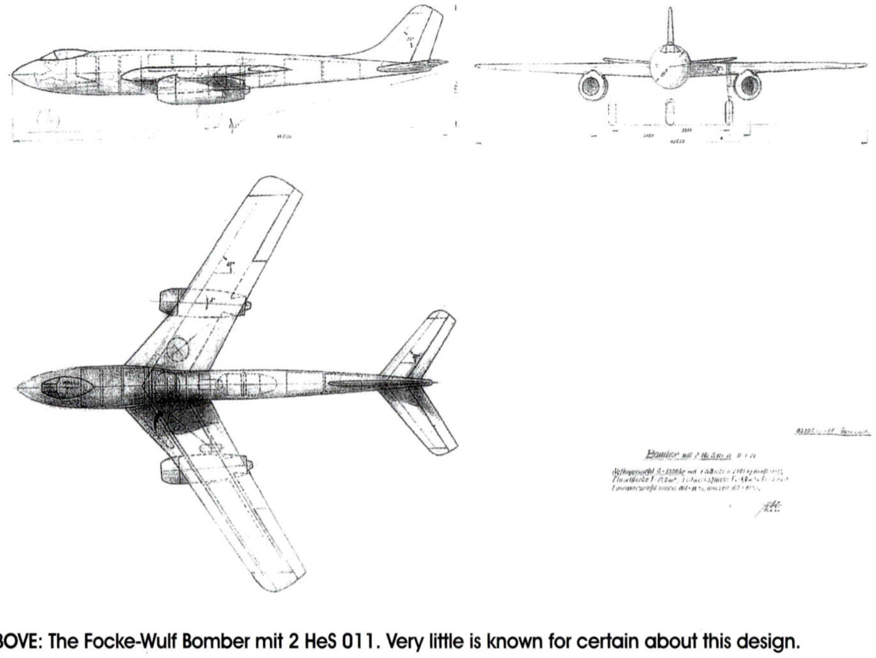

ABOVE: The Focke-Wulf Bomber mit 2 HeS 011. Very little is known for certain about this design.

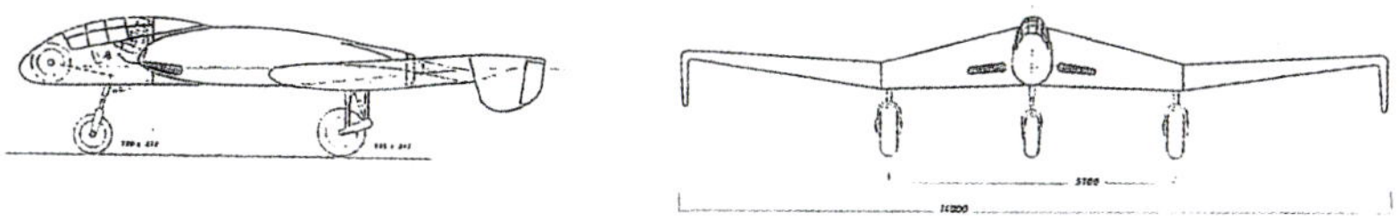

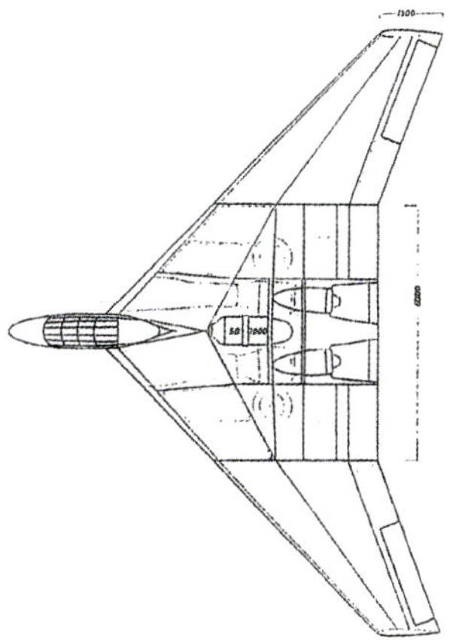

ABOVE: With its conventional fuselage counterpart, this all-wing bomber design is said to be the product of Focke-Wulf's designers – but information is sadly lacking. A close examination reveals some interesting design variations: the pilot is drawn very differently, there is no shading on the all-wing design yet its undercarriage is drawn in much more detail, and it seems odd that the nosewheel here retracts forwards into the nose rather than back into the fuselage.

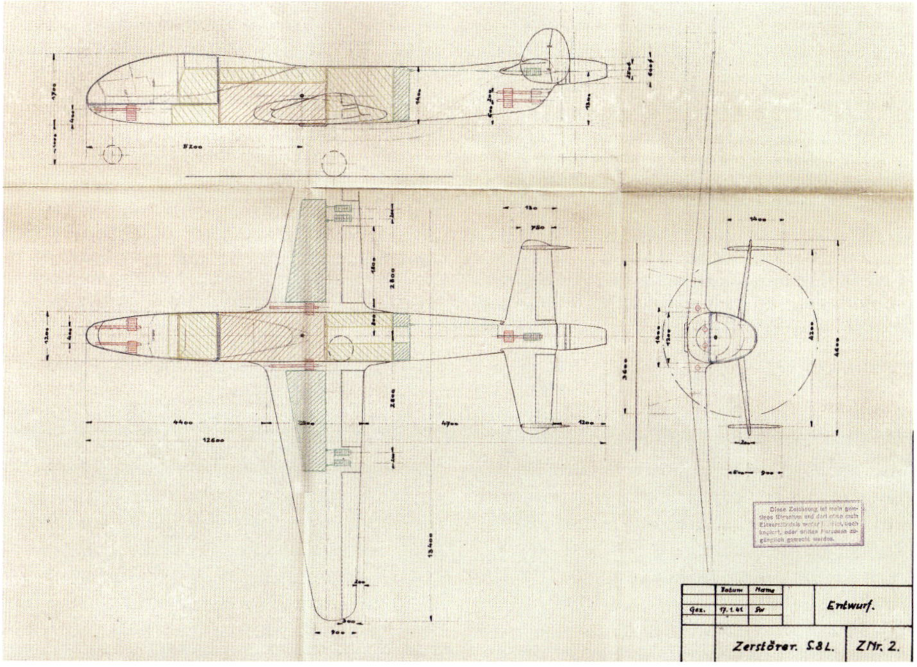

ABOVE: Franz Swaty's S.8L design crammed in a host of advanced features – particularly so given that it was designed in early 1941.

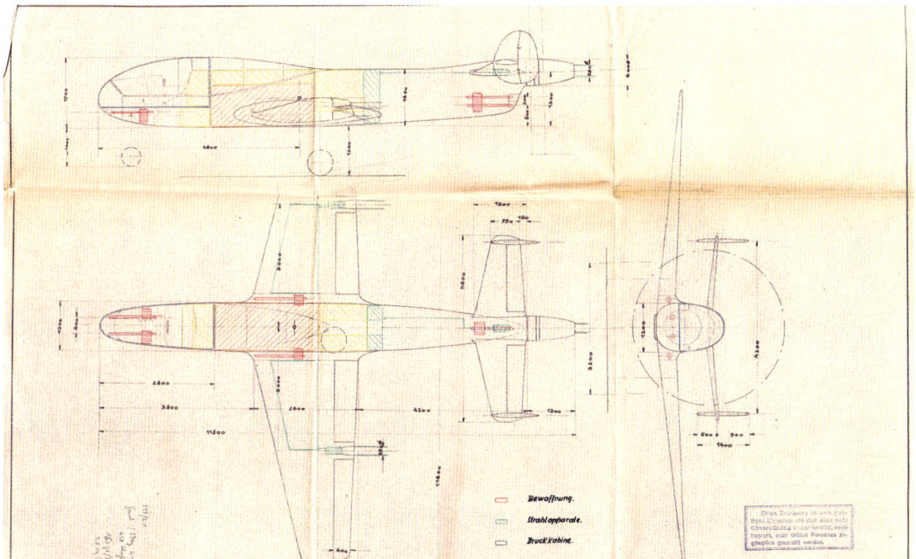

ABOVE: The S.8K was smaller than the 'L' but otherwise appeared very similar. Both would have afforded the pilot an excellent view.

fighter with the intakes for its jet engine on either side of the fuselage and the other having a single fuselage and a nose intake, demonstrates that this was not always the case.

Further research may eventually turn up more information on the Focke-Wulf Bomber mit 2 HeS 011 but for now it remains largely 'unknown'.

FRANZ SWATY S.8

During the war, engineers working at Germany's various experimental stations and testing facilities came up with bright ideas for future aircraft designs and attempted to interest the large manufacturers in them.

One such engineer was Franz Swaty of the DVL, based in Berlin. Towards the end of 1940, while working on tail units for the Messerschmitt Bf 110, he was inspired to design a new heavy fighter aircraft which he dubbed the S.8. His drawings of it are dated January 17, 1941.

It combined a host of advanced features in a layout designed to afford the pilot the best possible view of his surroundings. These included a bullet-shaped pressure cabin with an enormous canopy, a contra-rotating double pusher propeller, laminar flow wings with swept leading edges and a V-tail. The engine was "provisionally a DB 603 with a turbocharger" and top speed at 31,000ft was expected to be a fairly staggering 497mph.

Swaty further mentions that the performance of his design could be "much improved" with the addition of jet engines but he seems to have had little idea what these looked like, how large they were, or how much power they might produce. His drawings show the 'jets' as small units positioned within the aircraft's wings.

In the proposal document, two versions are offered - the S.8L and S.8K. The S.8L was the larger and heavier of the two with a wingspan of 43.9ft and a length of 41.3ft. All up weight was 7300kg. The S.8K had a 38ft span and was 38.7ft long. All up weight was 5000kg.

Armament was four forward-firing cannon - two in the nose beneath the pilot and two in the wing roots - and another two in the tail firing through the propellers.

While some aspects of Swaty's design were laughable and his figures on weight and performance were extremely optimistic, certain aspects of his design such as the high visibility cockpit and laminar flow wings seem to have endeared the design to the Heinkel company, since the sole surviving copy of his proposal was discovered among that company's design documents.

KARL STÖCKEL ROCKETS AND RAMMERS

Another DVL employee who dreamed up unusual concepts with advanced features was Karl Stöckel. During 1944, when the effects of Allied bombing were becoming increasingly significant for Germany, he began thinking of specialised aircraft that might be able to tackle the incoming enemy bombers.

It was noted in Luftwaffe: Secret Jets of the Third Reich that what was frequently referred to as the Blohm & Voss MGRP 'Manually Guided Rocket Projectile' might well be one of a series of 'rammer', ramjet and rocket concepts drafted by Stöckel - and ▶

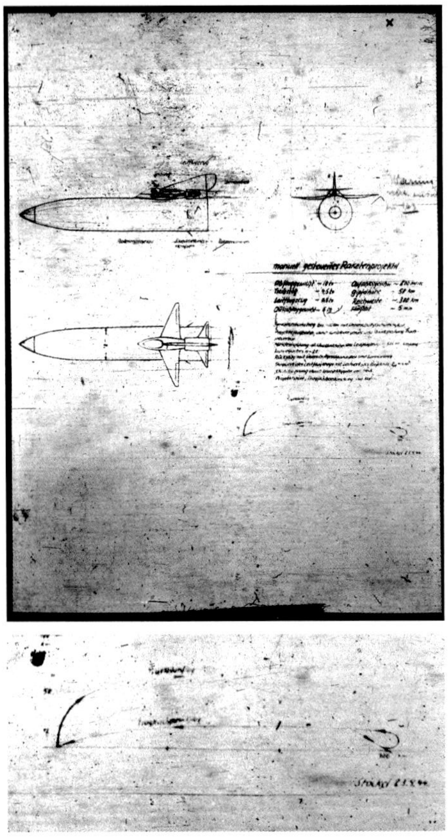

ABOVE: One of the most radical attack aircraft – if it can be called that – designed during the war was this combination missile/mini-aircraft. Just below the writing can be seen a quick sketch showing how the aircraft was intended to work. Designer Karl Stöckel worked for the DVL in Berlin.

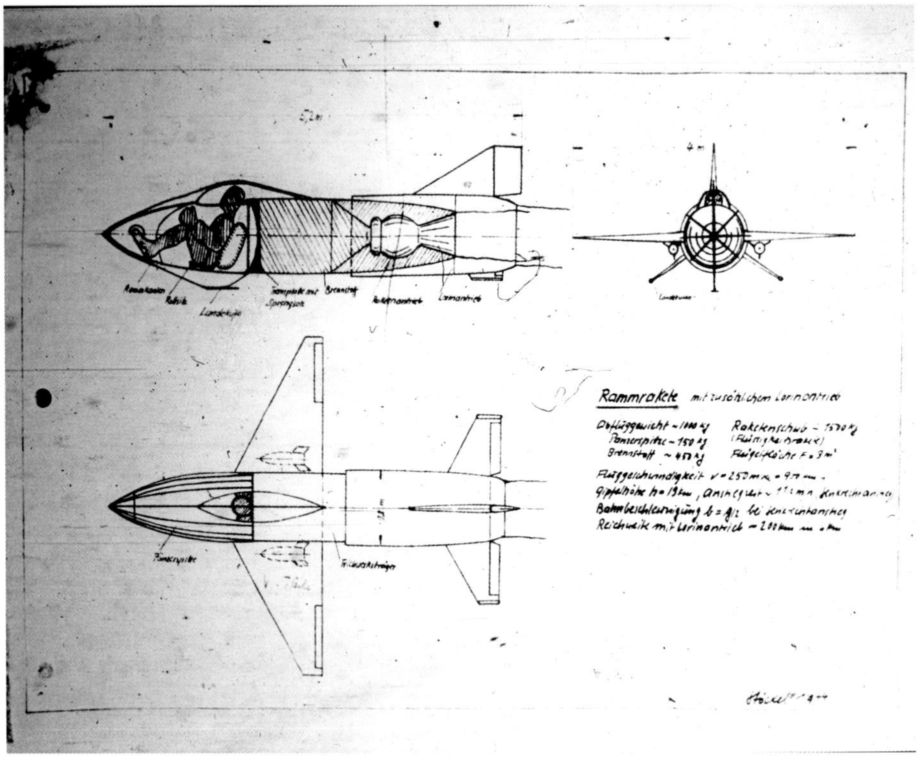

ABOVE: Another of Karl Stöckel's outlandish designs was this 'ram rocket'. The front section, housing the pilot, was more like a flying battering ram intended to slice through the weaker parts of Allied bombers such as the tail. This was no suicide attacker though – the pilot was afforded a parachute and a small explosive charge that offered a chance of escape from his ruined aircraft.

this can now be conclusively verified.

A drawing showing a 'Manuell gesteuerites Raketenprojektil' has been discovered, signed by Stöckel and dated August 23, 1944. It shows a large missile, similar in size to a V2, with a very small parasite aircraft attached at its base - barely large enough for one man. The missile would weight five tonnes, the aircraft 0.5 tonnes and the remaining 4.5 tonnes of the combination's all-up weight would be rocket fuel. A diagram and notes on the same sheet indicate how the MGRP was intended to operate.

After a vertical launch, the rocket would reach a speed of 1789mph or a little over Mach 2 at an altitude of 164,000ft. It would then be steered downward for a descent onto the target 300km away, with the tiny aircraft breaking away at the last moment to enter a climbing turn before flying back to base under the power of its own small ramjet engine.

This would no doubt have been just about the most terrifying or perhaps thrilling ride of the pilot's life, assuming he survived it. The Stöckel design shown in this publication's companion volume presumably would have operated the same way but on a somewhat less ambitious scale.

These were not Stöckel's only attempts at unorthodox aircraft design however. In September 1944 he came up with a 'Rammrakete' or ram rocket. This was another vertical launch one-man aircraft but this time fitted with a heavily-armoured front end shaped like a speartip. The idea, it would seem, was to crash through enemy aircraft and cause as much damage as possible before the aircraft was wrecked, whereupon a small explosive charge would separate the armoured cockpit from the rest of the fuselage and the pilot could parachute safely to the ground.

The Rammrakete measured 17ft from end to end and had a wingspan of just 13ft. It seems that the aircraft could be fitted with a pair of bombs too, although how it would have used these is uncertain.

A pair of rocket fighters of similar design, each powered by a different form of ramjet, were also envisioned by Stöckel, both drawings of them dated August 25, 1944.

After the war, Stöckel seems to have gone on to work for Bölkow, designing

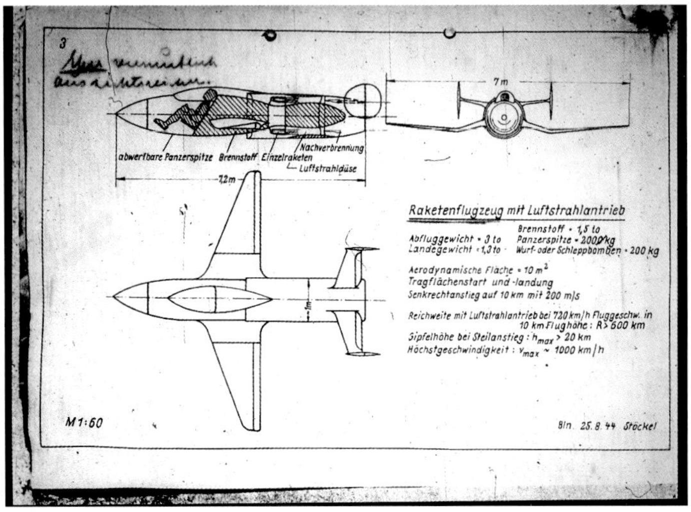

ABOVE: Measuring 23.6ft long with a 23ft wingspan, this ramjet-powered aircraft was typical of Stöckel's design philosophy.

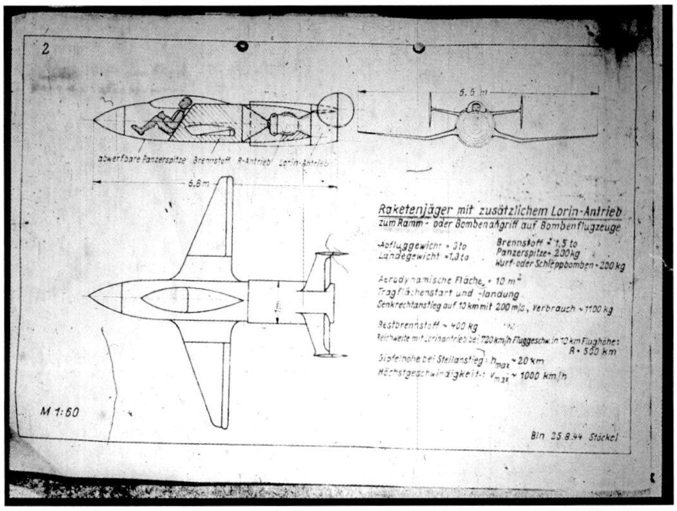

ABOVE: This tiny fighter was 22.3ft long with a wingspan of just 21.7ft. A Messerschmitt Bf 109, by way of comparison, had a 32.5ft wingspan. It was to be powered by a combination of ramjet and rocket.

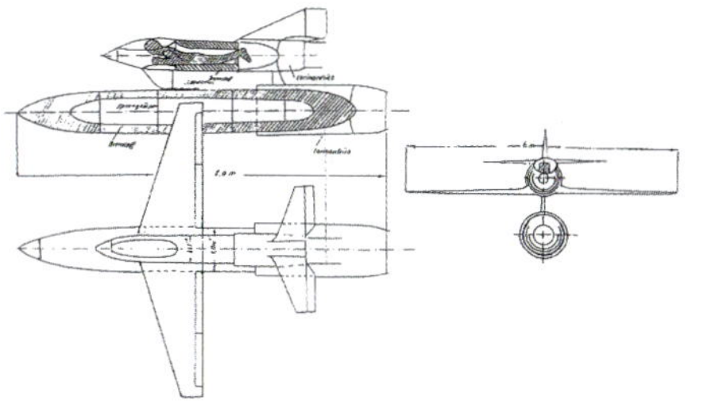

ABOVE: The fifth of Stöckel's five known designs was a less radical version of the 'MGRP'.

and patenting a series of rocket engine chambers during the 1950s and 1960s.

HORTEN 'COMMITTEE BOMBER'

The various controversies surrounding the Horten brothers and their Horten XVIII design have already been outlined but a footnote to the story is the idea that their design was tampered with and redrawn by a committee composed of leading figures from the large aircraft manufacturers - the result being the so-called 'Committee Bomber'.

During his interview with David Myhra, Reimar Horten recalled: "The committee had come up with a committee-designed aircraft. It took the wing form from my designs but the committee was unwilling to make it completely all-wing. So they added a huge vertical rudder to it. To make this bomber it would require more working hours. In my plane with its straight tapered wing took very few hours or if the wing was rounded (which aerodynamically speaking) the rounded wing is better. So when I went back to Dessau I was already thinking about a better form (which I did not tell the people there at the committee) and which later on came to be the Ho 18B.

"Another reason why I had chosen instead to produce the Ho 18B was that I was going to use the Heinkel-Hirth HeS 011 turbojets with their 1300kg of thrust instead of the Junkers Jumo 004Bs. Therefore I could eliminate two turbojets and now just get by with four HeS 011s. Plus, I did not like the use of the vertical fin on the model suggested by the Dessau committee."

And that appears to be all of the information that exists on the 'Committee Bomber'. A drawing of this bomber has surfaced which does indeed have a vertical fin - but rather than being the "huge vertical rudder" that Reimar describes, it has a sleek integrated fin/cockpit similar to that seen on the Lippisch P.13a. Whether this drawing genuinely depicts the 'Committee Bomber' remains to be seen since no contemporary source has yet been found that can confirm its authenticity.

BMW BOMBER PROJECTS

A series of four single-jet fighter designs were put forward by aero-engine manufacturer BMW some time towards the end of the war. These were intended to promote interest in the firm's products and perhaps offer suggestions for how they might be employed - particularly since the 003 jet engine programme had been plagued by problems and had resulted in a product that was significantly outperformed by its chief rivals.

At the same time, BMW also made suggestions concerning the potential use of its engines in jet bombers. Again, four design concepts were offered. The

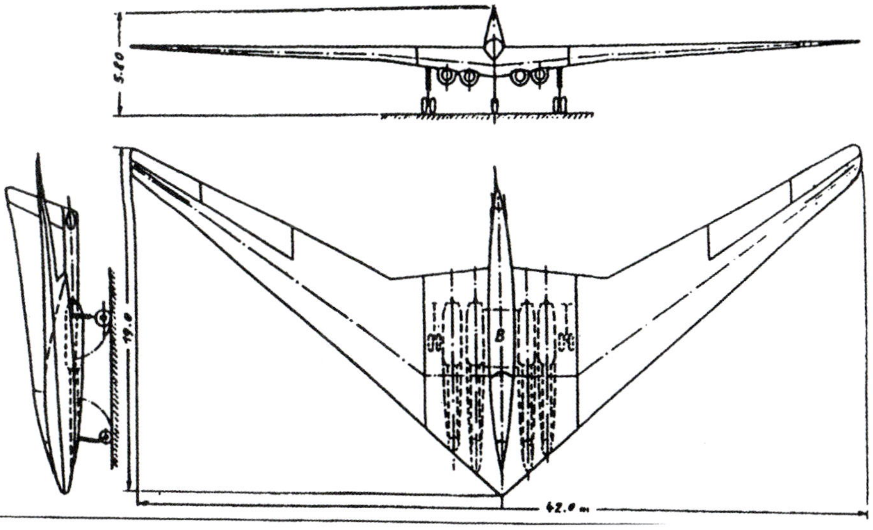

ABOVE: During an interview, Reimar Horten described how his all-wing bomber design had been mutilated by a committee of his peers and given a large vertical rudder. This design is commonly regarded as depicting this 'Committee Bomber'.

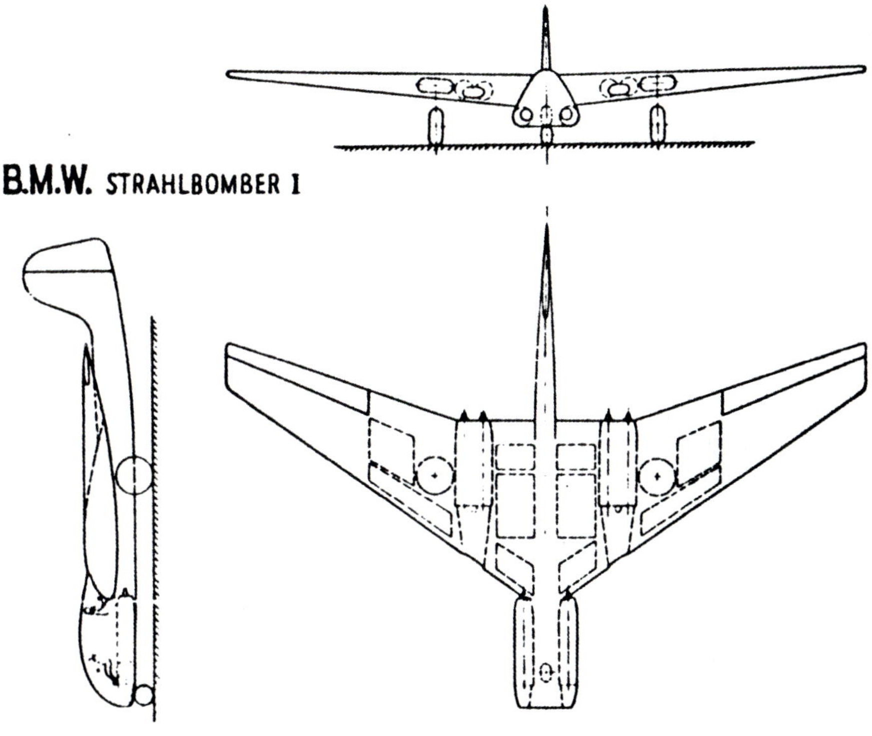

ABOVE: Eager to showcase its 003A jet engine, particularly after its protracted and expensive development, BMW offered this sample design concept, the Strahlbomber I, powered by six of them – four in the wings, fed by a pair of intakes, and two more in the nose with an intake each. A lack of horizontal tail surfaces, a bulbous cockpit and very narrow rear fuselage make this an aerodynamically interesting design.

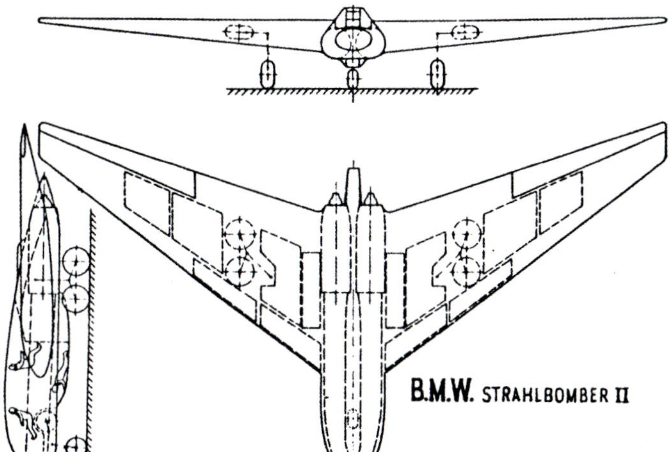

LEFT: Just two enormous 018 turbojets powered the BMW Strahlbomber II. It had a swept-wing form and no vertical tail surfaces. ▶

ABOVE: How the BMW Strahlbomber II might have looked if it had actually been built. The fuselage was very heavily built and the design had no tail. Art by Daniel Uhr

first pair were labelled 'Strahlbomber I' and 'Strahlbomber II', then there was a high-speed bomber and a 'large aircraft' fitted with BMW 028 turboprops.

The 'Strahlbomber I' was to be powered by no fewer than six BMW 003As - giving it a top speed of 552mph at 21,000ft. Range with a two tonne bomb load was 1680 miles but if it needed to carry a four tonne load this dipped to 1170 miles. The 'Strahlbomber II' had just two BMW 018 turbojets. This gave a maximum speed of 612mph at 13,000ft and allowed a range of 2600 miles with two and a half tonnes of bombs or 1950 miles with five tonnes.

Perhaps the most interesting design was the high-speed bomber. This was powered by a combination of two BMW 018s and two BMW 028s. The latter were mounted at the front of the wings and drove eight-bladed contra-rotating props with a 12.15ft diameter. The 018s were at the rear of the wing, on the underside, where they would be in the propellers' slipstream. The inner part of the wings - between the fuselage and the engines - was swept forward, while the outer part was swept back.

The British report German Aircraft: New and Projected Types noted: "The fuselage is very small in relation to the wing root thickness and is upswept to a surprisingly conventional empennage.

"On the other hand the undercarriage is anything but conventional. There are two pairs of main wheels under the fuselage, each pair being carried by a common oleo leg. In addition there is a wheel under each wing outboard of the propulsion units and retracting outwards, and a twin nose wheel. The bomb load - up to a maximum of 33,000lb - is carried in the wing roots. There is a large fuel tank in the fuselage and three tanks in each wing, with a total capacity of 7730 gal."

Maximum range, without any useful load, was 3030 miles at 51,000ft. Add a 20 tonne payload and this dropped sharply to just 560 miles at 43,500ft. Top speed with all engines contributing was 506mph at 26,000ft.

Finally, there was BMW's large aircraft with BMW 028s. This unusual creation had huge forward-swept wings and its engines were attached to outriggers projecting from the upper surface of the fuselage at an angle of about 45 degrees. Quite what purpose this might have been intended to serve may never be known since the original project documents no longer appear to exist.

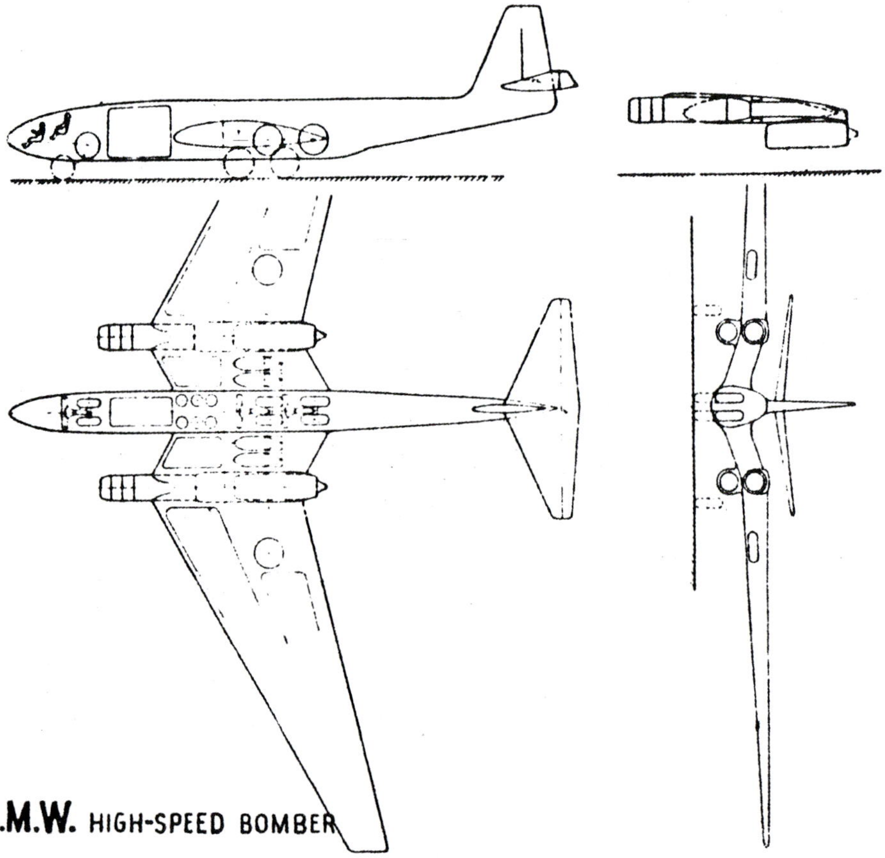

ABOVE: BMW's high-speed bomber was yet another highly unusual design powered by a combination of 028 turboprops and 018 turbojets. It was intended to carry very heavy loads - up to 20 tonnes - but its thirsty engines meant range was severely limited.

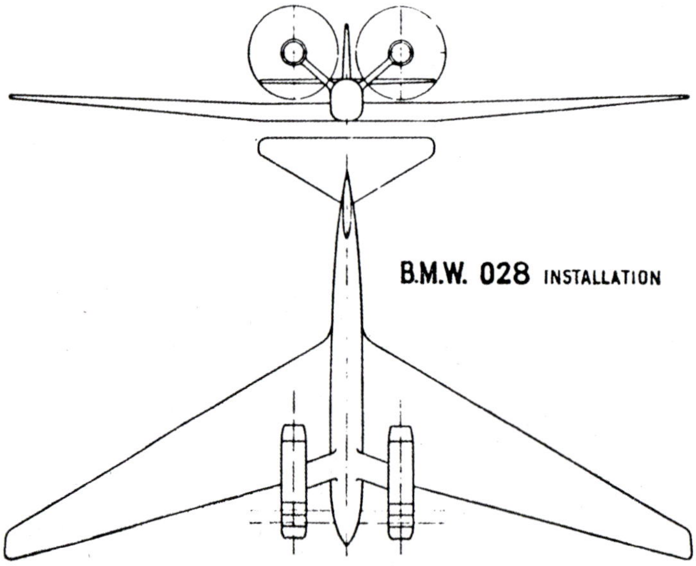

LEFT: The last of BMW's designs was little more than a showcase for the firm's 028 turboprops. It was billed as a 'large aircraft' and may or may not have been intended as a bomber concept.

LUFTWAFFE
Secret Bombers of the Third Reich

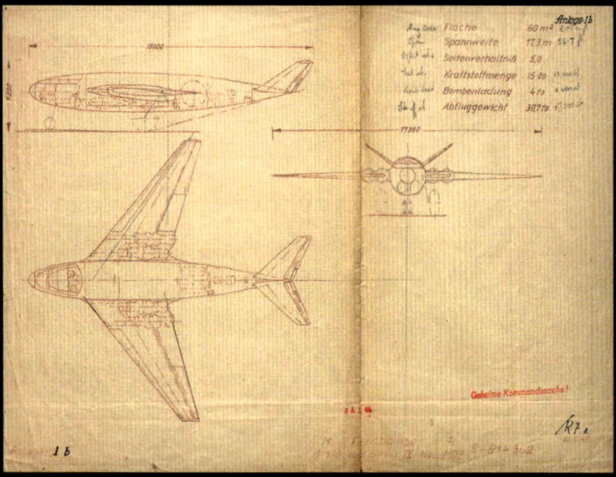

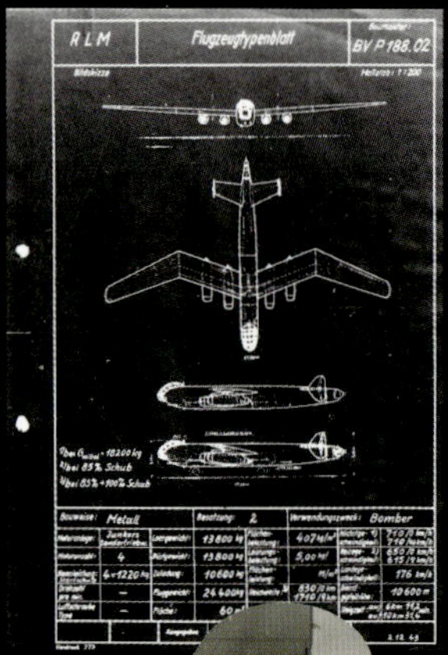

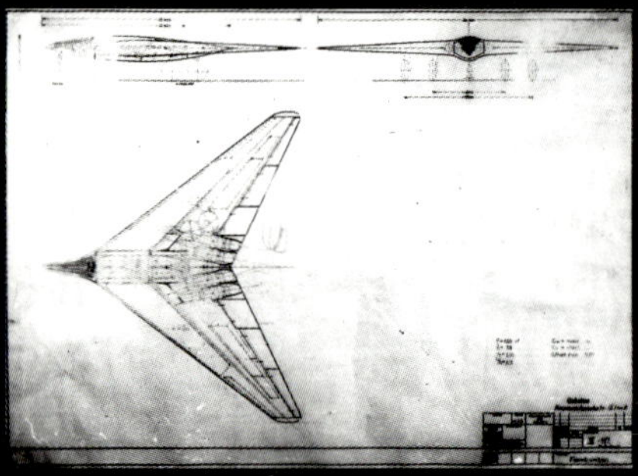

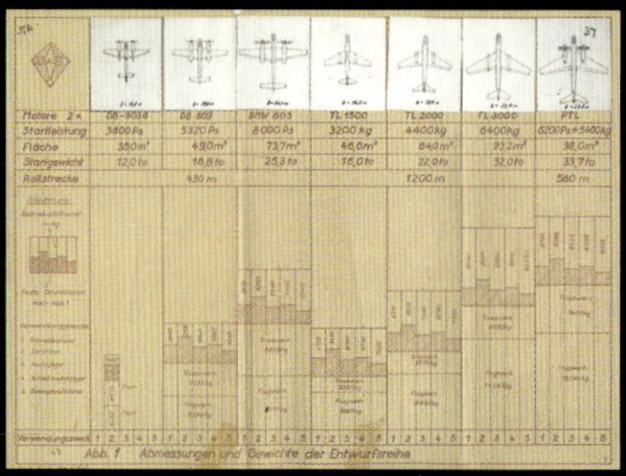

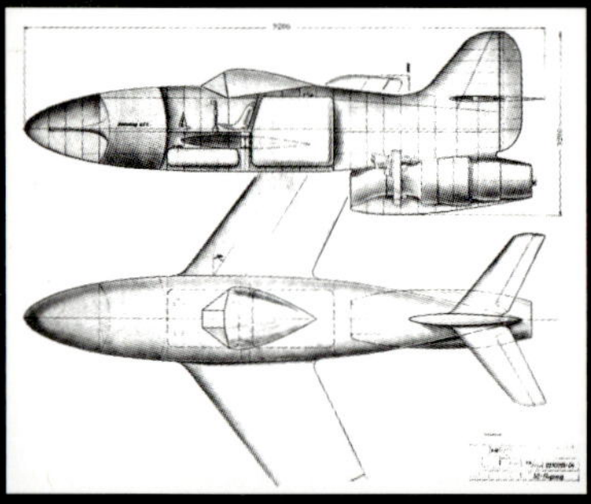

Dozens of top secret bomber designs were drawn up by the Germans during the Second World War, including gigantic flying wings, sleek jet bombers, asymmetrical bombers with the cockpit and weapons turrets on the ends of their wings and even enormous carriers for single-seat suicide bombers.

Starting with the He 177, the most advanced bomber design of its day in 1936, the huge variety of bomber projects produced during the days of the Third Reich are examined by aviation historian Dan Sharp including the Arado E 470, E 555 and previously unknown Arado types, Junkers Ju 488, Focke-Wulf Ta 400 and Fw 300, Blohm & Voss P 163 and BV 250, Messerschmitt P 1107 and P 1108, He 343 and the so-called Daimler-Benz projects.

Hundreds of original and previously unseen documents have been used to compile this unrivalled history of Germany's secret Second World War bombers, illustrated with a host of new and period drawings, illustrations and photographs.